Racisms

an introduction

Sara Miller McCune founded SAGE Publishing in 1965 to support the dissemination of usable knowledge and educate a global community. SAGE publishes more than 1000 journals and over 800 new books each year, spanning a wide range of subject areas. Our growing selection of library products includes archives, data, case studies and video. SAGE remains majority owned by our founder and after her lifetime will become owned by a charitable trust that secures the company's continued independence.

Los Angeles | London | New Delhi | Singapore | Washington DC | Melbourne

Racisms

an introduction

Steve Garner

Second Edition

Los Angeles | London | New Delhi
Singapore | Washington DC | Melbourne

Los Angeles | London | New Delhi
Singapore | Washington DC | Melbourne

SAGE Publications Ltd
1 Oliver's Yard
55 City Road
London EC1Y 1SP

SAGE Publications Inc.
2455 Teller Road
Thousand Oaks, California 91320

SAGE Publications India Pvt Ltd
B 1/I 1 Mohan Cooperative Industrial Area
Mathura Road
New Delhi 110 044

SAGE Publications Asia-Pacific Pte Ltd
3 Church Street
#10-04 Samsung Hub
Singapore 049483

Editor: Natalie Aguilera
Assistant editor: Delayna Spencer
Production editor: Katherine Haw
Copyeditor: Jane Fricker
Proofreader: Christine Bitten
Marketing manager: Sally Ransom
Cover design: Tristan Tutak
Typeset by: C&M Digitals (P) Ltd, Chennai, India
Printed and bound by CPI Group (UK) Ltd,
Croydon, CR0 4YY

© Steve Garner 2017

First edition published 2011. Reprinted in 2012 and 2013

This edition first published 2017

Library of Congress Control Number: 2016952263

British Library Cataloguing in Publication data

A catalogue record for this book is available from
the British Library

ISBN 978-1-4129-6176-9
ISBN 978-1-4129-6177-6 (pbk)

Contents

List of Boxes

List of Case Studies

List of Figures, Tables and Appendices

Figures

Tables

Appendices

About the Author

Steve Garner is Professor of Critical Race Studies and Head of the Department of Criminology and Sociology at Birmingham City University, UK. He has published widely on whiteness, as well as racism and its intersection with class and nation in a variety of geographical contexts, such as England, Ireland, the USA and Guyana. He is the author of *A Moral Economy of Whiteness* (Routledge, 2015), *Whiteness: An Introduction* (Routledge, 2007) and *Racism in the Irish Experience* (Pluto, 2004) as well as numerous book chapters and articles in such journals as *Ethnic and Racial Studies*, *Ethnicities* and *Sociology*. He is currently working on skin lightening practices and discourses.

Acknowledgements

Shout outs. Annie, my relentlessly ethical wife: always the good voice in my ear. I'd be lost without you. Dani: thanks for sorting out the references. At SAGE, thanks to the critical and positive reviewers of the first edition. Kudos to Natalie Aguilera for convincing me to resume a project that I initially didn't want to do, but ended up getting passionate about again.

Thanks also to nearly all my former colleagues at the Open University (especially Jacqueline Baxter, Vicky Canning, John Clarke, Kesi Mahendran, Steve Tombs, Sophie Watson and Louise Westmarland) and my new, inspiring ones at Birmingham City University. Thanks to everyone whose imprint this text bears because they have shaped my thinking since the last edition. There are too many of you to list but you know who you are, brothers and sisters, and I hope I've done you some semblance of justice.

Steve Garner, Bristol, August 2016

Introduction

As I reached the end of the final draft of this second edition in summer 2016, and the candidates for US president approached their official nominations, I remembered that damp evening in November 2008 when I watched Barack Obama's initial victory live on television as I worked into the night on the first edition. His term will be over and his successor in place by the time this book is published. My eldest daughter was in her second year of secondary school then. Now she is a young woman, starting university. All my hair was black … I could go on and on. It's a sobering reminder of the passage of time. And my acknowledgements last time ended soberly. Racism wasn't going away anytime soon, I wrote, and it still isn't. In fact, it feels like the screws have been wound so much tighter in the economic crisis societies we have been living in since 2008 that all kinds of discriminations have been intensified. As I neared the end of this writing, the UK voted to leave the European Union. One of the major issues in the campaign was immigration, and a wave of racist attacks, both physical and verbal have erupted (above and beyond business-as-usual), making a lot of people in England feel unsafe, unwanted and like they had gone to sleep in 2016 and woken up in 1980. In 1913, Irish revolutionary James Connolly foresaw a 'carnival of reaction' that would ensue when the North was partitioned from the Republic in 1921. I feel like we have been floating along in a 'carnival of reaction' for years now, and as of June 2016, with the Brexit vote and the astonishing reactions and political fallout, the UK has attained Rio Carnival-of-Reaction levels. Makes you wanna holler.

More than ever we need to be able to properly understand the social forces that divide us, in order to defend society and establish that black lives matter. If your first thought on reading this phrase is frustration because all lives matter, you really should try and engage with this text. This book is my tiny contribution to that ongoing and global attempt to understand and resist.

So What's Different About the Second Edition?

In response to readers' and reviewers' suggestions, there are two completely new chapters: 3 (Ethnicity) and 10 (Immigration), making 12 in total, as I also deleted the old chapter on Asylum, and used a little bit of it in the immigration and racialisation chapters. It's common practice to group 'race' and ethnicity together in titles of modules/courses, publications and statements on inequality. I hope to establish in Chapter 3 why I am sceptical of such a practice (while recognising that it brings together scholars and activists with similar objectives).

Although immigration was spread out across the first edition's text, people felt it would be appropriate to have a stand-alone chapter on immigration, which I have provided here. I have tried to let my hair down by putting forward some ideas about what the bases for immigration policies and attitudes toward immigration consist of, next to some historical and contemporary case studies.

In the first edition there were 27 boxes, 4 of which were deleted in the new mix. There are now 53 boxes, so there are effectively 30 new ones. These contain short case studies or ideas demonstrated through empirical research or theoretical positions, and are aimed at bolstering, or shedding further light on arguments developed within the chapters. There are also a few aimed at engaging with popular discussions about what 'race' is and isn't. The boxes are stand-alone, but for best results, please read in conjunction with the surrounding chapter.

For each chapter, there are also three or four 'Points for Reflection', plus three more for the whole book (located at the end of Chapter 12).

There are three further reading suggestions for each chapter. Sometimes these consist of work already referred to in the chapter, but mostly they are chapters, articles or books that would show the topic from an angle I didn't cover in the main text, expand on the arguments, or illustrate them in more depth (or any combination of those three things).

There were 6 tables and 3 figures in the first edition and 15 and 3 respectively in the second.

Although coverage is tilted toward the UK and the USA, there is now a little more on the rest of Europe, and definitely a few more Asian case studies. As I noted in the introduction to the first edition, there is another, 'ghost' book in a parallel world, containing all the areas not covered by this one.

Lastly, while some sections of chapters have been extensively revised, others have not. Although events since the first edition's publication have had immediate and far-reaching consequences in some areas, the basic points I am trying to convey mostly remain the same. It has certainly been a challenge to revisit this project, and I hope the text remains a useful and stimulating tool for teachers, students and researchers grappling with the complexities of racism in its twenty-first century guises.

1

The Idea of 'Race' and the Practice of Racisms

In this chapter we will

- Examine the history of 'race' as an idea
- Understand how 'race' has been theorised in the social sciences
- Look at definitions of racism and
- Arrive at our own definition, to be used for the remainder of this book

What is race? The striking element of all scholarly attempts to understand what 'race' is seems to be the impossibility of providing a definition. We think we know, obviously, who is in what 'race', even though we may try very consciously not to attach any further importance to it as an identity when we deal with other people. Clearly, dividing up people into 'races' is an act of categorisation. Yet when we look more closely at the kinds of assumptions this form of categorisation is based on, they do not hold water. We think 'race' is about physical appearance and has been a characteristic of humanity for centuries. But how many 'races' are there and what are they called? If you watch American crime shows, you may think 'Caucasian', 'African American' and 'Hispanic' are the main ones. Yet there are a number of problems with this understanding. First, these labels are all relatively new. 'Caucasian' was not used before the 1940s; 'African American' has only come into use since the 1990s; and 'Hispanic' has only been used since the 1970 Census. Second? Sorry my US readers, but the world really is bigger than the USA. What separates people's understandings of who is who in one place, at one time, is not necessarily the same logic that applies elsewhere at other times. Third, and we will come back to this many times, pursuing the idea that the world can be divided into 'races' requires a special suspension of logic.

What are the physical attributes we are really talking about in the discussion of 'race'? Skin colour, hair type and colour, eye colour, shape of eyes, shape of nose. Are there any more? Yet let's think for a moment about all the ways in which two human bodies could differ from one another. If you had to make a list of such elements, that list would be very long. Once you have proportions of limbs to body, shape of head, distance between eyes and muscle definition, I am sure you could come up with 20 before you have even started to struggle. That's just the external (phenotypical) differences. If we then start to think about genetic differences, the scale of the sleight of hand involved in dividing the world up into 'races' on the premise of biology becomes apparent. In Box 1.1, we can see some information derived from contemporary science about the various ways in which human bodies could be grouped together and it is counter-intuitive for people whose culture encourages the normalisation of 'race'.

Box 1.1   Race and Genes

While each human being has around 25,000–30,000 genes, the largest difference between two individuals seems to be in the region of 1 per cent. Although the biological basis of 'race' suggests distinct groups of people with more shared genetic heritage than genetic discrepancy, research into genetic differences shows that this is a false claim. The science does not stand up. Indeed, often there are geographical, social and medical reasons for the relatively small differences in genetic structure between people.

Example 1 – *Sickle cell anaemia*: often seen as a disease for which people of African origin exclusively are at high risk. The cluster of genes that means a person is likely to develop this form of anaemia is concentrated among groups of people whose ancestors came from sub-Saharan Africa, the Mediterranean, the Middle East and India. Thus, it is not solely a 'black people's' disease but rather closely linked to malaria; hence the geographical concentration of the pathology. Malaria exacerbates the illness, and so where malaria is not present, the rate of sickle cell sufferers drops. African Americans' rate is below that of West Africa, and falling as malaria has been eradicated in the USA.

Example 2 – *IQ testing*: the controversy about psychometric testing for Intelligence Quotient is ongoing. Introduced in the early twentieth century in the USA, its objective was to screen for intelligence among recruits for the armed forces. It was then used as a screening test for immigrants. The claims of those who advocate such tests are that different ethnic and racial groups score at different rates – even when environmental factors are taken into consideration. Those who disagree argue that there are a host of social class and culture-related issues around what is counted as intelligence and what is actually measured in these types of test. People can score at higher rates with training in the types of question asked, and in the case of immigrants, after longer exposure to the culture of the country in which the test is administered (Duster, 2003, 2006; Herrnstein and Murray, 1994; Fraser, 1995).

Ultimately, the judgement of science on 'race' as a way of definitively organising the human population into discrete groups, according to genetic make-up, is unequivocal:

> Modern genetics does in fact show that there are no separate groups within humanity (although there are noticeable differences among the peoples of the world) ... Individuals – not nations and races – are the main repository of human variation for functional genes. A race, as defined by skin colour, is no more a biological entity than is a nation, whose identity depends only on a brief shared history. (Jones, 1994: 246)

This is not to say that people do not share characteristics such as complexion, hair type, eye colour, etc., but instead it should draw our attention to the relatively tiny proportion of physical features that we use as criteria for our understanding of 'race': skin colour, hair type, eye colour, shape of mouth, shape of eyes, etc. Why, out of all the biological differences there *could* be between two people, do we only focus on half a dozen at most? Moreover, biological genetic similarity within a supposed racial group, and its distinction from another, represent only half the story: 'race' has always been about linking culture and behaviour to physical appearance. How we think about 'race' is to assume, for example, that Person X is part of group A, therefore she behaves in a certain way. There is more in this book about how the links were originally made, and on the idea of culture later, but here, we just need to underline the fact that the idea of 'race' is not merely about bodies looking similar to or different from one another, but about the ideological labour we invest into collectively interpreting those similarities and differences.

So, if we accept that there are many physical differences possible, yet when we think about 'race', there are only a few features that we are interested in, the problem for us becomes, 'why is this the case?' Moreover, the terms we use, like 'white', 'black', 'yellow', 'red', etc. are not even descriptions of what they claim to describe. Nobody living is actually white. Nobody is really 'black' in the sense of the ink on this page, although there are some people with very dark complexions indeed. Certainly, nobody's skin is yellow or red – unless they are sunburnt or suffering from particular diseases. So the conclusion must be that such terms have social meanings but not biological ones.

The same could be said for the idea of 'race'. Our social worlds are full of ways to distinguish between one group and another in a specific context, and 'race' is one form of categorisation. The interpretations of physical differences that we make in our societies are determined not by the indisputable fact of racial difference, but by the social imperatives that enable us to do so. In other words, the social world provides us with tools specific to both our culture and our period of history, which we then use to read 'race' from the bodies of human beings. We are bombarded with ways of admitting that 'race' is a *natural* part of our social world, one of the legitimate ways in which we try to make sense of difference. 'We hold these truths', it appears, 'to be self-evident': all people are created racial.

Indeed, 'race' has never been the object of consensus because of this slippery relationship to the facts. Throughout this book, we will examine geographical and historical contexts in which the interpretations afforded to 'race' differ. Michael Omi's conclusion is valid not just for the USA:

> ... the meaning of race in the United States has been and probably always will be fluid and subject to multiple determinations. Race cannot be seen simply as an objective fact, nor treated as an independent variable. (Omi, 2001: 244)

Paul Silverstein's anthropological perspective is that 'race' is a 'cultural category of difference that is contextually constructed as essential and natural – as residing within the very body of the individual' (Silverstein, 2005: 364). So, making sense of such clues, which we are primed to do in our cultures, is labelled a 'social construction' in the social sciences. Sociologists have long argued that 'race' is a social construction, but that the meanings attributed to it have concrete impacts on social relations. Although there might be strategic reasons why 'race' could be retained, as a basis for solidarity (Gilroy, 1987), I am convinced that as far as academic practice goes, Stephen Small's rationale (1994: 30) is the correct one. Contrary to the focus on 'race relations', he maintains, which first 'assumes that "races" exist and then seeks to understand relations between them', racialisation directs our attention to 'how groups not previously defined as "races" have come to be defined in this way and assesses the various factors involved in such processes'. These processes result in 'race' becoming a salient factor in the way social resources are allocated and how groups are represented, that is, *racialised*. The concept of 'racialisation' will be introduced and exemplified in detail throughout the next chapter.

Different Places, Different 'Races'?

As we said, these readings differ from one place to another and at different moments in time. Let's take an example of a person whom we shall hypothetically move from place to place. Using the racial terminology available to us in our understanding of the world seen through the lens of 'race', her mother is white and her father is black (UK), or Caucasian and African American (USA). This makes her either African American or bi-racial (USA) or black or 'mixed race' (UK). If we take this fictitious person with light brown skin to Brazil, there are at least four ways to categorise her racially: *parda, preta, morena* and *negra*. Each of these has different connotations, and the degree to which one is not white often affects your life chances in terms of education, employment, etc. Returning to the Caribbean via Latin America, she would pass through a set of cultures where the gradations between black, white and native American origins have an elaborate terminology: there would certainly be a term to describe her, possibly *mulatta* or *morena*, for example, and when she gets to somewhere like Jamaica, she might be referred to as 'red' or 'yellow'.

If we take her back to South Africa between 1948 and 1994, when the system called Apartheid was in place, she would have been 'Coloured'. This meant you were restricted to living in particular areas, barred from others, and this, in turn, meant restricted access to education, employment and other resources, in a context where the entire population was identified by 'race' and governed on that basis.

In such systems of attributing social value, therefore, everyone has a set of physical attributes that can get you categorised. However, in this form of categorisation, the outcomes are unequal. If you look like this person in the USA, South Africa, or Brazil, particular openings are closed off to you. Yet should she stay in a country where the vast majority of people are black, let's say Nigeria, her identity is much more likely to relate to religion, region of origin, language, professional status, etc. Lastly, if we took her back to 1930s Germany, she would have been a candidate for the forced sterilisation programme. After the First World War, the Rhineland (the industrial region bordering France) was occupied by American and French African troops, several of whom had children with German women. From 1937 onwards, as part of the 'racial hygiene' programme led by Dr Eugen Fischer, these 400 children were sterilised in order that they did not contaminate the Aryan gene pool. In each of those settings, the social and political distinctions between people have their own histories; the words used to describe groups of people based on culture and physical appearance have different meanings, and refer the individuals concerned to different positions of relative power in their society. 'Race' is therefore not a universal concept, but a particular and contingent one.

There are some significant elements to note from this small set of examples:

- 'Race' in biological terms (of simply what people look like) matters a lot. For example, it bears importantly on the way resources are made more or less accessible.
- It is not individuals alone, but also important institutions like the State, which have input in determining the meaning of 'race'.
- Different social systems and their cultures attach different types of meaning to physical appearance.
- It is not simply a case of some people being denied access to goods and resources, but of the corresponding easier access for others. Racism, as we shall define it below, is a social relationship. This means that there is always an imbalance of power, expressed through access to resources.

If racism's departure point is the idea of 'race', our first exploration must be into that term and its development. Once this is clear we can move on to the second aim of the chapter, to provide a working definition of 'racism'.

Some Key Moments in the Development of the Idea of 'Race'

The purpose of this section is to establish that the three foundational aspects of racism outlined above change over time, and from place to place. The meanings attached to 'race' and the practices it endorses are also specific to different eras and contexts. This is an important stage in the argument, because when we come to discuss configurations of racism post the Second World War, the idea that it consists of physical-based representations can be countered, and the debate moved forward. In later chapters, we shall go into some of these topics in much more detail. The three moments selected here are: the sixteenth century, the Enlightenment and classification, and racial science.

Although there were of course empires before the European expansion into the Americas, Africa, Asia and Australasia, the phase of empire that began in the late fifteenth/early sixteenth century is the key one for students of 'race'. Spanish and Portuguese involvement in establishing colonies, the slave trade and the subsequent struggle for advantage that dragged in all the European powers had immense historical consequences. In the realm of racism, this was the period which witnessed the encounter between European and native that was to frame the colonial epoch. Such an encounter was frequently violent. The Europeans held technological and military advantage, as well as pre-existing ideas about classifying groups of people by virtue of criteria such as religiosity, property ownership, communal property, government, nomadic and sedentary lifestyles, farming techniques, etc. What can be observed over the four centuries of European expansion is the construction of a set of ideas about the native/ indigenous people that placed them in a position of moral and cultural inferior- ity. This position was either borne out by, or led to (depending on how you interpreted such events), the corresponding political, economic and military inferiority institutionalised under the various forms of colonial rule.

The Sixteenth Century

References to 'race' prior to the eighteenth century were much more ambigu- ous than we might expect. Before there were 'black' and 'white' people, there were 'Christians' and 'Heathens'. In Christian symbolism, 'white' had positive connotations (purity), while 'black' had the opposite, hence the type of nega- tive meanings attached to the term black. The evidence suggests that ideas about explaining difference frequently focused on religion, climate and labour status, without giving the concept of 'race' the detailed content that it was to receive later.

How is this to be reconciled with the fact that the European colonial enterprises (including the conquest of Ireland) and the Atlantic slave trade had been under way for centuries before the Enlightenment? Surely ideas about superiority and inferiority revolved around physical as well as religious differ- ence? Physical difference was explained largely with reference to religion. This can be seen as a long-term process at its clearest in the 'sons of Ham' argument put forward by the Christian churches to justify the enslavement of Africans. The argument ran that the punishment given by God to Canaan (the son of Ham) in the Book of Genesis (9:18–27) involved servitude and blackness (to denote inferiority already present in the nature of servitude).

The frame of reference for educated Europeans until the Enlightenment was one in which:

- The dominant idea about origins was that everyone was descended from Adam and Eve (*monogenesis*), and signs on the body were read as judgements of God.

- The idea of separate origins (*polygenesis*) was a minority one among biblical scholars, and responded to the obvious physical diversity of the human race.

However, nowhere in Genesis does it say that all Ham's descendants were to be dark-complexioned, nor that the form of their servitude would resemble in any way the bondage of the Israelites in the Old Testament. In fact, the punishment was restricted to Canaan. The idea of the sons of Ham was added to the very broad lines in scripture in a manoeuvre by clerical scholars over centuries. For our purposes, we should note also that ideas about the inequality of classes and genders were also given justification by particular interpretations of the Bible (as well as the holy books of other religions). The logic ran: Africans could be enslaved in large numbers, therefore their slavery was natural and permitted by God. This is because they were the 'sons of Ham', designated by God to be servants.

Moreover, the military and technological power of the European states was underwritten by the unchallenged assertion that the rest of the world's land and peoples were available to be exploited. In the 1493 Treaty of Tordesillas, the Pope divided the 'New World' into two areas: one for Spain to control, the other for Portugal.

However, the most pressing problem facing sixteenth-century colonists in the Spanish New World, for example, was the requirement of workers in the labour-intensive enterprise of extracting primary materials such as gold, diamonds and silver. The debate between Spanish intellectuals Las Casas and Sepulveda over the fate of Amerindians, held in Valladolid in 1550, encapsulated early humanist thought and imperial imperatives. If Amerindians in the New World had 'redeemable' souls, they could not be used as slave labour; if they hadn't, then their labour could be passed off as penance for sinful paganism. Little of this discourse focused on what Amerindians looked like, and until the end of the sixteenth century, when Amerindian resistance had been quelled, there was certainly no consensus that their cultures were universally less developed than Europe's. Even when there was, there existed no consensus that any such developmental lag was due to an innate incapacity to become civilised. Indeed, the model of civilising by example was still a defensible (although minority) position in North America and Ireland during the British colonisations of those places into the seventeenth century.

The Enlightenment and Classification

Over the decades now referred to as 'the Enlightenment' (*c.*1720–1820), a dif-
fuse pattern of ideas expressed in relation to a number of disciplines including
biology, philosophy, history, economics and political science were transformed
into a coherent body of thought on humankind's place in the world, containing an elaborate typology of human beings. The Enlightenment thinkers were
engaged in a wide-ranging project of categorisation. Man's place in creation
was the object of study, and to this end, a series of classificatory tasks were
carried out, and inventories of living things (including peoples) were constructed.
The Swedish biologist Linnaeus, for example, wrote an epic work, *Systems
of Nature* (1735, in Eze, 1997: 10), in which the physical aspects of this
project appear clearly (see also Chapter 5):

> Man, the last and best of created works, formed after the image of his
> Maker … is, by his wisdom alone, able to form just conclusions from
> such things as present themselves to his senses, which can only consist
> of bodies merely natural. Hence, the first step of wisdom is to know
> these bodies.

In constructing the 'great chain of being', the fulcrum of Enlightenment reasoning was Linnaeus's 'bodies merely natural': that is, a set of common-sense
physical markers that expressed difference.

Indeed, a causal link was made by writers such as Hume, the Comte de
Buffon and Hegel, between climate, 'phenotype' (that is, physical appearance),
intellectual ability and capacity for civilisation. In this view of the world,
civilisation in its highest forms emanated from the version of human beings
dwelling in the temperate zones of Europe and America: they were pale in
complexion as a result, and as contemporary history showed, were capable of
mastering both nature and other species of man through the use of technology.
The differences between the categories of human being were explicable in terms
of appearance and culture: they were two sides of the same phenomenon.
Physical appearance became a marker of cultural development, not just in the
present, but also an indicator of the parameters of advancement (Eze, 1997).

There is a case that the 'Atlantic Protestant' Enlightenment was more conservative than its continental counterparts. There was less polygenist argument
and it was certainly less critical of the Church than the French Enlightenment,
which took place against the backdrop of the pre-revolutionary period.

However, ideas about racial difference, culture and climate gained
legitimacy and became part of elite ideology in the Atlantic world in the
context of the commodification of human beings in the Atlantic slave trade.
The conclusions arrived at by many of the Western world's most notable
minds acted to justify slavery after the event. Within the Enlightenment was
also an attempt to place secular rationalism above religion as the dominant

explanatory model for social phenomena. It did indeed achieve predominance, and the classifications proposed were honed in the industrial and scientific nineteenth century.

Box 1.2   Essentialism

A key relationship to be borne in mind is the one between the social and the natural worlds. When nature is employed to account for behaviour, the idea that this behaviour is unchanging, and therefore unchangeable, accompanies it. Identities are, in this perspective, constructed around an essence which cannot change.

   This is a particular source of tension: social science is about mapping and studying change and continuity, while discriminatory bodies of ideas are about fixing identity in time, and arguing that there is an essence that does not change. Some of the arguments against women receiving the franchise in the nineteenth and early twentieth centuries, for example, stated that they were naturally too emotional and irrational to be entrusted with the serious business of voting. This illustrates how unchanging and unchangeable 'essences' are advanced as part and parcel of collective identities. We refer to this kind of argument as 'essentialist', and the practice of arguing in this way as 'essentialism'. However, some argue that essentialism serves a purpose for the oppressed, of aligning them against a common enemy and promoting solidarity. Post-colonial critic Gayatri Spivak (Adamson, 1986) famously talked of deploying 'strategic essentialism' as a tool for liberation. Yet it is seen as having limited use. In his seminal paper 'New Ethnicities', Stuart Hall (1988) argued that essentialist constructions of blackness, and by extension other racialised identities, were ultimately deleterious for anti-racist struggles.

Racial Science in the Nineteenth Century

Nineteenth-century scientists built on the groundwork laid by the Enlightenment thinkers. Science began to eclipse religion as the legitimate authority for explaining phenomena in both the natural and social worlds. As the century progressed, the ideas that had been put forward linking appearance, climate and culture became the assumptions upon which new work was carried out, rather than themselves being the subject of scholarly debate. By mid-century, the idea that the causal link existed and explained behaviour was no longer debatable; it was instead the starting point for further debates about politics and inequality. If people's abilities were genetically determined and unequal, what was the point of trying to overcome these inequalities? They were natural, normal and must be the basis for the social world (see Box 1.3).

Box 1.3   Racialised Natural Sciences

Phrenology: the study of the structure of the skull (bumps and indentations) to determine a person's character and mental capacity. Promulgated by Franz-Joseph Gall (1758–1828), it correctly suggests that different parts of the brain are responsible for different mental functions. However, phrenology is based on the idea that these can be identified from the external surface, and people's behaviour thus predicted.

Craniology: the measurement of cranial features in order to classify people according to race, criminal temperament, intelligence, etc. The underlying assumption of craniology is that skull size and shape determine brain size, which determines such things as intelligence and the capacity for moral behaviour.

Anthropometry: the study of human body measurement for use in anthropological classification and comparison. In the nineteenth and early twentieth centuries, anthropometry was a pseudo-science used mainly to classify potential criminals by facial characteristics. For example, Cesare Lombroso's *L'Uomo Delinquente* (1876) claimed that murderers have prominent jaws, and pickpockets have long hands and scanty beards. From its earliest uses in identifying criminal types, anthropometry was later used specifically to research physical differences between the races (see Chapter 5).

Moreover, nineteenth-century science and pseudo-science further developed the central thesis of the Enlightenment, namely that the body is the key to culture. Sciences that flowered in the nineteenth century, such as craniology, phrenology and later anthropometry, involved the measurement of various body parts and the construction of classificatory typologies from these findings. The new 'social' sciences such as sociology, ethnology and anthropology which emerged in the second half of the century were equally influenced by the obsession with physical appearance and the meanings attributed to them by their colleagues in the physical sciences, within the contexts of colonial expansion and plantation slavery.

The texts produced by these natural science disciplines demonstrate that the notion of dispassionate and disinterested scientific endeavour held no sway over those interested in 'race': the logic underlying experiments is erroneous and the interpretations of data are so weighed down under the assumption of explicit existing hierarchies based on racial difference that the findings are not compelling. American craniologist Samuel Morton (1839), for example, filled the skulls of various 'racial' types with lead pellets to measure their capacity. He emerged with a league table showing that English skulls had the largest capacity, followed by Native Americans, and then Black Americans. His inference was that the English mind was larger, more powerful and superior.

Moreover, in addition to the inability of scientists to agree upon how many 'races' there actually were, and where the dividing lines between them lay (see Box 1.4), the cross-fertilisation of ideas and conclusions meant that the enterprise of racialising the population was carried out on the basis of a relatively small, scarcely challenged and scientifically dubious corpus. Yet the ideas contained in this corpus were referred to by contemporary scientists on both sides of the Atlantic, to the point where, by the middle of the nineteenth century, according to American historian Reginald Horsman, 'the inherent inequality of races was simply accepted as a scientific fact in America' (1981: 135). This is a crucial point: where the existence of unequal races passes from the area of discussion, to the area of accepted facts upon which further discussion is premised. French sociologist Pierre Bourdieu (1977) calls the latter *doxa*. Once an idea has become doxa, it is all the more difficult to challenge.

It was in mid-century that the crude racial hierarchies became more nuanced. Robert Knox's *The Races of Men* (1850) and de Gobineau's *Essai sur l'inégalité des races humaines* (1853–55) detailed the divisions within the 'white race', dividing it into categories including Aryan, Slavic and Celtic, for example. Although de Gobineau's appraisal of the various groups was not wholly negative, the elaborate nature of his treatise made it a work of reference for 'Social Darwinists' later in the century and eugenicists in the next. Indeed, he prefigured the latter group's phobia about mixing. All great civilisations, he argued, were maintained by pure 'races', and when these mixed with 'degenerate races', the result was inevitable decline and fall.

Box 1.4   How Many 'Races' Are There?

Even among those people engaged in the process of producing knowledge about 'races' through the seventeenth to the twentieth centuries, there is no consensus about where to place the lines dividing one 'race' from another, where to place the lines dividing the sub-races within each group, how many there are, and, indeed, what they are called. Nicholas Wade (2014) argues that modern science says there are five: Asians, Caucasians, sub-Saharan Africans, Native Americans and the original inhabitants of Australia and Papua New Guinea. Yet DeSalle and Tattersall's (2014) forensic critique of the science underpinning *A Troublesome Inheritance* ends with the statement: 'The central tendencies may be there, but the boundaries aren't. Which means that "race" is a totally inadequate way of characterizing, or even of helping us to understand, the glorious variety that is humankind' (DeSalle and Tattersall, 2014: 9).

For Linnaeus (1707–78) and Samuel Morton (1799–1851), there are four races: European, Asian, American, African.

For Johann Friedrich Blumenbach (1752–1840), there are five races: 'Caucasian' or 'white race'; the 'Mongolian' or 'yellow race'; the 'Malayan' or 'brown race'; the 'Negro', 'Ethiopian' or 'black race'; and the 'American' or 'red race'.

(Continued)

(Continued)

For Charles Pickering (1805–78) in *The Races of Men* (1854), there are 11 races: two white, three brown, four blackish-brown and two black.

For Joseph Arthur Comte de Gobineau (1816–82), there are three races: white, yellow and black.

Just for comparison, the US Census 2000 and 2010 have provided the opportunity for the US population to self-identify as members of at least 15 'races': white, black, American Indian, Asian Indian, Chinese, Filipino, Japanese, Korean, Vietnamese, Other Asian, Native Hawaiian, Guamanian or Chamorro, Samoan, Other Pacific Islander or 'some Other race'.

Like most official attempts to capture people's racial and/or ethnic identity, this schema is open to criticisms about consistency, among others. But one thing is clear. There is no consensus about how many 'races' there are, and never has been. This should not surprise us. 'Race' is a property of the social world and not of the natural world.

In other sections of this book we will examine some of the key racial ideas and practices in circulation in the late nineteenth and early twentieth centuries (eugenics in Chapter 7), as well as having a special focus on the 'new' racisms (Chapter 9) of the post oil-crisis West.

After the Second World War, most social scientists responded by making an official declaration via the United Nations (1950) according to which 'race' had no biological validity. Although the 'social' nature of 'race' rather than its biological substance has been emphasised in the decades since then, popular understandings, and it must be said, some strains of thought within the natural sciences, still identify bodies with racial messages (see Chapter 7). This is the context in which the production and reception of this text take place. I encourage the reader to not close off the world of academia or research from the rest of society and imagine that different rules apply to it. The struggle to establish dominant meanings and representations in the social world includes all the academic production of work based on the idea that 'race' is social, and all the work based on the idea that it is more than social. Claims that scientists and politicians are courageously telling it like it really is (Murray, 2014) instead of being held back by liberal intelligentsia and political elites are part of this ongoing struggle about the meaning of 'race' and its consequences for the societies in which we live.

My conclusion is that 'race' is social but has real impacts on the material world. Moreover, according to the historical record, 'race' has referred not to bodies or culture alone but – this is the key thing to take forward – to the process of linking them irrevocably to each other in the context of categorisation and hierarchical classification; as part of the expansion of European empires.

None of this is to say that racialisation is an exclusively European colonial technology, but that its grammar and vocabulary are developed to their most definitive – and globalised – form in the European and North American colonial settings. There might be a longstanding bestowal of privilege on lighter skin and the bloodlines that go with it in both Indian and Chinese cultures for example, but their versions of hierarchy were not exported and imposed on other areas of the world as a project aimed at establishing and maintaining control. The story of 'race' does not unfurl in a vacuum; power relations make it happen. This is evident in the seventeenth- and eighteenth-century ideologies referred to above, with European intellectuals explaining the classification and categorisation of the human race. Moreover, in all the sources identified here, 'race' is constructed as a *collective hierarchy*, rather than individual phenomenon.

Box 1.5   Who's Who? The Rachel Dolezal Case

It has been stressed so far that for mainstream social science, if not in popular discourse, 'race' is a social not a biological reality. But surely we know who belongs to which racialised group when we see them? In June 2015, a controversy erupted around Rachel Dolezal, a local organiser for the National Association for the Advancement of Colored People (NAACP) in Spokane, Washington State, when it was revealed that she was not actually African American, as she had claimed to be for the previous decade, but white, with European American forebears as far as could be traced. Dolezal used foundation and skilled hairstyling to produce a 'look' that succeeded in maintaining the pretence that she was – at least in part – African American.

This act of 'passing' is a puzzling one. The NAACP has always had a mixed membership, so there was no need to be black to participate in its activities. The revelation of Dolezal's whiteness led to her being fired from her temporary teaching position at a local university, her resignation from the NAACP and also split observers. Some of her former colleagues supported her, saying what she had accomplished was more important than who she was, while others criticised her for 'performing blackness', or doing 'blackface' (Box 11.3): a derogatory and mocking white performance of blackness that originated in the nineteenth century. Does Dolezal embody an extreme form of white guilt, acting black through over-identification? On one level, her story is commonplace: people have 'passed' as members of other racialised groups for centuries. Yet the objective of passing – as white – was to access resources from which people would otherwise have been excluded. Passing as a racialised minority, with no resource benefits, is not an equivalent practice, any more than tanning is the equivalent of skin lightening (see Chapter 7).

'Passing', in terms of 'race', gender and class, can be transgressive. A major criticism of Dolezal's behaviour is that instead of challenging white privilege, by declaring herself white but acting against the benefits accruing from that position, she opted to pretend to be black, which in no way challenged such a hierarchy.

Dolezal's case, like all passing, demonstrates the social and cultural aspects of 'race', and the impossibility of drawing hard and fast lines around physical appearance and using them to define 'race'. It also makes us think about what is at stake in a racialised identity: What does it authorise and prevent? What assumptions do other people make when you present yourself in a particular identity? What are the questions of power underpinning the relationship between the various identities?

Defining Racism

What *Isn't* Racism?

The systems of Nazi Germany, South Africa under Apartheid (1948–94), and the segregated Southern states of the USA ('Jim Crow') placed racial discrimination very obviously at the heart of the way that government and everyday life were carried out. We will return to these historical examples throughout this book, but it is important also to recognise that they are not paradigms (examples that serve as models) but rather extreme points on a continuum. A common misperception of racism is that it is only the severe examples that constitute the whole, in other words only violence, verbal abuse and deliberate segregation are actually racist; nothing else counts.

In the course of this book, an argument will be presented that the phenomenon is far broader and more complex than such a view would suggest. Indeed, the term has been bandied around in so much public discourse, particularly since the 1960s, that it appears to have lost some of its explanatory power. It gets divorced from power relations, so that terms such as 'reverse racism' (Box 9.4) gain currency. Indeed, one of the noticeable elements of the landscape of contemporary racism is the increasingly frequent assertion that programmes ranging from affirmative action to multiculturalism in the public arena end up placing white people at a *systematic* disadvantage in the realms of education and employment especially. Moreover, using the 'colour-blind' frame that we will explore in Chapter 9, many argue that racism is caused by continually addressing 'race' per se; there is really not a problem until activists and academics make a fuss about it. One such definition is that of Mike Adams (a University of North Carolina–Wilmington criminologist, writing as a columnist):

> Racism – is a pathological tendency to interject race into situations where it is not relevant, merely for personal gain. (Adams, 2006)

In case there is any confusion, this is categorically *not* the argument contained in this book! Indeed the whole project of writing it would be seen from Adams' perspective as an acting out of the 'pathological tendency'. That's a lot of wasted effort on my part, according to him. However, it is important to understand as a scholar of racism, that in many societies we are far from a consensus that racism even exists; and much further from agreeing that if it does, then it has longstanding, harmful effects. The core idea that I advance in this book – that racism is a set of social relationships rather than the outcomes of individual deviance and interpersonal interactions – is still a minority one. Indeed, popular understandings of racism can identify it as both 'natural' (people sticking together and preferring their own kind) and distributed equally through society, so that any member of a given group can be racist about a member of another group: what Miri Song (2014) has labelled a 'culture of racial equivalence' (Box 9.5).

However, through the interplay of claim and counter-claim about who is racist, the term comes to occupy a particular role. It is asked to serve as a normative description of something it is not – a level playing field (Doane, 2006). While it is perfectly possible that individuals have discriminatory opinions, the point of racism is that it constitutes much more than just personal opinions. What sociology has contributed to understandings of racism is that there are different levels of the phenomenon, some of which are to do with historical legacies and social formations that are not within an individual's capacity to alter. Like all forms of discrimination, racism is primarily an unequal *collective* power relationship.

In addition, there are the terms 'institutional racism', 'individual racism', 'cultural racism', 'indirect racism', and a host of other adjectives that qualify the noun. Faced with these competing understandings of racism, how can we take a step back and focus on the field as developed in the social sciences? Different expressions are used for phenomena, for groups and for outcomes in different periods. Indeed, terms like 'racialism' and 'race prejudice' were used in previous eras to describe more or less what the field of study is here.

We need a working definition to help us navigate this very broad terrain. My suggestion involves a two-part strategy. The first comprises looking at some existing definitions that undergraduates might find particularly helpful, and the second is an attempt to set out some criteria by which we can assess competing claims, and therefore, implicitly, develop our working definition.

Michael Banton (1997: 28) asks whether it 'is possible to discuss the sociology of race relations without using the term racism'. Banton advocates prudence in the use of the word 'racist'. It should be used carefully, he contends, and be attached to actions rather than to people, as labelling *actions* 'racist' leaves the possibility that *people* may be capable of non-racist or anti-racist behaviour as well. Whereas calling someone – rather than something that a person did – racist, can be a political tactic, which makes no attempt to illuminate the causes of racism. Moreover, according to George Frederickson (1988: 189), the popular idea that racism comprised a set of beliefs of biological superiority has gradually been replaced since the Second World War by 'patterns of action which serve to create or preserve unequal relationships between racial groups'. This new understanding of the term is concomitant with the development of a so-called 'new racism'. In a later chapter, we will explore this development, and argue that 'replace' might be the wrong word. However, putting the word 'racism' into the plural, to acknowledge the variety of forms it takes, might be worth considering.

The four definitions we shall use to begin the debate are the following.

I

[T]he attribution of social significance (meaning) to particular patterns of phenotypical and/or genetic difference which, along with the

characteristic of additional deterministic ascription or real or supposed other characteristics to a group constituted by descent, is the
defining feature of racism. (Banton, 1996: 310)

1. If we are to get to grips with racism as a sociological phenomenon, we have
    to address its existence in the social rather than solely the biological sphere.
    Banton stresses the process of attribution of social meaning to the body.

2. Racism tries to explain the social world by reference to the natural world.
    Nature, as we know, is in permanent flux, yet in racist social narratives, bod-
    ies and cultures are fixed and unchanging: everyone with certain physical
    characteristics naturally has a tendency toward certain patterns of behaviour.

3. As a model of the natural world, 'race' functions as a set of transmitted
    genes; some for appearance and some for behaviour. The range of these
    is fixed. We can never break free of our genes, would run the argument,
    because we are programmed to behave in particular ways. Determinism is
    the name given to the expression of this causal relationship.

II

Racism is a belief system or doctrine which postulates a hierarchy
among various human races or ethnic groups. It may be based on an
assumption of inherent biological differences between different ethnic
groups that purport to determine cultural or individual behaviour.
Racism may be described as a strong form of ethnocentrism, including
traits such as xenophobia (fear and hate of foreigners), views against
interracial relationships (anti-miscegenation), ethnic nationalism, and
ethnic stereotypes. (Wikipedia, until April 2007)

As every undergraduate knows, Wikipedia provides information, definitions
and links to further resources. While I generally try to guide students away
from using it uncritically, and especially cutting and pasting its contents into
essays, or even as a source of definitions in sociology (there are plenty of better
ones), the definition posted until April 2007 is useful for our purposes here, if
not very comprehensive.

1. It is crucial to our sociological understanding of racism that we realise it
    involves the expression of a power relationship. In the social reality con-
    jured by 'race', no two 'races' are ever on an equal footing. The history of
    the production of 'race' as a topic and the enactment of racism as a rela-
    tionship perpetually throw up hierarchies. These alter from one period to
    another and from one historical context to another. There is never usually
    a consensus about the exact intermediate positionings, but it is hard to find
    one in which white is not placed higher than the other racialised identities.

2. Another merit of this definition is that it suggests practical examples. It opens us up to the possibility that racism is not uniform but might contain various strands of ideas. It is therefore to be understood as a complex of ideas rather than a single monolithic one. The collapsing of ethnicity into racism is also a useful exercise ... in what not to do! Don't confuse the two! (Fenton, 2007) (see Chapter 3).

III

> The collective failure of an organisation to provide an appropriate and professional service to people because of their colour, culture or ethnic origin. It can be seen and detected in processes, attitudes, and behaviour which amount to discrimination through unwitting prejudice, ignorance, thoughtlessness, and racist stereotyping which disadvantage minority ethnic people. (*The Stephen Lawrence Inquiry* [MacPherson Report], 1999: para. 6.34)

The MacPherson Report (1999) was an inquiry into the (London) Metropolitan Police's handling of the investigation of Stephen Lawrence's murder in South London in 1993. The whole of section 6 of the report is worth reading because it sets out a genealogy of the term 'institutional racism' as developed in the context of what is referred to as British 'race relations'. We shall see in Chapter 6 that this is not the only context in which the term can be understood, but it is nevertheless very significant, because the definition provided by Lord MacPherson formed the basis of a controversial shift in defining racist crime in the UK (especially England and Wales) in the early twenty-first century. It was also fundamental to an important amendment to the law in Britain on racial discrimination (through the 2002 Race Relations (Amendment) Act).

1. MacPherson identifies that racism is not purely about the psychological processes of individuals dealing with each other (as most early work in the field suggested), but can be located at a broader, collective level, that is, as outcomes of an organisation's activities, rather than of one agent's activities.

2. The distinction drawn between 'processes, attitudes, and behaviour' is also helpful. It separates what people think (attitudes), from what they actually do (behaviour), and explicitly asserts that discrimination can result from long-term patterns (processes). All of these aspects can be addressed by different anti-discriminatory measures.

3. The idea that discrimination can be unintended, or 'unwitting', in Lord Scarman's terms, has proven controversial. Lord Scarman chaired an inquiry on the riots that took place in South London in 1981 (Scarman, 1986). His report suggested that actions and processes can be racist in outcome even if they are not intended to be. Because institutional racism has been developed

into a legal concept which has to be proven beyond reasonable doubt in a court of law, it must also have a clear definition. Defining something by its outcome rather than by its intention, as Scarman did, and MacPherson does here, has enabled institutional racism to become a workable legal concept. The other aspect of intentionality returns us to the idea that discrimination can occur at a level beyond the individual, and as part of a set of procedures that are unfairly loaded against some groups, while favouring others. In this way, by following the set procedures of an organisation, an agent can be performing an act that has racist outcomes, even if that agent has no intention of doing so (see more on this topic in Chapter 6).

4. Racism is popularly imagined as something someone *does to* somebody else. However, in this definition, it is also a failure to do something positive, rather than exclusively constituting positive and detrimental acts. As a result of the police force not carrying out its functions fully and rigorously, Lawrence's family and friends were dealt with in discriminatory fashion. This type of reasoning will not be news to the many people who have waited in vain to be protected by police forces, but it is a welcome addition to the understanding of racism we are trying to explore here.

5. An overview of this definition also suggests that the phenomenon of racism is multifaceted and cumulative: a number of aspects are identified along with a timeline that extends into the past. In a nutshell, this is well worth remembering, as the rest of the book serves to underscore these dual characteristics.

IV

Racism takes two closely related forms: individual whites acting against individual blacks, and acts by the total white community against the black community. We call these individual racism and institutional racism … When white terrorists bomb a black church and kill black children, that is an act of individual racism, widely deplored by most segments of society. But when in that same city – Birmingham, Alabama – 500 black babies die each year because of the lack of proper food, clothing, shelter and proper medical facilities, and thousands more are destroyed or maimed physically, emotionally and intellectually because of conditions of poverty and discrimination in the black community, that is a function of institutional racism. (Carmichael and Hamilton, 1967: 6)

Carmichael and Hamilton's book emerged out of the struggles for civil rights in the 1960s. Their stance was more radical than that of the mainstream civil rights movement. Indeed, the National American Association of Colored People and the Student Non-Violent Co-ordinating Committee (the principal organising bodies of national civil rights campaigning) both condemned Carmichael's philosophy as 'black racism'. Indeed, he ended up as a leading Black Panther and changed his name to Kwame Turé. Academic Charles Hamilton was a radical political scientist who held a professorship at Columbia University from the 1970s until he retired in the late 1990s. Together, they produced a book establishing a manifesto of black solidarity at a crucial juncture in US history.

1.   Their definition is compelling, detailed and empirical. It critically links economics and racism, or class and 'race', in a vision of mutually compounding, not exclusive, sources of discrimination. In it, we find the bones of what is later referred to as 'structural' or 'systemic' racism, later explored by academics (Massey and Denton, 1994; Oliver and Shapiro, 2006; Lipsitz, 1998; Feagin, 2006) (Chapter 6), involving society-level processes and contrasting them with what is popularly thought to exclusively comprise racism, that is, verbal abuse and violent attacks. It is a common discursive strategy in early twenty-first century Western societies to distance oneself from 'genuine' racism, as perpetrated by fringe extremist movements, and find ways of criticising the idea that anything other than this is really racism at all.

2.   Carmichael and Hamilton conjure up a conception of unequal and antagonistic social relationships involving two communities, the black and the white. However, implicit in their development of this concept is the idea that poverty also plays a role. Poverty is disproportionately concentrated in the African American population, although the largest proportion of poor people in the USA is white. By linking 'race' and class, they imply that racism is inextricable from class – in that people have multiple identities and locations.

Being poor in the USA would certainly lead to some of the housing and health-related problems they identify being experienced, but being poor and black would make them much more likely.

After examining these four attempts to define racism, we are a lot closer to something substantial. The point is really to demonstrate the complexity of racism. It cannot easily be reduced to a formula of the type 'racism is …'.

So far, we have the following elements of what racism is:

•   Distinctions have been made between the individual and the institution as sources, and between practices, attitudes and processes.

•   It is a phenomenon whose roots lie in the social meanings attributed to ostensible biological difference, and has an observable history.

•   It is a set of ideas organised hierarchically, and at its most abstract level, an ongoing power relationship.

The relative weights of these components can be argued about. However, we are moving to the kind of conclusion that definitions of racism are broad-ranging and numerous. Just a brief survey has highlighted this.

In his critique of the concept of racism, Robert Miles (1987) suggests that racism is primarily an 'ideology', an assertion which he and Malcolm Brown embed in their revamped second edition of *Racism* (2003: 17). It is arguable whether their definition is indeed a definition per se, but more of a five-part approach to a subject:

1. Racism is an ideology.

2. 'Race' and 'racism' as everyday concepts can be critiqued using a social science analysis of racism.

3. Racism should be flexibly defined so as to note the shifting emphases in meanings attached to it, and the constant importance in the political economy of migration.

4. The interdependence of racism and nationalism through the development of the capitalist system should be foregrounded.

5. Political and moral aspects must also be acknowledged alongside social scientific ones.

An 'ideology', in Miles' sense, is drawn from Marx, and can be understood as any discourse that distorts the truth about human beings and the social relationships between them. The search to avoid 'conceptual inflation' and 'conceptual deflation' that occupies two chapters in his book reminds us that too narrowly defining racism, or indeed overloading it so that *everything* is racism, leads to the rendering of the term as meaningless.

Miles' approach has been critiqued as lacking sophistication, being tied too closely to Marxism, and defining racism in too doctrinaire a fashion, as 'ideology'. These are arguments that he rebuts in the 2003 edition. For a student of the sociology of racism however, the work is of central importance as a critical contribution to the debate. There is rigorous attention to the specifics of the racial element that distinguishes racism from other ideologies (not necessarily a feature of much of the work in this field). Moreover, this approach is useful both in its insistence on a historical method, and in its emphasis on the intersections between bodies of ideas as being essential to understanding the way racism works *as an ideology*. Racism emerges in practice as inextricable from, but not reducible to, class relations, gender relations and nationalism. The focus is indeed on the material contexts in which racism is enacted, and less on the cultural expressions that racist ideas may take. The overlapping of -isms may be dizzying for those seeking conceptual clarity, but it rewards the reader interested in the dynamics of inequalities.

So if we want to use a definition, we should bear in mind the contributions above, and think, like Miles, of an approach that involves a minimal covering of the bases, so that we require certain elements to be present, no matter what other ones are included. The International Council on Human Rights Protection, for example, uses this strategy in an information pamphlet:

> Racism thus has three elements: (i) it is a vision of society that is composed of inherently different groups; (ii) it includes an explicit or implicit belief that these different groups are unequal by nature – often enough based on a Darwinian interpretation of history; and (iii) it shapes and manipulates these ideas into a programme of political action. Combined, these three components give racism its force. (International Council on Human Rights Protection, 2000: 4–5)

I think racism is a phenomenon manifesting itself in such a diverse spectrum of ways across time and place, that to properly anchor it theoretically, we need something of this type, which stresses foundations. Moreover, I would go as far as to recommend using the plural, racisms, to denote the variations on the main themes.[1] Indeed, my approach is akin to Wittgenstein's (1953) concept of 'family resemblance'. Elements are connected by overlapping features instead of one common feature, like the physical characteristics of the individuals comprising a family: no single characteristic is common to all members. Therefore in the case of racism(s), my suggestion is that whatever else your definition of racism includes, it must contain the following three elements:

1. **A historical power relationship** in which, over time, groups are *racialised* (that is, treated as if specific characteristics were natural and innate to each member of the group).

2. **A set of ideas** (*ideology*) in which the human race is divisible into distinct 'races', each with specific natural characteristics.

3. **Forms of discrimination** flowing from this (*practices*) ranging from denial of access to resources through to mass murder.

One element of racism is a set of ideas; the other is a set of practices, and we shall explore these in the following chapters. The gap between the social and the biological is to be emphasised. Racist ideas can be at least partly comprehended by returning to this basic adage: racism tries to explain differences in the *social* world by reference to *biological*, that is, *natural* distinctions (see Box 1.2).

Social scientists would argue that differences in the social world between groups are the result of historical, cultural and economic factors, that is, that the vast majority of the poor in any society are prevented collectively from advancing through the socio-economic hierarchy by factors largely outside the control of individuals. A racist argument would state that the poor are culturally inferior and genetically ill-equipped (through intelligence) for competition in the system we live in. Increasingly, as we will argue in later chapters, expressions of racialised difference have used 'culture' rather than 'nature' as their main vector. In discussions of immigration and multiculturalism, for example, people's collective culture is perceived as determining their behaviour, thus rendering them compatible or incompatible with the culture of the majority.

Conclusions

- There has been no satisfactory definition of 'race' yet offered. This is because it is a social rather than natural phenomenon. However, even though it has no basis in biology, the division of the human race into 'races' has very serious and measurable impacts on people.

- Racism is a multifaceted social phenomenon, with different levels and overlapping forms. It involves attitudes, actions, processes and unequal power relations. It is based on the interpretations of the idea of 'race', hierarchical social relations and the forms of discrimination that flow from this.

- Racism is not confined to extreme cases, but is present in a whole continuum of social relations.

- Specific societies see and do 'race' differently, and are organised in different ways. Therefore, discussions of racism *in the abstract*, without referring to particular conditions in particular places at particular times, are quite limiting. In this book, we will use the term racisms to acknowledge this diversity.

Having established a working definition of racisms and that there can be no single definitive one for 'race', we shall now turn to the dominant concept for understanding how 'race' becomes salient in the contemporary sociology of racism: racialisation.

Points for Reflection

Is 'race' a useful sociological concept?

Is 'race' about 'bodies', 'culture' or both?

'Racism' or 'racisms'? Which is the more appropriate and why?

Can you think of any ways in which 'race' and racism have impacted on your life?

Further Reading

Goldberg, D.T. (2009) *The Threat of Race: Reflections on Racial Neoliberalism.* Hoboken, NJ: Wiley.

Comprehensive and international comparative work emphasising the different historical contexts and development of racialisation across the globe, and its relationship with neoliberal forms of governance in the contemporary period.

Smith, L.T. (1999) *Decolonizing Methodologies: Research and Indigenous Peoples.* London: Zed Books.

An extended indigenous critique of what counts as knowledge and why in the Western academic tradition and makes power relations between coloniser and colonised very clear.

Essed, P. (1991) *Understanding Everyday Racism: An Interdisciplinary Theory.* London: Sage.

Interviews with women of colour in higher education in the USA and the Netherlands are examined through Essed's concept of 'everyday racism'; a framework that helps understand racism as a set of common and frequent experiences.

Note

1.   This is not a new idea. The term 'racisms' appears in early work such as: Husbands (1987), Satzewitch (1987), Anthias (1990) and Appiah (1990).

2

Racialisation

In this chapter, we will

- Examine the concept of racialisation

- Understand how and why racialisation developed as an analytical tool

- See how racialisation can be used as a tool to better understand social relations

We saw in the previous chapter that there is no consensus on the precise meaning of 'race'. This is necessarily the case because those meanings are not fixed by nature, but are instead dependent on historical, social and political contexts. What 'race' means in one place, at one time, is not necessarily what it means in another place, in another time. Even the official range of options to identify oneself racially – in countries that use such categories in their Census – is expanding. This lack of precision creates an epistemological problem for researchers (that is, one in which the status of knowledge is at the centre). As 'race' is a social but not biological category, what exactly is the subject of our investigation, and what can we actually know about 'race'?

If we want to understand the social meanings attached to 'race', rather than 'race' itself, then one solution is to use 'race' with inverted commas to highlight the concept's status as contingent and contested. Another is to adopt the approach whereby the researcher uses the concept to describe what the social actors see and talk about, namely race (with no inverted commas). A third option is to look at the social process by which 'race' comes to have meaning attached to it in a given context.

The concept of racialisation is based on the idea that the object of study should not be 'race' itself, but the process by which it becomes meaningful in a particular place at a particular time. In fact, racialisation has now become one of the key ways that academics make sense of the 'meanings of race'. Let's be clear what type of concept racialisation is before we continue. It is not an equivalent, either of 'race' or racism. 'Race' is about categorisation and classification. Racism is about the differential outcomes of those classificatory and categorising practices. Racialisation, however, is the process by which the classification and categorisation takes place: it is therefore ongoing. The racialised group is the outcome of that process. To draw on the vocabulary of grammar, it requires subjects (people, groups or institutions that generate or mediate them) and objects. This should not give the impression that racialisation is not resisted but denotes a power relationship. A group can be both a subject and an object of this process. The key point about racialisation is to note that it assumes that people make 'race', not that fully finished groups arrive at the field. Racialised identities emerge from the process of racialisation. Clearly however, the process does not start from scratch, but with the relevant historical, social and political baggage of the actors in play.

Stephen Small's (1994: 30) rationale for using the concept of racialisation is illustrative of this approach. Contrary to the focus on 'race relations', he maintains, which first 'assumes that "races" exist and then seeks to understand relations between them', racialisation directs our attention to 'how groups not previously defined as "races" have come to be defined in this way and assesses the various factors involved in such processes'. In this way, it has superseded the 'race relations' paradigm in both the UK and the USA. I am not certain that we can say all the groups emerging from racialisation everywhere and at all times were 'not previously defined as "races"'. However, the distinctions identified by Small have entailed a transition from studies that visualise society as groups of stratified 'races' engaging in competition over various resources ('race relations'), to those that seek to chart the ways in which race is constructed and made meaningful in the context of unequal power relations (racialisation).[1] In the twenty-first century, processes can result in 'race' becoming a salient factor in the way social resources are allocated, that is, racialised.

Different Understandings of Racialisation[2]

As noted by Barot and Bird (2001), the term 'racialisation' has a history going back to the end of the nineteenth century, and has since engendered a diversity of understandings. These range from Fanon's interpretation of it as an equivalent of dehumanisation (Fanon, 1967b) through Banton's (1977) suggestion that it describes Europeans' response to their encounter with people from the developing world from the fifteenth century onwards. Moreover, Miles and Brown assert that racialisation is a 'two-way process' (2003: 102), with which I concur – with qualifications.[3] Post-colonial scholar Patrick Wolfe (2002: 58) suggests distinguishing 'not too sharply, between race as concept – which, in this case, provided White men with an alibi – and the activation of that concept in the production of racial subjects, or racialization. *Racialization is an exercise of power in its own right, as opposed to a commentary that enables or facilitates a prior exercise of power*' (my emphasis).

There is thus a broad agreement that racialisation is something detrimental that *is done to* others as part of a power relationship. However, it should also be borne in mind that attaching meaning to one's own group as a 'race', and instilling this meaning with positive attributes (as we shall see below) is a common practice for subordinate groups seeking to defend and assert themselves collectively (see Spivak's 'strategic essentialism', Box 1.2). Clearly this form of valorisation and the process that Banton, Fanon and Wolfe are talking about are not equivalents. Let's begin by looking a little more closely at what Frantz Fanon argues (Box 2.1).

Box 2.1   Frantz Fanon

Frantz Fanon was born in Martinique in 1925. He joined the Free French army in 1943 and remained in France after the end of the Second World War. There he studied psychology at the University of Lyon and published *Peau Noire, Masques Blancs* (*Black Skin, White Masks*, 1967a) in 1952. He later went to Algeria, where he became head of the Blida-Joinville psychiatric hospital in 1953. His experiences there finally pushed him to withdraw from his relationship with the French state and he joined the Algerian independence movement as an activist. His written work was published in a variety of French-language sources in the late 1950s and early 1960s. In 1960, he was diagnosed with leukaemia and wrote *Les Damnés de la Terre* (translated as *The Wretched of the Earth*, New York, 1967b) in 10 months. He died in 1961 and was buried with full honours by the Algerian state. In the decade following his death, his work was translated into English. Fanon is one of the key writers influencing a number of liberation movements since the 1960s ranging from Cuba to South Africa and the USA, as well as the development of the multidisciplinary field of post-colonial studies. His work on black consciousness and revolutionary violence in particular has garnered significant critical attention.

Fanon's theory was that in the binary world of European thought, the development of which ran contemporaneously with colonisation, blackness came to embody bad and whiteness good. This process of psychological (as well as material and social) domination creates the categories 'coloniser' and 'colonised', and people who are identified (and come to identify themselves) as 'black' and 'white'. As part of this relational process, he argues, the European created the 'negro' as a category of degraded humanity: a weak, irrational barbarian, incapable of self-government. For Fanon, this psychological process, in the context of physical domination and oppression, was tantamount to dehumanising the oppressed. His understanding of racialisation was that it comprised the effects of a process instigated to relieve Europeans of guilt and to make the colonised responsible for their own oppression, because in this world view, they are too weak to rule themselves. To be racialised was thus to have been dehumanised as part of the colonial process.

Michael Banton (1977: 18–19) also links racialisation to the colonial project, although his emphasis is far from Fanon's, on abstract levels:

> There was a process, which can be called racialization, whereby a mode of categorisation was developed, applied tentatively in European historical writing and then, more confidently to the populations of the world.

Perhaps it might be useful to step back at this point from the historical specificity that is clearly emphasised by both Fanon and Banton. Not because their ideas are misleading, but because they suppose a certain amount of historical knowledge. Going back to a different starting point, David Skinner (2006: 460), writing on science's contribution to this discourse, argues simply that: '"Racialization" refers to the social and political processes whereby racially distinct groups are constituted.' In science's case, he stresses that this is not only in the past, but in contemporary science (Chapter 7). Indeed, it is important to stress that while historical methods are an integral component of this approach (how else can change be identified?), the process of racialisation is ongoing and multifaceted. It is very much part of the contemporary world and unfinished business.

This contemporary presence of racialisation is one of the points raised by Miles (1987), whose championing of racialisation as an alternative and improved paradigm to that of 'race relations' is one of the drivers of debate. Miles maintains that racialisation is closely bound up with labour markets; in particular with both internal and international migration of workers and the ensuing imbalance of the power relations characterising modern capitalism. While phenotype is an important marker in which groups get racialised in this process, it is not the crucial feature of a population: take the Irish in nineteenth-century Britain and the Eastern European Jews in early twentieth-century England. These examples demonstrate the intimacy of the way in which social relations of class and 'race' intertwine to attach a specific set of racial meanings to a given group's collective behaviour. This process, for Miles, is primarily to do with material context (that is, the labour market and perceived competition between workers). As can be seen from the examples below, the term has also been deployed outside this specific context, so it would be true to say there is no consensus either about the usefulness of racialisation, nor about its exact meaning – much like the vast majority of concepts in the social sciences, which are basically models-in-progress that help us understand different aspects of the social world, however imperfectly.

Indeed, whatever problems remain, racialisation represents an essential sociological tool because it draws attention to the *process* of making 'race' relevant to a particular situation or context, and thus requires an examination of the precise circumstances in which this occurs: who the 'agents' are; who the actors are. In other words, who does what and how? It provides us with an alternative to the binaries of racist/anti-racist. Racialisation does not necessarily include ideas of intention, but it does reintroduce ideas of 'race' and force us to look hard enough at our subject to realise that *making* racial identities also necessarily involves invoking other forms of social identification. It restores complexity to a world of either/or. Ali Rattansi concludes that:

Racialization tells us that racism is never simply racism, but always exists in complex imbrication with nation, ethnicity, class, gender and sexuality, and therefore a dismantling of racism also requires, simultaneously as well as in the long run, a strategy to reduce relevant class inequalities, forms of masculinity, nationalisms and other social features, whereby racisms are reproduced in particular sites. (2005: 296)

Racialisation as an Idea

Racialisation appears therefore to be a deceptively difficult idea to pinpoint. On one hand, the theoretical backing is relatively straightforward. Racialisation represents a significant strategic emphasis of 'race's' social nature, and an abandonment of the idea that it is exclusively a biological phenomenon. The next step is to argue that 'race' becomes a meaningful element in social relations because of the existing ideological funds. It is therefore a group-level theory reliant upon a particular understanding of 'ideology' (defined as a set of ideas that distort the representation of social relations). Arguing that there is a process with identifiable outcomes that can be labelled racialisation also necessitates historical perspectives. If not, how can it be proven that there is such a *process* (by definition, a long-term phenomenon)?

My main concerns about the current balance of understandings of racialisation are, first, the degree of intentionality conveyed, and second, the implicit assumption that racialisation is *always and only* something the dominant group does to the dominated one. For the architects of Apartheid, Jim Crow[4] or the Final Solution, which could all be categorised as 'racial projects' (Omi and Winant, 1994 [1986]), the separation, exploitation and/or elimination of people categorised as racially different was clearly the paramount driving force. However, it is an error to imagine extreme examples of racism as constituting the only ground for study and reflection. Racism does not always end in genocide or mass murder, and racialisation is not always an intended objective. Rather, it makes more sense to think of racism as an intrinsic feature of the modern State's functions of classification, biopolitics and governance (Goldberg, 2000; Foucault, 2003. We shall return to this in Chapter 5).

Box 2.2   Racialisation and the State: Philosemitism?

One of the current conversations within the field of race and ethnicity is about the extent to which engagement with the Israel–Palestine conflict entails anti-Semitism. Brian Klug's (2004) analysis of the 'new anti-Semitism' identifies a strain of thought that equates any criticism of the Israeli state's actions per se as anti-Semitism. It is the space between people's actions and the State's actions that is highlighted in Hourida Bouteldja's intervention. Bouteldja is spokesperson for the French *Indigènes de la République* (IdR) movement.

She speaks regularly on racism and politics and is a controversial figure in France because of the IdR's message that France is a racist colonial power that has not come to terms with its history. She frames her thought-provoking speech in Oslo in March 2015[5] in terms of racialisation. Her departure point is that the focus of anti-racists should be the structural level, an idea that is also identified in this book (see Chapter 6).

Central to the *Parti des Indigènes de la République* (IR) position is that Islamophobia and anti-Semitism are asymmetrical. Bouteldja maintains that Jews are no longer the victims of state racism in France, even if they are still not accepted as bona fide members of the nation. Instead, they are deployed as a shield, and exploited in various forms particularly Zionism. The State's investment in commemorating the Shoah, she maintains, antagonises the other communities of colour and Roma in France because the transatlantic slave trade, colonial history and the Gypsy holocaust are not commemorated. It singles out the Jews for special treatment. She finishes by suggesting that by occupying such a privileged position, Jewish French people (and by extension all other Jews) are pressured into supporting the Israeli state in its role of representing the West in the Arab world, and all that flows from that in terms of conflict over Palestine.

> Because they nowadays benefit from a 'positive racialization' on the one hand, and because the conflation of Jewish and Zionist is constantly fuelled on the other hand, they divert the anger of the wretched of the earth onto them, and at the same time protect the racial infrastructure of the nation state. They protect the white social body. Here lies the second source of resentment against the Jews which has nothing to do with European antisemitism as you can see.

David Goldberg (2009: 162) argues that 'mainstream European thought about race thus pursued three interrelated paths ... : denial of race as socially, politically, and indeed morally relevant; an overriding focus on antisemitism as the real (and almost only) manifestation of racism; and the radical delinking of the intellectual and political histories of colonialism and racism'. These three elements indeed underpin Bouteldja's intervention.

She thus concludes that the contemporary structures of Islamophobia and anti-Semitism are not parallels, and that geopolitics and the role of Israel make the closeness between the French government and Zionists unpalatable to many Muslims, but also to those French Jews who do not identify as Zionists. This is a political analysis that requires reflection. Critics might argue that attributing 'philosemitism' to the French state is a form of 'new anti-Semitism'. Apart from the specifics of the French case, Bouteldja's main theme, i.e. the exploitation of one subordinate group as proxy of the dominant one, to more effectively control the others, is quite common, even constitutive of colonial history. The questions raised are to do with the role of the State, the shifts in power dynamics, and the relationship between how 'race' is understood in the context of globalisation.

I understand racialisation, then, to be a process by which 'race' becomes a salient element of social relationships, frequently as a normal part of the actions of the State and its agencies regarding other social actors. However, the door should be left open to the idea that racialisation may also be a reflexive act initiated toward an emancipatory end – as a form of group solidarity. As examples, we could cite the Black Power movement and the formation of online fora aimed at, and run by, particular minority groups such as the Chinese and Asians in Britain (as Parker and Song [2006] argue; see below). So far, so good, yet this leaves us without any concrete examples that would help us understand and further critique racialisation. In the next section, we shall attempt to do this.

Racialisation in Practice

The contributions to Murji and Solomos's (2005a) collection on racialisation demonstrate a plethora of historical, sociological and psychological methods within the sociology of racism, analysing what is constructed as an uneven and contingent process. That it is uneven is about the only thing that emerges as a consensus. Ann Phoenix (2005), for example, shows how young white Londoners understand their racial identities in relation to those of their black counterparts through experiences of space and place. Deploying ideas from relational psychology, she observes how they theorise themselves as raceless individuals vis-à-vis raced Others. Tony Kushner (2005) argues that racialisation is the most effective tool to take into account the complexity of the responses to Jewish immigration to England at the end of the nineteenth and early twentieth centuries (by both British Jews and Gentiles). He notes how culture, the residential spatial distribution and the employment practices and experiences of new Jewish immigrants became understood as evidence of racial difference which was threatening to the English working class in particular. David Goldberg (2005), deliberately attempting to avoid using racialisation as what he calls 'an analytic', settles on the specificities of the USA, and contends that a more appropriate way to understand the topic is the 'Americanization of race'. However, it is revealing that even his critique of racialisation entails the examination of a long-term set of interacting processes involving the interplay of structures and agencies, as does racialisation. These three examples are merely to hint at the dizzying array of applications of the idea of racialisation. What we shall do now is take three themes: citizenship and belonging, welfare and the reflexive construction of minority identities, and apply racialisation to their understanding. It is, of course, not the only way to understand this process but a revealing one.

Box 2.3   Concepts of National Belonging

The two concepts governing most nations' citizenship regulations are derived from Roman law. These are ***ius soli*** and ***ius sanguinis***.

Ius soli refers to qualification for membership through birth within a given territory. *Ius sanguinis* refers to qualification through bloodlines (that is, parents' or grandparents' nationality). While most nations combine these routes in their contemporary legislation, this was not always the case. Until the 1970s, for example, French citizenship was gained through birth within France or one of its overseas *départements* or territories, regardless of parents' nationalities (*ius soli*), while the counter-case was Germany. The concept of German nationality is relatively new, as the country was only unified in 1871, then split again after the Second World War. It relied on the idea that German nationality was in the blood and expressed through culture. This meant in effect that after Germany's reunification in 1990, people of German culture who lived outside Germany (especially in Central and Eastern Europe) were granted German nationality (*ius sanguinis*). However, the children of immigrant workers from Southern and Eastern Europe and Turkey, who had been recruited to bolster the German workforce in the post-war period, and who had been born and educated in Germany, had no way of accessing German citizenship. This changed only in 2000, when a new piece of legislation guaranteed the right of access to nationality through birth in Germany and greatly facilitated naturalisation.

Racialisation in Practice 1: Citizenship and Belonging

Membership of a nation state is not determined by simply excluding people explicitly on the grounds of 'race'. Historically, nations might be dominated by groups who come to define themselves and others racially. Yet in the contemporary world, direct reference to race as a criterion for membership is highly unusual, and the citizenship rules for many nations now clearly state that this is not a determining factor. When legislators set the rules, they are effectively answering the questions: who is a member of the national 'family', and where are the limits of the 'imagined community' (Anderson, 1983)? In this case, racialisation works through the way in which routes to membership are regulated. In terms of broad patterns, the outcome is always to favour the access of some, while placing obstacles in the way of others.

There have broadly speaking been four principal ways to access citizenship since it became a modern phenomenon (accompanied by passports, immigration legislation, etc.). Two of these relate to Roman legal concepts: *ius soli* and *ius sanguinis* (see Box 2.3). The others are through changing citizenship through having complied with a residence qualification (naturalisation), or marriage to a national, possibly followed by a residential qualifying period (post-nuptial naturalisation).

The case of the United Kingdom illustrates that there can be movement between these two poles at different times, for different reasons. Until 1948, no distinctions were made in British law other than that between British national and foreign national (or 'alien'). People born in the vast British Empire were deemed British. Only in the post-war period did large-scale migration to Britain appear as a possibility, as the economy required a larger labour supply than could be satisfied from within the country. The 1948 Act distinguished between British, Commonwealth, Irish and Other nationals, without stipulating a difference in rights accruing to members of the first three groups. At this stage, citizenship was clearly based on *ius soli*.[6]

Between 1948 and the early 1960s, discussion of the pros and cons of immigration into Britain occurred at Cabinet level, and became a political issue. A minority of parliamentarians protested against continued 'coloured' immigration (from the former colonies in the West Indies, Africa and the Indian subcontinent). By 1962, immigrants from these regions had to have a work visa, for which there was a quota. The intensity of debates on immigration and what was referred to as 'race relations' in those days peaked in the late 1960s.

In February 1968, the 'Kenyan Asians' crisis occurred. Indian families resident in Kenya and their Kenyan-born children were forced to leave the country by its new leaders. Faced with the prospect of the arrival of tens of thousands of so-called 'coloured' immigrants with British passports (which was perceived to be a potential cause of hostility toward the government by the white UK majority), the British parliament passed a new piece of legislation with unheard-of rapidity: three days for all the readings of a Bill. The 1968 Commonwealth Immigrants Act deployed the concept of people with a 'substantial connection' to Britain. This was defined as having a parent or grandparent born in the UK. Those without this connection no longer had the right to automatic entry, residence and employment. The British passport-holding 'Kenyan Asians' were, at a stroke, rendered stateless. Note that the *ius soli* criterion now applied to a much smaller territory: the UK rather than the British Empire, or the UK and its former colonies. Here too is the introduction of the idea of 'patriality', or bloodlines (*ius sanguinis*) into the qualification for rights in Britain. However, all of this, and the ensuing 1971 Immigration Act referred only to immigration and not nationality per se. It was not until 1981, after the oil crisis that had reduced levels of primary immigration in Europe (and making family reunification a significant proportion of new immigration), that a British government incorporated the developments of the previous decades into citizenship legislation. The 1981 British Nationality Act set out three broad layers of citizenship (and is the only country's legislation that splits up rights accruing to nationals) and allows for eight hierarchical layers of rights-bearing nationals. At the top of this are those who were born in the UK on or after 1 January 1983, and whose parents are UK nationals or have permanent residence in the UK. So from a situation whereby all imperial subjects and those from the UK had been equally 'British' in legal terms until the 1960s, different criteria were steadily applied to people from areas of the world where non-white people were the vast majority, thus regulating employment opportunities and residence in the UK. Finally, in 1981, the pool from which British nationals with the full range of citizens' rights were drawn was fixed in order to limit access to it by people from the former empire. Take into consideration that after 1971 it had already become more difficult for former colonial subjects to enter Britain, making it less likely that they would form part of the pool of people born in the UK or who had permanent residence rights there. The intimacy of legislation with immigration and citizenship, as well as the racialised character of both, can thus be observed from this very short summary.

As a coda, when Britain signed up to the Single European Act in 1986, it granted freedom of residence and employment to the nationals (of whom the vast majority are white) of all the other EU member states.[7] In terms of rights, this group is now second of the nine (previously eight) levels set out in the 1981 Nationality Act. So while legislation and regulations can be talked about as though they are 'neutral' administrative categories, they do, in practice, favour some groups over others, and the reasons why they do so can be traced to political decision making at particular historical moments.

Box 2.4   Emotions and Racialisation

The earliest models of how racism works in the mid-twentieth century were based on the concept of 'prejudice' rather than racism. These models are psychological ones, focusing on individuals as much as groups. An initial model that saw prejudice as a rational response to 'inferior races' (Rooster, 1930) was challenged by Adorno et al.'s (1950) concept of an 'authoritarian society', but then supported by Allport's (1954) emphasis on the human need to use categories to understand society. The ambivalence over whether prejudice is best understood through the individual or the collective, and as rational or irrational has persisted. However, as is noted throughout this book, the main lines of enquiry for social scientists interested in racism have been underpinned by the idea that 'race' is social and structural, allowing less space for the social psychological insights and for the exploration of the rational/irrational binary.

In the 1990s and 2000s, a stream of work developed in which emotions are theorised as integral to understanding how and why people construct identities, and especially how that relates to racism. James Jasper (2006: 17) argues that emotions are 'clusters of feeling, forms of attraction or repulsion'. 'Affect' covers sustained and conscious love; hate; respect; resentment; solidarity; and negativity toward outsiders. For him it is the most politically powerful emotion. Margaret Wetherell, whose pioneering work analyses how racial discourses are constructed in New Zealand (Wetherell and Potter, 1992), underscores the importance of emotion in understanding identity-construction:

(Continued)

(Continued)

> Global political issues, multicultural futures, colonial history, immigration and national identity are being discussed. Yet what is fascinating is how we refract those conjunctions through domestic, ordinary, and wearing affective routines – through the well-worn and intimate practice of 'taking umbrage' and 'righteous indignation', intertwining with other practices such as the more poignant figurations that go with the sense of 'missing out', being a victim, and the discomfort of not having 'natural' claims recognised. (Wetherell, 2012: 7)

'Affect', and emotion more generally, are important for us as scholars of racism because of their 'immediate entanglement with very particular human capacities for making meaning' (Wetherell and Beer, 2014). Moreover, ideas about power function through affect, and indeed affect can be read through the ways people talk about power relationships. Sara Ahmed's (2001, 2004) stimulating work posits the model of an 'affective economy': in which emotions are circuits rather than responses to particular stimuli. In this process, ideas get stuck together by repeated proximity and association, producing 'affect' on the part of people exposed to the circuit.

Her starting point is that hate, for example, works first through a process she terms the 'production of the ordinary', where people are linked together as being ordinary, and at the same time threatened by a set of 'Others' (e.g. immigrants and ethnic minority groups) (Ahmed, 2001: 346). 'Hate', for Ahmed, is therefore an inexhaustible emotional circuit between the ordinary and the un-ordinary:

> The emotion of hate works to animate the ordinary subject, to bring that fantasy to life, precisely by constituting the ordinary as in crisis, and the ordinary person as the real victim … The ordinary or normative subject is reproduced as the injured party: the one 'hurt' or even damaged by the 'invasion' of others. The bodies of others are hence transformed into 'the hated' through a discourse of pain. They are assumed to 'cause' injury to the ordinary white subject, such that their proximity is read as the origin of bad feeling. (Ahmed, 2004: 118)

Paula Ioanide (2015) explores the similar idea of 'emotional economies' using the example of anti-immigrant legislators and protestors in Escondido, California. These groups produced and supported local legislation in 2006. The rationale put forward by the key actors for a law punishing landlords for renting to illegal aliens (immigrants bring dirt, crime, tuberculosis, and overcrowding is part of their culture) is not based on empirical facts, but on ideas that circulate, gaining potency as they pass on the circuit between entitlement, whiteness, Latinos, crime, dirt, overcrowding, etc. In Ioanide's argument, these circuits produce 'emotional economies' of hostility and white victimhood, in which – significantly – all Latinos are collapsed into the category 'illegals', against whom the legislation is aimed.

Emotion (especially 'affect') can thus help generate a morally advantageous victim position. In doing so, it depicts other people as perpetrators, embodying all the negative characteristics that the victims do not share. So it is not an empirical question of what the 'perpetrators' actually do, or do not do: the process works by clusters of associations that produce emotional responses.

Racialisation in Practice 2: Welfare and Nation

Although the development of welfare has slightly different histories in North America and Europe, it is recognised that from the last decades of the twentieth century, the models are coming under scrutiny and criticism in the currently dominant neoliberal discourses that prioritise the desirability of cutting state expenditure, and the reduction of the role of the State in individual lives. These ideas have the concomitant aim of making people more responsible for their economic lives. Three brief examples demonstrate how the payment of welfare can become racialised.

Harell et al.'s (2014) survey of attitudes toward welfare in Canada suggests that people are less likely to approve of welfare when the recipient is a member of the First Nations. These groups appear disadvantaged in a range of socio-economic data on health, housing, employment, etc., and the authors note that Aboriginals and Black Canadians experienced the worst concentrated urban poverty 'in older industrial cities' (Harell et al., 2014: 2584). For some Canadians, colonial policies including removing people from their lands, banning traditional industries and replacing the income with public assistance have caused the vulnerability of First Nations people, while others argue that dependency is inherent in their backward cultures. As the basis of the welfare system is reciprocity, the idea that a group does not subscribe to the idea of paying their way, but rather of acquiescing to a life on welfare is a very damaging one. In essence, it suggests that First Nations are as a group, a drain on Canada's collective resources. In the survey, 740 people were shown a case for welfare, half with no clue about the racialised identity of the claimant, and half with clues that the claimant was a member of the First Nations. The rate of rejection of the claim rose significantly in the latter case.

In the USA, research has demonstrated the unpopularity of welfare (Gilens, 1999), and its attachment in people's minds to Black and Latino Americans (despite the fact that the majority of recipients are white). Moreover, the discourse on welfare recipients has, in Hancock's study (2004), produced the figure of the single, black mother as 'Welfare Queen': welfare claimants are conflated around this stereotypical 'figure'. Hancock argues that this has significant impacts on policy, as the discourse around the new reforms to welfare in 1996 (Personal Responsibility and Work Opportunity Reconciliation Act) identified the Welfare Queen as the paradigmatic recipient, characterised by hyper-fertility and laziness.

A dislike of welfare is shared by many across class and racial backgrounds in the USA. Being on welfare is seen as choosing not to participate in the American dream, based on the values of individual industry. Single black mothers are understood as not contributing through work and taxation to the nation, bringing up children with the same anti-work values, and usurping the male head of household. Hancock maintains that the dominant ideas about single black women as recipients of welfare shaped and .03.00limited the policy options in discussions around the 1996 Act, by framing the welfare system as being defrauded, thus advantaging those actors who sought to reduce and add conditions to welfare. So by media and politicians generating and sustaining the idea that (contrary to the statistics) welfare recipients were overwhelmingly single black mothers, the legitimacy of cutting welfare and attaching a battery of conditions to it was enhanced.

Finland shares the deep investment in the social welfare state characteristic of Nordic countries, albeit to a lesser degree than Sweden. Suvi Keskinen (2016: 354) argues that 'the welfare state, egalitarianism and universalism became the central tenets of Finnish national identity'. Her study of political discourse on welfare reform in 2009–11 as a response to the rise in asylum-seeking, identifies three discourses: welfare nationalism, welfare chauvinism and welfare exclusionism. Her conclusion (2016: 355) is that welfare entitlements are a function of the debate about who belongs to the Finnish nation, and the three discourses draw the line increasingly narrowly. Welfare nationalism is more focused on Finland than on immigrants, whereas: 'Welfare chauvinism frames welfare provision as reserved only "for our own" in the sense that belonging or non-belonging is based on (ethno)nationalist, othering and often racialising criteria. In such discourses and rhetoric, focus on welfare is secondary to exclusionary and racialised understandings of the people/nation. The national identity, with its cultural aspects and the perceived deviance of migrants is central for the understanding of "our own".

There are no large numbers of indigenous ethnic minorities (Saami account for less than 1 per cent), and most immigrants are from the former Soviet Union, Russia, Estonia and Sweden. Maybe 3 per cent are from elsewhere. The far-right nationalist True Finns Party's position is characterised by Keskinen as 'welfare exclusionism'. Its focus is on asylum-seekers as non-contributing foreign nationals with backward cultures. For the True Finns:

> … welfare provision is reserved only for a part of those who live and work in the country, not for all with a residence permit. This includes views and policies that deny or condition access to income benefits or social services for migrants and their descendants even after they have lived in the country for several years and gained a permanent residence permit.

Indeed, citizenship, connected closely in this equation, should be contingent on the assessed 'level of the integration' of the migrant. Integration is defined as proper language skills, not living on social benefits and a wish to live according to the rules of Finnish society (Keskinen's translation of True Finns' policy paper, 2016: 361).

So the racialisation of Finnish welfare revolves around a definition of authentic Finnishness that is cultural and racial: only those with the desired characteristics can have access. The True Finns' racialised vision would have appeared extreme at the turn of the twenty-first century, but as the mainstream shifts rightwards, and since welfare exclusionism is rationalised in terms of economics, the discourse also appears race-neutral.

These three sketches demonstrate the significance of racialisation of public policy. Welfare is particularly emotive, evoking as it does the individual's relationship with the State, and crystallising ideas about belonging, reciprocity, solidarity, fairness, entitlement and unfairness. In all three places, ideas about what belonging to the nation should look like, and what responsibilities and entitlements are attached to it, function to produce an opposite idea of what it should not look like, and why people should not be entitled to it. All of these are racialised in terms of values: values that are, in the dominant discourses, unevenly distributed among the racialised groups within the national territory.

Box 2.5   'Police Lethality' in Sao Paolo

Costa Vargas and Amparo Alves (2010) beautifully develop a case study of racialisation of space in Sao Paolo, in which they demonstrate a set of overlapping social geographies enabling us to understand patterns of police killings not as the cause, but as a symptom of multiple social inequalities. Rates of police killings in Brazil's urban areas are enormous: 'In a month, Rio police kills more than two and half times more people than the New York Police Department kills in a whole year' (Cavallaro and Manuel, 1997). Rio's police killing rate in the early twenty-first century approaches the mortality rate of Baghdad, which is actually at war. Costa Vargas and Amparo Alves collate local and national data on 'race' in Brazil, which is already a contested political space: the dominant idea is that race has no meaning as the whole country is 'mixed'. They show that black Brazilians suffer worse child mortality, lower rates of employment, lower wages and are less likely to live in a dwelling connected to sewage than whites. Two-thirds of the inhabitants of favelas (shanty towns) are black, vis-à-vis one-third white.

Using a set of maps, the authors then show how the city of Sao Paolo's social geography concentrates the particular variables: social class, age, gender, race, and various forms of vulnerability (homicide, male homicide, teenage pregnancy, low educational outcomes, etc.). Specific areas of Sao Paolo have higher concentrations of working-class, younger, lower paid, black people with a higher risk of vulnerability and homicide. These are indeed the neighbourhoods where police lethality – uneven across the city – is highest.

In other words, as an expression of deeply ingrained social inequalities that are marked by spatial boundaries of belonging, police lethality is a manifestation of the state's complicity in reproducing such boundaries.

(Continued)

(Continued)

> At the extreme, the deaths caused by the police work culturally and prag-
> matically by constantly redrawing the racial lines of privilege and exclu-
> sion. As the result of multiply intersecting social vectors that become
> actualized in urban space, the lines of privilege and exclusion thus
> become reliable predictors – and, we claim, energizers – of violent death.
> Police lethality is a symptom, not a cause of social inequalities. (Costa
> Vargas and Amparo Alves, 2010: 632)

So this study enables us to understand that social inequalities are compounded along various axes, and that racialisation is always embedded in
other processes. It is never just about 'race', but always about how 'race'
articulates with other variables, and, here, in the case of what sense the
police make of these social geographies, seeing the people as more killable
than those in wealthier, safer, whiter neighbourhoods.

Racialisation in Practice 3: Self-Racialisation of Minority Identities

While it is clear that a group of people *can* be racialised by dominant groups,
and thus transformed into a subordinate social category by a combination of
ideological, cultural and legislative practices, inhabiting this social location
can sometimes be a rallying point for solidarity, campaigns against discrimination and more. In this section, I want to give two examples of this: the Black
Power movement and a set of online fora run by the British-born Chinese
community[8] represent diverse efforts to base social movements and explora-
tions of shared identity around the idea of belonging to a 'race'.

Black Power

For decades after the formal ending of slavery, African Americans endured
institutionalised discrimination in employment, housing and education. They
were also targeted for extra-legal punishments such as lynching and beatings
for transgressing, or appearing to transgress the Jim Crow legislation, and
were used as prison labour on the basis of flimsily evidenced law-breaking
(Blackmon, 2008). Wider social codes required them to behave in particular
ways, and keep away from particular places. One of the legacies of the slavery
and immediate post-abolition period was the social message that white was
still superior to black, and one of the ways in which this was expressed was
for some to physically engineer a 'whitening' process using a range of products
for the skin and hair.

   By the mid-1960s, however, one stream of thought in black America was
aimed at re-evaluating the term 'black', which had been so negatively endowed

for so long, with new positive meanings. Malcolm X recounts in his autobiography (X and Haley, 1969) how part of his conversion to Islam in prison in the 1950s involved a fellow inmate encouraging him to sit with a dictionary and read through the entries for 'white' and 'black' respectively, and to compare the meanings attributed to them. The domination of white Americans, ran the argument, involved not only physical but mental subjugation, making black Americans internalise ideas of inferiority. These expressed themselves in many ways, and one of them was by straightening natural hair and avoiding association with anything African. On the contrary, black people who were part of the Black Power movement allowed their hair to grow naturally, in Afro styles, sometimes wore clothing and took names associated with their African heritage. The phrase 'Black is Beautiful' was coined in this period, and people who identified with this project eschewed identification with white culture. The movement thus focused on both cultural resistance to the American norms, one that encompassed political action, and on economic self-sufficiency rather than integration into white society, but based on black solidarity. A range of figures such as Robert Williams (who first coined the term 'Black Power'), Stokely Carmichael/Kwame Touré,[9] Malcolm X, Amiri Baraka and Angela Davis were nationally prominent in this diverse movement, whose vanguard was provided by the Black Panther Party. A key iconic moment came at the 1968 Olympic Games, when two American medallists in the 200 metres, John Carlos and Tommie Smith, gave the Black Power salute (outstretched right arm and clenched fist, wearing gloves) during the playing of the national anthem, an action that provoked hostile mainstream media coverage in America, as did the Black Power movement in general.

Although the Black Panther Party, for example, was effectively closed down by the authorities, and influential figures were killed or imprisoned, many ideas attached to Black Power itself, such as self-reliance, the nourishment of collective self-esteem and the need to focus on developing institutions and economic autonomy have survived. Not that these did not exist before the 1960s. Black Power was never a homogeneous movement, and some of its critics were also Black Americans, who considered it a controversial anti-white path away from the policy of slow integration into mainstream America that they had been seeking over generations, and toward unnecessary confrontation. However, this does not detract from the idea that in this movement, the negative associations of blackness were confronted and an attempt was made to reverse them, to make black beautiful, in a context where it had not been, and to fix blackness as the rallying point from which people could campaign for equality.[10]

BBC

BBC does not only stand for the British Broadcasting Corporation but also 'British-born Chinese'. David Parker and Miri Song (2006) argue that British-born Chinese online fora constitute an example of 'strategic essentialism' (see Box 1.2), and this process of 'reflexive racialisation' helps a community orientate itself around shared experiences involving being racialised as Chinese in Britain. Both parts of this equation are significant. While ties with mainland China, Hong Kong and the global Chinese diaspora are acknowledged and engaged in, there is also a sense that the concerns of the contributors to the fora are specifically grounded in typical BBC experiences, such as facing verbal abuse at restaurants run by family (2006: 583), and inadequate police responses to harassment. Parker and Song contend that: 'Taken together the messages constitute a collective witness to the experience of growing up as Chinese in Britain' (2006: 584).

The complexity of racialisation is the result of the two-tier process of homogenisation (finding commonality) of BBCs, and critically examining the internal differences of the group. The ongoing discussion thus opens up the possibility of *reflexively* developing a broad identity with a racial or ethnic basis, that is, critically examining it rather than taking it at face value. Yet this construction of British-born Chinese-ness, is openly recognised as *not* constituting a homogenising plea for biological and cultural authenticity. Indeed, some members reacted angrily to what was interpreted as exactly such a plea from an American-based Chinese website. For Parker and Song, the 'offline' context is one of racism experienced in particular settings that are familiar to the vast majority of BBCs, and this background 'overdetermines' (2006: 584) both the content and process of racialisation.

Moreover, the now defunct britishbornchinese.org.uk website was the nucleus of campaigning against pernicious representations of the Chinese in Britain, as in the campaign to stop scapegoating Chinese food over the Foot and Mouth health scare in April 2001, as well as responses to other negative portrayals in the media. There are also offshoots of the site in civil society, with organisations representing BBCs developing out of it and sister websites appearing. It is also a site that is used as an obvious platform for groups campaigning around issues important to the membership. So, in this case, one of racialisation 'from below', as the authors put it, demonstrates that the social process does not always have to be carried out as a direct effect of power being exerted to frame representations of a minority and/or dominated group in a negative way. It can also be a response to this minority position: an attempt to create a space in which experiences are drawn on in order to resist dominant representations and forge a positive identity that recognises plurality within a specific social location.

Conclusion

- There is no consensus over the exact meaning or significance of racialisation, but there is broad agreement that it represents a step forward from essentialised 'race relations', and that seeing identity-building as a process is a useful perspective.

- There are a wide variety of meanings ranging from the largely descriptive one, the increasing salience of 'race' in a given context, to something imposed as a result of unequal power relations, on one hand and, on the other, something minority groups can do, on purpose, as part of their resistance struggles. Such diversity makes racialisation of limited use beyond a certain analytical level without qualification, which I hope to have suggested above. Allowing the understanding of racialisation as *potentially* a two-way process also moves us away from the one-way street model and toward the conclusion that raciali-sation is not a crude *synonym* of racism, but a means by which racism can be made functional and sustained, as well as resisted.

- The strong points of this concept are the historical dimension (a process cannot be understood without one); an openness to the idea that 'race' is both cultural and physical at the same time; and that racialisation is usu-ally transversal – in other words, it cuts across other variables.

- Racialisation usually shows that paradoxically, it is never just about 'race': the examples of police violence in Sao Paolo and discourses about welfare in Canada, the USA and Finland show that the variables are multiple, and they militate against simple readings of social relationships.

Points for Reflection

Can you explain the differences between 'race', racism and racialisation?

What does 'racialisation' offer us in terms of understanding racism, and what are its limits?

Is racialisation what dominant groups do to dominated ones?

Further Reading

Murji, K. and Solomos, J. (2005) *Racialization: Studies in Theory and Practice.* Oxford: Oxford University Press.

Still the most varied collection of social sciences work on racialisation.

Chakraborti, N. (2010) 'Beyond "Passive Apartheid"? Developing Policy and Research Agendas on Rural Racism in Britain', *Journal of Ethnic and Migration Studies* 36(3): 501–17.

Summary and synthesis of work on racism in rural spaces in the UK: demon-strates how different types of space (urban and rural) are differently racialised.

Torre, C.D.L. (1999) 'Everyday Forms of Racism in Contemporary Ecuador: The Experiences of Middle-Class Indians', *Ethnic and Racial Studies* 22(1): 92–112.

Shows how categories of 'mestizo', 'white' and 'Indian' are implemented in everyday situations. The middle-class Indians interviewed are usually assumed to be slow, dirty, rural peasants and treated accordingly by their white or mestizo interlocutors.

Notes

1. 'Race relations' are discussed by Kushner (2005) for the UK and Jacobson (1998) for the USA. Rex (1970) is the most complete sociological exposition in my opinion.

2. After this chapter, the reader may wish to turn to the excellent introductory essay by Karim Murji and John Solomos (2005b) that introduces their collection (Murji and Solomos, 2005a), and Rattansi's (2005) critical analysis in the same volume. While some of the argument presented above is covered, theirs goes into further detail about the distinctions made by more writers than I can deal with in an introductory text.

3. See Miles and Brown (2003: 102). Moreover, subordinate groups can make claims for representation and solidarity based on positive interpretations of 'race' – the 'Irish Race conventions' in twentieth-century urban America and the Black Power movement, for example. However, such strategies are responses to unequal power relations.

4. Jim Crow was the name given to the raft of state laws and practices that institutionalised segregation and violence against African Americans during the post-slavery period until the passage of the Civil Rights Act (1876–1964). See the *Jim Crow History* website at: www.jimcrowhistory.org/.

5. The text of Bouteldja's speech can be found in English ('State Racism(s) and Philosemitism or How to Politicise the Issue of Antiracism in France?') www.indigenes-republique.fr/state-racisms-and-philosemitism-or-how-to-politicize-the-issue-of-antiracism-in-france/.

6. Foreign Secretary Lord Palmerston's well-known speech in the House of Commons on the 'Don Pacifico' incident in 1850 encapsulates this: 'As the Roman, in days of old, held himself free from indignity when he could say "Civis Romanus Sum" [I am a Roman citizen], so also a British subject in whatever land he may be, shall feel confident that the watchful eye and the strong arm of England will protect him against injustice and wrong.'

7. This will be the case until 2018–19, at which point the UK is set to leave the European Union. What happens after that remains to be seen.

8. Some of the fora identified by Parker and Song (www.britishchineseonline.com and www.dimsum.co.uk/) are now defunct. However post-2010 online communities include the Chopsticks Club professional association (www.chopsticksclub.com/), and Nee Hao magazine (www.neehao.co.uk/), for which this point is probably equally true.

9. A text of a speech made at University of California at Berkeley in 1966 and an audio recording can be accessed at: www.americanrhetoric.com/speeches/stokelycarmichaelblackpower.html.

10. See Van Deburg (1992) and Joseph (2006) for examples of analyses, as well as the foundational text by Carmichael and Hamilton (1967).

3

Ethnicity

In this chapter we will

- Look at theories and definitions of ethnicity
- Compare the concepts of ethnicity and race
- Look at cases studies in which these theoretical definitions are tested
- Conclude as to the utility of 'ethnicity' and 'race' as explanatory concepts

Introduction

In Chapter 1 we looked at 'race' as a sociological concept, and found there were fundamental problems with using it. In this chapter we turn to ethnicity, an associated concept that many see as preferable to 'race'. While 'race' is to do with the body, it is argued, ethnicity is to do with culture. While 'race' is hierarchical, ethnicity contains no a priori ranking. While 'race' is an ascribed (imposed) identity, ethnicity is self-ascribed. While 'race' is a social construct masquerading as biological fact, ethnicity is based on real cultural production and interpretation. Let's keep this hypothetically neat set of binaries in mind as we explore ethnicity and its relationship to 'race'.

It seems to me that there are three outcomes of a comparison between 'race' and ethnicity as concepts. One possibility is that the binaries just outlined are valid, and this produces connected but distinct concepts that are useful in their own ways. Another is that the boundaries are not as clear as they first appear, and it is actually difficult to distinguish between the two ideas in practice. This outcome is also a question of degree. How much overlap can there be before the two ideas no longer function as distinct? A third outcome is that we learn something useful from the exploration. The latter of course does not depend on which of the first two is the result.

'Race' and 'Ethnicity'

The concepts of 'race' and ethnicity have genealogies to which we shall return in a moment, but let's look at some obvious and official ways in which they differ from one another. If we look at the US Census documents (see Box 8.2), the two are clearly demarcated. If you tick the category 'Hispanic' you may then tick another racial category. The former is an ethnicity, a cultural umbrella term that includes a variety of people who tick other boxes to do with race. 'People may choose to report more than one race group. People of any race may be of any ethnic origin', says the introduction to the US Census Bureau webpage on Race.[1] Similarly, the racial umbrella terms (White; Black or African American; American Indian or Alaska Native; Asian; and Native Hawaiian or Other Pacific Islander) branch out into more specific cultural groups. However, the US Census Bureau definitions are geographical: the category 'Asian' for example covers 'A person having origins in any of the original peoples of the Far East, Southeast Asia, or the Indian subcontinent including, for example, Cambodia, China, India, Japan, Korea, Malaysia, Pakistan, the Philippine Islands, Thailand, and Vietnam.'

If ethnicity is specific to culture, we might expect more detail. There are a number of groups with distinct cultures in India (more than 80 languages) alone, let alone China, Thailand and Malaysia. So let's step back and think analytically. The distinction between ethnicity and 'race' is made in these important official ways, by reference to a country of origin, which may in some people's genealogies, be a number of generations past. Also this categorisation is (unsurprisingly) specific to the history of the USA, reflecting indigenous people colonised; African-descended people whose ancestors were enslaved and brought to the colonies; indigenous people whose territory was acquired through treaties with other colonising powers; and waves of migration from virtually everywhere in the world. When we look at the UK Census we will see the same specificities. However, official ethnicity is quite limited. In this ultra-broad brushstroke, Nigerian Christian and Muslim migrants are grouped under Black African, while within the 'white' category in the USA, Amish and Cajuns join Northern African and Middle Eastern Muslims. This is a big difference from contexts such as France, where North African (Maghrebin) background is a subordinate position in the racialised hierarchy. All these groups obviously have class and gender differences within them, but they seem quite importantly distinct from one another considering they are in the same secondary category as each other after 'race', or share more with people in another racial and ethnic group.

In the UK Census, we find no mention of 'race' at all, but instead a section entitled 'Ethnic origin', which offers sections such as white, black, mixed, Asian, Chinese and Gypsy-Traveller, Arab. Subsections include terms that are geographical, exceptions to the geographical, racialised and cultural umbrellas. Like the US Census, the UK Census categories reflect a history of conquest (as does the existence of separate and slightly different forms for Scotland and

Northern Ireland) and migration. This UK Census question lies next to the one on religion, which was reintroduced at the 2001 Census after lobbying from faith groups from the Indian subcontinent, who argued that religion (i.e. a cultural distinction) outweighed for them the geographically suggested 'ethnic' one of being 'British Asians'.

This is by no means an engagement with the scholarly work on ethnicity, which we will address in the next section. I have merely used existing official categorisations, with which readers might be familiar, to demonstrate that the bases for using ethnicity, and indeed for distinguishing it from 'race' as a concept, might not be particularly clear, logical or consistent.

Theorising Ethnicity

The word 'ethnicity' is a neologism in English, dating back only to the 1940s. The term *ethnos* however, from which ethnic and ethnicity are derived, is a Greek word used to refer to those lying outside the *demos* (i.e. not part of the political community, and from elsewhere). I think this is an important departure point to store away while we go through other theories: ethnic is not, any more than 'race', a neutral term. In fact, if we think about how such collocations as 'ethnic minority', 'ethnic conflict', 'ethnic restaurant', 'ethnic jewellery', etc. (I'm sure you can add more) are actually used, then there is a pattern. The groups constituting the minority, engaging in conflict, running the restaurant and making the jewellery are not the dominant ones in a given society, but those with less political power, maybe migrants, maybe indigenous, maybe there because of the legacy of slavery or indentured labour, but it is seldom that the label is attached to the dominant group. Would anyone say that the largest 'minority ethnic group' in Ireland is UK nationals for example, even though that is technically true? The terms 'ethnic majority' or 'majority ethnic' are very recent additions to the lexicon.

Ethnos, Ethnie, Ethnic Group

It is this marginalised connection to the nation that was the starting point of the ethnos. However, ideas get transformed over time, and clearly, by the nineteenth century, when French historian Ernest Renan (1992) was teaching his classes on the composition of the nation in the modern world the *ethnie*, to use the French word for ethnic group, had assumed the opposite meaning. Indeed, Renan's point was that ethnicity established the nation: the common descent, cultural ties and a belief in a shared destiny were for him what defined the nation. He certainly was not conceptualising the French *ethnie* as marginal. However, we know that what might today be considered 'ethnic groups', such as the Bretons, the Alsaciens and Occitans on the various edges of Metropolitan French territory, were less inclined to feel French than others, and indeed according to Eugen Weber's (1976) research, the idea of being part of France (rather than part of a smaller group) was still an elite, mainly urban identification until the First World War. Moreover, Renan's observation that the ethnic bonds whose importance he underscored in the life of the nation were usually based on collective fiction links us neatly to Max Weber's early examination of ethnic groups (1978 [1922]).

Writing in the early twentieth century, a generation after Renan, Weber was clear that ethnic groups were an act of social interpretation (what we would today refer to as 'social constructions') rather than objectively identifiable groups that could be used in the analysis of society: 'We shall call "ethnic groups" those human groups that entertain a subjective belief in their common descent because of similarities or physical type or of customs or both, or because of memories of colonization and migration' (1978 [1922]: 389), and Weber goes on to add that: 'It does not matter whether or not an objective blood relationship exists.'

Weber focuses on the political community as the greatest stimulus for people to think of themselves collectively in this way, and notes the emotional charge of such identifications. The key element of belonging is belief in a common descent: that is, bloodlines and collective heritage, and the motivation for acting collectively is to secure resources.

Indeed, access to and control of resources is central to the story of ethnicity, and explains why it is a key topic in political science and social sciences, which are concerned with power and inequalities in different contexts.

Colonialism and Ethnicity

One of these contexts is the colonial one created by the European powers. In many places, the colonial project had involved manipulating the existing group hierarchies between local peoples in order to impede collective action aimed at resisting the colonising forces. These groups had typically distinguished themselves from one another by language, cultural practices, territory occupied, etc. Those distinctions can now be understood as 'ethnic', although this language was not used at the time. This manipulation often assumed the form of identifying one or more groups and conferring privileges upon them, such as the Tutsis in Rwanda under Belgian control, where distinctions between them and the majority Hutus and other smaller groups ended up being enshrined in a formal system of ethnicity, where people's identity was recorded and stated on ID cards. Moreover, understandings of cultural difference were actively used by colonisers as tools to facilitate control, as in the case of the categorisation and differential criminalisation of Indian hill tribes (Brown, 2002; Schwarz, 2010).

J.S. Furnivall's (1939) study of Indonesia (then part of the Dutch East Indies) marked the beginning of a particular implementation of the colonial legacies of control. Furnivall argued that the groups designated by the colonisers as the components of the nation, which, he noted, had lived separately under colonial rule, would seek political monopoly in order to control resource allocation in the newly independent decolonised states. Once the colonisers left, an ethnic scramble for resources would ensue. His term 'plural society', then, sought to capture a widespread form of colonial rule. It was picked up by social scientists in the decades that followed and applied to a number of developing world countries, particularly in the Americas, but then Africa and Asia (Freedman, 1960; Kuper and Smith, 1969: Despres, 1975; Milne, 1981). 'Plural societies' were thus demarcated from the norm by an excessive attachment to ethnic group rather than nation as primary site of loyalty. In relation to the nation state, commanding the loyalty of its citizens in return for protection and rights, a model that had blossomed into normativity since the French Revolution in North American and European political thought, plural societies thus represented a step *backward*, toward fragmentation and tribalism.

Ethnicity and Assimilation

However, we indicated above that ethnicity has an interestingly diverse genealogy. The first appearance of the word 'ethnicity' comes in William Lloyd Warner and Leo Srole's study *The Social Systems of American Ethnic Groups* (1945), which focuses entirely on white European migrant groups in a New England factory town. For Warner, a prolific student of status and stratification, ethnicity is a phase preceding assimilation. This is a clear example of how national understandings shape the questions researchers ask and the frameworks into which they insert them.

The model of assimilation put forward by Burgess and Park and their Chicago School colleagues is that migrants come to urban America and in succeeding generations move geographically from the most undesirable to more desirable parts of the town (heading for the suburbs); and socially from the poorest-paid, most dangerous work to the professions, as the children and grandchildren become absorbed into mainstream (white) American life. This story (which does not explain African Americans' ghettoisation) frames Warner and Srole's examination of how 1940s European white 'ethnics' become hyphenated Americans before ending up as unhyphenated white Americans. This gradual loosening of actual connections to the country and culture of origin thus becomes what Gans (1979) calls 'symbolic ethnicity', a cultural heritage to be dipped into, alongside the much broader mainstream offerings of the USA. Ethnicity therefore denotes a marginal position which is finally eschewed by assimilation into a racial category: white.

Both in colonial and metropolitan locations, then, ethnicity is viewed by mid-twentieth-century scholars as a sub-national identification that jeopardises the nation state, or is at best seen as the preliminary to the national identification (A.D. Smith, 1981). The political aftermath of decolonisation, from the 1950s to the 1980s, is a focus for researchers interested in the ways ethnicity becomes politicised, either as the dominant way of belonging, or as competing ways of belonging that end up in conflict for control of the state.

What is Ethnicity? The Boundary Process

It should also be noted that what I am referring to in this very brief and idiosyncratic tour of ethnicity is its political outcomes, rather than the details of which group does what, when and how. This latter focus was actually the dominant one, particularly in anthropology, until the late 1960s. Frederik Barth (1969) coined the term 'boundary process' to encapsulate the focus for studies of ethnic identity that he (and others) advocated; namely the means by which ethnic identity coalesces around particular elements, how it changes in response to events and how it is defended. For Barth (1969: 8), ethnicity is: 'a collective body with common ancestry, whether real or assumed, which shares the memory of a historical past, and whose essence is represented by one or more symbolic features'.

Barth's clarity of focus – the boundary is the game, not the content of ethnic identity – comes however at a price. 'Ethnicity' and 'ethnic group' become synonyms in this definition. Yet there are interesting elements to this definition. It does not matter which common ancestry is authentic as long as the group members share it, as they do a vision of a past. With Barth's work, we move from a situation where culture was examined per se for distinctions between groups, to one where ethnic identity is revealed at least in part as a socially constructed process.

Before going on to look at the relationship between ethnicity and the State, we should draw a line under the theoretical work discussed so far. Ethnicity is a social construction, drawing on bloodlines and culture – which raises the question for us as to how it differs from 'race'. It is associated de facto with loyalties and political mobilisation that can often override national belonging; by the mid-twentieth century this level of loyalty is viewed implicitly as historically backward. However, the story of ethnicity at the end of the twentieth and beginning of the twenty-first century is even more complex.

Box 3.1   Studying Ethnicity

Much of what we are discussing in this chapter is to do with epistemology (what counts as knowledge). 'Race' and ethnicity are not innate properties of nature, as much as some proponents of these concepts are convinced that they are. Scholars, whose job it is to produce new knowledge, have differing understandings, analytical tools, methods, etc. The approach adopted in this book is largely constructivist, which means that for me 'race' and ethnicity are fictions that we make with practices and ideas. It is quite a confusing process to understand what ethnicity 'is' if we think of it as a pre-existing natural object that researchers attempt to discover and then reveal truth about.

We noted that the word 'ethnicity' was only coined in the 1940s, although *ethnie* and *ethnos* have very long histories. So we can set out three main periods and understandings associated with the term 'ethnicity' alone, which will hopefully enable readers to make sense of how it has developed.

These are very loose categories and could easily be turned into a more detailed and complex genealogy. The point of this is to establish the idea that ethnicity is very much an academic 'subject', in that it is constructed and deployed from particular ideological positions. Scanning contemporary publications such as the international journals *Ethnic and Racial Studies*,

Idea	Indicative researchers and period	Comment
Ethnicity is a sub-racial grouping reflecting one stage of assimilation process	Warner and Srole 1940s	An American contextual understanding underpinned by the idea of assimilating.
Plural societies	R.T. Smith, M.G. Smith, Premdas (all referring back to Furnivall) 1950s onwards	A framework in which ethnicity is seen as the most potent form of post-colonial identity. Underpinned by idea that ethnicity is the fragmented outcome of decolonisation.
'Ethno-nationalism'[a]	A.D. Smith, Geertz, Horowitz, Connor, Kuper 1970s onwards	A version of plural societies, usually with a historical foundation, that sees the nation state as having ethnic roots. Nation states with more than one ethnicity are susceptible to fragmentation and conflict along those lines.
Boundary process	Barth Late 1960s onwards	The focus of study shifts from the content of culture to the boundaries between groups: how they are constructed, defended, advanced, etc. and in what conditions. Shapes post-1960s studies.
'Critical ethnicity'[a]	Hall, Enloe, Rex, Brass, Fenton. 1970s onwards	An approach that sees ethnicity as a dynamic feature of the social world intersecting with other forms of identity, particularly political ones.

Figure 3.1   Ethnicity studies: schools of thought

[a] 'Ethnonationalism' and 'critical ethnicity' are my own labels

Ethnicities, Journal of Ethnic and Migration Studies, Sociology of Race and Ethnicity and *Ethnopolitics*, for example, will soon alert you to the diversity of understandings and deployments of 'ethnicity' in the social sciences. Its proximity to the terms 'race' and 'racial' indicate the extent to which the fluidity around the terms, which I examine in this chapter, is prevalent.

Ethnicity and the State

Theories of the State can be divided into those that understand the State as autonomous (with its own interests), instrumentalist (used as a tool of external groups), or pluralist (a set of resources that can be captured by external groups in an interplay of power, but which also retains some interests of its own) (Bracey, 2015). Moreover, while a number of political sociologists have explored the relationship between class and the State,[2] few have attempted a theory of gender and the State (Pateman, 1988; Randall and Waylen, 1998; Anthias and Yuval-Davis, 1993) and even fewer 'race' and the State (Goldberg, 2000).

Ethnicity occupies a different space. While it might be technically true to say there is little explicit theory about how the State engages with ethnicity, there are numerous attempts to identify, describe and analyse how the State addresses ethnicity (apart from the 'plural societies' paradigm). This literature ranges from colonial creation and management of ethnic groups, through to the construction and management of immigration regimes, and the management of 'diversity' within the nation state, both in countries of immigration and de facto 'multiethnic states'. Indeed, researchers are spoilt for choice in relation to ethnicity and the State, ranging from states that refuse to acknowledge ethnicity as a valid form of social identity at all (France), to those where it is a principle of governance at a formal or informal level (Belgium), and places where conflict has become organised around political affiliations expressed through ethnic belonging. Justice cannot be done to the entire range of perspectives, so in this section I will identify two key theorisations of politics and ethnicity: 'consociationalism' (Lijphart, 1977) and 'ethnopoliticisation' (Kandeh, 1992). These might not strike scholars of ethnicity as particularly important or mainstream theorisations, but I think they reveal interesting elements that enable us to develop our understandings of what 'ethnicity' means in practice.

Some of the debate about ethnicity (as with other single-dimensional identity studies) revolves around the degree to which studying one aspect of identity encourages neglect or downplaying of the importance of others. Consociationalism and ethnopoliticisation seem to me to span the spectrum of these positions. The first deals with an attempt to capture ethnic identity as a political instrument and make a system of governance reflect this; while the second identifies ethnicity as an affiliation that can absorb other sources of collective identity in particular conditions. Consociationalism seems to take ethnic identity for granted and seek to incorporate it in governance; while ethnopoliticisation flags it up as a 'patsy' for more complex forces.

Consociationalism, as Arend Lijphart (1969, 1977) defines it, sees ethnic politics as a source of social fragmentation, and thus destabilisation for the State. It seeks to mitigate this competition for resources and the exclusion of minorities from power by instituting a system of quotas and consensus decision making. 'In fragmented systems', writes Lijphart (1969: 214), 'many other decisions in addition to constituent ones are perceived as involving high stakes, and therefore require more than simple majority rule.'

Elites in this system have the role of negotiating with those of other ethnic groups and brokering deals whose outcomes are not viewed as benefiting some groups and not others. Where nations are fragmented along ethnic lines, suggests Lijphart, a different way of doing democracy is required, one where the bare minimum 51 per cent majority is not commensurate with the task of leadership. Consociationalism thus begins with the idea that ethnic groups are valid forms of political organisation, and that there are such things as ethnic interests that can be negotiated around in order to avoid the fragmentation and alienation of constant opposition for some groups, and constant power-holding for others. Thus collective ethnic identification becomes the departure point, and no longer a question for critical analysis. Other ways of doing politics (cross-ethnic, and by issue or political principle) become harder to do in practice.

'Ethnopoliticisation', on the other hand, sees the political manipulation of ethnic group membership as a process to be analysed rather than the starting point. Kandeh's (1992) study of Sierra Leone politics demonstrates the activation and instrumentalisation of ethnicity as a means to form coherent and effective voting blocs. Kandeh terms the outcome of this process 'political ethnicity', which, he argues, 'tends to collapse the distinction between ethnic identity on one hand, and political choices, affiliation and loyalties on the other' (1992: 98). The concerns of voters are the usual ones around access to resources, but the point is that powerful political actors can frame struggles in particular ways that seem more or less relevant to the voters. The key element of ethnopoliticisation is that despite the existing alternative sources of identity, ethnicity can capture and propel a political struggle. We know of conflicts that get labelled 'ethnic' in media and academic studies, such as those in Northern Ireland, Sri Lanka, Lebanon, the former Yugoslavia and Rwanda, for example. There is a strong case that these conflicts have been ethnopoliticised, in that they are based on access to power and resources, yet assume a form tied to ethnic identity rather than anything else, because of specific historical events and contexts. In other words, the form of conflict (ethnic) is not an 'inevitable' outcome of centuries of wars and skirmishes, but that is an easier narrative to understand than the more complicated one suggested by ethnopoliticisation.

Box 3.2   Ethnicity and Governance: Consociationalism

In most systems of government, it is political ideology that (at least ostensibly) forms the basis of political parties. One party might well be associated with a geographical area, a social strata, a religious group or combinations of these. However, that system is not formally organised to reflect a balance between areas, groups, classes, etc. In Dutch political scientist Arend Lijphart's design

(Continued)

(Continued)

of 'consociationalism', ethnicity is the basis on which governance functions. This system is designed for post-conflict societies, or those where the threat of 'ethnic' conflict is serious, and is aimed at institutionalising cross-community working and equity. It also, in its more formal forms, eschews majority voting, granting a minority veto. Consociational governance is formally implemented in the Northern Ireland Assembly for example, whereas versions of it also work in Suriname, Switzerland, Belgium, South Africa and Lebanon. It was used in the Netherlands from 1917 to 1967 (Lijphart's formative context). Consociationalism has plenty of critics, who argue that it reinforces, rather than moves away from, ethnic division; institutionalises instability; ignores other important social divisions; and focuses entirely on internal to the exclusion of the external forces. However, it does enable and instigate a degree of power-sharing based on ethnic parties in situations where it would otherwise be difficult to start such processes.

In Northern Ireland, for example, the 'ethnic' groups are (mainly Catholic) Nationalists, who ideally want to secede to the Republic of Ireland, and (mainly Protestant) Unionists, who wish to remain in the UK. The First Minister and Deputy First Minister must be drawn from different groups and one cannot be in office without the other. They have equal powers. The Cabinet is composed of elected Unionist and Nationalist deputies. Particular issues can only be addressed in a cross-community format, which means that a de facto minority veto exists: a certain proportion of either Nationalist or Unionist members of the Assembly must agree to a proposition before it can be accepted, even if a majority of the whole Assembly has already been attained. Consociationalism thus translates ethnicity into a method of governance.

Critical Case Study 1: Anti-Semitism and Ethnicity

So far I have argued that retaining ethnicity and 'race' as completely distinct concepts is difficult to sustain. If the argument is that ethnicity is only about cultural and/or national variations within a larger racialised group (as Warner and Srole [1945] suggest), this perspective does have a certain validity. Using intersectional analysis to explain that 'ethnic' models of entrepreneurship are rare, Zulema Valdez (2011) argues vis-à-vis minority groups in the USA that variation within the racialised 'Asians' and 'Latinos' groups (by country of origin, gender and class, for example) is conceptually valid: business and community practices within the Korean community differ from those within Japanese communities, while Mexicans' history of migration and community solidarity differ from those of Guatemalans or Colombians. Moreover, class and gender impact significantly – in ways that are relevant to entrepreneurial activity and the success of that activity. These nuances indicate the bluntness of using 'ethnicity' alone as an analytical device.

The ambiguity and tenuousness of the distinction between 'ethnicity' (the cultural) and 'race' (the physical) have already been alluded to (Chapter 1). In this section, I will take the case of anti-Semitism to explore the competing claims of 'race' and ethnicity, and suggest a way out of the cul-de-sac to which they bring us.

Using ethnicity, there are three possible binaries which can be used in combination to produce frames through which we understand the social world:

1. 'Ethnicity' exclusively covers culture; 'race' exclusively covers the phenotypical (thus ethnicity accounts for cultural variations within a larger 'racialised' group).

2. 'Ethnicity' is an avowed identity; 'race' is an ascribed one.

3. 'Ethnicity' is dynamic; 'race' is fixed in time.

Let's add to this the critical assertion that I favour: both ethnicity and 'race' are social fictions that cover more common ground than they possess distinct areas. Neither is an adequate analytical tool.

Of course, these are all in their own way simplifications of more complicated arguments, but the object of this exercise is to enable us to better understand the broad lines of the model rather than its fine lines.

If we take 'Jews' as a global group, there are two ways, even under (1) above, to see them. From one perspective they are a cultural sub-group of white people. Indeed, nineteenth- and early twentieth-century race theorists such as de Gobineau and Chamberlain saw them as just this, but as a dangerous element that would bring down other whites if it were not excised. From another perspective, the cultural variation within the group means that 'Jews' is the umbrella term, and that the variant ethnicities would be something like Sephardic (originating in the Iberian peninsula), Ashkenazy (originating in Central/Eastern Europe), Orthodox, secular, etc. Specialists would be able to identify the religious, social and linguistic distinctions between these groups that all refer to themselves as Jews (much as the various Christian and Muslim denominations would all see themselves as Christians and Muslims). However we should note two things about even this relatively uncontroversial statement. First, if we are using ethnicity to describe the variations *within* a racialised group, the concept of 'race' is the necessary yin to ethnicity's yang. Second, is a methodological point, as Nasar Meer (2013: 386) indicates, the amount of scholarly work using 'race' to examine groups that religiously self-identify is very small: growing, but small compared to the cultural-based work. The underpinning dominant line of argument is that religion is all about culture, and that this is a separate sphere of scholarship from that of 'race'.

(Continued)

(Continued)

Jews define themselves clearly in a number of ways: to do with their relationship to secularity; the State of Israel; the status of the Torah (divine or not), etc. This is fascinating fare for those concerned with cultural distinctions, and invites further scrutiny for those, like Zulema Valdez and myself, who are also interested in the empirical material distinctions manifest in how those identities get played out. However, looking anthropologically at how Jews make themselves Jewish in different ways is not the whole story. In the chapter on racialisation, I noted that my understanding of that concept included strategies by groups aiming to generate and bolster group solidarity by socialisation processes in which group membership by bloodlines is stressed. Indeed, Jewishness is generally passed on through the mother's line,[3] making the absolute distinction between bodies and culture impossible to sustain. Moreover, the distinction between avowed and ascribed is quite fluid. Jews identify as Jewish, but in situations where it is not a neutral or advantageous social position, Jewishness has been ascribed: to prevent access to resources; as a preliminary for elimination from territory; and as a triage system to facilitate mass murder.

In terms of the final of the three binaries put forward above, the dynamic/static might be the most interesting. There is a tension already between anthropological and sociological understandings of change (typically as a dynamic object per se), and the actors' perspectives, in which it is frequently the case that ethnic group membership is structured around a static, ahistorical understanding of culture as an unchanging, quasi-natural 'essence' (Box 1.2). Let's look briefly at the central elements of anti-Semitism, and see how they map onto the dynamic/static binary. Here are the statements encapsulating the main currents of anti-Semitic thought (Harap, 1987; Poliakov 2003a, 2003b, 2003c, 2003d; Flannery, 2004 [1985]):[4]

- *Disproportionate love of money*: Jews have been linked with accumulation of capital since medieval times. They are often depicted in anti-Semitic thought as physically bloated as a metaphor for wealth. This also feeds into the conspiratorial theme.

- *Killers of Christ*: Christian anti-Semitism revolves around the notion of Jews as Christ-killers.

- *Child sacrifice*: Jews are also identified in medieval Europe as poisoners and child-sacrificers, using the blood of Christian children in their rituals.

- *Dirty*: Like many other subordinate groups, Jews are often depicted as 'filthy', both as a representation of cultural difference and to designate otherness and trigger affect. Dirt elicits a powerful emotional response as a moral and physical sign of undesirability.

- *Conspirators*: Jews are accused throughout history of being relentless and expert conspirators, through international finance (as bankers), as Bolshevik revolutionaries, or shady figures pulling the strings of media and government in various countries such as the USA (the so-called 'Zionist Occupation Government'), according to far-right nationalists.

- *'Holocaust Denial'* (Lipstadt, 1993) can be seen as one of the conspiracy theories. Holocaust deniers argue that not only was the Holocaust an exaggeration and misrepresentation of facts (they say Jews were deported but not systematically worked to death and murdered in gas chambers), but that the Holocaust is actually a fiction propagated by Jews to give them an advantage vis-à-vis other groups.

In each of these cases, there is an argument that culture *alone* is the key element of the equation between Jewishness and behaviour understood as threatening to other groups in anti-Semitic thought. However, displaying these statements exclusively in textual form, without the array of visual enhancements used in their actual presentation – in leaflets, manifestos, posters, books, in films and on webpages – gives the impression that culture is exclusively at play, in other words, that anti-Semitism is inherently a cultural (Taguieff, 1990; Modood, 1992) form of racism. I would argue that the effort to portray Jews as physically different from Gentiles, as a way to underscore their cultural difference, has occupied anti-Semites in the period since the term 'anti-Semitism' has existed, from the late 1800s.

So we are here at a confluence of binaries: these listed characteristics seem static – they are purported to attach to all Jews everywhere and at any time, in other words, to be a natural essence of *ascribed* Jewishness.

Just as the function of Islamophobia is to reduce the complex and diverse bodies of people who follow Islam to a narrow set of identities based on particular representations of them, so the function of anti-Semitism is to make all Jews everywhere into 'dirty Jews', 'money-grabbing Jews', 'child-sacrificing Jews', etc., each version more or less relevant to what the representation of them is supposed to produce in the mind of the target audience.

The problem for anti-Semites is that unless Jews are wearing particular clothing, hairstyles or participating in specific activities, they are not distinguishable from Gentiles – hence the intellectual effort invested in anti-Semitic political activities toward making Jews physically different, not just in the bountiful anti-Semitic visual propaganda of the 1870–1939 period, but in the Nazi regime's objective of making the Aryans a 'race' apart by using relational methods.

Michael Burleigh (2001) argues that German Jews were particularly well culturally integrated, and that, on the spectrum of physical differences that can be shorthanded by 'race', it was not often possible to distinguish between them and the Aryans. Burleigh suggests that the Jews whom German soldiers encountered in Eastern Europe were more differently Jewish (in terms of clothes, hairstyles and customs) than those that had lived within Germany. In any case, if it had been so easy to tell European Jews apart from other white Europeans, the compulsory wearing of the Star of David would have been unnecessary. Nazi propaganda effort went into anthropometry and the production of images depicting German Jews as physically distinct: with large noses and fat lips, wearing particular types of hats and coats. The anti-Semitic caricature was designed to make racialised difference apparent externally whereas by all failed anthropometric measures, it remained a cultural difference.

(Continued)

(Continued)

Indeed, even the sophisticated German propaganda film effort struggled to make physical differences 100 per cent reliable. In the 1940 film *Der Ewige Jude* (The Wandering/Eternal Jew), shot principally in the Warsaw Ghetto, 'difference' is translated as poor (dirty) living conditions and clothing. The point is even made that, according to the film's script, Jews can change their dress and pass almost indistinguishably in non-Jewish society, and that this is one of the dangers that must be countered (Schulte-Sasse, 1996: 60).

In the case of anti-Semitism then, it is not possible to say that culture is its exclusive strand, but neither can we argue that it is entirely about bodies: indeed the lack of physical difference is a source of crisis of recognition. Thus, even a form of racism about distinguishing one ostensibly white European group from another is not entirely cultural. Both Jews and anti-Semites accept that Jewishness can be passed from one generation to another by bloodlines, not solely by learning the culture. Whether the bodies express difference or not, the putative cultural traits that constitute the contemporary anti-Semitic stereotypes are denuded of dynamism and placed in a constant ahistorical perspective that sees the 'eternal Jew' as a clannish conspirator aiming to disadvantage all other groups to his/her own profit.

My suggestion to make sense of this failure to distinguish 'race' from ethnicity *in practice* is to see them as equally inadequate tools. Ethnicity and 'race' cannot be kept apart in the real situations in which we use them, and should be seen not as ways to help us understand the social world, but as part of what we aim to understand. Racialisation is the analytical tool capable of making sense of anti-Semitism because its departure point is that 'race' has always been comprised of both culture and biology, and thus sees culture vs body as a false dichotomy. Moreover, racialisation demonstrates that all racisms are dynamic but historically situated processes. The end result of a form of racism is to construct a group identity in which all its members are reduced to the display of the same characteristics.

Box 3.3 'Tiger Moms' and Cultures of Success

One of the longstanding debates in both popular culture and academia is over the role of ethnicity as a key to social advancement. Edna Bonacich's theory of ethnic 'middlemen minorities' (1975) cites cultural distinctions attaching to a particular set of groups as being key to their entrepreneurial economic success. Asian, Middle Eastern and Jewish settlers in a variety of locations, for example, are cited as 'middlemen minorities'. These groups are seen to have entrepreneurial values of industriousness, thrift, emphasis on education and capacity for collective solidarity and sharing funding. Other minority groups are often compared in disadvantageous terms to these 'model minorities'.

A classic use of the middleman minority narrative is Amy Chua's 'Tiger Moms'. Chua is a Yale law professor who wrote a popular parenting memoir, *Battle Hymn of the Tiger Mother* (2011), in which she extols the Asian values of strict parenting and results orientation (particularly in education) that trump the development of children's self-esteem as the goal of a parent in the West. The book sparked controversy about the relationship between child-rearing, parents' values and educational and professional success. The book's arguments have more subtle interpretations than can be dealt with here, but the key point in popular debates was that some groups have values that predispose them for success, while other groups' values (e.g. African Americans and Mexicans) have the opposite effect. Indeed, in the 1990s Richard Herrnstein and Charles Murray published their extremely controversial *The Bell Curve*, in which they argue that Latinos and African Americans have lower IQs than Asians and whites, and that public spending on social and economic initiatives for disadvantaged groups is therefore a waste of money. This is clearly an ideological and racialised debate. However, this reading is challenged by scholars for whom ethnic identity is one of a number of contextual factors and not the only explanation of success and failure. Sociology Professor Jennifer Lee has argued extensively that social class explains more about educational outcomes in the USA than ethnicity (a finding replicated in the UK). She goes as far as to say that in fact, the class backgrounds of Asian migrants are generally higher than those of Latino migrants, and they are also disproportionately high compared to their countries of origin. The achievements of Latinos are actually more 'value added' than those of Asians, who overwhelmingly retain their middle-class positions rather than being socially mobile. Lee went on to co-author with Min Zhou the award-winning *The Asian American Achievement Paradox* (2015), a rebuttal of the Tiger Mom thesis.

Critical Case Study 2: Gypsy-Travellers

To mirror the case study of Jewish groups, it should be pointed out that the utility of ethnicity is its focus on the cultural distinctions within the diverse groups of people covered by the term 'nomadic' (as opposed to sedentary): Gypsy-Travellers, Sinti, Rom, Pavee, Tsigane, Gitane, Saami, inter alia.[5] The charting of these groups, their origins, cultural distinctiveness and commonalities is therefore especially pertinent to the groups themselves, who struggle against representations of them constructed from more powerful institutions such as the State and the media. Indeed, the question of power is what makes ethnicity such an interesting and difficult construct for scholars. Ostensibly then, Traveller groups are Europeans. Yet their histories have been variations on a theme of being identified as standing outside mainstream whiteness, in a position of vulnerability marked by lack of capitals and property, and thus being open for discrimination ranging from

(Continued)

(Continued)

exclusion to genocide. In the context of this chapter, the question is, which concept is more useful to analyse the processes by which this discrimination occurs: ethnicity or 'race'?

If ethnicity is deployed to distinguish cultural differences and similarities between the various groups of Travellers, and at a push, between the sedentary groups and the Travellers, it tells us about language, family organisation and geographical reach, for example, but little explicitly about power relations or even the terms on which they develop. The starting point is to note that sedentary urban culture was put forward as being superior to nomadic and semi-nomadic cultures by the sixteenth century (Quinn, 1966). As the history of Jews in Europe also demonstrates, these Othered groups become the object of discourses and practices that seek to construct them as simultaneously weak and aggressive, and threatening to the bodies and property of sedentary people. It is difficult to mobilise populations against a range of groups qualified by anthropological nuance, and much easier to do so against homogeneous groups that are turned into 'figures'. In this way, Travellers are racialised by the State, i.e. the valid distinctions that different groups make between themselves and others get collapsed, and they are viewed as having common characteristics, drives and behaviours that can be known and predicted. That this passes through cultural vectors does not mean that it is not racialisation, as I have already argued in previous chapters. As one can see from the legislation passed in different countries to outlaw travelling lifestyles and Jewish religious practices, and exclude Jews from guild professions, Travellers and Jews became the 'marginal whites' of Renaissance Europe.

As noted in relation to Jews (above), a number of stereotypical characteristics are associated with marginalised groups. Travellers are identified as:

- *Dirty:* the norms of travelling life emphasise cleanliness inside the dwelling place and don't apply it to the area surrounding that space (Okely, 1983). Moreover, as Sibley (1995) points out, the trend in industrialised countries is for marginal land to be used for building, storage and transport. The spaces left for temporary settlement are residual and often associated with dirt, as are some frequent economic activities such as recycling.

- *Thieves:* Travellers are viewed as incorrigible thieves.

- *Idle:* At the same time as Travellers are identified as thieves and or workers who do not pay taxes, their lack of engagement with the mainstream workforce leaves them open to the accusation of being idle. Of course, idle and unproductive in industrial and post-industrial society being such key stigma, they are thus connected to the absorption of public funds. This is particularly striking in the coverage of Eastern European migrants to the UK, for example (Greenslade, 2005).

- *Tax-avoiders:* Following on from the above, Travellers' entrepreneurial norms, combined with distrust of sedentary financial institutions, mean that their economic interaction with the settled population usually comes as self-employed traders or service providers. The perceived combination of self-assessment taxes and lack of fixed abode, required for tax purposes, together with the practice of consumer spending rather than saving, leads to the conclusion that the only way they can 'afford their lifestyle' is through avoiding tax.

- *Tribal:* Travellers' family structures, the emphasis on defending territory, refraining from mixing and the controls exerted on women's autonomy by men lead to them being understood as 'tribal', and therefore less civilised than mainstream society, which is characterised in this binary as individual and autonomous.

- *Superstitious:* Gypsies have long been associated with supernatural powers, or at least the manipulation of this perception, such as fortune-telling and the ability to set effective curses. Popular representations of these abound. Their link with the supernatural is another compounding element in their backwardness and lack of modernity.

- *Women:* representations of Traveller women as oppressed, chaste and traditional coexist with those that construct them as sexually uninhibited and exerting dangerous pressure on sedentary men (e.g. Carmen, 'Gypsies, Tramps and Thieves').

As we could note from even such a brief overview, there are plenty of overlaps between representations and dominant ideas about subaltern groups: the connections between ideas about Travellers, Jews and Muslims in the twenty-first century are particularly prominent, for example.

However, the language of ethnicity, albeit implicitly linked to power, does act as a political stake in states where this terminology is used. Where gaining recognition as an ethnic group leads to negotiating space in the national struggle for resources, ethnicity itself becomes a resource developed for access. For Amerindians in French Guyana (Collomb, 1999), or for Travellers in Ireland (McVeigh, 2009), for example, groups that see themselves at the bottom of league tables can become incorporated however imperfectly into the formal negotiations over resources. Becoming an 'official' ethnic group where that guarantees a place at the table is therefore one strategy by which a degree of autonomy can be obtained, restricted as it is by the State's definitions and rules surrounding access.

So while an ethnicity perspective shows different ways in which nomadic groups carry culture, this does not push us to investigate the politics around the groups' individual positions. Crucially, this means how Gypsy-Travellers get amalgamated into a homogeneous representation that reproduces longstanding ideas but also incorporates some contemporary twist, such as the struggles between Travellers and local authorities over control of land under the planning regulations (Chapter 6), and the place of the media in propagating racialised ideas about Travellers. This process, of transforming a complex set of identities and positions into a homogeneous, necessarily weak and threatening unproductive Other, demonstrates racialisation rather than ethnicisation.

Box 3.4   Removing Travellers' Children

If ethnicity is *all* about culture, that subtlety has escaped the Gardai (Irish police) who removed two children from their parents in separate incidents in October 2013.

Officers took the blue-eyed blonde children of Roma in Dublin (a seven-year-old girl) and Athlone (a two-year-old boy), and put them temporarily into care because they suspected the adults of stealing the children, such was their physical difference from their parents. According to Channel 4 (2013), the information was passed on to the police by journalists working for TV3 who were investigating the kidnapping of children used to claim child benefit in the EU: a case had been highlighted in Greece. Those journalists had responded to an anonymous tip on their television company's Facebook page (McDonald, 2013). The children were both later returned after DNA tests.

There is a history of the State removing children from Travellers, alluded to by Brigid Quilligan (Irish Traveller Movement, 2013) in her response to these two cases, as Travellers' own memoirs testify (Reid, 2008; Whyte, 2009). Indeed, the State has for a long time removed children from working-class women, unmarried women and mothers of mixed race children in the British and Irish islands (and of course the planned removal of Aboriginal children in Australia in the first half of the twentieth century lies at one end of the spectrum).

Travellers' physical attributes can clearly also be assumed: unless they have dark hair and eyes they appear to be suspect, which seems to under-mine the case that ethnicity is only about cultural difference. The casual linking of all Gypsy-Travellers by the authorities is also evident. The logic underlying the interventions in Ireland seems to have been that a case involving Roma had occurred in Greece (BBC News, 2013), so some other Roma might well be working the same 'scam'. Finally, the premise of a single anonymous report through Facebook seems a relatively tenuous departure point for an operation entailing removing a child from a family. These issues suggest that Travellers are subject to different assumptions and standards of evidence than other groups.

So What's the Point of Ethnicity?

Max Weber (1978 [1922]: 395) concludes that: 'All in all, the notion of "ethnically" determined social action subsumes phenomena that a rigorous sociological analysis ... would have to distinguish between carefully ... It is certain that in this process, the collective term "ethnic" would be abandoned, for it is unsuitable for a really rigorous analysis.'

Weber's stance on ethnicity therefore is at odds with the majority of the social science work on this subject, which is much less critical. Ethnic groups form the building blocks of 'consociationalism' and the 'plural societies' theories, while the original usage of the term in the 1940s (Warner and Srole, 1945) is to distinguish white sub-groups from a larger racialised white population. Steve Fenton's perspective (Fenton, 2007) is that 'race' and ethnicity are equally contingent; ethnicity is a lens through which society can be studied: but the context is the most important variable. Ethnicity is not a frame through which identity can be understood as if it is a unit of analysis.

Then what is the utility of the term 'ethnicity'? Up to a point, Warner and Srole's use does tell us something descriptive and raises questions that have to be answered. It gives us specifics, and is in dialogue with 'race'. In other words, it helps if we need to know that we are talking about Korean diaspora practices rather than 'Asian' ones; or referring to Nigerian Christian religious observances in contemporary London instead of those of black people in general; or to understand the dynamics of the Rwandan genocide. It never hurts to have cultural specifics highlighted vis-à-vis a necessarily broader racialised group, as social scientists often have to talk in generalities. Yet the problem is, where does ethnicity stop and 'race' start? Without this tension between group and sub-group, ethnicity seems to sit precariously close to 'race', and inexorably slipping toward a place where it can be a tool of description but not analysis. Moreover, 'ethnic' is not a neutral term but is overwhelmingly applied to non-whites and whites with non-normative cultural or national characteristics.

Conclusions

When we use 'race' or 'ethnicity', we are dealing essentially with forms of categorisation that have been developed in Western academic traditions. This is absolutely not to say that the social practices these terms attempt to describe and summarise are restricted to the West, but to indicate that neither of them are go-without-saying universal theories of identity and power relations. So it might not be the most ridiculous thing in the world to acknowledge that one is not more useful or more authentic than the other.

- If we begin with the notion that ethnicity is all about culture, then it assumes that 'race' isn't. Yet we have already seen that 'race' has never been exclusively about physical appearance and bloodlines. It is a serious error to assume that 'race' is not about culture, and the historical record demonstrates this. Culture is and always has been a constituent of 'race', just as bloodlines are also contained within the ethnic stories of groups that are allegedly disposed to work hard, be good at business, be good at studying, or be timid, suited only for lower-level labour.

- Maybe we can think of ethnicity running along a spectrum from the symbolic to the political, with at one end, food, drink, dance, marriage, language and the other specific mobilisations around projects aimed at defending or accessing resources. However, are the ways in which people see themselves and others as part of, or lying outside of ethnic groups, different to how people do the same with 'race'?

- The limits of both concepts are also similar. They both assume community where there might well be community, but draw our attention always toward the group-ness of the group thus conjured up, and away from the different slicings of the same cake that might be equally relevant, such as class and gender, among others. Indeed, the intersectional theorists we encounter in the next chapter tell us that social identities are rarely so simple as 'just' one thing or another.

- The claim that ethnicity is self-ascribed rather than ascriptive is more credible, but does not hold up often enough under scrutiny for it to be a coherent element of ethnicity. The ease with which groups such as Mexicans in the USA, indigenous people (in Latin America), Muslims in the West, Maghrebins (in France), inter alia, are transformed into objects of scorn and analysis (regardless of how members of that group enact their group-ness and dispute it in ongoing conversations within the group) should make us query the self-ascribed nature of ethnicity.

- The question of power. As ethnic groups tend to see themselves as chosen or at least better than the next one, it's hard to see how, other than in the abstract, ethnic groups are all on a level footing. Indeed, the development of ethnic political mobilisation and representation is typically generated by a perceived need to defend or attain a particular position in the hierarchy, and/or eliminate opposition.

- The multicultural states that proclaim themselves as such are riven in different ways by the tensions described as 'ethnic': Singapore, Malaysia, the UK, the USA, Canada, South Africa, as much as those steadfastly refusing to engage with the concept of ethnicity are, e.g. France. Others still, like Canada, Belgium and Switzerland, base governance on forms of consociational politics in which ethnicity becomes the authentic basis for politics.

- The problem with the concept of ethnicity is that once the argument is propounded that a particular framing of the social world is ethnic, not racial, the argument thus advanced slips away from a nuanced attempt to emphasise cultural aspects of the politics of identity, toward a more exclusive statement meant to establish borders where the border is shifting or incomplete. The physical structure of the two ideas is too connected to be completely separate: there is absolutely no currency in the idea that 'ethnicity' is real and 'race' is fiction, or in the claim that they cover entirely different landscapes. Both ideas have their histories (Fenton, 2007), which makes them objects of enquiry more than objects that can aid our enquiry. In the investigation into 'race', ethnicity is a 'person of interest', and vice versa.

- My opting for racialisation as the key concept for understanding derives from the embeddedness of both bodies and culture in it. However, implicit in racialisation is the attention to culture that ethnicity denotes.

- The way to deal with the problem of understanding ethnicity as distinct from 'race' is to recognise that ethnicity is a context-based social process. We could try and understand that process, rather than accepting the outcome of the process (ethnic identity at a given moment) as if it were unproblematic in a way that 'race' is not.

- Ethnicity is a social construct, and although it has been used as if it were at all times distinct from 'race', in practice it would be more accurate to say that they are sister terms with a large overlap and maybe a slightly different focus. I would suggest, however, that given the understanding of 'race' outlined in Chapter 1 – 'race' is the biologicalisation of the cultural and the culturalisation of the biological – that 'race' can exist without ethnicity, but ethnicity cannot exist without 'race'. Ethnicity operates in a space below and parallel to 'race' but if 'race' were not there, what would be the point of ethnicity?

Points for Reflection

What are the differences and similarities between ethnicity and 'race'?

Can you make a case that ethnicity is a useful concept for understanding society?

In contemporary Europe, how does anti-Semitism differ from anti-nomadism, and what might they have in common?

Further Reading

Fenton, S. (2007) *Ethnicity*, 2nd edn. Cambridge: Polity Press.

By the far the best exploration and critique of the concept of ethnicity, using a variety of historical and geographical contexts.

Valdez, Z. (2011) *The New Entrepreneurs: How Race, Class, and Gender Shape American Enterprise*. Stanford, CA: Stanford University Press.

Study of a variety of Latino/a entrepreneurs showing the complexities of the variables influencing their success: ethnicity, 'race', class and gender.

Hall, S. (1988) 'New Ethnicities', in K. Mercer (ed.) *Black Film Black Cinema*, pp. 27-31. London: Institute of Contemporary Arts.

Groundbreaking essay that sets out and explores the tension between racialised and ethnicised identities: looks at the variety of positions within blackness arising from post-colonial migration to the UK.

Notes

1. US Census Bureau: www.census.gov/topics/population/race.html.

2. Leading political sociologists traditionally conceptualise the State in terms of class relations (Offe and Ronge, 1982; Jessop, 1990).

3. There are a variety of distinctions and small groups who wouldn't recognise themselves in this.

4. Poliakov's is the most detailed discussion of anti-Semitism throughout history. Harap's contribution is to add 'social anti-Semitism' to the categories of 'ideological' and 'economic', 'religious', 'nationalistic' and 'racial' that had been put forward by Flannery.

5. 'Roma' is an EU umbrella term covering a set of peoples.

4

'Race', Class and Gender

In this chapter we will

- Examine some ways that social relationships of 'race', gender and class are connected

- Find out what analysing more than one of these relationships at a time can add to our understanding

- Look in detail at the concept of 'intersectionality'

- See case studies of scholarly work that examine intersections

The main thrust of this book is to suggest ways in which racism (as defined in Chapter 1) can be conceptualised, analysed and understood. None of this is possible in a model where *only* 'race' matters in the construction of identities. Nobody is 'just' an Asian, a white or a black person. They are, for example, a middle-class professional Asian woman; a working-class white man; a lower middle-class black woman. If we separate these identities out, ignore, underplay or overplay elements of them, we miss the messy combinations that make social identities and racism such complex phenomena. 'Race, class, and gender', argue Anthias and Yuval-Davis (1993: 63–6), 'are not independent variables that can be tacked onto each other or separated at will … They are concrete social relations … enmeshed in each other.'

Around this simple and compelling argument lie the investments of scholars in vast corpuses that focus on class, or gender, or 'race', or sometimes combinations of two of these. A smaller group have been committed to the theory of 'intersectionality', which combines class, gender and 'race'. In this chapter, we will look at some very basic outlines of class and gender. Then we will introduce the idea of *intersecting* identities and forms of discrimination (class, 'race' and gender), before examining some case studies drawn from scholars' work on these sources of identity. This will illustrate what is useful about understanding social relationships through the prism of multiple identities (used here to mean taking class, gender and 'race' into account as *a normal practice*).

Class and Gender

Both class and gender are, at the abstract level, hierarchical systems of global power relations with national, regional and more local configurations. However, there is a great deal of contestation about their relative significance. There is, for example, a corpus of writing on social class in the Marxist tradition, going back to the nineteenth century, whose focus has been on the overriding salience of class as a system produced by the capitalist market economy in its various guises. In relation to *that* global set of relations, gender would appear as having limited significance, as its main role is to play a part in ordering the composition of the workforce and its reproduction (through accomplishing the domestic work that enables families and workers to continue their productive lives). However, the critique that has developed from academic work on class is based on the conditions of that work's production. The male-dominated academy, it is argued, prioritises class over gender, not necessarily because there is intrinsic merit in doing so, but because men hold relatively privileged positions in what is termed a patriarchal society and are therefore less aware of and interested in examining male privilege. The production of knowledge is a reflection of the existing power relations. In reference to women, Donna Haraway (1988: 578) comments that Marxist sociology has been impotent 'in historicizing anything women did that didn't qualify for a wage'. Indeed, one of the principal critiques of Marxist sociology is its relative neglect of areas of life outside the workplace. It is unsurprising then that some of the first attempts to demarcate territory in feminist studies included a focus on the home (as an unpaid workplace) in which housework is accomplished on a gendered basis (Oakley, 1974; A.Y. Davis, 2001b).

For scholars of racism, such as Omi and Winant, this over-emphasis on work has had the effect of turning racism into a secondary effect of class domination, or an 'epiphenomenon of other supposedly more fundamental categories of socio-political identity' (1994 [1986]: 66). Engagements with racism from the Marxist tradition go back to the 1940s (Cox, 1948), through to Robinson's (1983) attempt to draw the two together in the American context. In relation to the UK, there is also Miles' (1982) reformulation of racialisation as the key concept to use, and the way he embeds it in the labour process, particularly migrant labour (Chapter 2), from the nineteenth century onwards. San Juan (2001) notes that the left-wing line was always that racism is functional to capitalism because it hides and confuses the oppressive social relations of capitalism, turning worker against worker to the benefit of the capitalist class. The solution to racism is therefore the end of capitalist relations per se. Indeed, the problem for progressive sociologists studying racism is that most of the available models are either the very deterministic orthodox Marxist view (which reduces all other struggles ultimately to class), and those postmodern cultural-based explanations that have very limited historical specificity or relation to the material world. 'Race' can be deconstructed effectively in the world of ideas, but it still remains embedded in the material social relations of twenty-first century capitalism. In the Marxist tradition, the labour process and class relations are everything, yet in the cultural turn, they account for virtually nothing.[1] The space in between these poles has been filled by attempts to set out 'race' as the primary organising principle in American life, in 'racial formation' (Omi and Winant, 1994 [1986]) and 'critical race theory' (Delgado and Stefancic, 1995, 1997),[2] and by an absence of a particular unifying school in the UK.

Box 4.1   Black Marxist Scholarship

For Marxists, such as Gramsci, Althusser, Negri, etc., class is the dominant frame and set of experiences while for critical 'race' scholars, either 'race' is a more significant paradigm, or there is at least parity or a complex link (or articulation) between the two. Marxists interested in 'race' often theorise it as an 'epiphenomenon' (or secondary effect) of class. This is a major stumbling block for engagement with black scholars and activists, many of whom do not necessarily recognise such a hierarchy of identities as pertinent to their life experiences – and this is not even to mention gender.

Yet many black scholars have also been part of the very broad Marxist tradition, have critiqued early Marxism's lack of interest in 'race', and especially its clumsy determinism: where class is the main game and so resolving class exploitation necessarily resolves racial exploitation. It should be clear that black scholars' interventions in Marxism are as varied as the number of interveners: there is no single 'black' position.

Oliver Cox's *Caste, Class and Race* (1948) analyses caste systems and class systems, and makes the link between capitalism in the Americas and racial slavery so that the two processes are inextricable. Cedric Robinson's *Black Marxism* (1983) is an attempt to place black radical traditions in a historical context, and develop a critique of Marxism from a variety of black positions. He argues among other things: that class is not the key paradigm; that the Marxist model over-emphasises how forces determine action; that culture is as important as material elements in struggle. C.L.R. James, the Trinidadian writer, also critiques Marxism's historical sequencing. He states that the large workforces of Africans in the New World were a proletariat centuries before such a formation occurred in Europe. James is also the author of a unique book on 'race' and class understood through the prism of cricket, *Beyond a Boundary* (1963). Charles Mills (2003) critiques what he sees as the 'whiteness' of mainstream Marxism, neglecting the importance of 'race' in the American context, and indeed in the historical development of capitalism. He advocates instead a critical race theory approach in which discriminations articulate, but class does not subsume 'race' in all places at all times.

(Continued)

(Continued)

We shall look more closely at Angela Davis's work on the Prison Industrial Complex elsewhere (Box 6.4), but we should note that her engagement with Marxism has taken the form of membership and leadership of the US Communist Party, and involvement as an activist in a series of campaigns of resistance against oppression of women, racial minorities and particularly, and especially, the system of incarceration that she sees as institutionally racist.

The importance of culture as a site of oppression and resistance is alluded to by Robinson. Cultural theorist Stuart Hall's highly influential work centres the articulation of 'race' and class. He has theorised the development of 'mugging' as a racialised crime in the UK that demonstrates the State's implication in racism through methods of control (Hall et al., 1978), and suggested that the 'race'/class relationship is the significant social relationship in contemporary societies (Hall, 1980). Indeed, for Hall, 'Race is, in short, the "modality" in which class is "lived," the medium through which class relations are experienced, the form in which it is appropriated and "fought through"' (1980: 342). He argues that racism impacts not only on those discriminated against, but also acts as a brake on development for those white members of working classes who are prevented from achieving progressive change.

Black Marxist interventions then are part of a radical critique of Western thought, and a durable engagement with the West's major critique of itself. The principal tenets of Marxism are viewed as open to debate. While the idea that class a priori trumps 'race' is resisted, there is subtle investigation and attempts to re-theorise the relationships between class and 'race'.

On the other side of the Atlantic, Charles Mills' work (2003) is the most recent engagement with Marxism from a 'critical race theory' scholar. He sets out very clear arguments (2003: 156–60) for 'race', rather than class, to be considered the key social division in the USA. His claim is that, among other things, 'race' is 'the stable reference for identifying the "them" and "us" which override all other "thems" and "us's"' (2003: 157). Gender is not the most acute contradiction because the majority of American women benefit from the family structures of whiteness, and in terms of gender relations, 'sleep with the enemy'.

Whiteness provides a cognitive and experiential shell protecting white people against knowing about discrimination due to the largely segregated living patterns in the USA. The radical European political tradition, Mills maintains, was forged in a context where 'race' was about the interface with the colonial world, and is thus not equipped to deal with the New World context of the Americas, constructed upon the collective theft of land, slavery and a racialised system of white supremacy. I am expecting that these terms and ways of talking about the topic will be difficult to accept for some of the American readers, which in fact underscores Mills' allied assertion that the 'dominant categories' of the 'white cognitive universe … block apprehension of the centrality of race' (2003: 157).[3] Mills' provocative claims continue with his argument that there is no universal rule of symmetry between different forms of oppression (class, gender and race). Using the example of Nazi Germany, he contends that in *that* case, racial oppression was worse than the other two. 'So the point is', he contends, 'that the relative badness of oppressions in a given country is an empirical matter to be settled by looking at its structure' (2003: 166). The causal relationships and genealogical roots of forms of oppression do not determine 'continuing causal preeminence' (2003: 164), so although it could be argued that capitalism brought racism into being, this does not mean that in every place at every moment, class is the most potent form of oppression.

Moreover, Mills has continued his attempt to theorise the institutional exclusion and deprioritisation of racism within academia and American political discourse by collaboration with key political theorist Carole Pateman (Mills and Pateman, 2007), who has pursued a similar line of argument in relation to gender with *The Sexual Contract* (1988). Their arguments derive from the understanding that the formal Enlightenment social democratic contract of rights was empirically rather than theoretically exclusive. It was based on a rigidly hierarchical set of norms in which both all women and all black people were chattel, whereas all white men were potential, if not actual, citizens. One of their insights is that not only does the ensuing normative exclusion impact on society in a way that produces disadvantage for the marginalised groups, but it also generates concomitant advantages for the dominant group, whether individuals are in support of it or not. In other words, white people benefit from racism even if they disagree with it because the way society functions at a collective level is not affected by their personal beliefs: there are different levels of action. All men benefit from sexism in the same way. The amount by which people benefit depends on other factors, but this principle is a challenge to the theories of racism and sexism as merely forms of individual prejudice.

The second challenge is to the way gender and 'race' are discounted in mainstream models of social theory, particularly that of dealing with rights, which seem to suppose that both racism and sexism are either absent or are relics of the past (Rawls, 1971; Nozick, 1974). Indeed, it is the critique of mainstream models of social sciences that brings us to the connected sets of arguments about the status of the concept 'woman'.

The Critique of 'Western' Feminism

The 1970s saw the rise of 'women's studies' and 'gender studies', both as courses at universities and as corpuses of academic theory. The feminist critique of mainstream sociology was that it ignored women's experiences, and focused on areas of male dominance such as employment. A feminist perspective developed, whose minimum parameters were, according to Ann Denis (2008), that:

- Women are legitimate subjects of study;

- Their identities, like those of men, are socially constructed rather than biologically determined;

- As a social category, they have been subordinated (at least since private property as a concept came into existence);

- There is a commitment to social change aimed at the elimination of women's subordination.

The point for feminist sociologists was to examine social phenomena from a feminist 'standpoint' – a methodological stance that relies on the position of the researcher as having experienced social relations from a particular, relevant perspective (Haraway, 1988; Harding, 1991). This recognises that all positions are partial, rather than one being impartial and objective. The experience of living out social inequalities means that standpoints differ from one person to another, with a pattern of experiences shaping particular positions, such as 'woman'. Standpoint feminism then is aimed at injecting knowledge of women's experiences into research problematics, rather than imagining that it will make research less objective to incorporate their points of view.

By the late 1970s, however (Combahee River Collective, 1982 [1977]), the various streams of feminism (e.g. liberal, radical, Marxist) were being criticised in a similar way to that in which mainstream sociology had been critiqued. In other words, it represented the experiences and priorities of the dominant minority, in this case, white, middle-class (straight and able-bodied) women.

Alongside this raised profile, however, flowed a stream of criticism from scholars and activists within the feminist movement in its broadest sense. These concerns were voiced by women 'of color' in the USA and 'black' women in the UK (with the broader meaning of black in use at that time, covering all minority groups). The critique identified a discrepancy between the priorities of 'Western' feminism and those of minority groups. Historically, the feminist movement had campaigned for a set of rights: freedom from chattel status, to own property, reproductive rights, access to higher education, employment, etc. Because of the hierarchical way in which these societies were structured, the priorities of minority women were different, geared toward combating racism; freedom from slavery, from low-paid work, from sexual abuse by employers; and in the developing world, freedom and justice, bread and peace. In short, these differences of priority highlight fundamentally different experiences, and thus perspectives from which research is undertaken.

Box 4.2   Background to the Split in the US Women's Suffrage Movement

The women's suffrage movement officially began in 1849 at the Seneca Falls (NY) congress on the abolition of slavery. The campaign for the vote for women ('woman suffrage') thus developed out of the movement to abolish slavery. Indeed, some people were part of both organisations, and the social background of activists in both was often similar: professional, wealthy and with religious leanings. In 1865, after the Civil War, with the abolitionists' objective achieved, women's rights campaigners expected to resume where they had left off, with the added support of the former abolitionists. However, the Fourteenth Amendment then led to a split within the women's rights movement. Section 2 of the Fourteenth Amendment proposed full voting rights for all males (not just whites). Women's rights activists were therefore split between opposing the amendment in order to argue for votes for women, or supporting it, and placing white women behind African American men in the pecking order of voting rights. Campaigners such as Julia Ward Howe, Frederick Douglass and Lucy Stone backed the Fourteenth Amendment, while others like Susan B. Anthony and Elizabeth Cady Stanton led the opposition. After the Amendment had been ratified, they unsuccessfully pressed for an amendment introducing universal suffrage.

Supporters of each side of the argument viewed the others as having betrayed a principle of equality (either racial or gender equality) and the split lasted for decades. This tension, argue critics like bell hooks (1982), Patricia Giddings (1984) and Angela Davis (2001b), characterised the women's movement well into the contemporary period.

Whiteness and the Feminist Movement: USA

Moreover, not only was this discrepancy the subject of debate, but the social relations of the world outside the feminist movement were, in the eyes of the critics, being reproduced within it. bell hooks' (1982) historical study of the American feminist organisation (which was referred to as 'woman suffrage' – see Box 4.2) excluded black women (although it fêted high-profile black men, such as Frederick Douglass). The two simultaneously functioning hierarchies were those of gender and 'race', and hooks argues that American feminists opted for the solidarity of 'race' (i.e. whiteness) over that of gender. Women workers in the same industries and workplaces as black women segregated the latter; the priorities of the mainstream movement catered for white middle-class women who formed the core of the movement; yet, ideologically, the movement projected the image of a bloc of homogeneous sisterhood. For hooks, this homogeneity is based on white being the norm. She illustrates this by reference to a book on women in the Southern states (hooks, 1982: 137–8) – Julia Cherry Spruill's *Women's Life and Work in the Southern Colonies* (1938). As she finds no reference to black women in the book, hooks contends that the title should begin with the word 'white', rather than assume that white women's experiences are the only or most important set. Moreover, hooks observes that if an author had written a book focusing only on black women (as opposed to only white women), the publisher would have insisted on a title beginning with 'Black'.

The American feminist movement failed to manage the tension between the hierarchies of 'race' and gender (as well as class). It was imperative for the strategic purposes of the feminist movement for it to be recognised as respectable (which meant middle class): 'Negative attitudes toward black women were the result of prevailing racist-sexist stereotypes that portrayed black women as morally impure. Many white women felt that their status as ladies would be undermined were they to associate with black women' (hooks, 1982: 130). Indeed, the theme of the critiques that hooks so concisely summarises is the ongoing gap between lip-service paid to equality for all women and the practical sidelining of women of colour within the movement. 'The women's rights movement', she concludes, 'had not drawn black and white women close together. Instead, it exposed the fact that white women were not willing to relinquish their support of white supremacy to support the interests of all women' (1982: 136).

Whiteness and the Feminist Movement: UK

In Britain, similar notes of frustration are sounded by Carby (1982) and Amos and Parmar (1984). The latter point to the family, sexuality and the women's peace movement in the early 1980s as three arenas illustrating the mismatch of priorities and the underlying racist assumptions of mainstream feminism – what they call 'the "imperial" nature of feminist thought and practice' (Amos and Parmar, 1984: 10). They contend that black and Asian families are constructed as deviant (through the figures of dominant single mothers and submissive women in arranged marriages respectively). In terms of sexuality and reproduction, it is noted that white British feminism (like the American version) has been complicit with eugenics and imperialism, through support for population control and of uncritically accepting ideas of blackness as sexual threat (from men and women). Amos and Parmar critique the women's peace movement as nationalist and parochial, reliant on defending 'our country', in which minority women have to struggle to justify their presence, and not being interested in wider global offshoots of the nuclear industry with its impact on developing world nations.

Along the same lines, in what is now one of the key texts of post-colonial studies, Mohanty (1988) argues forcefully that the construction of third-world women in the Western academy is of people 'outside history'. They appear as a pre-constituted product of backward culture. The reference point is Western women (usually middle class), against whose norms putative distance is measured. One of the key points Mohanty makes is that Western feminism is often stuck in a binary set of understandings that fail to grasp the complexity of the social realities experienced by women from the developing world. She critiques the practice of understanding things as signs that can only be read in one way (such as wearing the veil, which is only ever interpreted as a sign of oppression – see Chapter 12) and the practice of universalising social relations by understanding them from a white European woman's perspective and assuming homogeneity.

However, we find Avtar Brah (1996) still having to argue against the homogenisation of women and especially that of developing-world women. She uses the 1991 Gulf War as an example of how gendered experience is also raced and how women are not a unitary subject. She contrasts European expatriates who lost property in Kuwait with immigrant Asian women forced into the Kuwaiti desert, and then out of employment. This outcome has an important impact on remittances, etc., thus worsening the economic position of those women's families in the country of origin.

She goes on to make two sets of distinctions about how 'difference' is conceptualised. First, she separates social relations from social position. Even though black and white women are nurses in Britain, for example, and thus linked by occupation and income, their experiences of exploitation (status) are different. Second, there is what she calls 'experiential diversity', that is, the distinctiveness of collective experience contrasted with personal experience, which may exemplify or contradict the collective experience, depending on other factors. Cultural difference, she contends, is open to both positive and negative uses. It is more usefully conceptualised as a process than a static set of artefacts. There can be opposition to various forms of cultural practice from within the culture. To illustrate this, she gives the example that you can be against *suttee* without being 'positioned within those colonial and postcolonial discourses which represent such practices as symbols of inherent barbarism of Indian cultures' (Brah, 1996: 92). So, just as feminists had once argued that male standpoints had become the invisible norm, and were partial, these contesting voices have been raising questions about the standpoints of the female protagonists in debates about what it means to resist sexism. One epistemological solution to the problem of standpoint is that of the approach called 'intersectionality'.

Intersectionality: Theory and Methods

The term 'intersectionality', coined by Kimberlé Crenshaw in her essay 'Mapping the Margins' (1991),[4] addresses the articulation of class, gender, language and immigration status. Over the decades since this term was first deployed, there has been an uneven take-up of the methods internationally (Denis, 2008) with American, then UK and Canadian and more recently French scholars trying to adopt its tenets. These, put very briefly, state that focusing on 'race' (or ethnicity), class or gender alone cannot capture the diversity of women's experiences. This perspective was adopted most readily by African American academics, indeed Angela Davis's pioneering *Women, Race and Class* (2001b) prefigures this without using the term 'intersectionality' itself.

Although theoretical studies and discussions of intersectionality are a growing corpus, there is relatively little critical attention paid to methodology within that strand. Leslie McCall's (2005) systematic analysis of the strands of intersectional theory is worth looking at in order to help us gain purchase on this area. Her analysis can be loosely broken down into the two principal 'complex' methodologies she identifies. These are 'anti-categorical' and 'intra-categorical'.

'Anti-categorical complexity' is aimed at *deconstructing* the abstract analytical categories used in discussions of discrimination and identity such as 'gender', 'masculinity', 'femininity', etc. The constructed nature of categories can be demonstrated with the various methods drawn from the disciplines such as anthropology and sociology. This involves a degree of reflexivity about representing people as being part of categories at all. The idea is to leave open the question of what the categories mean, and not to take them for granted as social realities.

However, argues McCall, the beginnings of intersectionality came with 'intra-categorical complexity'. This method 'interrogates the boundary-making and boundary-defining process itself', and focuses on 'particular social groups at neglected points of intersection' (McCall, 2005: 1773–4). Examples of these are the works of Davis, Crenshaw and Hill-Collins cited below. The intersection is often explored from the perspective of an individual, which is then used to illustrate the broader collective experience of this particular set of intersections. There may also be comparative work comparing classed experiences of 'race' or 'raced' experiences of gender, tempered with the recognition that categories might be restrictive and oppressive in their own right. 'The point is not to deny the importance – both material and discursive – of categories, but to focus on the process by which they are produced, experienced, reproduced, and resisted in everyday life' (McCall, 2005: 1783).

Patricia Hill-Collins (1990) sets out the three propositions that underpin what she terms 'black feminist thought', which can be seen as one version of intersectionality:

- The forms of oppression experienced as 'race', class, gender, sexuality and nation are inextricably linked to each other.

- Negative definitions of black womanhood imposed from outside have acted as obstacles to black women's development.

- The world views created by black women have been generated out of the need for self-definition, and with the aim of working toward social justice.

Hill-Collins argues, with reason, that this constitutes 'a fundamental paradigmatic shift in how we think about oppression' (1990: 221). Where it gets challenging for people involved in progressive struggles, however, is when she talks about people's multiple positioning within different frames of domination:

> Although most individuals have little difficulty identifying their own victimization within some major system of oppression – whether it be by race, social class, religion, physical ability, sexual orientation, ethnicity, age or gender – they typically fail to see how their thoughts and actions uphold someone else's subordination ... In essence, each group identifies the oppression with which it feels most comfortable as being fundamental and classifies all others as being of lesser importance. Oppression is filled with such contradictions because these approaches fail to recognize that a matrix of domination contains few pure victims or oppressors. Each individual derives varying amounts of penalty and privilege from the multiple systems of oppression which frame everyone's lives. (1990: 230)

Moreover, a different way of thinking about forms of oppression is required because they not only all function simultaneously, but are mutually dependent. This is why Hill-Collins advocates thinking in terms of 'both/and', rather than the dichotomous 'either/or' model. 'No one group has a clear angle of vision', she contends. 'No one group possesses the theory or methodology that allows it to discover the absolute "truth" or, worse yet, proclaim its theories and methodologies as the universal norm evaluating other groups' experiences' (1990: 237).

This set of interlocking oppressions (a 'matrix') then alters the paradigm in which 'race', class and gender, for example, are understood to operate *independently*. The emphasis on reflexivity pushes actors to identify themselves as oppressing as well as oppressed along different lines, and explicitly calls for dialogue and empathy: a radical shift. How does this play out? We can see by looking at Crenshaw's original (1991) essay.

Crenshaw discusses domestic violence as inscribed in the matrix described above. 'The problem with identity politics', she contends, 'is not that it fails to transcend difference, as some critics charge, but rather the opposite – that it frequently conflates or ignores intra-group differences. In the context of violence against women, this elision of difference is problematic, fundamentally because the violence that many women experience is often shaped by other dimensions of their identities, such as race and class' (1991: 1242). Crenshaw illustrates this in the second half of her article, by recounting the story of an immigrant Latina woman who was unable to find a place in a domestic violence shelter (1991: 1262–4).

The shelter refused to take non-Anglophone clients, and she wanted to bring her young son, who would translate for her. However, it was against the shelter's policy of not allowing clients to be isolated by language difficulties. Moreover, her immigration status compounded the position of powerlessness she was in. The woman was obliged to stay married in order to be able to apply for US citizenship. The 1990 amendments to the marriage fraud provisions of the Immigration and Nationality Act meant: 'a person who immigrated to the United States to marry a United States citizen or permanent resident had to remain "properly" married for two years before applying for permanent resident status, at which time applications for the immigrant's permanent status were required by both spouses. Predictably, under these circumstances, many immigrant women were reluctant to leave even the most abusive of partners for fear of being deported. When faced with the choice between protection from their batterers and protection against deportation, many immigrant women chose the latter' (1991: 1247).

Eventually, the woman did not call back to the shelter about being housed and nothing more was heard of her. She had previously reported living on the street and being mugged, so the shelter had failed in its mission to protect her. In this case, the complexity of gender, class, language group and immigration status meant there were fewer choices available to her, and these had more detrimental outcomes.

Crenshaw's initiative then is aimed at making visible a set of social locations that are rendered invisible in scholarly work that is derived from both white male and, crucially, white feminist epistemological models. The 'approach' of intersectionality – 'a method and a disposition, a heuristic and analytic tool' (Carbado et al., 2013: 303) – is designed to draw attention to and explore experiences erased from mainstream academia and anti-racist practice:

> Although racism and sexism readily intersect in the lives of real people, they seldom do in feminist and antiracist practices. And so, when the practices expound identity as woman or person of color as an either/ or proposition, they relegate women of color to a location that resists telling. (Crenshaw, 1991: 1242)

Box 4.3   Race, Class, Gender and Housing

Stigma (Goffman, 1963) is often attached to places and, by association, to people who live in them. It has real effects, such as 'postcode prejudice', hampering people's attempts to find employment or move into rented accommodation elsewhere. At the same time, individuals in classed, gendered and/or racialised categories know they may be seen as 'undesirable populations' in some neighbourhoods or by property owners. In the former case, when stigma is attached to places, people resist being 'stigmatised-by-association' by 'passing' as members of groups viewed as privileged and unproblematic. For example, the white American working-class women on welfare studied by Macdonald and Twine (2013) manage their presentation of self in order to move from inner-city Boston to more desirable middle-income suburbs. Within the US housing market that is highly racially segregated, they are already advantaged by being white. However, they must conceal their welfare status, present themselves as middle class (by dress and speech patterns) when they visit the rentable properties, and do not reveal to prospective landlords that they are in receipt of welfare vouchers that grant them entitlement to housing subsidies.

However, even middle-class respectability is not always enough. Karyn Lacy's (2007) study of the African American professional middle class in the suburbs of Washington, DC shows that estate agents are frequently racially selective about properties they show to such families, regardless of the latter's high purchasing power. If they are not assertive, they may end up being shown only properties in areas with higher concentrations of African Americans, and not the full range of properties that meet their search criteria. These African Americans make a point of dressing in smart clothes when meeting estate agents, to emphasise their status. In both of these examples, the actors are well aware of the rules of the game, and how they are stacked against them. This status-based subterfuge reveals the unofficial regulations about 'race', class and gender in access to housing markets. Within these parameters, they advance strategies for subverting these practices.

Intersectional Analyses: From Domestic Work to the Global Sex Trade

Part of critical feminist epistemology involves stressing that employment is not the only starting point for studies of oppression. Yet focusing squarely on employment can be just as revealing about class, 'race' and gender. My argument is not either/or, but both/and. Angela Davis's chapter on black women's employment in the post-abolition period (2001b: 87–98) demonstrates the enduring power of categories developed under one structure (the slave mode of production) to influence people's lives long after that structure has been dismantled.

Often, the abolition of slavery in various countries is simply understood as a point where everything changed for the better in terms of the formerly enslaved people's life chances. The reality was very different. In the British Caribbean, the sugar plantation owners attempted to keep the former slaves dependent on the plantation system for an income by making it difficult for them to create a viable peasantry. In the USA, similar strategies were deployed, all aimed at making former slaves into dependent and often indebted peasant farmers reliant on their relationship to land. Moreover, the practice of arresting black people on spurious charges and renting them out as convict labour (the 'convict lease system') was widespread in the post-abolition Southern states, and in some places, lasted well into the twentieth century (Blackmon, 2008). In this context, as people left the land to work in cities, what were the employment options available for Black Americans? Of the 2.7 million black women over 10 years of age counted in the 1890 Census (35 years after abolition), more than a million were in paid employment. Their distribution is presented in Table 4.1.

Table 4.1   Percentage of African American women in various forms of employment at the 1890 Census

Agriculture	Household domestic service	Laundries	Manufacturing	Others
38.7	30.8	15.6	2.8	12.1

Davis argues that the main types of work that African American women did were similar to that which they had carried out under slavery: agricultural and domestic. Also, they were often subject to sexual advances from the white men for whom they worked. This cultural aspect, in which white men could force themselves on black women with impunity, is another continuation of slavery-period relations. She cites a domestic worker from Georgia in 1912:

> I believe nearly all white men take, and expect to take, liberties with their colored female servants – not only the fathers but in many cases the sons also. Those servants who rebel against such familiarity must either leave or expect a mighty hard time, if they stay. (Aptheker, 1946: 49, cited by A.Y. Davis, 2001b: 92)

By 1890, domestic service was the largest single occupation for black men and women in 32 of the 48 states of the USA, while an 1899 study of Pennsylvania found that 60 per cent of black workers in total (and 91 per cent of women) were employed in some kind of domestic service. These women worked long hours in an unregulated, virtually non-unionised sector, in which the only competition was newly arrived European immigrant women, the only other group who would perform this kind of low-status labour. The obstacles before women seeking better-paid work in other industries were formidable. Over the 1890–1940 period, the figures show that there was little mobility. The 1940 Census shows that 59.5 per cent of black women were still in domestic service with another 10.5 per cent in other service occupations.

While the Second World War altered the conditions of entry and movement within the labour force for all women, the pattern was not completely broken. As late as 1960, more than one-third of black women were in domestic service and another 20 per cent were in other forms of service employment (A.Y. Davis, 2001b: 97–8). Davis maintains that this concentration of black women in domestic and other forms of service demonstrated that genuine emancipation was far from being achieved, as women were still tied into slavery-period social relations, and blackness was still synonymous with 'servant'.

Masculinities

Intersectionality is not only about women, of course. Gendered roles and structural positions belong to both men and women. Lois Weis's work analyses the transition from the types of masculine identities derived from being the breadwinner in a single income family in the post-war period (because of the prevalence of jobs for life in heavy industry), to those available for men in the post-industrial landscape of service-sector and casualised employment. She argues (Weis, 2006) that the re-making of this segment of the working class is accomplished through ongoing changes in gender relations.

Comparing the ideas about gender roles from her interviewees in 1985 (then aged 15–16) and in 2001 (aged 30–31), she concludes that the gender regime has been transformed. The dominant model of the mid-1980s involved a continuation of the heavy industry job, the family constructed around male employment, and for younger men, a certain lack of accountability and responsibilities. By the beginning of the twenty-first century, men in 'settled' jobs are those who no longer correspond to the hard-living stereotype of the 1980s, but those employed in 'feminised' areas (e.g. hospital work) or whose work is based on going back to adult education to learn new skills. They also typically share childcare with a partner in similarly paid work. Talking of one of her two exemplary case studies, she concludes that 'John's "stable" or "settled" new working-class existence, which he values highly, is wholly dependent upon his breaking away from hegemonically-constructed white male masculinity' (Weis, 2006: 268).

This is contrasted with the traditional male breadwinner's guarantee of his sacrifice made for provision (of food, clothes, cleaning, etc.). There are no men in Weis's sample who think gender roles have stayed the same, yet a few cling to the construction of self that is based on strength and unaccountability. The example in her article is 'Clint', who has failed to engage either with the world of work, or a stable emotional life. He lives between parents' and girlfriend's homes, has a tenuous relationship with the labour market, and is not accountable to anyone. He recounts how he spent $15,000 on a motorbike instead of on a house, as his girlfriend had suggested, and predicts the imminent and subsequent demise of his relationship with her. This is a minority position, however, with most men negotiating childcare and work roles with a partner in an equal position. Weis writes: 'Ironically … while the old industrial order rested upon a stable gender regime, it is the unsteady fulcrum of gender (roles, definitions, and hierarchy) that lies at the very heart of reconstituted white working-class life' (2006: 271).

Class, Identification and Disgust

Indeed, working-class identities can also be viewed using an intersectional frame that seeks to identify their gendered dimension. This project might not always be as easy to accomplish, given the dominance of frameworks that reject class as a useful point of focus, as in the UK since the late 1980s. Beverley Skeggs' work with young working-class women in the North-West of England shows that the fraught relationship of gender to class is characterised by rejection and dis-identification, as the women realise that they are being judged by standards they feel are unfeasible (1997). They rarely embrace working-class identity unequivocally. However, Skeggs goes on to argue (2005) that in the 1990s and 2000s, the place that class used to occupy has been usurped by other discourses covering ostensibly the same object, but which are to do mainly with culture (especially visual and popular culture). In this domain, class values are represented in the tension between middle-class norms (from which judgements are made) and working-class bodies and habits.

The British term 'Chav' embodies this switch to culture, and for Haywood and Yar (2006: 16), it is 'a term of intense class-based abhorrence'. For Skeggs and Wood (2008), this process is particularly visible in contemporary reality television show formats in which working-class subjects are made to reflect upon their behaviour and 'improve' it in order to attain middle-class norms of restraint and femininity. The drama for the audience is the struggle of the working-class body to shake off its association with working-class culture, and the frequent inability to accomplish this goal. This is presented as a personal failure, and the social world of economics and material obstacles remains insulated from the personal 'journey' in which the participants of the shows engage. Skeggs' argument is that in early twenty-first century Britain, the focus on culture is a proxy for class.

'Chavs'

This substitution of culture for class emerges strongly from Imogen Tyler's study of the use of the term 'Chav' as a way to say 'underclass' in contemporary Britain (2008). She demonstrates the gendered nature of the process of division, and how it intersects with racialisation. The subjects of this discourse are white working-class British people. In this context, the term 'underclass' has been used relatively little in public and academic discourse since the mid-1990s. The use of 'Chav' and its regional variations since the early twenty-first century has now become, for Tyler, 'a ubiquitous term of abuse for white working-class subjects' (2008: 17). She argues that the Chav has become a representative 'figure' of classification accumulating power through repetition.

The disgust that is a central feature of class relations (Ahmed, 2004; Lawler, 2005, 2012) is attached to bodies through talking about culture. Laughter and disgust create a community of non-Chavs, distinguished by not sharing Chavs' excessive and tasteless consumption. In other words, white poor people are rendered abnormal in the constant repetition of the themes that 'make' the Chav. They are instead 'hypervisible "filthy whites"' (Tyler, 2008: 25). Moreover, the bodies of Chavettes (female Chavs) are most explicitly objects of disgust. The figure of the Chavette begins to absorb a number of 'disgusting' practices: wearing garish and excessive clothes, revealing too much flesh, being overly sexualised, having children out of wedlock and frequent 'race' mixing. Tyler suggests that one reading is also that the Chavette's extra-fecund and sexualised body is read as a mirror of middle-class, middle-aged and possibly infertile women who have put their careers first:

> Indeed, the disgust for and fascinated obsession with the Chav mum's
> 'easy fertility' is bound up with a set of social angst about infertility
> amongst middle-class women, a group continually chastised for 'putting

career over motherhood' and 'leaving it too late' to have children. The figure of the Chav mum not only mocks poor white teenage mothers but also challenges middle-class women to face their 'reproductive responsibilities'. (2008: 30)

This eugenicist theme, of the 'wrong' people reproducing and the 'right' people not, is taken up again in Chapter 7. What Tyler seems to be indicating is that the term 'Chav', and the many negative practices associated with it, now occupy a space in which to express overtly racist comments that is now shut off elsewhere in public discourse, except maybe in relation to Gypsy-Travellers (see Chapter 3).

Box 4.4   Paradigm Intersectionality

Ange-Marie Hancock has worked on intersectionality over the period since 2010 in a series of pieces of work (2011, 2012, 2013). In relation to the Trayvon Martin case, she identifies what she calls 'paradigm intersectionality', as distinct from Crenshaw's. There are five dimensions of paradigm intersectionality (Hancock, 2012): Categorical Multiplicity; Categorical Intersections; Diversity Within; Individual-Institutional Relationships; and Time Dynamics. She rejects the following three questions, as representing standard lines of enquiry:

1   Was it Martin's race that drove Zimmerman to claim a justifiable response (shooting and killing) to the presence of an unknown black man?

2   Was it Martin's race or Martin's gender or Martin's (perceived) class or age that drove Zimmerman to his acts?

3   Was it Martin's race, gender, age and perceived class together that drove Zimmerman to his acts?

The *paradigm intersectionality* question is: How do inegalitarian traditions interact and emerge in our understanding of the meaning of George Zimmerman's shooting of Trayvon Martin?

Hancock's rich reading cannot be done justice here, but its principal interlocking elements focus on the bodies of young black males at intersection of: police policies (historically often lethal and reckless toward black life); the 'stand your ground' law in Florida; and the 'politics of disgust' (expressed as a white consensus around the expendability of black lives).

Commenting on Du Bois' invitation to the reader from *Darkwater* (2003 [1920]: 227) to 'imagine spending your life looking for insults or for hiding places from them', Hancock writes:

As Du Bois says, it is a threat that can't ever be fully anticipated nor benignly ignored, for race (and, I would add, other analytical categories) continually render marginalized people's movement through space 'suspect' in a context where the rules are purportedly as 'fair' as a lottery, with those in need having the highest probability of fighting to the death.

Gender, Sex and 'Race'

So intersectional analyses, whether explicitly inserting themselves into the 'matrix of domination' paradigm or not, can reveal plenty about the ways that discrimination compounds 'race', gender and class. Our last two examples move the frame of analysis from the national to the global.

Intersectionality and Global Mobilities

Joanne Nagel (2003) locates the intersection of global inequalities, gender, racialised identities and class squarely within the domain of US military imperialism in the latter part of the twentieth century. The US military in Asia, she asserts, has generated an extensive sex trade. Off base becomes an arena for the enactment of masculinities. Moreover, the 'military-sexual complex' (2003: 177) spreads this dimension of the sex trade to the USA because of relationships with women who are then brought back. Moon (1997) estimates that at least 100,000 women came to the USA as brides of servicemen from the 1950s to the early 1990s. The US bases in Asia, Europe and Central America since the Second World War have spawned a dependent industry of sexual services catering to servicemen. The longstanding images of Asian women as docile, mysterious, exotic and subservient serve as the backdrop to this for US servicemen:

> ... the sexual recreation areas that surround US military bases, especially in Asia, are ethnosexual sites where Western fantasies of Asian female sexuality meet material manifestations of Asian women and where the marriage of geopolitics and racial cosmologies is consummated nightly. (Nagel, 2003: 179)

Moreover, the growth of sex tourism in Asia is linked to the US military presence, as the post-conflict relations are constructed on the economic foundations built for the 'Rest and Recreation' (R&R) programme of the US military. The most obvious example to put forward in this respect is Thailand. Bishop and Robinson (1998) argue that in 1971, World Bank President Robert McNamara, who had been Defense Secretary when a contract was signed with the Thai government to provide R&R services to US troops in 1967, 'went to Bangkok to arrange for the bank's experts to produce a study of Thailand's post-war tourism prospects' (Bishop and Robinson, 1998: 9). The Thais took the advice of the World Bank experts and developed the tourist industry – but on the basis of the go-go bars and brothels that had been created to service the US military. In this relationship then, Thai (and the other poor, young Asian) women who become sex workers in Thailand's major cities and resorts are placed in a position of subjugation by Thai men who economically exploit them and foreigners who sexually exploit them.

This has not been a historical accident but an outcome of US military presence, just as Japanese men's use of Asian sex workers both in Japan and abroad is, for Watanabe (1995: 506), a continuation of the war-time activities engaged in by the Imperial Japanese army from the 1930s, whereby women from occupied countries (from China to Burma [Myanmar]) would be taken and forced into prostitution to service Japanese troops.

Ronit Lentin (Lentin and McVeigh, 2006) explores the position of developing-world women in the rapidly expanding Irish economy of the early twenty-first century.[5] Her study demonstrates the interconnectedness not only of gender, 'race' and class, but also that of the first and developing worlds in how these are articulated. She starts with the murder of Paiche Onyemaechi, a Malawian woman (and mother of two Irish citizens) to highlight some of these relations. Onyemaechi was a sex worker and former asylum-seeker and was constructed in media coverage as a bad 'm/other', to use Lentin's formulation, against which white married Catholic women can be contrasted as good mothers.

The movement of women in global migratory flows – into low-paid work, as domestics, nannies and sex workers (Ehrenreich and Hochschild, 2003) – reaches places that had not previously been destinations for mass migration. The Republic of Ireland became one of these in the mid-1990s (Garner, 2004).

Until 2005, any child born on the island of Ireland became an Irish citizen regardless of the nationality of his/her parents. For Lentin, Irish women are seen as representing the nation (through Erin, Hibernia, etc.), and reproducing the nation through giving birth. Yet foreign women's bodies in twenty-first century Ireland mark a crisis for Irish identity. They are seen as transgressive, threatening the integrity of Irish nationality through 'unnaturally' giving birth to Irish nationals (through their non-national bodies). These women are accused of putting strain on Irish maternity care provision, and unfairly getting access to resources through residence and citizenship (Lentin, 2004; Luibhéid, 2004; Garner, 2007c). Their giving birth is also portrayed by politicians and the media as a threat to the integrity of the Irish citizenship system. The bodies for whom the residence rights acquired through mothering an Irish national are a worthwhile asset are from outside the EU (specifically Africa, Asia, Latin America, the Middle East and Eastern Europe) so, primarily, this means women of colour. Responses go as far as people spitting at them, abusing them and perpetrating physical violence on them.

In the end, the 2004 Citizenship Referendum closed off the avenue of birth right for Irish children with foreign parents, as 80 per cent of the voters accorded the Minister of Justice the right to exclude children born to foreign nationals the right to access Irish citizenship (unless a condition of three years' residence prior to the birth, not including time spent as an asylum-seeker, was satisfied).

Ireland has a history of regulating women's bodies (unmarried mothers, women seeking abortions, etc.), and the focus on the sexuality of foreign women in the discourse of impurity continues the process of displacing problems onto external sources, and in thus removing responsibility from the nationals. Absent from the exposure given to female migrants is the fact that the Irish sex industry is sustained by mainly Irish men paying to have sex with mainly foreign sex workers, many of whom are trafficked. Ireland's expanding economy 'needs' highly mobile low-paid workers, women like Paiche Onyemaechi, to continue to grow, and allow white Irish women to forge careers:

> ... the globalisation of domestic work brings ambitious and independent career-oriented western women and striving women from the Third World together, though not as sisters, rather as mistresses and maids. (Lentin and McVeigh, 2006: 105)

This reminder that power relations suffuse social relationships that may seem ostensibly relatively equal ends our brief introduction to intersectional analysis.

Conclusions

These small slivers of much more complex and dense work, along with the much more bountiful theoretical discussions on intersectionality, bring into view the idea of a multiplicity of axes of domination.

- Intersectionality (at least in terms of 'race', class and gender) cannot be understood as an approach in which people add each element of their identity onto others like layers of a cake, but as a three-dimensional re-lationship, a matrix, in which all these identities are constituents of the others, and create specific experiences and oppressions.

- The reframing of the approach as a critique of mainstream social sci-ences is not meant to be deterministic (assuming that all black working-class women, or all middle-class Asian men have the same experiences, for example). Nor is it an attempt to replace one false universalism with another. Intersectionality is therefore not a mechanical reading of what the actors will think and do, but of the *structural conditions* they are likely to have faced, and therefore the sometimes pitiful options avail-able the lower down the local scale of status the actor(s) may be.

- Intersectionality is the product of tension between the (white male) epistemologies of mainstream academia and feminist research in its broadest sense. At the heart of the critiques of feminism, racism is seen not as an aberration from the humanist post-Enlightenment tradition of liberalism, but as an intrinsic dimension of how capitalism functions as business-as-usual.

- The types of historical and local specificities thrown up by such research seem to me to turn the search for a general Marxist theory of racism into a wild goose chase. The principles are that these forms of exploitation cannot be readily distinguished in practice: they are permanently *in articulation* with each other. Class is, to borrow Stuart Hall's formulation, the 'modality through which' 'race' is lived, and 'race', the modality through which class is lived.

- Moreover, 'race' is not just for people not racialised as white, nor is gender only for women.

Points for Reflection

Are class, 'race' and gender all equally important sources of identity?

In what ways does looking at 'race', gender and class together rather than separately provide a more complex model?

In terms of 'race', class and gender, where are you located, and how might this affect and influence your perspectives on racism?

Further Reading

Crenshaw, K. (1991) 'Mapping the Margins: Identity Politics, Intersectionality, and Violence against Women', *Stanford Law Review* 43(6): 1241–99.

The essay that launched intersectionality as a concept: identifies race, gender, class and immigration status as factors in women's experiences of violence.

Davis, A.Y. (2001a) 'Race, Gender, and Prison History: From the Convict Lease System to the Supermax Prison', in D.F. Sabo, T.A Kupers and W. James (eds) *Prison Masculinities*, pp. 35–45. Philadelphia: Temple University Press.

Davis links the history of slavery to the development of prisons and the penal regimes surrounding them. She identifies race and gender as key elements in this story, and asserts that the penal regime aims to punish and control black bodies, while making profit from their labour.

Yuval-Davis, N. (2011) *The Politics of Belonging: Intersectional Contestations*. London: Sage.

Yuval-Davis studies the intersection of the sociology of power and the sociology of emotions: casting the net wide, she demonstrates the complexities of making political projects about 'belonging' to various social groups (nations, religions, racialised groups, etc.).

Notes

1. For a general critique of the cultural turn's impact on sociology, see Rojek and Turner (2001). More specifically on racism, try Mac an Gháill (1999).

2. See Ladson-Billings and Tate (1995). In the UK context, the attempts to integrate Critical Race Theory (CRT) into British theory by Gillborn (2005) and Hylton (2005) are also worth consulting, with multidisciplinary interventions from law, philosophy and cultural studies.

3. The objection might be that if you do not accept the centrality of the assertion that there is a separate racialised 'cognitive universe', then none of the rest follows. However, the statistical basis of differential outcomes (income, wealth, educational achievement, segregation, life expectancy, etc.) for people in different racialised groups in the USA is surely by now incontestable. Denial that this matters is proof in Mills' term of inhabiting a separate cognitive universe.

4. Crenshaw had set out a draft of the concept of intersectionality in a previous article without actually using that term (Crenshaw, 1989).

5. See Chapter 6: 'Black Bodies and Headless Hookers: Women and Alternative Narratives of Globalisation', pp. 97–111.

5

'Race', Nation, State

In this chapter we will

- Distinguish between the nation, nationalism and the nation state
- Focus on the nation state and examine its relationship with 'race'
- Examine some of the theoretical work on 'race' and state
- Demonstrate that nation states shape our understandings of 'race', and play a role in the generation of racist practices and ideas

Nation states are a product of what sociologists refer to as 'modernity', the period of global changes starting from around the turn of the sixteenth century and ending in the late twentieth. This period includes processes such as secularisation, industrialisation, urbanisation, democratisation, and the division of the world into the nation state system. Regardless of the extent to which people in various nations argue over how long their nation has existed, and what the roots of nationalism are, the nation state as we know it today dates to the French Revolution. The nation state is a political entity that claims legitimacy to control and represent a territory full of people who owe allegiance to that state, and who share aspects of culture, language and history. The nation state makes sense now as one unit of many in a world of around 200 states: the nation state system. Indeed, reference to this system of states is a widespread practice in locating one-self individually in the contemporary world ('I'm English', 'I'm French', 'I'm 'American', 'I'm Chinese', etc.). We shall first look at how we talk about member-ship of nations and how we arrive at the conclusions that we do in fact belong to them, before moving on to the study of how nation states shape our understand-ings of 'race', and play a role in the generation of racist practices and ideas.

Nation

Belonging to a nation has been conceptualised by academics in different disciplines in a number of ways. For nineteenth-century political scientist

Ernest Renan (1992 [1882]) a nation is 'a daily plebiscite' in that people elect to remain part of the nation by not challenging this format or replacing it with something else. This formulation raises the question that scholars have been trying to answer ever since: what keeps all these people together, when objectively there are all kinds of potential lines of division such as wealth, class, region, ethnicity, gender, political viewpoint, religion, language and cultural orientation? For Renan again, this is a secondary issue:

> What makes a nation is not speaking the same language or belonging to the same ethnographic group, it is having done great things together in the past and wanting to do more great things in the future. (1992 [1882]: 54)

So being part of a nation requires both a collective act of imagination and an emotional investment in belonging. Nation states are constructed by people, and are not natural units into which groups of people fall without being pushed. Convincing people that they legitimately belong to a community so large that they will never know all its other members, but to which most have a strong allegiance, and for which many are prepared to die, requires a variety of methods. Looking backwards and forwards in time involves placing oneself among people who are either already dead or not yet born, and allying oneself with them all. The language of the nation is all about this emotional response, whereas that of the State is more about interests. Indeed, the nation state and people's multiple bonds and allegiances to it are terrain in which the ideas that are crucial to that of 'race' are embedded. Nations are often talked about as biologically 'natural' units, whether this is in relation to the world of plants or people. German historian Herder argued that:

> The most natural state ... is one nation, with one national character ... a nation is as much a natural plant as a family. Only with more branches. Nothing therefore appears so directly opposite to the end of government as the unnatural enlargement of states. The wild mixture of races and nations under one sceptre ... (1784–91: 249–50)

Nascent concerns with the problems allegedly posed by multilingual and multicultural populations within the territory of a nation state are foreshadowed in Herder's comments. Language is also a key factor in one of the most often quoted commentaries on nationhood, Benedict Anderson's 'imagined community' (1983). Anderson, a historian of South East Asia, studied Indonesian nationalism and focused on the way that nationalist activists managed to create a shared language, using the printed word, from a set of cultures with a multitude of languages. 'Indonesian-ness', if you like, had on one level to be invented in order for all Indonesians, in their various parts of what is a huge territory, to feel as though they belonged to one unit. Indeed, the role of invention in this process is underscored by the historians Eric Hobsbawm and Terence Ranger, in their famous collection of essays, *The Invention of Tradition* (1983), containing case studies drawn from the British Isles, Continental Europe and colonial India and Africa. They argue that it is a function of the nation state to create national traditions rather than merely observe existing ones, and that this is part of the process of constituting nationhood and inculcating the idea among its people that nations stretch back in time, thus legitimising the present situation.

Box 5.1   Nations and Nation States

The nation is a self-defining cultural and social community. One of the most dominant, normative ideologies is that which sets out that the natural unit for groups of populations is the nation. In theory, the members of a given 'nation' share a common identity of some kind. The idea of a nation stretches across time to include the dead and the as yet unborn in a continuous narrative of belonging. Thus, the use of 'we' and 'our' to describe history, heritage, armies, victories, etc. is a normal part of this idea. Although the term 'nation' is informally used as a synonym for a *state*, there is a distinction between the two.

A **nation state** is the political and legal structure of a state that has jurisdiction over a particular nation. Nation states therefore differ from previous forms of governed entity such as city states. Although nation states have defined themselves as relatively homogeneous cultural groups, this was never the exclusive model. Moreover, since the European expansion into the developing world, and the accelerated movement of migratory flows, I would argue that the multicultural nation (as a *description*) is now the norm. Every nation (group of people) is associated with its own specific territory, the national homeland, although some territories may be part of other nation states, e.g. Kurds, and Jews prior to the foundation of Israel. There might also be arguments over the legitimacy of particular territories, e.g. Israel/Palestine, Northern Ireland. A nation state's nationality and citizenship laws determine who is a member and under what conditions membership is allowed. This is usually a combination of bloodlines, residence periods and/or marriage (Chapter 2).

Craig Calhoun, taking a concept from Foucault, calls the nation a 'discursive formation', 'a way of speaking that shapes our consciousness' (1997: 3). This does not have to do necessarily with using the term 'nation', but to do with:

> ... whether participants use a rhetoric, a way of speaking, a kind of language that carries with it connections to other events and actions, that enables or disables certain other ways of speaking or acting, or that is recognised by others as entailing certain consequences. (1997: 3–4)

So the nation is an implicit presence in how we frame our talk about identity and social problems, for example. What I am trying to get at is the quality of taken-for-grantedness that the nation state now assumes in our talk and actions. Greek sociologist Alexandria Halkias (2003) finds, in her interviews with women about the low birth-rate crisis (*demografiko*), that:

> The need to have at least one child in order to be considered a good Greek woman, which is implicitly underscored in the official public sphere's articulations of the *demografiko*, is never challenged by the women interviewed. (2003: 224)

So while they talk about their careers, the problems of bringing up children in an expensive place, etc., the supposed role of women as 'reproducing the nation' (Anthias and Yuval-Davis, 1993) is not questioned.

We find both the language of essentialism (Box 1.2) and of the natural world in the discourse on the nation shot through with references to family, community, kinship, bloodlines, homogeneity and purity (key elements of 'race'). We have, from this perspective, a series of undeniable bonds with the other members of the nation, as an extended family, with whom we face other nations, equally constituted, in the global competition of nation states. As part of that bond, we owe allegiance to the State, which 'protects' borders against incomers, and provides us with signs and symbols of membership, such as passports. How have we arrived at the point where this all seems natural and the only way the world could be?

Nation States

French political philosopher Etienne Balibar argues that the link between 'race' and nation is actively made by the State (Balibar and Wallerstein, 1991). Nations are constructed as 'natural' entities, as we have seen above, in which the human race can be broken down into homogeneous groups. Thus, blood (genealogy) and soil (territory) combine to make nationals who 'belong' in that place to that group. However, this process does not happen on its own. Instead, the State 'produces' both 'nationals' and 'non-nationals' (Balibar and Wallerstein, 1991) through its institutions, particularly the legal and education systems. This happens by socialising people into the idea that those in a given nation are intrinsically different from those of other nations, and that any internal divisions are less important than this principal one. Indeed, social psychologist Michael Billig (1995) argues that nationalism is not all about wars, sport, national heroes and flag-waving, but also the innumerable ways in which the idea of belonging to the nation state is transmitted and picked up by the nation's population on a daily basis, through maps, oaths, school curricula, language, official procedures, the use of 'we' to talk about the nation, etc. He terms this 'banal nationalism'. What both he and Balibar underline is that nations are necessarily *exclusive*, established as they are in permanent opposition to all other nations. In saying 'we', the nation simultaneously says 'they'.

Scholarship on 'Race' and the State

The bodies of academic writing on racism and the State seldom overlapped before the late twentieth century. We will look at some exceptions to that rule before focusing on Omi and Winant's (1994 [1986]) and Goldberg's (2000) explicit attempts to flesh out the racialisation of the State in modernity. Racism in the Western view is still popularly seen as an aberration, something that marks *individuals* as deviant. In short, racism is viewed as a marginal and undesirable outcome that the State now (in the twenty-first century) strives to combat. However, I am going to argue in this section that 'race' has been for centuries an important part of how Western society governs itself *normally*, and that racism is, as Bauman (1989) suggests, politically inseparable from the project of modernity, due to the imbedded process of *categorisation* undertaken in the Enlightenment.

To understand racism in the contemporary period, it is essential to engage with two ideas. First, although racism is an historical process, it is an ongoing one and cannot be located wholly in the past (Box 6.3). Second, the State is not a neutral arbiter in the way that 'race' becomes pertinent in various fields, but a significant player in defining membership of the nation. It does so using concepts deriving from essentialism and attaching these ideas to bodies deemed different, both physically and culturally.

The idea that the State plays a role in racialisation was first explored explicitly by the German political theorist Erich Voegelin, publishing in the 1930s and 1940s (Voegelin, 2000 [1933], 1940). W.E.B Du Bois, in his history of the decades following the American Civil War (1998 [1935]), also addressed this issue. A refugee from the Nazis, Voegelin sought to understand the process of state formation, and, unlike any other political theorist before him, concluded that racialisation was crucial to this. Nations, he argued, have to put themselves forward as unique entities, natural groupings of people each different from the other nations. The idea of 'race', with its spurious scientific basis, provides ideal fuel for such ideological labour. So by making the idea that the nation represents a racial group, what Lentin and Lentin (2006: 3–4) call 'the theoretical glue' binding people to each other, and to the otherwise abstract State, is provided. 'Race' therefore emerges as one of the principal factors underlying the legitimisation of nation states as the accepted, appropriate and 'normal' way to organise societies.

Zygmunt Bauman (1989) has suggested that the act of classification is a crucial element of modernity, and especially of the Enlightenment, which itself is a crucial phase in the idea of 'race'. One of the activities engaged in by the Enlightenment thinkers was the hierarchical classification of all forms of life.

The incarnation of this desire to order and list was Linnaeus's taxonomy of people based on skin colour, 'humour' and geographical location (Box 7.1).

By the time that the Enlightenment was in full swing on both sides of the Atlantic, in the last quarter of the eighteenth century, the Triangular Trade of slaves, raw materials and finished products that linked Europe, Africa and North America, was at its most profitable juncture, and the United States had already written its Constitution. The US economy was based upon the slave mode of production, and this was recognised as intrinsic to the country's form of governance. Senator Henry Wise, in the debates on anti-slavery in the 1830s, argued that: 'they [our northern brethren] cannot attack the system of slavery without attacking the institutions of our country, our safety and our welfare' (Nye, 1949: 34, cited by Feagin, 2006: 12). Indeed, 10 presidents between 1790 and 1869 had been slaveholders at some point in their lives (Feagin, 2006: 12). Although the Constitution holds the 'truths to be self-evident', all men were not created equal in terms of their right to live in the absence of servitude. Moreover, the annexation of territory that the first 13 states of the Union would later claim for itself, to the north and the west of the initial colonies, involved violently usurping Native Americans from their ancestral lands. Elsewhere, other imperial powers, acting first through private companies, then through state powers covering colonial possessions, were involved in similar activities of mineral extraction and the creation of economies serving Europe under armed rule. As the beginnings of what we recognise as modern nation states with varying degrees of democratic participation began to emerge across the West, the ideas incorporating 'the people' as citizens with rights excluded the poorer, the female and enslaved members of those societies, and cast the colonial subject as the opposite of the rights-bearing citizen. Summarising this process, Lentin and Lentin write:

> Because the idea of universal humanity was constructed in the image of the white European, against the non-European, the blacks in the colonies and the internal others, the application of the essence of humanity, as it was defined by European thinkers, to all men and women was impossible from the outset. It is simply not possible for those who do not comply with a definition of humanity – rationality, individuality, white aesthetics – to be considered (fully) human. (2006: 6)

This is the context of the instigation of the modern nation state system. The very invisibility of these groups in the original vision of the citizen is the basis for the 'racial state' described by Omi and Winant (1994 [1986]), Goldberg (2000), and explored further in Lentin and Lentin (2006).

The State's role is to control its population, and in Foucault's merciless expression, to 'make live' and 'let die' (2003). Bauman had earlier captured this necessary cruelty in his metaphor of the 'gardening state'. Here, the State represents rationality and order. To maintain the garden's order against chaos, the gardener must weed out 'every self-invited plant which interferes with his plan and vision of order and harmony' (Bauman, 1989: 57). What this means in terms of 'race' and the State is that the former comprises the plants and grass, while those seen as weak or alien constitute the weeds. The procedure and mechanisms for deciding who is an insider, and subsequently sorting insiders from outsiders, constitutes the work of this gardening state.

In this racialised vision of the nation, there are people who are 'weeds in the garden', preventing the superior plants from flourishing. It is clear from historical work on 'race' in the Victorian era, for example, that in nineteenth-century Britain and America, very similar ways of talking about the working classes and slaves or colonial subjects were in use. These are essentialising discourses, identifying reasons for the existing status quo (the weakness of one group and the strength of another, measured in terms of industriousness and moral codes), and thus fixing working-class bodies to a culture that represents the opposite of middle-class virtue, restraint and dynamism. For Hartigan (2005), a discourse that explained fecklessness and moral turpitude by reference to environmental factors of socialisation and heredity was grafted onto an anti-immigrant ideology in the works of the well-funded and communicative eugenics lobby. We shall see how the 1924 US Immigration Act was influenced by such ideas, in Chapter 7.

Box 5.2   Michel Foucault

Foucault (1926–84) was a French philosopher, much referred to in sociological and political theory because of his groundbreaking historicising work on the social construction of key concepts such as 'discipline', 'sexuality' and 'madness', and for his complex theorisation of power. For Foucault, new forms of power are generated by and developed through the emergence of the modern nation state. He coined the term 'bio-power' to explain this state form of power.

Bio-power is a 'technology' (or mechanism) of power, that is, a means of managing an entire population. Foucault argues that the phenomenon he labels 'bio-power' emerged in the seventeenth century. It has two constituent elements: scientific categories of human beings and 'disciplinary power'. The categories are based on gender, sexuality, nationality, etc., while 'disciplinary power' is targeted on regulating bodies (a process he analyses in *Discipline and Punish* [1977]). Traditional types of power, he maintains, were derived from a sovereign's power to kill his/her subjects. However, in the period after feudalism, where there has to be a rationale for the exercise of power beyond that of divine right, bio-power is implemented by emphasising the protection of life instead of the threat of death. Foucault summarises this alternative as the passage from 'let live and make die', to 'make live and let die'.

When the State is so heavily involved in protecting the lives of 'its' people, it can use this to justify anything. Bio-power is therefore an essential characteristic of modern nation states, and ties in neatly with eugenics (Chapter 7). Groups viewed as inferior and thus threats to the life of the nation (like Bauman's weeds) can be eliminated with impunity. This idea is explored most fully in Foucault's lecture on 17 March 1976, reproduced in *Society Must Be Defended* (2003), in which he analyses what he terms 'race struggle' and the modern state.

In the contemporary period, scholars have grappled with the concept of the State influencing the struggle for power between groups that organise around the basis of 'race', in order to obtain social justice for those groups. Michael Omi and Howard Winant's pioneering thesis (1994 [1986]) situated the US federal state as an active player in the racialisation of its population in different ways. They first provide a working definition of what they mean by the State:

> The State is composed of institutions, the policies they carry out, the conditions and rules which support and justify them, and the social relationships in which they are imbedded. (Omi and Winant, 1994 [1986]: 83)

This definition is interesting in that it moves away from the strictly material to encompass the ideological, and for us, interested in the ways in which states encourage people to think about social relationships in terms of closed and natural groups, is a very appropriate one.

Much of what the authors describe focuses, as their book's subtitle indicates, on the period from the 1960s to the 1980s, the civil rights and backlash period. However, in order to understand their claims, we have to go back to their historical model, in which they deploy Antonio Gramsci's (1971) concepts: 'war of manoeuvre' and 'war of position'. In the former, the civil society actors have no legitimate outlet because they are excluded from the democratic community. The mission there is to establish spaces and counter-cultures in which their own group can be valorised, and in which oppositional ideology can be developed. In the 'war of position', however, they are enabled to influence the democratic process from within. This allows political and ideological projects to be developed. These are aimed at contesting the dominance (or 'hegemony', to use Gramsci's term) of the most powerful group, and of the ideology it uses to justify its dominance. In terms of American history, the authors see the period before civil rights as that of the 'war of manoeuvre', whereas the 1960s usher in the 'war of position', which the authors maintain is ongoing.

In the model that Omi and Winant establish, 'race' is never stable, and indeed 'racial formation' is crucial to understanding it as an unfinished process. The process of attaching meaning to 'race' is engaged in by the State in the form of legislation, Census, immigration and citizenship rules. Social movements generally focus on the State as an entity from which to extract concessions in a struggle for equality and the politics of recognition. So instead of starting and finishing with group identities that are set in stone, social movements engage the State and other civil society actors in a struggle over meanings that results in steps forward and backwards being made at different moments. Progressive social movements may influence the State to the point where the very idiom in which they are conducting the war of manoeuvre is appropriated and used for non-progressive ends (such as a blanket opposition to any affirmative action-derived programme on the grounds that they constitute 'reverse racism'). Conservative social movements may also have 'racial projects', and can use the language of previous progressive campaigns for their own ends. The widely held view that affirmative action (fought for during the 1960s to compensate for generations of discrimination) constitutes 'reverse discrimination' against white Americans, and the attempts to eliminate quotas through state legislation and the courts since the 1970s, are examples of this process (Harris, 1993).

While Omi and Winant raise interesting questions about contemporary America (1994 [1986]), David Goldberg (2000) is concerned to trace a historic trajectory of the State in the West, and how it has addressed 'race' as a normal part of its existence, rather than as a marginal and specific activity. From a complex, dense piece of work, there are a number of useful points, three of which I summarise here.

Racial States

Goldberg's starting point is that the everyday ways in which Western states function sustain the idea of 'race', even in the official ideology of racelessness. So the 'racial state' is the norm. However, most political and academic focus under the heading 'racism' has been on states where 'race' has been made into an explicit rather than implicit tool of governance. So, 'racial' states can become 'racist' states, as did Nazi Germany, Apartheid South Africa and the Jim Crow states of the USA.

Second, he conceptualises a distinction in the racialised attribution of difference from the Enlightenment era onwards, between 'naturalist' and 'historicist' racism. In the 'naturalist' view, racialised groups are naturally and unbridgeably different from one another, and structured into a hierarchy of civilised and not-so-civilised states. Those at the bottom of the pile can never attain the sophistication of those at the top. 'Historicist' racism, on the other hand, uses the same hierarchical template, but understands 'race' as a relative developmental time lag: the less civilised may catch up, given time. He argues that while each approach was dominant at different moments, they are both still used to explain the state of the world.

Third, the difference between civilised and less civilised, which has been an intrinsic part of the way in which people in imperial countries are socialised to see themselves, is now a condition for the contemporary scenario. For the modern Western state, the aspiration is for a 'raceless' society in which the past divisions no longer have an impact (cf. classlessness). To attain this aspiration, states have education, public information and special equality legislation aimed at squeezing out the residual racism in each nation state. In this model, argues Goldberg (2000), the State places itself outside the field of racism, unconnected to it except in its interventions aimed at ridding society of this 'disease'. The only way that states and people can arrive at such conclusions, suggests Goldberg, is from uncritical acceptance of the dominant paradigms of 'white' thought. These paradigms, or what Joe Feagin (2006) calls 'white frames', filter out and neutralise evidence that the State actually plays important roles in structuring the terrain on which nationality, citizenship and immigration statuses are defined, how Censuses are designed, etc. These roles have developed over centuries of European and North American domination of military, financial and technological arenas, and are based on the Enlightenment project of creating 'universal man'. In the context of that project (Eze, 1997), only whiteness can be racially neutral, and therefore 'universal': everyone else is 'ethnic', and the only residual racism is caused by aberrant individuals.

Western states now aim to be 'raceless', that is, where 'race' plays no role in the allocation of social positions, which, ideally, are all down to the capacities of the individual. This ideology of the raceless society, pursued to different degrees in different places, denotes the triumph of Western liberal thought, and there is little recognition of the contradiction between official State objectives in this regard and the racialising work carried out by the State in the fields of immigration, citizenship and now, increasingly, security. However racism is defined by Western states, it excludes consideration of citizenship laws that include genealogical criteria; immigration regimes that place obstacles in front of developing-world nationals but which are not placed in front of other people and/or apply different laws to people who have asylum-seeker or migrant statuses; and security regimes that use racial profiling.

Goldberg's work (2000) makes it impossible to claim that the State is a neutral arbiter in the field of racial politics. He presents us with a timeline, a qualified and historicised commentary, and how this helps us make sense of the contemporary world.

The Gendered Nation and 'Biopolitics'

Theses such as those of Goldberg (2000) and Omi and Winant (1994 [1986]) break new territory in terms of attaching a major role to the State in racialising its populations across time and place. However, there are other dimensions of this process neglected in their work, such as the importance of gender. Nira Yuval-Davis (1997: 26–38) makes an important contribution to plugging that gap. She focuses on 'the intersections between women's reproductive roles and the constructions of nations' (1997: 26). The international market for, and technology surrounding, egg donation has developed at a furious pace since Yuval-Davis's book. The ramifications of this for membership of national collectivities have become ever more complex (Nahman, 2008; Twine, 2011). Here, I will simply draw out the distinctions she makes between varying forms of natalist policies that states impose on women, who comprise the 'natural', physical borders of the nation.

First, she notes that some states have tried to encourage higher birth rates at different moments in order to strengthen the nation. Examples of this are Israel, France (Camiscioli, 2001) and Australia. Often the political rivalry over territory is engaged in through exhortations to maintain or increase a birth rate, as in Lebanon, Bulgaria and the former Yugoslavia. These exhortations can also be aimed at increasing one racialised group in the face of perceived growth in another, as identified by Angela Davis in early twentieth-century USA (2001b). President Theodore Roosevelt, whose 1906 State of the Union speech she quotes, blamed white middle-class women exercising reproductive choices for endangering the USA by practising 'race suicide':

> ... wilful sterility is, from the standpoint of the nation, from the standpoint of the human race, the one sin for which the penalty is national death, race death; a sin for which there is no atonement. (Roosevelt, 1906)

Second, Yuval-Davis identifies the 'eugenicist discourse', which is aimed at improving the quality rather than quantity of the population (see Chapter 7). In positive eugenics, groups seen as more valuable in terms of genes (typically the wealthy, able-bodied, better-educated) are encouraged to have more children. In 'negative eugenics', the focus is on preventing groups considered less valuable (typically, poorer, maybe with disabilities, ethnic minorities) from having children. The State's role in this is to construct a legal framework in which particular actions are given legitimised rationales and carried out through the courts, from compulsory sterilisations at one end of the spectrum, to cash incentives at the other. The association in eugenics practice is for culture, values and genes to be naturalised as a connected trinity.

The third point, which overlaps with negative eugenics, is the idea of population excess. This fear of overstretching existing resources provokes a set of policy responses based on the objective of reducing or at least stabilising population through birth control. The fear of a mismatch of resources and population is drawn from the ideas of English clergyman and economist Thomas Malthus (1798), who argued at the end of the eighteenth century that population increased at a much faster rate than food supplies. Only natural disasters and wars, he maintained, would control population growth. Yuval-Davis (1997) points to China and India as key Malthusian states in this respect, and highlights the fact that Western governments, as well as multinational companies, have long provided the wherewithal for population-control policies. In more contemporary versions, well-funded key nativist scholar-activists relentlessly disseminate the idea that Mexicans, for example, are culturally inclined to over-breed and therefore absorb more resources than European Americans (Ioanide, 2015: 295–300).

The other salient point to note is that women have become key 'combatants' in civil wars because of their role as reproducers of the nation. In both the former Yugoslavia and Rwanda, women were targeted for mass rape (sometimes with the transmission of AIDS as an objective). The rationale for this is to destroy the nation's border, populate the nation with non-nationals, bring shame on the women, and by extension shame on 'their' men for not defending them properly. This functions within a masculine world view where women are the cultural property of men and of the nation. To acknowledge this tactic and the context in which it was being used, the International Criminal Court made rape a 'crime constituent of genocide' in 1997.

As noted in Box 5.2, Foucault's lectures at the Collège de France in 1976 contained a series around the development of the State's power to control its population. The striking change brought about, argues Foucault, is that by the nineteenth century, the State had accrued the power and right to make some live and let some die. Who falls into which category and why is really the subject of this chapter, and indeed of all the work on 'race' and the State. An important element of Foucault's (2003) way of discussing the topic of the State is that he has developed a set of concepts to refer to the process he identifies, most importantly 'bio-power' (see Box 5.2). Moreover, his use of the word 'race' is primarily drawn from the European context, holding within it the older connotations of 'stock' and 'people', and he explicitly notes that he is not using racism to refer to the kind of social relationships between the European powers and colonial people. This is an important qualification to make, but one that enables us to focus on a significant part of the equation that we will see anchoring the concept of 'new racism' (Chapter 9): the way biological difference is made cultural and vice versa. Indeed, Foucault sees 'race' as one of a number of 'technologies' (or mechanisms) enabling the State to control populations and their behaviour:

> It [race] is primarily a way of introducing a break into the domain of life that is under power's control: the break between what must live and what must die. The appearance within the biological continuum of the human race of races, the distinction among races, the hierarchy of races, the fact that certain races are described as good and that others, in contrast, are described as inferior: all this is a way of fragmenting the field of the biological that power controls. (Foucault, 2003: 255)

So the biological and cultural distinctions between human beings are used in Foucault's theory as ways of first establishing, then justifying, control over the population of a nation state. At one end of the spectrum of State powers lies the protection of the good (defined racially, that is, biologically and culturally), yet this contains its opposite, the genocidal dream of eliminating the bad, whether through the very rare opportunity to actually kill the membership of an outgroup, or more likely, to prevent them from reproducing, or at the least, stopping them living as a distinct cultural group. 'In the bio-power system', he contends:

... in other words, killing or the imperative to kill is acceptable only if it results not in a victory of political adversaries, but in the elimination of the biological threat to and the improvement of the species or the race. There is a direct connection between the two. In a normalizing society, race or racism is the precondition that makes killing acceptable. (2003: 256)

He could quite easily be talking about social class as 'race' in the European nineteenth-century context, but Foucault has carefully selected 'race' because of its capacity to melt the biological into the social and the cultural, and throw up hierarchies that are both partly embedded in and partly independent of class.

So much for the theories. How do these processes actually work? Ideas about power, 'race' and nation manifest themselves in popular culture as much as in official state policies, so in looking at practical examples we will begin with beauty contests, before going on to: the classification of populations, legislation on equality and citizenship policies.

Beauty Queens: Representing the Nation?

When I was growing up in Britain in the 1970s, televised beauty contests were unremarkable elements of the entertainment industry. However, by the 1990s it was rare to see them – at least on terrestrial television – although there are live events covered by cable channels. They have been relentlessly criticised for rendering women as passive sexualised objects who have to fit a particular set of narrow and imposed criteria to be considered 'beautiful'. If you dismiss beauty pageants as demeaning to women, you may have a political point. However, if you are a sociologist, you are also missing an opportunity to engage with a serious connection between 'race' and nation if you do not take the discourses around such competitions seriously. Moreover, while attitudes toward beauty contests have altered in Europe and North America, they are not necessarily the dominant ones globally. Many countries and minority groups within countries take such contests seriously, and are much less dismissive of them, as we will see here.

Beauty queens are chosen to be racialised and idealised representations of the nation, and the competitions are about gender, purity, sex, discipline, and struggles over the meaning of tradition. Beauty is both gendered and raced (and some would argue, classed). Conflict has arisen over who is authentic enough to represent that nation; or a diasporic group within a nation. Moreover, there are beauty contests specifically for transgender people and for other marginalised groups. Each story has its own context: and the stakes for the competitors are not the same. Some are claims for representational power and recognition of alternative forms of beauty. A few examples of contests can suggest the richness of the area for studies of nation. Here they are drawn from Ecuador, Jamaica, Trinidad and the USA.

In 1995, Monica Chala was crowned as the first black Miss Ecuador. In a country where the dominant ideology is of a mixed nation *mestizaje*, and the components of this mixture are indigenous people and Europeans, Rahier (1998) suggests that black people are not part of the national story. They live principally in two geographical areas and are identified as being backward and associated with crime, and a litany of other characteristics that one finds in racist ideas for centuries are attached to them. Rahier's argument is that Chala is atypical of Black Ecuadoreans and that this explains her success. She grew up in the capital, Quito; her sister is a well-known athlete; she is connected to media and modelling circles; and did not turn her victory into a platform for addressing racialised inequalities experienced by Black Ecuadoreans. In this story then, the dominant set of ideas about blackness in Ecuador is not really challenged despite Chala's victory.

Box 5.3   Miss Jamaica

The dynamics of the beauty pageant were similar in Jamaica, where a succession of white and light-skinned black women won Miss Jamaica for decades. This pattern reflected the domination of the white/light business and political elite (Barnes, 1994), who sponsored and organised Miss Jamaica contests after independence in the 1940s. The stakes of the beauty contest are described by Barnes:

> The real test of the anti-colonial struggle was thought to be measured not only in concrete material gains, but in the success that the centuries-old stigma attached to black skin could be eradicated. And it is in this regard that the beauty contest, more so than any other arena of cultural production, was seen as the ideal place where the readiness to accept these values could be tested. (1994: 474)

However this was an ongoing issue: Lisa Mahfood, the 1986 champion, had bottles and fruit thrown at her on stage after winning the title because she was identified as unrepresentative of a black nation. Barnes points out that one response to this monopoly had been the pluralist initiative of holding 10 beauty contests simultaneously, each reflecting a different 'racial' component of the island's population. This multi-contest was sponsored by the main daily newspaper's evening edition. In 1955, the *Star*, the evening news tabloid of the *Gleaner* announced its sponsorship of the 'Ten types; One People' contest. The 10 types were:

> 'Miss Ebony' for black-complected women, 'Miss Mahogany' for women of 'cocoa-brown complexion,' 'Miss Satinwood' for 'girls of coffee and milk complexion,' 'Miss Golden Apple' for 'peaches and cream' Jamaican women, 'Miss Apple Blossom,' for 'a Jamaican girl of white European parentage,' 'Miss Pomegranate,' for 'white Mediterranean

girls,' 'Miss Sandalwood,' for women of 'pure Indian parentage,' 'Miss Lotus' who was to be 'pure Chinese,' 'Miss Jasmine,' for a Jamaican of 'part-Chinese parentage,' 'Miss Allspice' for 'part-Indian' women. (Barnes, 1994: 476)

Yet the pattern of lighter-skinned champions is still present. There are relatively few contemporary dark-skinned Miss Jamaicas, even in the twenty-first century, which suggests that the dominance of the lighter-skinned elites is still in place.

If you are part of a diasporic group, however, your appearance and culture are the objects of a different kind of scrutiny, one that seeks to find the most 'authentic' and 'traditional' woman. Japanese American beauty contests (King-O'Riain, 2006) demonstrate the emphasis placed on purity. Miss Japanese America had to be much more Japanese than she was American, and the entry and success of mixed race women caused anxiety among the more traditionally minded community members, who wanted a 100 per cent Japanese. Mixed contestants were careful to demonstrate robust cultural competences (language, behaviour, clothing, interests, etc.) in order to fit into the required mould.

A similar set of expectations falls on Indian women entering contests in Trinidad and Tobago. They are required to perform traditional Indian-ness, where that means distinction from African-ness and creolisation (viewed as leading to more independent, assertive, sexualised womanhood). Ragbir (2012) suggests that such beauty contests are the cultural opposite of 'chutney' music (Indian-based soca), whose practitioners are 'raunchy' and creolised. The modernity of Indian women (against whom these contests were judged) has now in some ways exceeded that of the diaspora – in terms of dress and the sexuality of women – so that there is some fluidity about which role Indo-Trinidadian women are to perform. The competition's ban on swimsuit sections (that's only for Miss Trinidad) means that revelation of small amounts of flesh, and the movements of the body now perform more work in the Trinidad Indian beauty contests. Ragbir's ethnography shows how the tension between versions of national authenticity expresses itself around women's bodies, in a way that it does not around men's.

Lastly, it should be noted that diaspora identities are, as in the case of Trinidad's Indians, often much more traditional than the more fluid ones found in the 'mother country'. The 1999 Miss Ireland, Emir-Maria Holohan Doyle, whose mother is from the Middle East, reported being booed in New York and Chicago when she was on her tour of the Irish diaspora in 2000. However, the Rose of Tralee competition saw its first mixed winner in 2011 when the Filipina-Irish-Australian Tara Talbot won. The annually televised contest is designed to emphasise the qualities of Irish womanhood in the Irish diaspora, in a very traditional way, yet within that quite narrow set of parameters, the recognition that the Irish diaspora is now a much more diverse space, is something worth noting.

Orders: Classification, Census

How do states 'make race' formally? How do they introduce 'a break into the domain of life that is under power's control', to use Foucault's terminology? Census categories are not a neutral reflection of a country's population. They are simultaneously a political response to social pressures, and a means of exerting one strand of Foucault's bio-power. If such categories were merely a reflection of the natural world, we would expect them to be universal, their boundaries to be uncontroversial, and their substantive content and naming easy to rationalise.

Instead, categories differ from one country to the next, so that a person categorised in one way in one country falls into a different category in another (e.g. a UK national whose parents were Nigerian might tick the box saying 'Black African' in the British Census, but in Nigeria, they would more likely select a religious grouping and/or cultural or ethnic affiliation). Second, where the line between different groups falls is also open to debate, the most obvious example being people whose parentage lies in more than one of these categories. The idea of somebody not fitting clearly into a category usually disturbs the hierarchical construction of racial groups in a given society (Chapter 8). Responses can range from attentive detail to neglect. In the colonial Americas we find absurdly detailed language to cover every possible combination of European, Amerindian and African origins. In the contemporary USA, there has been a political campaign to have the category 'bi-racial' included on the Census (Chapter 8). In the 1981 UK Census, there was originally a catch-all box labelled 'Other', which in 2001 became 'Mixed' with no specification, and by 2011, people could choose from a small number of combinations of mixedness (Tables 8.3–8.5).

In Apartheid South Africa (1948–94), people in this category might have ended up in any of the major official categories used: 'Black', 'White', 'Coloured' or 'Indian'. The consequences of being in one rather than another seriously impacted on people's life chances, their treatment by authorities, their access to healthcare, employment and education, and their freedom to move around.

The latest US Census invites people identifying culturally as 'Hispanic' to also identify 'racially'. The 'ethnic' group Hispanic (which itself appears only at the 1981 Census) is thus comprised of people whose origins lay anywhere between Tierra del Fuego, Puerto Rico and the Mexican border, and is overlaid by the racial categories of 'African', 'Caucasian', 'Asian', 'White' and 'Bi-racial' among others. The question of what it actually means to identify oneself with any of these categories cannot be captured here, but the point remains that the State uses categories that have varying degrees of relevance to how the people it enumerates live their lives, and the social processes in which they are agents.

Finally, the categories themselves are not arbitrary, but rather attempts to enclose something that might not be enclosable. The substantive groups may not be meaningful in themselves, or may not make sense in the context of the other categories. Take 'Indian' in the UK Census, which is put forward as an ethnic group to choose as an option. In India, there are around 80 linguistic groups, all the major world religions plus a number of smaller ones. Even this small amount of information seems to make the idea that 'Indian' is a relatively homogeneous ethnic group somewhat implausible. It is more of a nationality than an ethnic group. When in the same Census (1981) another option is 'White', it can be argued that 'Indian' and 'White' are not of an equivalent order. One is a nationality, the other a racialised group. Moreover, the headline category 'Asian' does not include 'Chinese', which geographically belongs to Asia. There is, clearly, even at this fundamental level, something illogical about the breakdown of the British Census that should alert us – in looking at other Censuses – that they are social interpretations of given societies rather than incontestable versions of social reality reflecting nature.

When we step back and look at the Census categories, we ought to ask, what assumptions are such categories based upon? The assumptions are that such ethno-racial distinctions are socially meaningful, and that the data collected aid in a State-led process of amelioration of particular problems associated with the social divisions that are put forward as real. In other words, if there was no associated or potential social division attached to the categories, why collect demographic data in this way? The Census is an ongoing outcome of a historical process that has national distinctiveness, reflecting struggles over experiences of racialisation.

The State, through its Census, introduces ways of thinking about the social world that are made meaningful in official policy-making circles and upon which services, employment and the legal system are based. Most of it is ostensibly driven by social policy on equality. However, there are also political stakes in being made into an ethnic category if you live in a nation state where some form of multicultural governance is operated, as political-community power-related projects can be embarked on with legitimacy. The case of the Irish in the UK in the 1980s (O'Keeffe, 2007), and Travellers in the Republic of Ireland and Northern Ireland at the turn of the twenty-first century, illustrate the way in which access to resources via the State are considered motivation for a targeted campaign in which the ethnic group is put forward as authentic and deserving of recognition.

Social Policies on Equality

Nation states provide minimum resources through welfare and social security programmes, services and employment (through the provision of such services). They also intervene in a variety of ways, one of which is that of formal pro-equality work, a relatively recent area. As we will see in Chapter 6, the introduction of legislation aimed at providing equal access to employment, services and other resources dates back only to the 1960s in the USA and the mid-1970s in some European countries.

In order to enact and implement such policies, there has to be, first, a consensus that there is structural discrimination (or institutional racism) to overcome, and a division of the population into ethno-racialised groups through the Census. This is because the data from the Census are used to establish the parameters for policy. If the object is to make the workforce approximately reflect the national population, for example, then the targets for the employment of minorities would be set at around the national levels or possibly at local levels. All the collection of data by human resources departments or external monitoring organisations in the UK is based on the Census categories. Moreover, with statutory bodies being obliged to collect data on their workforces and clients in order to establish that they are carrying out such a duty, the importance of ethno-racial categories starts to overtake the social realities they are supposed to cover. As the focus is on the quantitative and statistical production of records, the other questions lose importance: this production becomes to a certain degree 'fetishised' (pursued as if the categories were real and distinct entities rather than outcomes of other processes). This is not to say that formal anti-discrimination legislation and practice do not achieve some of their goals, but that there are also unintended consequences. From our viewpoint as critical sociologists, we also have to be aware of, and be interested in them.

One significant outcome is the way that equalities legislation has divided the field of the social into particular sub-fields of inequality. Currently, the EU directive of November 2000 (European Union, 2000) has encouraged this pattern, and there are between seven and nine grounds currently used by national semi-state agencies responsible for enforcing equality legislation. None of them, anywhere, explicitly includes social class. This is significant for two reasons: first, it demonstrates that one of the most obvious sources of inequality (and possibly the most ubiquitous) is not considered feasible ground for remedial action. Second, for us, interested in 'race', it reveals the liberal democratic framework of the Western democracies that we are primarily studying here in this book. The orthodox thinking is that ameliorative measures carried out by redistributing resources through taxation, social security welfare, education systems, etc. are all valid actions for government, but the redress of collective inequalities by individual cases does not fit the model. In the majority of cases, equalities legislation is about individuals proving cases of discrimination.

Box 5.4   Japanese Nationalism

Bruce Armstrong (1989) argues that over the period from the Meiji Restoration (1868) to the 1940s, Japanese nationalist ideology became racialised in different ways. The new unitary state needed a unifying language, a project, which developed around a combination of Shinto myths and the idea of the Japanese people as a family headed by the Emperor. Japanese culture was viewed as uniquely the property of those born into this family, and contrasted with other Asian people colonised in the Japanese Empire (e.g. Taiwanese and Koreans) who were not phenotypically distinguishable from the Japanese. In the late 1800s and early 1900s, prominent intellectuals explained ideas of Japanese cultural and technological specificity by biological traits, as the ideas of Social Darwinism developed from the European imperial enterprise were adapted to explain Japan's military domination. The reasons given for Japan's superiority were both genetic and cultural, and indeed Japan's destiny was to lead and control. This was so ingrained by the 1940s that even though direct references to 'inferior races' in the Empire were dropped, in favour of 'Japan overseas', the underlying racialised distinction remained important. Moreover, the large number of Koreans resident in Japan (due to the forced labour migration that followed Japan's annexation of Korea in 1909) remained distinct from the Japanese nation. Japanese citizenship is based primarily on *ius sanguinis*, although naturalisation was possible, conditional upon taking Japanese names (which most Koreans found unacceptable).

Armstrong's example of Japan shows interaction with global discourses of colonialism (the master race dominating others and Social Darwinism); the proximity of biological and cultural forms of racialisation; and the prominence of the idea of bloodlines in forging ties as part of the nation-building process.

Conclusions

- The nation, nationalism and the nation state are topics that have fascinated scholars from a wide range of disciplines for a long time. However, only since the mid-twentieth century has attention been paid to the idea that there might be a link between expressions of nationalism and racism, or between the construction of national and racial identities. Moreover, this has been a relatively late and minority interest among sociologists.

- The main contention in this corpus is that the State influences racial identities through setting the rules of engagement, legislation on membership of the nation and access to various resources that can be either explicitly or implicitly constructed along racialised lines. This is backed by the authority and legitimacy derived from the exercise of power within a democratic electoral system.

- Race and nation is a gendered and cultural relationship – women are constructed as performing different roles to men in the reproduction and defence of the nation. They are effectively the border between one nation and the next. Moreover, as representatives of the nation they embody particular values, ideas and specifics that men and women cherish as part of their shared heritage. One way in which tensions over belonging are expressed is in beauty contests, where membership of communities, both national and diasporic are affirmed and sometimes contested.

- The State is a key actor in making 'race'. Although most states now promote themselves as anti-racist, they effectively racialise their populations through various types of social policy, such as equality, welfare (Chapter 2) and immigration (Chapter 10), inter alia.

Points for Reflection

What degree of overlap might there be between nationalist and racist ideas?

To what extent does the State contribute to creating 'race'?

Think about the nation(s) of which you are a member: is it possible for the nation to be represented (in textbooks, on television, national holidays, etc.) without 'race' as a constituent factor?

Further Reading

Anderson, W. (2003) *The Cultivation of Whiteness: Science, Health and Racial Destiny in Australia*. New York: Basic Books.

This book examines some of the policies – based on science and ideas of racial destiny for the Australian nation in the twentieth century – that framed Australia's settlement by Anglophone Europeans.

Rivers-Moore, M. (2013) 'Affective Sex: Beauty, Race and Nation in the Sex Industry', *Feminist Theory* 14(2): 153–69.

Article based on ethnographic fieldwork demonstrating ways in which people construct ideas of the nation and sexuality through 'race' and gender.

Zakharov, N. (2015) *Race and Racism in Russia*. London: Palgrave.

Applies the concept of racialisation to post-Soviet Russia, and extends to cover nationalism, taking into consideration its distinct meanings within the Russian context.

6

Institutional Racism

In this chapter we will

- Define 'institutional' racism
- Provide working examples of institutional racism
- Develop the idea of 'structural racism' as an approach to understanding racisms

In earlier chapters, I outlined the development of the idea of 'race', provided working definitions of racism, and explained the process of racialisation. We now turn to the concept of 'institutional racism', a term that has come to occupy an increasingly significant space in public discourse in the English-speaking world since it was coined by American authors Stokely Carmichael (Kwame Touré) and Charles Hamilton in their 1967 work, *Black Power* (see Chapter 1). We shall look at definitions, and note the two broad strands of the core idea (which is a separation of *individual* from *collective* forms of racial discrimination) that have developed in two different directions.

Definitions

The definition put forward by Carmichael and Hamilton (1967: 6) deals with the parallel processes of individual and collective forms of action, the latter being exemplified as follows:

> ... when in ... Birmingham, Alabama – 500 black babies die each year because of the lack of proper food, clothing, shelter and proper medical facilities, and thousands more are destroyed or maimed physically, emotionally and intellectually because of conditions of poverty and discrimination in the black community, that is a function of institutional racism.

Compare this with the MacPherson definition (1999: para. 6.34), which was used by the British government as the basis of the 2000 Amendment to the Race Relations Act:

> The collective failure of an organisation to provide an appropriate and professional service to people because of their colour, culture or ethnic origin. It can be seen and detected in processes, attitudes, and behaviour which amount to discrimination through unwitting prejudice, ignorance, thoughtlessness, and racist stereotyping which disadvantage minority ethnic people.

The key elements are a failure to act properly and unintentional actions. We will come back to these below when we look critically at how this definition is put into practice.

What Does 'Institutional Racism' Mean?

Carmichael and Hamilton repeatedly associate social structures with systemic forms of discrimination and disadvantage. For example, they make very close links between the economic structure of the USA and the patterns of racialised discrimination they describe. Their concept is an analytical tool that contributes to understanding the collective practices of a society, and the thrust of their argument constitutes part of what I refer to here as 'structural' racism (see below pp. 115–16).

What we now call 'institutional racism' in Europe is not *necessarily* this at all, but rather a *legal concept* that has developed since the mid-1970s. To make sense of this confusion, we need to understand one crucial point.

The original distinction (Carmichael and Hamilton, 1967) was made between 'individual' and 'institutional' forms of racism in the American context. This meaning of institutional racism was dominant until the mid-1970s, when some European countries started to introduce legislation to combat racially discriminatory practices in the provision of services and access to resources, such as employment and housing. One example is the UK's Race Relations Act (1976), which built upon previous legislation (Race Relations Acts 1965 and 1968) that had made it illegal for individuals or organisations to discriminate on the grounds of 'race'. The Netherlands ratified the International Covenant on the Elimination of All Forms of Racial Discrimination (ICERD; United Nations, 1965) in 1971, and it was officially transposed into Dutch law in 1976. Moreover, the 1983 Dutch Constitution made discrimination illegal and formulated a general objective of equality. Since this period, the use of 'institutional racism' in the European context has tended toward a legal instrument rather than a social scientific analytical tool. We have to understand where it went after this fork in the road. To do so, it is vital to grasp the difference between 'structure' and 'agency' in sociological terms (Box 6.1).

Box 6.1   Structure and Agency

Social structure may be seen to underlie important social systems including the economic system, the legal system, the cultural system and others. Examples of what are considered structures in sociology are: family, religion, law, economy and class. These are long-term observable patterns that are beyond the reach of an individual to alter. The structure allows us to understand the parameters within which we, as social actors, operate. In contrast, the idea of **agency** is the degree of freedom to act that each of the social actors enjoys.

Throughout the history of sociology as an academic discipline, there has been disagreement about the relative explanatory power of each. Some schools and methods lay the emphasis more on agency, some more on structure. Interpretivism would tend toward the former position and Marxism toward the latter, but this is merely a guide. There have also been attempts to formulate a theory in which these two understandings interact more explicitly, such as Anthony Giddens' 'structuration' (Giddens, 1984). For him, it is the fact of the individual social actors repeating the practices that actually creates the structures.

In terms of the sociology of racism, the utility of the idea of structures is that it enables us to move away from the older psychology-dominated paradigm of racism, which conceptualised it as the aberrant behaviour of individuals, that is, where agency was dominant over structure. Using the structural lens, we can identify patterns of action at social and national (as well as international) levels, which do not appear if we focus exclusively on some people's behaviour patterns. In short, the structural approach sees racism as a problem of society, manifest in the way things function *normally*; the agentic approach sees it as innate to particular types of abnormal individuals. Clearly, the type of solution proposed in each case differs.

Legal Terms and Practice

The UK and Dutch governments were among the earliest to deploy specific legal forms as a response to the changing demographics of their populations in the late 1960s and early 1970s. A generation of people born to post-war migrant parents from the former colonies of the Western European countries began to contest the informal segregation and discrimination that their parents' generation had faced (Sivanandan, 1990). Liberal politicians and civil society organisations supported the legal moves to ban discrimination, on principle, by the use of legislation. Since that point, the story of institutional racism has been the slow adoption of a principle and, with it, a set of organisations and agencies to monitor and implement equality plans at national and European Union level. The idea of racial equality has become a mainstream one within the EU now, and member states have had to implement the ICERD by transposing it into national law. There are three things to note about this:

1. The definition that derives from institutional racism in this context is necessarily simple – it has to be operational in a court of law.

2. In doing this, the concept of 'race' has to be uncritically accepted. If not, how could you prosecute an organisation for institutional racism without proof that someone was being discriminated against on the basis of 'race'?

3. There is an intersection between racial equality and some other grounds for discrimination, which are organisationally brought together due to legislation.

Box 6.2   Casework for The Equality Authority, Republic of Ireland, 2006

To illustrate the three points above, we will look at the example of the Irish **Equality Authority**,[1] the semi-state agency set up in 2000 (and which ran until 2009) to monitor the effectiveness of new legislation on discrimination in the provision of services and the access to employment. The Republic of Ireland was one of the last EU member states to ratify the ICERD. The model the Irish adopted was to organisationally combine the nine grounds for discrimination enshrined in legislation within one body – the Equality Authority.[2]

1 Definitions, Reports, Publications

The definitions of discrimination and 'indirect discrimination' used by the Equality Authority (2006) demonstrate its focus on the specific areas for which it was established: employment and the provision of services. The following definitions must be capable of being proven or disproved in a tribunal setting:

> *Discrimination* is defined as the treatment of a person in a less favourable way than another person is, has been or would be treated in a comparable situation on any of the nine grounds which exists, existed, may exist in the future, or is imputed to the person concerned. The instruction to discriminate is also prohibited.

> *Indirect discrimination* happens where there is less favourable treatment in effect or by impact. It happens where people are, for example, refused employment or training not explicitly on account of a discriminatory reason but because of a provision, practice or requirement which they find hard to satisfy. If the provision, practice or requirement puts people who belong to one of the grounds covered by the Acts at a particular disadvantage then the employer will have indirectly discriminated, unless the provision is objectively justified by a legitimate aim and the means of achieving that aim are appropriate and necessary.

2 The 'Race' Grounds

'Race' was the most frequently used grounds for Employment-related case-work: for example, the 2006 casework included 103 out of 404 cases on these grounds (26 per cent, of which 40 per cent are to do with working conditions), while in Equal Status (provision of and access to services), the proportion is lower (41 of 366, that is, 11 per cent in 2006). In Ireland, the 'race' grounds are not used for Travellers (an indigenous nomadic minority group). They were recognised as an ethnic group by the Equality Authority (2000–09) but not by the Irish government. This Equal Status legislation has instead been used primarily by migrant workers (including white Eastern Europeans). In the example year, 2006, Travellers accounted for only 2 out of 404 (0.55 per cent) of Employment cases, but 88 out of 366 (24 per cent) for Equal Status. Also, more than half the cases dealt with under the Intoxicating Liquor Act 2003 (which addresses treatment in hotels, restaurants, pubs and nightclubs) are to do with Travellers' claims of discrimination.

Officially, then, there is a discrepancy here. An indigenous cultural minority, the Travellers, do not apply for justice through 'race' grounds, yet white European groups such as Poles and Lithuanians do. It is argued elsewhere (Chapter 3) that Gypsy-Travellers are racialised.

Critical Responses to the Legal Form of Institutional Racism

Confusions

Another point to note is the *combined effect* of differing forms of discrimination, which was identified by the Equality Authority (Zappone, 2003). A small proportion of claims are based on multiple forms of discrimination, even if they are not always deemed to have been proven. In 2006, in the case of *Czerski v. Ice Group*, a Polish woman claimed that she had been overlooked for a factory job (Equality Authority, 2006: 34). She had been employed in a similar position with a different company since 2000. When she asked why she had not been interviewed, she was told there was heavy lifting involved and the firm were looking for male employees. Moreover, she had only been able to find one employment-related referee (as opposed to the two requested) due to the relatively short period for which she had been working in Ireland. The Equality Authority found that there was insufficient evidence to support the claim on the basis of gender, but there was enough to support indirect discrimination by 'race': it was easier for an Irish national than a non-Irish national to find the required number of employment-related referees, and that no argument had been put forward by the employer that the demand for two referees was more justifiable than one.

Looking at the work of the Irish Equality Authority, even as briefly as we have done here, raises some of the issues arising when the concept of 'institutional racism' is applied within a legal framework. There first have to be definitions that can be proven or disproven in a tribunal (the Equality Authority is not a court of law but a tribunal whose rulings can ultimately be rejected). In this process, 'race' is necessarily used in an instrumental and essentialist way. In other words, it gets 'reified'. The term 'reify', taken from the work of Marx, means turning something that is produced by ideology (rather than a real thing) into an object itself. Reification therefore occurs when an abstract concept (e.g. one created to describe a relationship) is treated as a concrete thing. Georg Lukács (1971: 83) contends that:

> Its basis is that *a relation between people* takes on the character of a thing, and thus acquires a 'phantom objectivity', an autonomy that seems so strictly rational and all-embracing as to conceal every trace of its fundamental nature: the relation between people. (my emphasis)

In the case of 'race', this means that the social relationship (the idea that 'race' is a biological rather than a social fact that has been produced by centuries of unequal power relationships) becomes treated as a real thing with an autonomous existence, empirically provable and used as a given in a court of law.

The example of *Czerski* (see above) illustrates some of the limits and advantages of the use of institutional racism. On the one hand, the practice of asking for a certain number of employment-related referees from within the nation state discriminates indirectly against workers who are just as capable as others, but whose employment history lies outside the State. Whether this is to do with 'race', however, could be seen as questionable, as anyone who had not been working in the Republic of Ireland for very long would presumably have encountered the same issue. On the other, the discriminatory practice seems more glaring in terms of gender, with the supposition that women cannot lift heavy weights being a longstanding justification put forward for the recruitment of male staff in industry. The complexity of the story requires attention to both practices (gender and nationality) rather than simply looking at the fact that Czerski was a foreign national. The same problem could theoretically have arisen for a returning Irish emigrant. Moreover, the fact that there is no 'nationality' grounds among the nine specified by Irish law means that a certain proportion of claims that might be dealt with under such a heading end up coming under the 'race' grounds instead. Of course, there are arguments about which groups of nationalities are more likely to be migrants in Ireland and to be affected disproportionately by such practices.

Returning to the legal definition, MacPherson's 'failure to act properly' is a partial one. Surely, the range of actions that can have a discriminatory outcome is broader than a set of inactions. Alongside the inaction are a set of actions. For example, in the case of *Buenaventura and 15 Others* v. *The Southern Health Board* (Equality Authority, 2006: 46), 16 Filipinos working as care assistants had been ranked 14–29 in the list of prospective candidates for full-time positions behind 13 Irish candidates. The Health Board told the Equality Authority tribunal that the Filipinos had been ranked below the Irish nationals *as a matter of course* because they had work permits. This was ruled an incorrect interpretation of a government guideline that had urged employers to look within the EU before employing non-EU nationals. All the Filipinos were, as of the 2006 report, in full-time employment with the Health Board.

Aside from this, there is a certain amount of confusion engendered by the idea of 'unwitting action'. It is always difficult to prove or demonstrate 'intent', either philosophically or in a legal context. When, in the wake of the MacPherson Report, the British police redefined a 'racial incident' as one in which the victim interpreted it as such, the emphasis shifts to an area where it is hard to go further. How can this be proven or disproven in the majority of cases? One of the reasons that Robert Miles (1987) objects to the term 'institutional racism' is that it supposes that a racist outcome can be disentangled from other sources of discrimination such as class and gender, whereas for him (and others – see the 'intersectionality' interpretation in Chapter 4), these forms of discrimination are bundled together.

Moreover, as Floya Anthias (1999) argues, there is a difference between organisational processes whose result is the exclusion of particular groups, and policies that are implemented on the basis of individual police officers' assessments of situations. She writes of the MacPherson Report that:

> ... it fails to distinguish between mechanisms that indeed unwittingly exclude and disadvantage groups through criteria which are non-ethnic but where ethnic categories may be over-represented (for example, in terms of skills, language, period of residence, lifestyles, etc.) and mechanisms that actually specifically and 'wittingly' are applied to different groups on the basis of ethnic membership or its perception (this includes 'stop and search' of more black people than white, more arrests, etc.).

Opponents of the concept of institutional racism, and there are many, often argue that it injects 'race' where it has no place, thus perpetuating racism rather than addressing it. They also suggest that tarring all the employees of an entire organisation with the same brush, as 'institutionally racist', is unfair and counter-productive. The line of argument used by the then British leader of the Opposition, William Hague, in a speech about institutional racism delivered in December 2000 (which caused a minor controversy) was that the institutional sensitivity of having to tread carefully around minorities, and of the requirement for employees to undergo training in racism awareness and such like, confers 'victim status' on minorities, and actually ends up preventing the police from doing their job. A set of essays arguing along these lines can be found in Green (2000). Its basic thesis states that focusing on 'race' detracts from the ideal outcome, which is justice for all. Ignatieff's essay, for example, critiques the Report's recommendation that the victim should define the incident's nature:

> The MacPherson definition will 'racialise' every encounter between the
> police and the non-white public to the benefit of neither, while the white
> public, often badly treated by the police too, will feel that they have no
> recourse for the indignities they suffer – and will resent the perceived
> 'positive discrimination' towards non-whites. (Ignatieff, 2000: 22)

Indeed, the logics of the critiques of institutional racism as a concept are
diverse, but the colour-blind one outlined by Ignatieff is a common thread. It
supposes that we have passed through the phase of correcting the most discriminatory aspects and emerged the other side on a roughly level playing field.
Green, in the same volume (2000: 38–40), pursues this logic further to construct the concept as a system of racial preference geared to giving an advantage
to ethnic minorities. He approvingly cites economist Thomas Sowell (1990),
who theorises that the claims of indigenous and minority groups in the political
realm are not in fact for equality, but for racial preference. In this interpretation, then, institutional racism is a concept whose use actually enables a reversal
of the (begrudgingly acknowledged) discrimination prior to its introduction
into the public domain.

   In relation to the Stephen Lawrence case, it is hard to see how two parents'
quest for a properly conducted investigation of the murder of their son is a
claim for *differential* treatment. Indeed, the basis of the original claim was for
justice like anyone else, which is exactly what Ignatieff seems to be arguing for.
However, the misreadings upon which these sorts of criticisms are based are
revealing about the heart of what we are looking at: the idea of a level of social
action which it is beyond an individual's power to alter significantly. The first
thing to note is that neither the MacPherson Report nor its predecessor, the
1986 Scarman Report (which had first raised the possibility of institutional
racism if not naming it as such), state that individual employees of institutionally racist organisations are racist. The point of the way these reports
establish the concept of institutional racism involves distinguishing collective
practices of a culture that discriminates from the actions of all individual
officers. The latter can act in discriminatory ways without this affecting the
practices and culture.

   The second point is that the concept's objective is to make 'race' visible
as a factor in how an organisation and its staff operate. In Anglo-American
colour-blind public cultures in the late twentieth and early twenty-first centuries, the norm is for 'race' to be avoided. From the perspective where not
talking about 'race' solves the problem of racism, the opposite, that is, rein-
troducing 'race' as an explicit topic in public policy and discourse, actually
encourages racism. This 'race-neutral' approach argues that, for example,
police practices should be geared toward serving everyone regardless of
'race'. However, this supposes that using the term 'institutional racism' necessarily impedes this outcome, and that the type of inequalities that separate
people's experiences do not play a role in how they are policed. Simply put,
the power relations (of class, gender and 'race') in the wider society already

have a major role in how different groups are policed. The objective of using the concept of 'institutional racism' to understand power relationships is to reduce that inequality.

Yet, a major problem here with 'institutional racism' as a concept in legal terms is ambiguity about the relationship of racism to power. The focus on unintentionally discriminatory actions carried out by an organisation (covered by the 'indirect discrimination' clause in Ireland) is a necessary corollary of the way the concept has been framed. Organisations not set up to be specifically racist can, in practice, discriminate in their service provision, employment procedures, etc. However, the term 'unintentional' poses a problem. On the one hand, it gives the impression that racist outcomes are clearly identifiable effects of clearly identifiable causes that can either be intentional or unintentional. This is true up to a point because the legal framing has to make such outcomes empirically provable and/or deniable. If not, the legal concept would be unworkable in its own context. However, while broadly recognising power relations as important, this implementation ignores the power relations *outside* the particular company, government agency, pub, etc. that is being called to rights. Indeed, they are beyond the scope of the precise legal battle involved in the discussion at a tribunal. It is at this point that the distinction between 'institutional racism' *as a legal concept*, and 'structural racism' *as a sociological one* become apparent. The latter includes and emphasises what goes on outside the case in question.

Institutional Racism as 'Structural' Racism

Within sociology, there have been longstanding distinctions between various understandings of how society functions and what counts as knowledge. The different schools of thought have suggested variously that sociology is a natural science of society, with problems/truths that can be unearthed and analysed (positivism); that there is no single social truth but rather a competing set depending on the interpretation of individual social actors (interpretivism); or that no individual social actor is aware of all there is to be aware of, so that the most important role of a sociologist is to construct models of how society functions at a theoretical level (critical theory) through structures (Box 6.1).

The account presented in this chapter owes more to the latter than the former two ideas, but discounts neither the importance of the empirical (enshrined in positivism), nor the way groups make sense of their own social positions. However, the idea that social processes function at a level above the individual lies at the heart of this side of 'institutional racism', as coined by Carmichael and Hamilton (1967). Thus theorists and activists have been engaged for decades in efforts to reformulate and develop understandings of racism that move beyond the personal or even the institutional, like Feagin's (2006) systemic racism, or Bonilla-Silva's structural racism (see Box 6.3). In an address in 2015, for example, Hourida Bouteldja of the French anti-colonialist and anti-racist movement Parti des Indigènes argues that:

Structural racism cannot be understood if you don't understand the
nature of the relationship between the North and the South and the
global racialization of humanity for the needs of imperialist exploitation before anything else. In other words, you cannot understand
islamophobia if you don't understand the war in Afghanistan and Iraq,
as well as you cannot understand negrophobia if you don't understand
France's post-colonial/neo-colonial approach to Africa ('Françafrique').

So what ingredients should a study of structural racism contain? Let us examine
Bonilla-Silva's concept of 'structural racism'.

Box 6.3   Bonilla-Silva's 'Structural Racism'

Eduardo Bonilla-Silva's (1997) groundbreaking reformulation of racial theory
is aimed at breaking with the dominant models in US social sciences. The
key elements that he identifies as obstacles are:

1 Individual-focused social psychology deficit models;

2 The idea that racism is an irrational aberration; and,

3 The idea that racism necessarily refers to *past* social structures.

For Bonilla-Silva, the point is that racism is ongoing business-as-usual, and
social scientists have to use that as a departure point for looking more
broadly at the ways in which differential experiences and outcomes are generated. His six conclusions are reproduced here:

1 'Racial phenomena are regarded as the "normal" outcome of the racial
   structure of a society.'

2 'The changing nature of what analysts label "racism" is explained as the
   normal outcome of racial contestation in a racialized social system.'

3 'The framework of racialization allows analysts to explain overt as well as
   covert racial behaviour.'

4 'Racially motivated behaviour, whether or not the actors are conscious of it,
   is regarded as rational – that is, as based on the races' different interests.'

5 'The reproduction of racial phenomena in contemporary societies is
   explained in this framework, not by reference to a long-distant past, but
   in relation to its contemporary structures.'

6 'A racialization framework accounts for the ways in which racial/ethnic stereotypes emerge, are transformed and disappear.' (Bonilla-Silva, 1997: 475–6)

Bonilla-Silva's concise iteration of the arguments in favour of racialisation
tie it very firmly into structuralist accounts of society: in other words, a way
of conceptualising racism as something in the present that is not exclusively the province of aberrant individuals.

There are relatively few examples of individual states or sections of states with legal authority using division by 'race' as an explicit tool for organising the life of its people. Examples such as South Africa under Apartheid (1948–94), the Southern states of the USA (formally until the mid-1960s) and Nazi Germany (1933–45) are understood not as end points on a continuum, but as completely separate *sui generis* forms of governance. Indeed, they are in a way constitutive of racism: in these models, there are superior and inferior 'races', and life is organised around that principle. However, these examples are by no means the whole story (as we noted in earlier chapters). The idea of institutional racism may well have been shaped by the experiences of activists in segregated Southern US states, but its general applicability lies in the form of structures.

   We are now going to look at three interlocking areas of discrimination and suggest how they can be interpreted as examples of structural racism.

Loans for Housing

In the USA, as in the UK, most people own their homes (more than 60 per cent in both countries). The vast majority of home-owners need to borrow money to purchase them, usually in the form of a loan from a financial institution. In two important pieces of work, George Lipsitz (1995, 1998) analyses the racialisation of the granting of loans for housing purchase. He found that even when the sample was controlled for social class (white working-class compared to black working-class applicants), more money was made available, for longer and under more advantageous conditions to white applicants than to black ones. Other research focusing on this has demonstrated similar findings. A study of housing on Long Island, New York carried out by the Institute on Race and Poverty (IRP, 2002) concluded two things. First, that in the 1999–2000 period, the rates at which conventional home loan applications were denied rose by more than 20 per cent for both African Americans and Latinos. Second, that higher income had less impact on the likelihood of obtaining a loan for minority applicants. In 2000, for example, Latinos in Nassau-Suffolk County in Long Island who earned in excess of $91,800 were more likely to be turned down for conventional home loans than were whites earning less than $38,250. This kind of lending practice is a partial explanation of the patterns of racialised residential segregation observable in cities across the USA. Indeed, there is a clearly identifiable pattern of differential group access to home-ownership, which appears in Table 6.1, compiled from US Census Bureau data.

   While the discrepancy between the different 'racial' groups lessened over the 11-year period captured in the table, the differences are still statistically significant and point to structural discrimination.

   Such practices have a major impact in determining who gets to live where. In the USA, the most expensive housing is generally found in suburban areas, and the failure to obtain loans means that black and Hispanic Americans remain primarily in cheaper neighbourhoods where they can afford to buy. Moreover, the difficulty in obtaining loans is only one of a set of obstacles to minority integration into more affluent neighbourhoods. 'Restrictive covenants, explicit or implicit threats of violence, and generally adverse social conditions kept blacks out of white areas', argue Cutler et al. (1999: 496). When placed alongside other segregationist practices such as 'redlining', this results in the development of areas that black and other minority people cannot easily access (Gotham, 2000). They are therefore over-concentrated in other areas. The practice of 'redlining', for example, lies at the root of later versions of segregation. Lipsitz (1995) identifies the functioning of the Federal Housing Authority (FHA), set up in 1934, which lent virtually exclusively to white families in the post-war period. He points to the organisation's area reports and appraiser's manuals (drafted by the Home Owners Loan Corporation [HOLC] in the 1930s) as maps of discriminatory practice. The maps colour-coded 239 American cities into areas of greater or lesser risk for lending, not according to criteria related to people's capacity for repayment, but merely to the demographics of the areas concerned.[3] Areas in which minorities were concentrated thus frequently appeared in red on the maps, indicating the highest level of risk, and therefore, the smallest chance of obtaining loans, even for home improvements.

It should be noted that the peak in home-ownership came in 2006, before the economic crash fuelled by sub-prime lending, which disproportionately disadvantaged minorities (Beeman et al., 2011; Wyly et al., 2012). The combination of these structural patterns with the deterrent factor facing the first black families to move into an area (captured, for example, in Lorraine Hansberry's play, *A Raisin in the Sun*, 1959) means that there are tangible material and ideological factors at work, granting privilege to white Americans and impeding the mobility of African Americans and other minorities (Massey and Denton, 1994).

The Institute on Assets and Social Policy (IASP) at Brandeis University tracked household income from 1984 to 2009. The median net worth of white households in this study rose to $265,000 over the 25-year period compared with just $28,500 for the black households. In terms of income the average African American household earned 64 per cent, and Latinos 73 per cent of the average white one (Sullivan et al., 2015)[4] as of the 2010 Census. However, if you look at wealth, rather than income, the economic positions of racialised Americans are even more starkly polarised. In terms of wealth, African American households have 6 per cent of the wealth of the average white household, and Latino households have 8 per cent (Sullivan et al., 2015).

Residential Racial Segregation

To illustrate the distinction between structure and agency in relation to housing segregation, we can first reduce them to their extremes and then suggest how they function in a more complex way. The patterns of segregation in urban America could be interpreted as outcomes of the long-term historical processes referred to above: a structural understanding in which the individual has no power to brook the rule.[5] On the other hand, if housing location was

Table 6.1 Home-ownership by 'race' in the USA, 1994–2014 (in per cent)

Race	1994	1996	1998	2000	2002	2004	2006	2008	2010	2012	2014	% change since 1994
White (non-Hispanic)	70.0	71.7	72.6	73.8	74.5	76.0	76.0	74.8	74.2	73.6	72.3	+3.3%
Asian American	51.3	50.8	52.6	52.8	54.7	59.8	60.8	59.5	58.9	56.7	57.3	+11.7%
Native American	51.7	51.6	54.3	56.2	54.6	55.6	58.2	56.5	52.3	51.1	52.2	+0.97%
African American	42.3	44.1	45.6	47.2	47.3	49.1	48.2	46.8	44.9	44.5	42.1	-0.47%
Hispanic or Latino	41.2	42.8	44.7	46.3	48.2	48.1	49.5	48.6	46.8	45.0	44.5	+8%

Source: US Census Bureau, 2014.

merely a question of individual choice of an area to live in, a different pattern would emerge. One of the common-sense understandings of 'race' is that people stick together 'with their own', neatly explaining why there is residential segregation: it's all the minorities' choice. However, if social class rather than 'race' were thought of in these terms, it would appear more problematic: after all, everyone knows that different types of housing and locations command higher prices on the housing market. It is therefore a lot more difficult for those on more modest incomes to buy in an expensive area. However, while this is acknowledged, the key idea that seems more compelling for many people is the rule of individual responsibility. This means that you get what you deserve, both for hard work and for idleness. Forms of this logic appear in a lot of discussions about class and 'race' (Lamont, 2000; Bonilla-Silva, 2013).

Yet, to go back to the examples captured in the research referred to above, if you are a Hispanic in Nassau-Suffolk County, earning US$90,000 and not getting loans that are offered to white people earning US$38,000, there is obviously a breakdown in that logic. This is not to say that the latter do not work hard for their incomes, but simply, that there is not a level playing field. This outcome has not emerged from nowhere. During the periods either side of the Second World War, there were higher levels of union membership among American workers than today, and far lower proportions of women in the workforce. The majority of these labour unions operated colour bars, excluding black and Hispanic workers from protection and access to much of the better-paid work. The benefits of industry were thus transferred *disproportionately* to white male workers. Additionally, the Federal Housing Authority channelled more money and loans into predominantly white counties, which then developed white suburbs, obtained government funding for services and often sought independent status (Lipsitz, 1998). Massey and Denton (1994) note that although black people also moved to the suburbs, this process was uneven. In the 1960–77 period, 0.5 million African Americans and 4 million white Americans moved to the suburbs from inner-city areas. Of the latter, 86 per cent were living in highly segregated areas (that is, those with a maximum of 1 per cent African Americans) by 1993.

So there is no simple automatic relationship between income, ambition and social mobility. That is an aspirational element of the dominant ideological model of contemporary classless and raceless society in which anyone can achieve anything if they try hard enough. The idea of personal development and responsibility becoming the basis for identification is largely covered by the 'individualisation' thesis most famously put forward by academics such as Ulrich Beck (1992, 2000). However, if you have less chance of accessing the type of employment that leads to loans being granted, and even then, less access to the loans on top of that due to the financial organisations' lending practices, then how, practically, do you move out of the ghetto? Your failure to move is refracted through the atomised prism of late capitalism in which people are seen as exclusive agents of their own destiny. If you are not successful, runs the logic, it must be because there is something wrong with you, personally, or your cultural values. This is true even for people who tick all the boxes for the American dream. Lacy's middle-class African American home-owners (2007) tell stories of being directed away from particular areas in their home search, and of having estate agents question their capacity to buy property in some areas. Indeed, they are quite aware that convincing white Americans of their middle-class status (and acceptability as potential homebuyers) requires specific patterns of dress and behaviour.

This leads us back to the sociological problem: is residential segregation in the USA caused by class inequalities or racism? If it were a question of class alone, we might predict three things:

First, as racialised minorities climb the socio-economic ladder, and can afford more expensive housing, segregation diminishes.

Second, attitudes about which 'race' lives where do not play an important role in choice of residential area. Massey and Denton's work (1994) indicates that for African Americans, class is irrelevant to their degree of residential segregation, although it is a factor for Hispanic and Asian Americans. The segregation indices for African Americans in three income bands are very similar, and very high, particularly in the Northern cities. Yet this is not true of all minority groups. For Hispanic and Asian Americans, the degree of segregation reduces as upward social mobility increases. Racism seems therefore to be relatively more compelling in explaining patterns of African American settlement than it does in explaining those of Asian and Hispanic Americans.

Third, although it is often suggested that people choose to live with 'their own' (thus bolstering segregated patterns of settlement), the information collected from surveys on this topic shows that if people had a choice, the opposite pattern would be the outcome. African Americans express the most favourable responses to scenarios where a district is 50 per cent black. 'All black' or 'all white' neighbourhoods are the least enticing options (Massey and Denton, 1994). So while African Americans see a mixed neighbourhood as more appealing, white Americans see homogeneous white areas as the best option. In the same survey quoted by Massey and Denton (the Detroit Area Survey, 1976), half the white respondents said they would be unwilling to enter an area where 21 per cent of the residents were black, a number rising to 73 per cent for an area with a black population of 36 per cent. Maybe some do choose to live with what they consider to be 'their own' people, but it is not necessarily the minorities who self-segregate.

So, in summary, there are observable socially constructed mechanisms for restricting the housing mobility of non-white people, which develop from the practices of white decision-makers, and fellow white residents as well as their own individual choices. As a result of these mechanisms, all white people, regardless of class and gender, are ostensibly granted an a priori advantage over everyone else, even if it consists primarily in *not* encountering as many obstacles.

The other side of this process is how the inner-city areas became more impoverished in the post-oil crisis era. Lipsitz identified four trends that result indirectly from the decline of industrial zones in inner-city areas (1995, 1998):

1. The process of urban renewal involved clearing former industrial belts of cities and replacing them with commercial and more expensive residential units. Many of the people previously living in such relatively cheap areas (disproportionately minorities) were displaced.

2. The business development in these areas means that greater taxes are levied (to pay for redevelopment) on a smaller number of households, as redevelopment reduced the number of residential units.

3. There is more commercial dumping of waste in the poorer areas, which are again disproportionately home to minorities. Even when such illegal dumping is penalised, the penalties meted out are weaker than those for dumping in mainly white, especially suburban areas.

4. The type of criteria used for the organisation of space in newly developed downtown areas are business-friendly. The priority is the defence of capital and high-return housing units built for the wealthier middle classes, often in gated communities. For an in-depth argument about Los Angeles, for example, see Mike Davis (1992). He maintains that downtown space has been reorganised to suit business interests, so that the urban poor are policed away from the business core and the residential blocks. As a result, they enjoy increasingly smaller areas in which they are free from police intervention.

If we stand back from this chain of interrelated consequences, we can see that decision making on one issue (here the system of access to financial loans) has a series of ramifications. These work to prevent people from being as geographically and socially mobile as they would like. The areas that most minorities live in will be more likely to be deprived, where local taxes are higher, and there are associated social phenomena such as the increased probability of crime and under-funded and low-achieving schools. These in turn limit the choices open to people who are educated in them. In brief, there is a structural chain of impacts that ends up impoverishing the life chances of those with less likelihood of accessing funds for loans. In this ongoing scenario, those in the dominant racialised group (which for Europe and North America means white people) emerge as beneficiaries. This is true even if they neither support the idea of such a system nor benefit much from it in other areas. There is no such thing as a neutral white person in this process because it is a *social* process, which means an individual cannot remove him or herself from it, solely by wishing it away or changing behaviour *as an individual*.

Box 6.4   The Prison Industrial Complex

The Prison Industrial Complex (PIC) is Angela Davis's concept based on the model of the 'Military Industrial Complex'. She deploys it to talk about a system of mass incarceration that disproportionately impacts on young minority people, and involves the criminal justice system; expanding prison populations; increasing privatisation of prisons; the globalisation of incarceration through transnational private companies; and the racialisation of the prison population. In short, the PIC describes the increasing overlap between State and the industry that enables the State to hide social problems without resolving them, and enables industry to turn incarceration into profit. Davis argues that:

> Imprisonment has become the response of first resort to far too many of the social problems that burden people ensconced in poverty. These problems are often veiled by being conveniently grouped together under the category 'crime', and by the automatic attribution of criminal behaviour to people of colour, especially Black and Latino/a men and women. Homelessness, unemployment, drug addiction and illiteracy are only a few of the problems that disappear from public view when the human beings contending with them are relegated to cages. (Gordon, 1999: 146–7)

She points to the reservation system, the mission system, slavery and internment camps as four examples of racialised punishment systems (Davis, 1998) ensnaring Native American, Latino, African American and Japanese Americans respectively.

Feeding into the PIC is the 'school-to-prison pipeline', in which schools have increasingly engaged the police and the juvenile criminal justice system as ways to address school offences since the 1980s, through 'zero tolerance' policies and expulsions. Mallett (2016: 4–5) points out that minority school pupils are three times as likely as white peers to be expelled, while one in four African American schoolchildren are suspended per year, compared to 6 per cent of their white peers. Indeed, tens of thousands are in juvenile detention for truancy, breaching liquor laws, disobedience, fighting, etc. Although this phenomenon has primarily been explored in the American setting, work is beginning to emerge on it in the UK (Graham, 2016).

The institutional settings of the various elements of these 'systems' ultimately function (as a structure) to disproportionately imprison minority groups – as their normal practice – making them an example of both structural and institutional racism.

Travellers, Planning Rules and 'Cheating'

When it comes to Gypsy-Travellers, there is a blind spot in popular understandings of racism. They are white Europeans, runs the logic, therefore the antipathy felt by other white Europeans (and their descendants elsewhere) toward Gypsy-Travellers cannot be 'racist'. However, I argue first that Gypsy-Travellers have been racialised in a number of different ways (Garner, 2007a); and second, that this racialisation can assume an institutional form.

Gypsy-Travellers have been viewed as dirty, dangerous and lazy thieves with a relationship to nature and the world of passions and emotions that is more acute than that of people in sedentary cultures (Sibley, 1995; Holloway, 2003, 2005). Gypsy-Travellers have a distrust of sedentary society and its institutions, and there is a historical tension between the two ways of life (Okely, 1983). Nation states require people to be rooted (with fixed abodes); to share loyalty (expressed through compliance with rules and regulations and obligations such as taxation) and aspirations (to employment, home-ownership, etc.). In different places at different times, Gypsy-Travellers have lived in marginal or 'residual' spaces (Sibley, 1995) that sedentary society did not use all the time: there was not a competition for living space. However, in twenty-first century Britain, this separation is no longer always the case. Policies impact on Gypsy-Traveller mobility and settlement.

First, legal spaces for Travellers (as Travellers) to stop at are shrinking. The Office of the Deputy Prime Minister's report in 2004 (ODPM, 2004) found that 90 per cent of Gypsy-Travellers' halting sites had been shut down in the decade preceding the enquiry (1994–2003). This is since the 1968 Local Government Act's mandatory element of providing accommodation was made optional. Moreover, the Criminal Justice and Public Order Act (1994) gave the police the power to prevent people staying on land if it might lead to disorder.

The impact of these regulations is that, increasingly, Gypsy-Travellers do not have a space in which to legally perform their culture of mobility. Consequently, they have pooled resources and purchased land for development into places to live, at least temporarily. At the same time, increasing numbers (around 200,000 of the 300,000 Gypsy-Travellers living in the UK) are no longer mobile, and have settled. Some live in houses, but still adhere to other aspects of Gypsy-Traveller culture. To further make it difficult for Travellers to access accommodation, the 2015 UK government regulations (Smith, 2015) stipulate that Travellers seeking to access accommodation set aside for Gypsies and Travellers are only defined as Travellers if they are of 'a nomadic habit of life' (2015: 9), a definition that does not correspond to Gypsy-Travellers' own broader definitions involving lineage and culture. Compare this with Ireland (Fanning, 2002), where local authorities have historically used the practice of nomadic movement itself to exclude Travellers from entitlement.

The key point is that Gypsy-Travellers are often forced onto illegal sites because of the lack of provision and the difficulty of getting planning permission to build their own. The number living in illegal sites in Britain is estimated at between 20,000 and 25,000 (Eccleston, 2016).[6] Moreover, they do not compete on a level playing field with sedentary people in terms of planning permission. In 2015, there was still a noticeable discrepancy between the success rates of Travellers' and sedentary people's applications. Using figures from the official Planning Statistics Data (2010–15), the Traveller Movement argues that:

> Between 2010–2015, major Traveller site applications were on average 11.6% less likely to be granted when compared to applications for major Dwellings. For the same period minor Traveller site applications were on average 17.8% less likely to be granted permission when compared with applications for minor Dwellings. (Traveller Movement, 2015)

The ongoing issue of how Gypsy-Travellers access sites revolves around perceptions of cheating. *The Sun* newspaper's famous 'Stamp on the Camps' campaign in 2005 (Richardson and O'Neill, 2013) urged the authorities to clamp down on Gypsy-Traveller settlements with the rationale that: 'The rule of law is flouted daily by people who don't pay taxes, give nothing to society and yet expect to be treated as untouchables' (*The Sun*, 9 March 2005).

The context to this increasing focus on Travellers' settlement is that rural and semi-rural land is increasingly expensive, particularly in the South of England, while in neoliberal ideas of self-managing and responsibilised citizens, the importance of contributions is underscored: Gypsy-Travellers don't fit this mould. They are depicted as never contributing and only absorbing resources. The confrontation between settled society and Travellers around access to land is staged around a set of policies, and a set of binaries (unproductive vs productive; entitled vs unentitled people; unfairness vs fairness). The former disadvantage Travellers, while the second render them vulnerable to attacks as punishment for their perceived 'sponging'. The outcomes of planning applications seem also to disadvantage Travellers. Circumnavigating these laws and applying for retrospective planning permission is seen as breaking the law, or more emotively, 'cheating'. It generates anxiety, hostility and violence.

Once content to see Gypsy-Travellers as traditional and rural (Holloway, 2003) or at least residual dwellers (Sibley, 1995), settled society now reads them as threatening sedentary people's space, and cheating in order to occupy it. Moreover, although the discussion is framed as one over public finances (Travellers cost the taxpayer money – as if Travellers are not also taxpayers) (Richardson and O'Neill, 2013), the amount of money spent on bailiffs and law cases to evict and prosecute Travellers, plus clean-up, costs around £20 million per year in the UK, according to Friends, Families and Travellers (Eccleston, 2016): significantly more than providing enough halting sites would cost.

The issue then is not purely financial, but one of management. How can local authorities and central government discourage and minimise Gypsy-Travellers' access to space, and punish encroachment, by using the rationale of fairness? Public resources are thus spent annually – and within a national framework of policies – on the social control of one particular group.

Conclusions

We have identified institutional racism as an important development in both *conceptualising racism* and in *public policy responses to inequalities*. However, while drawing from the same pool of resources for argument, these two spheres are quite different.

- The institutional racism concept used for public policy is basically a legal tool used to combat inequalities directly arising from employment and service provision by both state and private sector organisations, on a case-by-case basis.

- It is frequently discussed and critiqued in the media and the world of formal politics. The ideological battle consists here of a clash of two main sides. On one side are those who seek to valorise the concept's capacity to bring about more equal outcomes, and oblige organisations to address discriminatory practice as a matter of course. On the other, the arguments focus on the concept's alleged clumsiness and its inappropriate use: this term brands a whole organisation, it is claimed, where only a minority of individuals are actually behaving in racist ways. There are a number of ways to understand this struggle, but I suggest that a starting point for a sociologist is to focus on the main problem that 'institutional racism' has helped to resolve.

- There are two distinct dimensions of racism – the individual and the collective. One makes no sense without the other. People must use the cultural stuff available to them, and that includes the ideas on 'race' that we recognise as dividing groups of people into categories based on appearance and culture. One of the most difficult things that undergraduate students and lay people experience in trying to come to terms with the topic of racism is the idea that there is a level at which it (like all other forms of discrimination) operates *counter* to individuals' intentions and regardless of their personal convictions. In the argument against institutional racism, there are individual actors who do bad things and those who do not. The objection is that within an organisation, the two are grouped together.

- Yet this type of response really misses the point of what the concept of institutional racism can do for us. 'Institutional racism' underscores the idea that the individual and collective dimensions of social action coexist, yet are distinct at the theoretical level. It can therefore be said to be a real sociological concept that illuminates otherwise more muddied waters.

- When 'institutional' is used as a synonym for 'structural', as it has been in the lineage of ideas derived from Carmichael and Hamilton (1967), the utility can be more widely applied outside the legal realm and in the social world, where, like class and gender, 'race' is one of the main vectors along which discrimination is channelled at a collective level.

Points for Reflection

What's the point of the concept of institutional racism?

How can you explain wealth discrepancies like those observed in the USA?

As a researcher, how would you go about examining the proposition that a country's higher education system, or criminal justice system is structurally racist?

Further Reading

Phillips, C. (2011) 'Institutional Racism and Ethnic Inequalities: An Expanded Multilevel Framework', *Journal of Social Policy* 40(1): 173–92.

Sets out a synthesis of institutional racism and puts forward an alternative framework (using racialisation) for understanding it.

Lipsitz, G. (2011) *How Racism Takes Place*. Philadelphia: Temple University Press.

A detailed and compelling account of how racial segregation has occurred in urban spaces, and how whiteness ensures that the ideas attached to the process remain crucial in continuing the segregation process.

Golash-Boza, T. (2015) 'A Critical and Comprehensive Sociological Theory of Race and Racism', *Sociology of Race and Ethnicity* 2(2): 129–41.

Concise but wide-ranging essay that incorporates ideas of systemic racism into a broader theorisation of the current state of American critical race scholarship.

Notes

1. The nine grounds are: gender, marital status, family status, sexual orientation, religion, age, disability, race and membership of the Traveller community. The relevant pieces of legislation are the Employment Equality Acts 1998–2004 and the Equal Status Acts 2000–2004.

2. See www.equality.ie (Equality Authority definitions can be found on this website).

3. See, for example, the City of Charlotte: www.blackpast.org/aah/redlining-1937. However, many examples can be accessed by googling 'HOLC' and 'redlining'.

4. These IASP reports build regularly on the original set of data developed and interpreted by Melvyn Oliver and Thomas Shapiro (2006).

5. There are a number of maps available to visually understand the segregation data. Here are three: A map created by Dustin Cable at University of Virginia's Weldon Cooper Center for Public Service, based on 2010 Census figures: www.wired.com/2013/08/how-segregated-is-your-city-this-eye-opening-map-shows-you/.

   24/7 Wall Street constructed a map based on households from the same survey, which can be accessed here: http://247wallst.com/special-report/2015/08/19/americas-most-segregated-cities/.

   Pew Research Center's work on Texas (2015): www.pewresearch.org/fact-tank/2015/06/29/in-greater-dallas-area-segregation-by-income-and-race/.

6. *Source:* Friends, Families and Travellers: www.gypsy-traveller.org/.

7

Science

In this chapter we will

- Look at how scientists have contributed to defining race

- Present case studies on eugenics and the marketing of racialised drugs

- Examine science's ongoing input into racialised understandings of the social world

- Look at contemporary practices like cosmetic surgery and skin lightening from a racial science perspective

In Chapter 1, we briefly looked at some examples of how the natural sciences gave support to racial theory in the late eighteenth and early nineteenth centuries. In this chapter, we shall examine in more depth the role that the natural sciences have played in racialising the world's population.

At first glance, science might seem an unlikely place to investigate 'race'. Aren't the natural sciences a set of arenas in which the objective truth is more important than the social inequalities and political ideologies of the world we look at elsewhere in the book? Many practitioners of the natural sciences would argue that their work is concerned only with facts and the quest for knowledge, that their 'knowledge and the assumptions that guide knowledge production, now, as never before, transcend the times' (Duster, 2006: 487). So what to make of the occasional controversies around the scientific status of 'race'? In 2007, Nobel prize-winning James Watson, who discovered the structure of DNA in the 1960s, told us that African Americans were less intelligent than other groups. In 2011, Satoshi Kanozawa, a London School of Economics Professor of Evolutionary Psychology, concluded that black women were less attractive than others, while Nicholas Wade's *A Troublesome Inheritance* triggered anger and controversy with its insistence in 2014 that race has real biological and genetic dimensions.

In Brazil, the campaign for affirmative action has been ideologically hampered by genetic science (Kent and Wade, 2015). For the Afro-Brazilians, the discovery that many of them have a great deal of European DNA enables the anti-affirmative action lobby to argue that there is biologically no such thing as 'Black Brazilians' as a distinct group, therefore no need for affirmative action. Yet Alondra Nelson (2016) reports that DNA testing is used in a variety of ways to connect diasporic communities. Perhaps there is more to the story than we thought.

In this chapter we will look at a series of fields and episodes in which 'race' is effectively made by and through science in particular contexts.

We shall return to the period of 'race science' in the late eighteenth and early nineteenth centuries and ask what contribution scientists of the day made to establishing 'race' as a fact in the natural and therefore social world. Then we shall consider the role of eugenics, particularly in the first decades of the twentieth century, and its relationship with the political ideology of Social Darwinism, followed by a section dealing with medicine's relationship to 'race'. Finally, we will look at cosmetic surgery and skin lightening, and suggest that part of what these practices do is recast people's bodies racially to more closely resemble the somatic norms of the dominant racialised group. It is worth pointing out before we begin that although 'race' has been designated a social reality rather than a biological one by most social scientists and many natural scientists, it is still used as a variable in contemporary scientific research in a way that suggests that it has biological validity. People are frequently asked to self-report their 'race'/ethnicity in relation to medical treatment, for example, so, in the practice of science, the social often overlaps with the natural. In the examples below, we will try to unpick some of this confusion.

'Race' Science

The fields of science that can be encompassed by this term stretch from the pseudo-sciences of craniology and phrenology (the study of skull shapes and bumps) through biology, and the origins of anthropology, sociology and ethnography, which developed in the middle of the nineteenth century. We shall use two examples: a classificatory system still used today, and some particular applications of the very broad science called anthropometry, which involved measuring body parts and extrapolating social conclusions from them. This is a clue to why science is important to the student of racism. In the nineteenth century, science overtook religion as the legitimate source of authority in explaining natural and, by extension, social phenomena in the Western world. For something to be established by scientists henceforth meant that it had entered into the set of assumptions that people held about their world and which they used to decipher it.

Box 7.1   Linnaeus (1707–78) from *The System of Nature* (1735)

Man, the last and best of created works, formed after the image of his Maker, endowed with a portion of intellectual divinity, the governor and subjugator of all other beings, is, by his wisdom alone, able to form just conclusions from such things as present themselves to his senses, which can only consist of bodies merely natural. Hence, the first step of wisdom is to know these bodies; and be able, by those marks imprinted on them by nature, to distinguish them from one another, and to affix to every object its proper name ...

Mammalia

Order 1: Primates

HOMO

Sapiens. Diurnal; varying by education and situation

Four-footed, mute, hairy. *Wild man.*

Copper-coloured, choleric, erect. *American.*

Hair black, straight, thick; *nostrils* wide; *face* harsh; *beard* scanty; obstinate, content, free. *Paints* himself with fine red lines. *Regulated* by customs.

Fair, sanguine, brawny. *European.*

Hair yellow, brown, flowing; *eyes* blue; gentle, acute, inventive. *Covered* with close vestments. *Governed* by laws.

Sooty, melancholy, rigid.

Hair black; *eyes* dark; *fever,* haughty, covetous. *Covered* with loose garments. *Governed* by opinions.

Black, phlegmatic, relaxed.

Hair black, frizzled; *skin* silky; *nose* flat; *lips* tumid; crafty, indolent, negligent. *Anoints* himself with grease. *Governed* by caprice. (Eze, 1997: 10)

Linnaeus's classification schema is still used in biology. It uses a binomial system (two words: one denoting genus and one a specific title), plus it is arranged hierarchically. Prior to Linnean classification, animals were categorised according to their method of movement. So what he is doing here, logically for an Enlightenment scientist, is classifying people in the same way as plants, fish and animals. In this schema, however, we see the rationale: there is a typology of phenotype informed by innate characteristics, which then enables an appropriate level of governance. The hierarchy runs from rational to capricious. The 'bodies merely natural' can be read as mediations of capacity for civilisation. A causal relationship between these things has developed and been locked into place. The legitimacy and authority of science is crucial to this understanding becoming accepted. Once this relationship is deemed a natural fact, there can be no changing it, and no rational argument against it.

Box 7.2   Comte de Buffon (Georges-Louis Leclerc) (1707–88) from *A Natural History, General and Particular* (1748–1804)

The most temperate climate lies between the 40th and 50th degrees of latitude, and produces the most handsome and beautiful men. It is from this climate that the ideas of the genuine colour of mankind, and of the various degrees of beauty ought to be derived. The two extremes are equally remote from truth and from beauty. The civilised countries situated under this zone are Georgia, Circassia, the Ukraine, Turkey in Europe, Hungary, the south of Germany, Italy, Switzerland, France and the northern part of Spain. The natives of these territories are the most handsome and most beautiful people in the world. The climate may be regarded as the chief cause of the different colours of men. But food, though it has less influence upon colour, greatly affects the form of our bodies. (Eze, 1997: 17)

Buffon links climate with appearance and capacity for civilisation, locating the apex of the latter in the temperate zone of Southern to Central Europe. We can see here a version of Linnaeus's ideas, and what is noteworthy is not just the assertion of causal links between observable differences in climate and physical appearance, but the process of reiteration. Scientists, philosophers, economists and historians of this period read each other's work and framed their own through it. By force of repetition, assertions enter into the realm of indisputable facts. Here also we have a standard of authenticity: the 'genuine colour of mankind', and of beauty proposed as part of the ideological domination of the West over the presumably inauthentic and ugly others. European and North American elites read the work of the Enlightenment thinkers, and this formed the basis of consensus about what 'race' meant in terms of the social world. If you could successfully argue that some types of people were naturally inferior to others, and this was marked on their bodies, then what could mankind do but respect this divine pattern? The baton is picked up by the Social Darwinists later in the century.

Anthropometry

Anthropometry is the study of human body measurement for use in anthropological classification and comparison. It has a number of benign uses to do with
monitoring health and development, for example. However, it also had another
strand that was aimed at producing empirical evidence for the establishment of
hierarchical typologies of people. One of the best known is the 'criminal types'
typology constructed by Italian physiognomist Cesare Lombroso (1876) that
links physical traits (nose shape, length of chin, ear size, distance between eyes,
etc.) to different criminal tendencies. Lombroso believed that people were born
criminals and that if the types of physical feature were analysed, then criminals
could be identified before they reached the stage of actually committing crimes.
His understanding was an evolutionary one: human beings were evolving and
criminals were a throwback, degenerating and therefore the bearers of physical
deformities that betrayed their inner natures. Lombroso's socio-biological interpretations of crime were part of a much wider set of assumptions held by
scientists about the link between civilisation and appearance.

Scientists constructed bodies as the clue to meaning about whole groups of
people. How could they be read? What 'social sense' could be made of them? In
Australia, as late as the 1920s and 1930s, the effort to understand who and what
Aboriginal Australians were entailed an intensive anthropometrical effort
described by Warwick Anderson (2006). The various understandings of them –
childlike savages, Caucasian throwbacks, people who die out when confronted
with civilisation, people who die out when confronted with disease (especially
from contact with 'immunologically incompetent' poor white males [2006:
221]) – were put to the test by researchers from the Adelaide University
Institute. They measured, weighed, photographed and took samples from hundreds of people. While there was a concentration of the rare type B blood (like
Northern Europeans), intelligence tests showed 'childlike levels' of achievement. These findings were significant because they were taken on board by
policy-makers, who then understood Aboriginals as Caucasians, who were
therefore redeemable, rather than irredeemable savages genetically incapable
of attaining civilisation. Particularly interesting to these scientists was the discovery and analysis of what they termed the 'half-caste', people with one white
European and one Aboriginal parent. An entire project was constructed
around this exploration and involved researchers from Harvard as well as
Adelaide University in 1938–9. As a result, the anthropologists involved rec-
ommended that absorption, rather than isolation, of the native Australians
was the way forward. Their conclusion about what studying 'half-castes' could
tell us was that it was not particularly revealing. However, once it had been
scientifically established that Aboriginals were racially close to Europeans, the
path of absorption was taken across Australia. The policy developed aimed at
civilising them by forcibly separating 'full-bloods' from 'half-castes' in the
form of wide-scale adoption to bring them up in all-white environments, and
reservations to protect the 'full-bloods' from civilisation. In an uneven process

across the states, around 100,000 Aboriginal children were removed from their own families and brought up by white families up until the early 1970s (the 'Stolen Generations').

The debate about this is ongoing. A national report, *Bring them Home*, was published in 1997 (Australian Human Rights Commission, 1997). A South Australian won the first compensation from the Federal government in 2007, and in February 2008, Prime Minister Kevin Rudd gave an official apology to the Aboriginal and Torres Strait Islanders. We thus arrive at the 'Stolen Generations' via 'race' science.[1] Regardless of the intentions of any researcher involved in the data-gathering process, the ultimate consequences of their work were catastrophic for large numbers of Aboriginals. Yet within the context of their profession, these scientists were not deviant but mainstream practitioners, probably even located toward the more progressive end of the scale. They did, however, share the general assumption that 'race' was a matter of blood, bodies and genes, and that it was an accurate predictor of civilisation and development. The Australian case clearly demonstrates the power relations of racial science: the dominant measure the dominated, not the other way around. The production of knowledge flows in one direction, and feeds into policy in which the dominated have no voice. This conclusion sets us up for the next example, that of eugenics.

Eugenics

Eugenics is the idea that the State can and should intervene in demographic development by encouraging some groups to breed and/or preventing other groups from doing so. It also extends into the domain of euthanasia, where such a policy can be defended, like the previous ones, through claims to protect the national interest. Although eugenics per se is now seen as a historical phenomenon, there are still existing national eugenics societies, a small but vocal pro-eugenics lobby (examples can be found on www.eugenics.net) and a legacy of the ideas put forward and made central to policy in the twentieth century. The origins of eugenics lie in the last quarter of the nineteenth century, when the ideology now called Social Darwinism was dominant. Darwin's ideas about evolution, competition and adaptation in the natural world, as published and popularised from the 1860s, were extrapolated into an ideology applicable to the human world.[2] This kind of 'social' interpretation of Darwinism claimed that existing hierarchies (class, gender, 'race') were the result of the natural tendency for the strong and adaptable to dominate the weak and inflexible. War and conflict were seen as ideal mechanisms for accelerating the process of sorting the strong from the weak, which fitted perfectly with the strand of imperialism that was blooming. This idea was deployed to rationalise massacres of colonised people and even their extermination: the last native Tasmanian died in 1868, for example, and some commentators argued that this merely demonstrated the workings of Darwin's model in the human world. Those unable to adapt run to extinction.

The development of Social Darwinism, however, should really be more associated with the work of the pioneering sociologist and philosopher Herbert Spencer, whose work (prior to and contemporaneous with Darwin's) popularised similar ideas. Spencer sold nearly 400,000 copies of his books in the USA and UK. In the nineteenth century, that represents astounding sales, and indicates the extent of his appeal. Spencer, for example, used Darwin's phrase 'survival of the fittest' in *Principles of Biology* (1864) a number of times to refer to the social struggle for survival, whereas Darwin used it as a metaphor for 'natural selection'. Spencer understood society through natural frames, organic relationships, struggle and development by means of this struggle.

Against such an ideological background, the application of similar principles through state policy would receive a sympathetic hearing. The word 'eugenics' was coined by Francis Galton in 1883 (Pearson, 1930: 348). Galton's idea of eugenics, as expressed to the Royal Anthropological Society, was the following: 'Eugenics is the study of agencies under social control that may improve or impair the racial qualities of future generations, whether physically or mentally.' Galton and his growing group of supporters, which included people from across the political spectrum of the day, from right-wing imperialists through to Fabian socialists, worked hard to popularise the idea of eugenics as public policy, but found the going difficult. Two decades later, Galton was still talking hypothetically, arguing that it should be 'first an academic matter, then a practical policy', and finally, 'it must be introduced into the national consciousness like a new religion' (Galton, 1905: 50).

The basis of the eugenic standpoint was twofold. First, there was a belief in the State's powers to improve society, and second, an understanding of social hierarchies as deriving from nature: the professional classes were seen as the fittest, most competitive and able section of society, with neither the indolence nor the weakness of the poor, nor the vices and lack of dynamism of the aristocrat. Yet this group's birth rate was diminishing, while that of the lower classes was increasing. The eugenics response was couched in terms of the positive and negative. 'Positive eugenics' consisted of measures aimed at promoting higher birth rates among the middle classes, and 'negative eugenics' entailed measures aimed at reducing it among the poor and those with serious congenital problems. While the British eugenicists were unable to effectively move these ideas into the arena of public policy, their counterparts elsewhere were more successful.

The extent of eugenic practice reached from Scandinavia (Broberg and Roll-Hansen, 2005; Andreassen, 2014) through Germany across the Atlantic to North and South America in the period 1910–40 especially. It took a variety of forms on a continuum: with increased European immigration and educational programmes at one end (Latin America), through mass sterilisation (USA) to genocide (Nazi Germany) at the other. The Latin American republics such as Mexico, Argentina, Brazil and Uruguay, for example, saw the problem of governance in different ways, but shared the general assumption that European genes were stronger and more desirable than indigenous and African ones. Educational policies aimed at civilising the working classes were deployed alongside immigration policies targeted at Europeans in order to demographically whiten the nation (Stepan, 1991; Appelbaum et al., 2003; Dávila, 2003).

Eugenics in the USA

The case of the USA is interesting in that it preceded the Nazis and provided models that were later acknowledged by German scientists. The success of the American eugenicists is owed to the funding and organisation provided through, first, the Carnegie Institute, and then, after 1910, through the New York-based Eugenics Records Office (ERO).[3] The director, Charles Davenport, and his deputy, Harry Laughlin, were dedicated lobbyists with a message that people were willing to hear. The work of the ERO was focused on three areas: population control, anti-miscegenation legislation and immigration control.

Population Control

The ERO was concerned to put in place measures to stop people it considered a public menace from having more children. The groups targeted were those with antisocial and/or immoral habits and genetically transmittable illnesses. Since the mid-nineteenth century, a body of work had been growing that sought to locate the source of America's ills in the family environment and bad genes of its poor (Hartigan, 2005; Wray, 2006). Moreover, alcoholism was in those days considered an immoral behaviour rather than an illness, and conditions such as 'feeble-mindedness', later dropped by medical practitioners as being without substance, were still in circulation. The Commonwealth of Virginia was the most eager state to take on board the ERO's arguments, and in the landmark *Buck* v. *Bell* case in 1927 (an appeal to the Supreme Court by Buck), the state government was granted its right to compulsorily sterilise a young woman called Carrie Buck. She had been raped by a family member, and her child, Vivian, had been 'tested' at seven months by a child psychologist who argued that she was 'feeble-minded', like her mother and grandmother. The case revolved around the Commonwealth's duty to act in the public interest by preventing the Bucks from continuing to produce mentally ill children, and it had modelled its statute on Laughlin's draft in 1924. In the Supreme Court, Judge Oliver Wendell Holmes' summary was that: 'Three generations of imbeciles are enough.'

The Buck case set a precedent for state powers of compulsory sterilisation, and by the next decade, more than half the states in the USA were following Virginia's lead. The compulsory sterilisation procedures were carried out disproportionately on African American, Native American, Hispanic and on white working-class women (A.Y. Davis, 2001b). This practice went on into the 1970s before it was recognised as being inappropriate. The head of the Federal government's Department of Health, Education and Welfare admitted in 1974 that between 100,000 and 200,000 sterilisations had been performed in 1972 alone (A.Y. Davis, 2001b: 218). From the various inquiries into forced sterilisation, it appears that the proportions of Native American, black and Latina women sterilised by the mid-1970s lay at upwards of 20 per cent (2001b).

The Nazis also ran sterilisation and euthanasia programmes (Burleigh, 2001) aimed at people with disabilities and alcoholism, etc. in Germany in the 1930s. Indeed, the so-called 'Final Solution' can be read as a eugenics project: aimed at eliminating the unwanted 'races' and sub-humans from Europe. The shared understanding among eugenicists and the policy-makers they influenced was of a natural genetic order of things that shapes the social world. This period (the 1920s to the 1940s) seems to have been the one in which federal and local governments felt they had the authority to act according to that order. What distinguishes it from the earlier period is not so much the ideological underpinning, but the target populations. Prior to the 1920s, colonial powers or their agents had either allowed high death tolls because the natural and social order suggested the colonised groups were expendable, or inflicted mass killings for the same reasons. This can be seen, for example, in the responses to nineteenth-century famines in Ireland and Bengal for the former (M. Davis, 2001), and the Philippines (1899), the Congo Free State (1902–10) and German South-West Africa (1904–7) for the latter. The movement of eugenics into policy *at home* shaped a remarkable three decades of State terrorism against elements of its own population, and it was based on racial logic: first, that people are genetically different (superior and inferior) and second, that the superior have the right to impose policies, including execution, on those it deems inferior (Foucault, 2003).

Miscegenation

'Miscegenation' was a term invented by two political journalists in the 1860s to talk about 'race mixing', specifically between black and white, in order to exacerbate white anxieties over the abolition of slavery (see Chapter 8). The ERO was interested in protecting what it saw as the white gene pool, both from defective whites (like Carrie Buck) and from non-whites. Mixing was held to lead to degenerate individuals more susceptible to illness and the supposed flaws of the inferior partner's 'race'. The important eugenics theorist and activist Madison Grant argued in his *The Passing of the Great Race* (1915) that great races were undone by not protecting their gene pools. Although Davenport found that by 1913, 29 states already had anti-miscegenation laws on their books, he offered support for tightening them and extending them to other states. Again, the Commonwealth of Virginia was first to benefit from this expert advice, and its Virginia Integrity Act (1924) banned marriage between a white person and anyone 'with a trace of blood other than Caucasian'. All the country's anti-miscegenation laws were abolished in 1967, and in 2001, the Commonwealth of Virginia publicly renounced its role in American eugenics.

Immigration

Davenport stated early in the ERO's existence that the organisation was concerned about the future shape of American demographics. In a 1911 publication, *Heredity in Relation to Eugenics*, he argued that:

> ... the population of the United States will, on account of the great influx of blood from South-eastern Europe, rapidly become darker in pigmentation, smaller in stature, more mercurial, more attached to music and art, [and] more given to crimes of larceny, kidnapping, assault, murder, rape and sex-immorality. (Davenport, 1911: 219)

To understand this statement, we must look at the changing character of immigration into the USA after 1890. Increasing proportions of Southern Europeans (Italians, Greeks, Yugoslavs) and Eastern Europeans (Poles, Lithuanians and Russians, especially Jewish Russians) were immigrating to America at that time due to the poor economic conditions in Europe and the phase of labour-intensive expansion experienced by the US economy. The ERO, with its eye for putative natural/genetic distinctions that would play out in cultural terms, found it dangerous that so many poor Catholic and Jewish Europeans from the East and South were outnumbering the Northern and Western, mainly Protestant stock. Harry Laughlin's role in the formulation of the US 1924 Immigration Act is extraordinary. The ERO was contacted in 1911 by the Immigration Restriction League and successfully lobbied the government to take such bio-cultural consequences into account when setting quotas. The ERO had powerful allies: the Public Health Service (whose officials dealt with incoming immigrants at Ellis Island), and labour organisations fearing a drop in working conditions for their members. Laughlin carried out research on the mentally ill and prison population with a view to arguing that the immigrant population were causing the degeneration of American standards, and in 1920 he appeared before the US Congressional Committee on Immigration and Naturalization, where he gave evidence suggesting that the US gene pool was being polluted by defective genes. He was appointed as an expert by the Committee, and for the next decade had his research funded by the taxpayer. He was instrumental in determining the 1924 Act's content. The result was that the 1924 Immigration Act granted quotas to the various countries based on the levels of the US population as of 1890. This date was deliberately chosen because it preceded the peaking wave of Catholic, Slavic and Jewish European immigration from 1890 onwards, and therefore established quotas for such sources of labour at very low levels. That Act remained in place until 1965.

The interpretations of genetic diversity made by eugenicists were backed up by seemingly scientific analyses and impressive amounts of statistical research. However, their understanding of what constituted a 'race' is far from consistent, even from one researcher to another. Moreover, according to the ERO's work, entire nationalities were prone to particular types of crime; a clear line was established between worthwhile and useless members of society, and into the latter category fell people with physical and mental disabilities, as well as pseudo-categories such as the 'feeble-minded'. Deciding that a given group is worth less than another, based on a medical condition (for reasons of money/collective security), is saturated with assumptions resulting from racialised thinking (blood determines culture, and cultures are arranged in a hierarchical order). The main thrust of eugenics discourse is to argue for the common good, for the improvement of society. However, in practice, it is the relatively powerless who are the victims, so the questions that must always be asked about eugenics are: 'improvements for whom?' and 'who will lose out in the improvement process?'

Racialised Bodies and Medicine

Early racial science sought to measure, and thus interpret, the meaning and value of bodies through a framework of a division of the world into civilised and savage cultures and people. According to the prevailing logic, members of the inferior cultures, had, by extension, physical and intellectual capacity inferior to those of others. This made their bodies interesting to anthropometrists and anthropologists, as we have seen above, and also to medical practitioners. Once you begin with the assumption that some generic types of phenotype are vehicles for a different and distinct biology (within the body and not just its surface), then other things also become possible, such as the placing of thresholds of deviancy and normality in places where it might now, with the benefit of centuries' more scientific research and social change, be thought very odd. One example of this 'medicalisation of deviance' is given by Troy Duster (2006). In an article setting out the links between the legal profession, science and medicine, he points to the invention of a new mental illness, *drapetomania*, coined by prominent American surgeon Samuel Cartwright. It represented Cartwright's assertion that slaves' repeated attempts to escape the plantations constituted a mental health condition whose source was a particular deviant psychological state. While it might appear perverse to characterise such behaviour as anything other than normal, it has to be understood that the diagnosis stemmed from a particular interpretation of the social world. In this view, black men were naturally prone to violence, against their own women and children (Duster, 2006: 490–1), and had to be treated with a balance of familiarity and discipline, but not too much of either. Imbalance in either direction could create the conditions for 'drapetomanic' behaviour:

The cause in the most of cases, that induces the negro to run away from service, is as much a disease of the mind as any other species of mental alienation, and much more curable, as a general rule. With the advantages of proper medical advice, strictly followed, this troublesome practice that many negroes have of running away can be entirely prevented. (Cartwright, 1860: 707)

This only makes sense if black people are understood to be biologically and psychologically inferior to white people and to require governance that only disciplinarian whites can provide; if the violence inflicted by white slave-owners and their staff does not therefore count as violence; and if this is a natural state. Why else would the quest for freedom from slavery be viewed as unnatural? Indeed, the inferiority of black people is made a material reality in the US Constitution of 1790, which categorises them as chattel rather than people, and the equation of black personhood with the 1787 'Three Fifths Compromise'[4] which went unchallenged until the 1856 *Dred Scott* Supreme Court ruling upheld the principle.

Further examples of scientific practice predicated on the idea that European and African Americans have such different physiognomies as to allow differential pathologies, can be seen in the 'Tuskegee Syphilis Experiment', where controlled experiments were carried out on black subjects, and in the recent developments in pharmaceuticals such as BiDil, the so-called 'ethnic drug' (see Box 7.3).

The 'Tuskegee Syphilis Experiment'

The experiment, whose full title is the 'Tuskegee Study of Untreated Syphilis in the Black Man', is notorious: President Clinton publicly apologised in 1997. Its notoriety derives from both its assumptions and its conduct. The experiment was aimed at studying the effects of syphilis and its remedies on the human body. A number of studies have been written (e.g. Jones, 1993). However, the African American sample group were not told about any treatments that developed during the lifetime of the trials, and were used de facto as a control group without their consent. This contradicts the ethical responsibility to inform patients, and not to do them harm, which is part of the Hippocratic Oath taken by medical practitioners.

The experiment, funded by the Public Health Service (PHS), was run from the University of Tuskegee in Alabama, and began in 1932. The nearly 400-strong African American sample consisted of peasant farmers from the surrounding area (Macon County) who were suffering from syphilis. They were observed and tested at various intervals over a 40-year period. However, they were not told what illness they had, merely that they had 'bad blood'. At the outset, they were given very small amounts of the contemporary remedies such as bizmuth and mercury. Yet these were soon replaced with aspirin.

Moreover, even when some of the men joined the armed forces in the Second World War and were required to have treatment, the PHS obtained an exemption from treatment for them. When penicillin became the standard remedy for syphilis in 1947, the men were not informed, and were allowed to go untreated for the purposes of the experiment. Scientific papers on the men were presented and published throughout the experiment, but the sample were mainly illiterate and in any case not likely to read the specialist medical journals in which the papers were published. Basically, the real data could only be retrieved once the person had died and his body could be inspected in a post-mortem, to gauge the effects of untreated syphilis on the body. The medical interest in them therefore began after death, and so it was actually in the researchers' interests for them to die! Eventually, details of the experiment's conduct were leaked to the media by concerned public health workers, but by the time the experiment ended in 1972, 28 of the men had died directly of syphilis, and 100 had died of related complications. Forty of their wives had been infected, and 19 children had been born with congenital syphilis. In 1973, the National Association for the Advancement of Colored People (NAACP) won a $9 million settlement in a 'class-action' lawsuit. Free healthcare was extended to the remaining sample, and to infected wives, widows and children.

The Tuskegee experiment changed the way research ethics were conceptualised and controlled. Its legacy was serious distrust of the government among African Americans over any area relating to public health (Freimuth et al., 2001). There are also complicating factors in this story. Tuskegee University was a black college founded by Booker T. Washington. It lent the PHS access to its laboratories and amenities without question, and a senior black nurse was one of the project's key staff throughout. This does not change the assumptions behind the research, or its overall functioning, but raises troubling questions about Tuskegee's institutional involvement. If we compare the Tuskegee experiment with the policies implemented in response to the work of the American eugenicists, the power relations are evident. The powerful research the powerless and, in this case, virtually wield power of life and death.

Box 7.3   BiDil: An Ethnic Drug?

One of the rationales put forward for continuing to do race-based medical research is to target illnesses specific to different racial groups in order to improve their life chances (Bliss, 2012). The marketing of the drug BiDil (isosorbide dinitrate/hydralazine hydrochloride), approved by the US Food and Drugs Agency (FDA) in 2005 as a drug specifically for African Americans, is a case where commercial practices, scientific reasoning and research methods and concepts of 'race' intersect. BiDil was not a new drug but a combination of two old ones. However, the marketing plan, run by NitroMed, Inc., was new: it exclusively targeted African Americans.

The new marketing plan was based on a clinical trial in 2004 that used only African Americans in the sample group. As there was no control population (for comparison), there is nothing to sustain the company's claim that 'race' is a useful variable. Moreover, if the principle is to market a drug by a group who it is tested on, all other drugs would have to be marketed as 'white drugs'. Jonathan Kahn (2006: W3) explains that: 'NitroMed holds at least two patents to BiDil. One is not race-specific, but it expires in 2007. The other is race-specific; it does not expire until 2020. With its race-specific patent in hand, NitroMed can even block the marketing of the generic components of BiDil specifically to treat heart failure. NitroMed therefore has a vested interest in framing BiDil as a race-specific drug – regardless of the limitations imposed by the actual evidence.'[5]

The use of figures in convincing customers comprises a sleight of hand. The company quotes a higher ratio of overall African American to white deaths from heart failure than is the case. However, the age cohort in relation to which the ratio is actually true (45–64) accounts for only a maximum of 6 per cent of all heart attacks. The vast majority (94 per cent) occur at age 65 and over. In that older age group, there is virtually no difference in mortality rates between whites and African Americans.

Moreover, factors other than what scientists call 'race' or ethnicity affect the body's responses to drugs. It would be possible to arrive at a technical profile of these factors. However, a drug cannot readily be marketed to a technically defined group, only a social group. Therefore, the marketing of BiDil is part of a commercial rather than medical and research-driven agenda. Even if the set of markers that people have traditionally considered 'racial' were clear and unequivocal (which they are not), there is no consensus among scientists about the response rates to drugs being only to do with those markers.

The BiDil episode demonstrates how science naturalises 'race' by passing it off as being reflected in nature (it thus racialises nature). Could this type of marketing usher in a trend? Kahn (2007a: 387) thinks this is possible.

Figures show that 65 patents have claimed a racial basis since 2001. There were zero in the 1976–97 period, and 12 between 1998 and 2005 (Kahn, 2007b). Kahn's conclusion about science, marketing and 'race' in the twenty-first century is troubling: 'In the context of gene patents, genetic race is becoming a commodity as race-specific patents allow biotechnology corporations to raise venture capital and develop marketing strategies that present a reified conception of race as genetic to doctors, regulators, and the public at large' (Kahn, 2007a: 416).

The racialisation of pharmaceuticals therefore appears to be emerging as a strategy for marketing medicines, and this is not based on rigorous science. Indeed, as an editorial in the science journal *Nature Biotechnology* puts it: 'Race is simply a poor proxy for the environmental and genetic causes of disease or drug response ... Pooling people in race silos is akin to zoologists grouping raccoons, tigers and okapis on the basis that they are all stripey' (*Nature Biotechnology*, 2005).

Cosmetic Interventions

In the video for Michael Jackson's 'Black or White' (1991), people morph into different 'racial' bodies, as he sings 'I don't want to spend my life being a colour'. Indeed, with cosmetic surgery increasingly lucrative and popular, Jackson's own problematic relationship with the racialisation of his body seems to be an increasingly mainstream concern. The video-enhanced morphing has become, in a way, a reality for some people ready to make the financial commitment required. However, the contention in this section is that a specific set of cosmetic procedures are not really about refining features toward a neutral universal version of what a beautiful face and/or body should look like, but a heavily racialised reproduction of dominant culture. Cosmetic surgery can be a project of whiteness for those who recognise the cost of it and are prepared to make an investment to profit from it. It can be seen as an advantage in employment, in business, in the marketplace for partners and as a way of avoiding some of the obstacles that are placed in front of people who are not white.

Skin-whitening creams have been available as products at least since the late nineteenth century. By 1930, over 230 brands of skin lightener were available (Peiss, 1999: 149). At the outset, these were mainly marketed at white women in America through magazines but this does not mean that they were the only people to use these products. The creams usually contained either hydroquinone or mercury or derivatives of the former (Box 7.4). They function by suppressing the production of melanin in the basal layer of the skin. These creams have been used to lighten skin shade in Africa and Asia, and latterly also Europe. As Amina Mire (2005) points out, skin-whitening creams are an integral part of a global cosmetics trade, earning large multinationals such as L'Oréal, Ponds and Garnier billions of dollars annually. She calls the emerging skin-whitening industry 'a lucrative globalized economic enterprise with profound social and political implications'.[6] Just as an indicator, estimates suggest that as of 2001, the Japanese skin-whitening market was estimated to be worth $5.6 billion, and China's market (the fastest growing) was estimated to be worth over $1.3 billion. India is another huge market for such products. By 2007, skin lighteners were worth around $318 million, a rise of 43 per cent since 2001. Melwani (2008) reports that the country manager for L'Oréal India told *The Times* that half of this market was accounted for by skin-whitening creams, and that 60–65 per cent of Indian women were daily users of these products.

There are two parts to this market. One is for cheaper products, often containing excessive amounts of the two main constituents, which are sold to less well-off customers. The other is a 'high end' market aimed at the affluent. The creams are marketed to white women as 'anti-ageing' products, and to non-white women as a means to make themselves radiant, attractive and Western. Considerable argument has occurred within African American circles about the use of skin-lightening products, and they are now marketed as ways to even out skin tone (by removing blotches) and to slow the ageing process rather than directly as skin whiteners. The link in Asian and American cultures between whiteness and success is used as a ploy to draw in more customers (mainly women, although there is a growing market for men).

Box 7.4   How Skin-Lightening Products Work

Two chemicals found in skin-lightening products are particularly problematic:

- hydroquinone ($C_6H_6O_2$) – a highly toxic chemical used in photo processing, rubber manufacture and hair dyes
- mercury – in the form of mercury chloride and ammoniated mercury, which is carcinogenic.

Both appear on the list of toxic substances that can only be purchased via pharmacies with prescribed labels of toxicity. Both products perform a similar process. In the short term, they will initially cause the skin to lighten by inhibiting the production of melanin. Many contemporary forms of skin lightener use derivatives of hydroquinone or compounds with a similar structure. If the products contain too high a proportion of either hydroquinone or mercury, they cannot legally be sold in many countries. In the 1930s, US products contained around 10 per cent mercury. It is now illegal for products to contain more than 2 per cent. Amina Mire (2005) reports that in developing-world countries and 'ethnic' grocery stores in North America and Europe, many of the creams are cheap and toxic, exceeding the toxin thresholds set out by the US Federal government, for example.

   Indeed, overuse of skin lighteners can irreparably damage skin, and even paradoxically produce darkening (ochronosis). Moreover, while hydroquinone and mercury can be absent from the ingredients of the product, this does not guarantee that it is safe to use. Repeated use of products that actually suppress melanin production (as opposed to creams that are marketed as lightening the skin but do no such thing) is lowering the body's level of protection against UV rays.

There are occasional organised critiques of how advertising marks whiteness as the aspiration and darker skin as something to get rid of, such as #unfairandlovely and the 'Dark is Beautiful' campaign, but this has not stopped advertisers from blatantly promoting their whitening products as a way to attract the opposite sex and to gain financial success. A series of mini films used to market the subtly titled Pond's 'White Beauty' cream in India in 2008 attracted a controversy. In it, a trio of prominent Bollywood actors (Saif Ali Khan, Priyanka Chopra and Neha Dhupia) perform. The story is that the darker-skinned Chopra splits up with Khan, who years later becomes famous and goes out with the pale-skinned Dhupia. Chopra uses Pond's product to make herself more attractive, that is, whiter, and wins Khan back. A film with a virtually identical storyline (Pond's 'Flawless White') was also used in the Japanese market. Another advert, for men's cream this time, was also the subject of controversy in India months prior to this.

Other Asian countries are experiencing similar cosmetic bonanzas, and often witness racist ad campaigns (Holmes, 2016). Fuller (2006) claims that 40 per cent of women in Hong Kong, Malaysia, the Philippines, South Korea and Taiwan use a whitening cream, according to market research company Synovate, and that more than 60 'new skin-whitening products were introduced in supermarkets or pharmacies across the Asia-Pacific region' in 2005, This is above the average of 56 new products introduced annually since 2000. New technology is also using lightening as a selling point, with some camera/mobile phone companies selling 'magic' selfie-filters that lighten the subject's skin to Chinese consumers (Sin, 2016).

While there are different explanations within each culture as to exactly why a lighter complexion is so desirable that people use toxic chemicals to achieve this goal, the main role must go to the legacy of Western domination of the rest of the world for centuries. Regardless of existing social stratifications such as caste in India, and the negative associations attached to darker complexions elsewhere, possibly partly to do with class (as in Europe until the mid-twentieth century, outdoor work activities meant a darker complexion), the European practices and ideas of 'race' connected with and altered them, so that the available ways of understanding colour as a social marker are a combination of local and imported systems.

In the USA and other plantation societies, the social correspondence between fairer skin and social prestige led to increased differentiation between darker and not so dark-skinned people, both on plantations and off them, as small 'coloured' or 'mulatto' middle classes developed (Lacy, 2007). The profound legacy of vilification of blackness in the Americas, which grew out of the slave system and has long outlived it, cannot be ignored – the hierarchical social relations in which lighter skin is afforded more value, known as 'colorism', are still pertinent (Morrison, 1970; Yancy, 2001; Hunter, 2007). Although the civil rights movement and its message of Black Power marked a cultural shift in the way African Americans could evaluate themselves culturally and physically in the public arena, that legacy has not disappeared. Meanwhile, increasing awareness of the physical and psychological impacts of skin-lightening products in Africa has resulted in bans on such products by Côte d'Ivoire and Ghana since late 2015.

It is not only skin-whitening creams but also cosmetic surgery that enables people to racially alter their appearance. I am not claiming that every surgical operation such as reconstruction after injury or illness, or tummy tucks or breast enlargement/reduction is solely to do with expressing a desire to be whiter. I am concerned here only with surgeries undergone by minorities (including Jews) that are aimed at changing the body shape or features in a way that makes them appear closer to white Western norms. This is not merely taking place in larger numbers in the two centres of world plastic surgery, the west and the east coasts of the USA, but also in a number of Asian countries, where new racial surgeries are being improvised (Box 7.5).

The number of surgeries in Asia, for example, is increasing. Countries such as South Korea and Thailand are situating themselves as surgery tourism sites for international customers, while developing economies and cultural messages encouraging self-improvement have created a boom. The surgeries available to Asian clients are clearly focused on approximating to the white ideal, of larger breasts, a different appearance of the eyes, and paler skin. Indeed the *Wall Street Journal* reports that 67 per cent of those polled in a 2014 Korean consumer survey on cosmetic surgery said they had had double eyelid surgery (Evans, 2014). The search for a whiter body also encompasses longer, thinner legs, as the example of Korea (Box 7.5) demonstrates.

Box 7.5   Special Surgical Procedures for Asian Women

Just as Asian faces require unique procedures, their bodies demand innovative operations to achieve the leggy, skinny, busty Western ideal that has become increasingly universal. Dr Suh In Seock, a surgeon in Seoul, has struggled to find the best way to fix an affliction the Koreans call *muu-dari* and the Japanese call *daikon-ashi*: radish-shaped calves. Liposuction, so effective on the legs of plump Westerners, doesn't work on Asians since muscle, not fat, accounts for the bulk. Suh says earlier attempts to carve the muscle were painful and made walking difficult. 'Finally, I discovered that by severing a nerve behind the knee, the muscle would atrophy,' says Suh, 'thereby reducing its size up to 40 per cent.' Suh has performed over 600 of the operations since 1996. He disappears for a minute and returns with a bottle of fluid containing what looks like chopped up bits of ramen noodles. He has preserved his patients' excised nerves in alcohol. 'And that's just since November,' he says proudly. (From 'Nip and Tuck', a special feature in *Time* magazine, Asia section, 2006)

Meanwhile, back in the USA, the numbers from the plastic surgeons' professional associations are revealing a growing trend among minorities for cosmetic procedures since the turn of the century.

In the period 1999–2015, the overall number of cosmetic surgeries increased massively, from 4.6 million to over 15 million. Of this, the ethnic minority customer share rose from 15 per cent to 31 per cent (Table 7.1). This seems to reflect increasing affluence on one hand but also a pattern of surgeries (Table 7.2) reflecting a desire to move toward a 'Caucasian' standard (especially nose reshaping for all and eyelid surgery and breast augmentation for Asian Americans).[7]

Table 7.1 Percentage of US cosmetic surgery patients, by ethnicity, 1999, 2003, 2008 and 2014

Ethnic group	1999	2003	2008	2014
Caucasian	85	80	73	69
Hispanic	6	8	10	10
African American	4	6	8	8
Asian American	3	4	7	7
Other	1	2	2	5

Sources: American Society for Aesthetic Plastic Surgery (1999: 3) and (2003: 2); American Society of Plastic Surgeons (2009, 2015).

Table 7.2 The three most commonly requested surgical procedures for 'ethnic' patients, 2007

African American	Asian American	Hispanic
1 Nose reshaping	1 Nose reshaping	1 Breast augmentation
2 Liposuction	2 Breast augmentation	2 Nose reshaping
3 Breast reduction	3 Eyelid surgery	3 Liposuction

Source: American Society of Plastic Surgeons (2009).

We should not be surprised that the origin of cosmetic surgery is a wish to change one's appearance to something closer to the dominant phenotype. The 'nose job', or rhinoplasty, to give it its medical term, was invented in India in the sixth century as a reconstructive procedure. However, rhinoplasty as a *cosmetic* surgery was pioneered by German Jewish surgeon Jacques Joseph in Berlin in the 1890s. Many of his operations were responses to Jewish patients' experiences of anti-Semitism (Gilman, 1991). The 'Jewish nose' was seen as an ethnic giveaway by German Jews of the day, and Joseph became aware that it was as much in the minds of some of his patients as an observable fact. The surgery seemed to serve psychologically reassuring ends, although it was no guarantee against further anti-Semitic violence. Joseph's textbooks on cosmetic surgery that were published in the 1930s became landmark medical texts.[8] The rhinoplasty went on to become the stock cosmetic surgery until other procedures, such as liposuction and breast enlargement, became more popular from the 1990s. A point of comparison is the blepharoplasty: a procedure developed to alter the appearance of Asian eyes by inserting a permanent crease in the eyelids. It is the most popular procedure in Asian clinics, and among Asian clients in the USA it has moved from 3rd to 2nd most popular between 2009 and 2014 (see above, and Tables 7.2 and 7.3).

Table 7.3   The three most commonly requested surgical procedures for 'ethnic' patients, 2014

African American	Asian American	Hispanic
1 Liposuction abdominoplasty	1 Breast augmentation	1 Breast augmentation
2 Abdominoplasty	2 Eyelid	2 Nose reshaping augmentation
3 Breast augmentation	3 Nose reshaping	3 Liposuction

Source: American Society of Plastic Surgeons (2015).

So there is a pattern according to which some of the cosmetic procedures chosen by many minority women in the USA make the patient's body approximate more closely to a white norm than their starting point. So what does this tell us about standards of beauty, individual agency and collective understandings of beauty? I think that whatever else cosmetic surgery is about, such as the search for the self (Elliott, 2008), it can also be about racialisation and white supremacy. Mire's (2005) conclusion about the skin-whitening industry is just as apt in relation to the cosmetic surgery one, albeit with a more complex dynamic. It is, as she argues, 'part and parcel of our old enemy, the "civilising mission"; the violent moral prerogative to cleanse and purify the mind and bodies of the "dark/dirt/ savage"'. The added complexity of skin lightening and specific cosmetic surgeries is that they are part of the post-colonial internalisation of this civilising mission, among those whose ancestors were the original objects of the mission. Is the object to approximate to whiteness, or to stave off blackness and Asian-ness? The fact that people risk their health and spend considerable amounts of money on cosmetic products and services indicates that there is something significant at stake.

Conclusions

- The field of the natural sciences is actually a very fruitful one for understanding the construction, dissemination and translation of ideas about 'race' into popular culture. Science does not reflect a single objective truth but is itself the result of social struggles with material and cultural resources: science therefore often reflects and participates in dominant groups' understandings of how society works. The longstanding debates about nature vs nurture, for example, which have framed the idea of 'race', lie at the heart of what science does: fuel our understandings of what is 'natural' and what is 'social', and when the ambiguities are.

- The enterprise of categorisation may well be for scientific purposes, but the categories used by scientists are not always neutral and objective ones: 'race' is never a neutral variable, and its use in scientific projects relating to health, or genomes, for example is bound to throw up the kinds of questions explored elsewhere in this book to do with equality and the distribution of resources.

- Once 'race' is attached as a variable to risk assessment of health, and then to pharmaceuticals, commercial logics are also evidenced: the object becomes selling products rather than responding to actual health needs or resolving them, as the case of BiDil shows us.

- Moreover, a key element of how 'race' is constructed is physical appearance. The capacity to change one's appearance through surgery and cosmetics therefore enables people to engage with 'race' in very material ways. Again, by using medical technology and cosmetics, those people are entering the arena of consumption of products and services, in which commercial logics predominate. Skin lightening products are created to make profits for their producers, not to provide improved health outcomes for the consumers. Similarly, cosmetic procedures not necessitated by medical situations are also profit-making strategies, and those aimed at moving people's bodies closer to a perceived ideal type of appearance are obviously part of that logic.

- Indeed underlying the cases set out in this chapter is the uneven playing field of 'race'. Some of the numerous ways in which the concentration of power and resources around bodies racialised as 'white' as a result of historical social relationships such as colonialism still play out, is in what might be called the 'internalisation' of whiteness as a desired social location. How this works in different cultural contexts is the subject of much more detailed studies, but the key point to retain is that the very lucrative skin lightening industry revolves around the idea that paler skin is more desirable than darker. Marketing departments have not created that idea and surrounding practices.

Points for Reflection

What links did Enlightenment thinkers make between the natural and the social worlds (look at Chapter 1 again also)?

How do gender, class and race configure in the reality of eugenicist policies?

How could you argue that the natural sciences are actors in the definition of 'race'?

Further Reading

Duster, T. (2003) *Backdoor to Eugenics*. New York: Routledge.

A dazzling critique of the social and political implications of genetic technology in American culture, particularly in relation to 'inherited disorders'.

Wade, P., Beltrán, C.L.L., Restrepo, E. and Santos, R.V. (eds) (2014) *Mestizo Genomics: Race Mixture, Nation, and Science in Latin America*. Durham, NC: Duke University Press.

A study of the relationship between ideas about nation, 'race', culture and science in Colombia, Brazil and Mexico. Shows how natural/social understandings of 'race' slip back and forth between the scientific and non-scientific contexts.

Roberts, D. (2011) *Fatal Invention: How Science, Politics and Big Business Re-Create Race in the Twenty-First Century*. New York: The New Press.

Critical study of the return of 'race' as a scientific category in the twenty-first century, primarily through State-funded research, pharmaceuticals and the criminal justice system.

Notes

1. Resources are available from the Noongar people's cultural site: www.noongarculture.org.au/stolen-generations/ and testimonies of stolen people can be accessed at: http://stolengenerationstestimonies.com/index.php/testimonies/index.1.html.

2. The two major works are *On the Origin of Species* (1859) and *The Descent of Man* (1871).

3. See a superb online collection relating to the ERO at: www.eugenicsarchive.org.

4. At the 1787 Constitutional Convention, an argument between the Northern and Southern delegates took place over whether to count slaves as property or people. The reason was that they were discussing each state's representation to the US Congress. The greater the population, the greater the relative representation and therefore power that a state could wield. The delegates from the non-slave-owning Northern states wanted slaves not to count, and the Southern delegates held the opposite view. James Madison's compromise meant that each slave would count as three-fifths of a man, that is, 15 slaves would be counted as 9 voters. The obvious irony is that slaves could not vote anyway.

5. Arbor Pharmaceuticals bought the marketing rights for BiDil from NitroMed in 2011.

6. See also Glenn (2008).

7. These figures however need further research as they are just raw numbers. Eyelid surgery for Asians and whites might not be of the same type.

8. For further information on Joseph, see www.jacques-joseph.de/.

8

Mixedness

In this chapter we will

- Look at how 'mixed race' has emerged as a category

- Examine the ways in which people in the 'mixed' category identify themselves

- Reflect on the implications of 'mixedness' for racialisation and racism more broadly

One of the most noticeable phenomena in terms of demographic trends in the West is the increase in the proportion of people identifying themselves as 'mixed race' or 'bi-racial' or the equivalent. While this pattern is far from news in many countries outside Europe and North America (and I suggest not really new there either), it is a point that poses three interesting questions for students of racism. The first is the challenge to existing racial categories in which the State, groups and individuals invest politically and emotionally. The idea of people belonging simultaneously to more than one group, or not, depending on the context, undermines the racialised boundaries that most people now recognise. Indeed, this is a key point advanced in the inaugural issue of the *Journal of Critical Mixed Race Studies* (Daniel et al., 2014: 8):

> Multiracials become subjects of historical, social, and cultural processes rather than simply objects of analysis. This involves the study of racial consciousness among racially mixed people, the world in which they live, and the ideological, social, economic, and political forces, as well as policies that impact the social location of mixed-race individuals and inform their mixed-race experiences and identities.

Critical mixed race studies (and associated scholarly organisation[1]) developed in the first decades of the twenty-first century, acknowledging the very long tradition of studies of 'mixedness'. The second question to look at is what are the implications of 'bi-racial' becoming a bloc in itself, or what are the implications of those individuals consistently finding themselves marginalised by the mainstream groups? Third, what does a growing mixed race population tell us about today's patterns of sociability and about tomorrow's national identities? Is there a classic postmodernist blizzard of hybridity and options, or is it more a case of people strategically juggling and choosing identities on a political basis? While I was writing this chapter for the book's first edition, in 2008, the United States elected its first non-white President, and some of the early public responses questioned whether he was 'black' or 'mixed/bi-racial', which, I suggest, is a false dichotomy. We shall look at what is at stake in these types of debates in more detail in the later sections of this chapter.

We are going to begin at a relatively abstract level, then move on to some case studies from fieldwork. Throughout this section, readers should bear in mind that the discussions about multiraciality/bi-raciality/'mixed race' in the UK and the USA are derived from some quite different social realities and dynamics, which will be explained as we go along. For the purposes of this chapter, I am going to use the terms 'mixedness' and 'mixed race' in inverted commas, which reflects my British habitus, and the lack of really good alternatives. This is an area of contestation in the literature, with some preferring the use of other terms (bi-racial, multiracial, *mulatto*, *métisse*, etc.). However, as important as this might be, there are other equally important elements to this field that need contextualising and attention. The starting point will be historical and comparative.

Historical and Comparative Frameworks

Jane Ifekwunigwe (2004) has worked on international comparisons of the phenomenon of 'mixed race', and puts forward two overarching frameworks. The first is that there are 'four pillars' of international comparative studies, and 'three phases' of attention paid to 'mixedness', each characterised by a different understanding of it. Figures 8.1 and 8.2 represent my interpretation of these frameworks in a tabular format.

I am going to use Ifekwunigwe's historical and thematic framings in this chapter because they represent a theoretical intervention that enables us to approach this very diverse set of writings and perspectives from a position of cohesion and awareness of the comparative dimension. Although there are British and American-based essays in some of the edited volumes, much of the writing in the latter two 'ages' is extremely focused on the national conditions of the USA, as in the sub-field of 'whiteness', with notable exceptions (Parker and Song, 2001; Aspinall and Song, 2013; King-O'Riain et al., 2014). Using an internationally and historically comparative perspective therefore will provide a starting point.

Pillar	Function	Details
European expansion, settler colonisation and imperialisms	Political power-producing	Since 1500. Settler colonisation, in some cases displaced and subordinated indigenous peoples.
Slavery		The process of importing a labour force from Africa to the New World. This led to the economic development of Europe and North America, and the underdevelopment of continental Africa.
'Race'/colour hierarchies	Structural/status-defining	White superiority and non-white inferiority assumed and bolstered by racial science in the nineteenth century. Local social conditions determined whether mixed population would be assimilated or cultivated as a 'buffer' group between Europeans and Natives.
Gender hierarchies		White men, then white women, then non-white men, then non-white women. This hierarchy led to the production of a 'mixed race' population through the sexual exploitation of non-white women by white men.

Figure 8.1   The four pillars of international comparative work on mixed race

Source: Ifekwunigwe (2004: 7).

The age of ...	Themes	Questions
Pathology	Miscegenation and moral degeneracy	What does 'race-mixing' mean for individuals and societies? Should 'race-mixing' be regulated or legislated?
Celebration	Contingency of identifications: 'actor-centred' approaches; social constructionism	What do 'mixed race' identities look like from the perspectives of the actors? What options for identity construction are open, where, when and why?
Critique	'Multiraciality'; the politics of identification	What are the political implications of counting 'mixed race' in the Census? What is the future of 'mixed race' studies?

Figure 8.2   The three 'ages' of 'mixed race' studies

Source: Ifekwunigwe (2004: 8–9, 137, 201).

The Idea of 'Mixed Race' in History

It is in the colonial contexts of the New World that the idea of 'race' became salient as a way of dividing up people by status and employment. This is not the same thing as saying that prior to the sixteenth century there were no people who were what might now be described as 'mixed race'. Indeed, as 'race' is about *political and social interpretations* of bodies and culture, it is these that form the focus of this section. This is why the expansion of Europe into the Americas, Asia, Africa and Australasia is the key moment. In the Spanish New World, for example, the social hierarchies were imported. The feudal nobility of bloodlines, represented in the ideal of *limpieza de sangre* (biological and cultural purity) could be extended to cover 'race' as well as class. However, the practical impossibility of keeping Spaniard, Native and African from producing children with each other (a gender and power relations framework) meant that the authorities responded by constructing a complicated human typology, using terms such as *mestizo, castizo, mulatto, quadroon* and *zambo* to describe various mixtures. This status typology (in which the paler complexion was afforded higher status) signifies the entry of such phenotypical groups into public life. Soon, factors other than bloodlines also began to enter into the social equation, such as occupation, wealth, religion and education. In particular areas of labour shortage, 'mixed race' people were afforded marginally better status than others who lived where there was no such shortage. 'Mixed race' people could, as Ann Twinam (2006) demonstrates, also petition the authorities for the right to be officially designated white, which gave access to more lucrative opportunities for employment and higher status.

In North America, there was no shortage of labour in the seventeenth century due to the indentureship of poor white Europeans and the growing trade in enslaved Africans. The mixed population grew through the planter and his staff's access to African women. At this time, children born to an enslaved woman were the property of the slave-owner, so there was even an economic interest in this type of forced and imposed race mixing. At the same time, fugitive Africans frequently mixed with Native Americans across the Americas. However, laws against having children across the colour line were introduced at the end of the seventeenth century in the slave states. This was primarily aimed at black men and white women, as the opposite combination continued to generate children until the abolition of slavery. Indeed, this was the case wherever there were plantation societies. Ifekwunigwe points out (2004: 16–17) that in a BBC documentary, *Motherland* (2002), which focused on tracing mitochondrial (m-DNA), that is, female DNA, and Y chromosomes (male), a very strong pattern emerged. The sample comprised 228 American and British people whose grandparents and parents were all Afro-Caribbean. Only 2 per cent of British Afro-Caribbeans have m-DNA that can be traced to Europe rather than Africa, while 25 per cent have a Y chromosome that can be traced to Europe rather than Africa. For Ifekwunigwe, this demonstrates 'the particular gendered, economic and erotic politics of the transatlantic slavery enterprise' (2004: 17).

So laws against black men marrying white women were attempts to mark out a gendered and racialised limit to race mixing, and as with *limpieza de sangre*, suggest the basis of such legislation was the fear of threats to white purity. From this perspective, whiteness can be made impure by mixing with others, whereas the other identities cannot be.

As the era of 'race' science blossomed in the mid-1800s, those theorists interested in 'race' concurred (with very few exceptions) that 'mixed race' people were degenerate and more prone to the supposed racial characteristics of the darker partner. Although the idea that mixing between the human races produced infertile offspring was quickly disproved, it was argued that whole civilisations were doomed to cultural as well as physical degeneracy if they allowed such mixing. This was a constant theme in writing on 'race', from de Gobineau in the 1850s, to H.S. Chamberlain (1911 [1899]) in the late 1890s, to Madison Grant in the twentieth century.

The idea of degeneracy is combined, according to Robert Young (1995), with the desire for exotic difference. His thesis is that the development of the concepts of 'hybridity' and 'sexuality' in Victorian England and America was essential to the development of the Western world's image of itself as all-conquering and civilising at that moment in the nineteenth century. While these were elements supporting the push for English cultural domination, they simultaneously fuelled a desire for interracial sex. So the paradox, claims Young, is that Victorian disgust with sexuality and the inferior alien 'Other' is constantly in tension with the profound desire for interracial sex, as played out in the Empire. This tension then 'destabilises' the idea of Englishness derived from the avowed disdain for dirt and impurity.

By the time of the American Civil War (1861), the word 'amalgamation', borrowed from metallurgy, was in use as a general term for ethnic and racial inter-mixing. It would be superseded by the new term 'miscegenation' around the 1864 presidential election. Two pro-Democratic Party journalists, David Goodman Croly (managing editor of the *New York World*) and George Wakeman, a *World* reporter, produced a hoax pamphlet called 'Miscegenation: The Theory of the Blending of the Races, Applied to the American White Man and Negro'. The pamphlet was aimed at scaring voters away from the pro-Abolition Republican Party (led by Abraham Lincoln) by suggesting that race mixing was a Republican policy. In the climate of the day, with tension between pro- and anti-abolition forces, and with even anti-slavery supporters unlikely to see 'miscegenation' as a positive, such a piece of propaganda was highly inflammatory. Of course, it focused only on black men having children with white women; the other groups were omitted from the account. Ifekwunigwe's 'four pillars' are thus demonstrated here: European expansion brought Europeans to the Americas; slavery was instituted as a device for supplying and controlling labour; within the society, a colour hierarchy developed in which white was at the summit and black at the bottom; and within this hierarchy was a gendered one – white men's relationships with black women were neither legislated against nor socially policed, whereas much was emotionally invested in preventing relationships between white women and black men. It is in this context that the function of the rule of hypodescent (see Box 8.1) can be understood as an attempt to protect the line that was white women.

Box 8.1   Hypodescent and National Frameworks

'Hypodescent' is the social and legal idea that fixes whiteness as a pure identity that cannot be claimed by anyone with an ancestor who is not white. Also referred to as the 'one-drop rule', this was the dominant practice in the USA, where a variety of terms came into use to describe people with varying amounts of what was called 'negro' blood: mulatto (one non-white parent), quadroon (one non-white grandparent), octoroon (one non-white great grandparent), etc. This was bolstered by 'anti-miscegenation' laws, passed in many US states in the inter-war years which made it illegal for white people to marry anyone who was not white (a set of laws not overturned until the *Loving* v. *Virginia Supreme Court* case in 1967). As there were no laws against non-white people marrying each other, it can be concluded that these laws were aimed at protecting the purity of whiteness.

F. James Davis, in his 1991 book, *Who is Black? One Nation's Definition*, argues that while the one-drop rule may be the dominant one in mainland USA (thus consigning children of 'interracial' unions to the social status of the non-white parent), it is not so in other places. Davis produced a typology of statuses for the children of such unions, which he updated for David Brunsma's (2006) edited collection on 'mixedness' (Davis, 2006). The seven status positions are:

1 Hypodescent – the dominant frame for the USA, except Louisiana.

2 In between both parents – this is to do with the reclassification of mixed race people, e.g. under South Africa's Apartheid laws (1948–94), and the creation of mixed groups as buffer groups under colonial rule.

3 Bottom of the ladder – this is true when a previously 'in-between' status group suffers economic dislocation, like the Métis in Canada, or where there is strong cultural antipathy toward 'mixedness', as is the case for the descendants of US servicemen in Korea and Vietnam.

4 Top of the ladder – in some colour-conscious majority black societies, a lighter complexion confers high social status which then gives access to greater resources so that after a while, lighter-complexioned people are the economically and politically dominant group. This is the case for Haiti, Liberia and Namibia.

(Continued)

(Continued)

5 Highly variable – this status depends on other contextual factors (such
   as education and wealth), but is found in Latin American and Caribbean
   societies. Davis makes a distinction between former Spanish and
   Portuguese colonies, where he argues there is more mixing between
   whites and mixed race people, and the former British, French and Dutch
   colonies, where there is less fluidity.

6 Egalitarian pluralism – the special history of Hawaii, where there have
   been frequent and successive waves of migration from Asia and Europe,
   as well as internal migration from mainland USA, meaning that there is
   no ethnic majority. Moreover, there is a higher proportion of *hapa* (people
   of mixed origins) than elsewhere in the USA. The status afforded to
   people of mixed origins is no different from that of white, black, Asian
   or indigenous Hawaiians.

7 An assimilating minority – this status is for people with mixed descent
   (with no black component), often with one non-white grandparent. The
   person becomes (in the terminology of the one-drop rule) three-quarters
   white in the second generation, and is treated as an honorary white.

I am not sure that the line between Spanish and Portuguese colonies
and British and French ones is as stark as Davis maintains. In the latter,
I would place 'mixed race' people (with white as part of the mix) in
the 'in-between' status, and possibly, if their complexion and features
are European, in position number 4. However, Davis's typology demonstrates the social, geographical and historical contingency of 'mixedness', which is very easy to lose sight of in the relentlessly parochial
American discourse.

Therefore, if we can understand race mixing as representing a threat to white
purity and supremacy, it becomes more comprehensible why black–white mixing was socially problematic. Simply put, little was challenged in either the
idea of people of colour mixing with each other, or of white men exercising
patriarchal rights. The penalty for even being perceived as threatening the
gender and 'race' hierarchy could be extrajudicial killings, which of course was
the case in the USA, especially in the post-Civil War era. A frequent pretext for
lynching African Americans was the protection of white women from their
rapists, potential rapists, or occasionally their husbands (Wells, 1893).
Moreover, riots in the UK ports of Cardiff, Liverpool and South Shields in
1919 are also partly explicable through reference to this fear, as well as
demobbed soldiers' and unemployed workers' concerns about scarce employment and competition.

'Won't Somebody Please Think of the Children?'[2]

This kind of comment about mixed relationships, suggesting they should not result in children because the latter would be unable to integrate into society, is still heard in British and American culture (Childs, 2005; Sims, 2007). We might, in the light of the preceding description of the gendered and structured nature of social hierarchies, read this as a mechanism for reiterating racial boundaries, in the same way as the Spanish administrators' attempts to classify and rationalise the extended legacies of the newly settled territories: by recreating and reasserting the boundaries between groups as something natural, with social outcomes. Transgressive behaviour has a penalty. European and North American white women may lose their racial privileges by having mixed children (they and their children can be insulted in the street). Black women with light-skinned mixed children (Ifekwunigwe, 2001) may also lose their place as mother when they are seen together. Obviously, this is all in the eyes of other people; such ruptures are social and psychological. By falling outside the established order, people are identified as deviant and then 'corrected' by being fitted into an 'either/or' category.

The marginality of 'mixed race' children and adults (which is one step further along from their degeneracy and infertility) was developed in the inter-war period. Rich (1990) relates the story of the 1930s Liverpool enquiry into 'mixedness' that concluded that 'mixed race' people were prone to childishness and psychological weakness. A similar theory was being worked on across the Atlantic by the Chicago School sociologist Everett Stonequist (1937). His position was that people can become stuck between two cultures, are therefore marginal and consequently suffer identity problems that are expressed psychologically. There are three stages to this process of marginality. First is a lack of awareness of difference, followed by some crisis in which the person is rejected and comes to know their real place. The pain this causes then leads to a third stage in which they choose to adopt one or other of the identities open to them. As Tizard and Phoenix (2002: 44–5) note, this 'plot' heavily echoes those of stereotypical American novels about mixed race people from the late nineteenth century onwards, in which the central protagonist goes through these traumatic stages. Often in the academic literature this scenario is referred to as the 'tragic mulatta' figure (Raimon, 2004), a theme updated and critically interrogated by Streeter (2012). A key work is the film *Imitation of Life* (1934) starring Fredi Washington as a mixed race woman 'passing for white'.[3] Stonequist's framework of in-built marginality is applied not only to 'race' but to other scenarios as well. The point is that this marginality is the result of a dual set of identifications that divides the self, rather than a lack of identification that would cast the person adrift. In any case, the pathologisation of people due to their mixed ancestry is the most salient characteristic of academic attention paid to the experience of mixing in this phase. Even in Latin American states where *mestizaje* is officially the national philosophy, the reality is closer to a search for whiteness, which acknowledges white supremacy and regards mixing as impurification (Garner, 2007a).

Terminology, Contingency and Identification

We will now look at some fieldwork after a brief examination of the terminology. There is no consensus on what term to use for people who are variously labelled 'mixed race', 'bi-racial', 'multiracial' or 'of dual heritage' in English (as well as a host of other place and time-specific terms). We noted in Chapter 1 that the study of 'race' is inherently paradoxical in that the focus is always something that is both simultaneously real (in the social world) and not real (biologically speaking). One of the many consequences of this central fact is that any effort to name a state, process or product that emerges from crossing or mixing reflects what the origins of the 'mix' are. In other words, the source is individuals from different (mixed) 'races'; two distinct 'races' (bi-racial); more than two distinct 'races' (multiracial); two separate 'heritages' (dual heritage); more than two 'heritages', and so on and so forth. Some American writers note the use of the term *hapa* drawn from Hawaii, or *haafu* from Japanese, in specific contexts. However, both these words approximate to the meaning of 'half'. The lexicon of French, Spanish and Portuguese terms (*mulatto, zambo, mestizo, griffe, sang-mêlé*, etc.) deployed in the Americas also refers to breeding, animals and fractions. Ifekwunigwe's flirtation with the French term *métisse* (1999) ended two years later. Indeed, Mengel summarises the terminological bind:

> ... all of these terms perpetuate notions of blood division that can be quantified in fractional terms, and, in a race-conscious society, serve to reinforce the ideology that the mixed race individual is somehow less than a whole person. (2001: 100–1)

While the fact of 'mixedness' challenges the boundary between racialised groups, there is no discursive escape from the treachery of the 'r' word or its synonyms. I have opted in this book to use 'mixed race' in inverted commas, not because I think it is an especially appropriate term to use, but because there are none that strike me as any less tainted by the illogicality of deconstructing 'race' through a concept rooted in the fetishisation of 'race', or what Paul Gilroy (2000) calls 'raciology'. Talking about the social identifications made in a racialised world without using the concepts upon which that process is built presents a significant challenge.

The picture that emerges from fieldwork on the social and personal identities of people classifying as mixed race/bi-racial/multiracial/of dual heritage, etc. is far from that which could have been expected from the 'marginal man'. We will look at two sets of qualitative fieldwork, one based in Britain and the other in the USA.

Barbara Tizard and Ann Phoenix's (2002) updated study of young people in London reveals some thought-provoking and counter-intuitive patterns. They interviewed 58 young people in London with one black and one white parent. Their findings contradicted the prevailing assumption in social work practice, according to which mixed children had to be brought up by black parents in order to feel properly black. Very few of those they spoke to felt marginalised or wanted to consider themselves white. Just under half considered themselves 'black', while just over 40 per cent felt 'both', 'brown' or 'mixed'. This is contrasted with how they are viewed by the black and the white samples. Only 30 per cent of the former and 16 per cent of the latter saw the mixed-parentage people as 'black' (Tizard and Phoenix, 2002: 220). The children's identities were analysed using responses to a number of questions about how they identified with different people and groups. In their search for causal relationships, it emerged that one predictive factor for having a strong black identity was a politicised background within the home, where racism was a topic for discussion. This was a better indicator than just having at least one black parent per se. Having a problematic identity though seems to be related to a variety of factors, from the racial composition of the child's school through to the quality of the relationship with one or other of the parents.

Indeed, the contrast between the young people's personal image of themselves and those of others was an important theme, with as much racism experienced by mixed as by black interviewees. The distinguishing feature is that mixed-parentage young people report encountering prejudice from *both* white and black people. Moreover, there are distinctly classed and gendered patterns to the experiences. Many people with a black parent in this sample were in private schools, so benefited from class privilege. Moreover, boys and working-class students report more frequent experiences of name-calling and other forms of racist behaviour than do middle-class students and girls. The authors thus conclude from the stories told that the experience of being of mixed parentage is more difficult for working-class boys than middle-class girls.

The gendered nature of 'mixed race' experiences in the USA also comes to the fore in the work of Kerry Ann Rockquemore and her colleagues (Rockquemore, 2002; Rockquemore and Arend, 2002; Rockquemore and Laszloffy, 2005). They note that in the USA, there are constraining factors on the identity of mixed-parentage individuals:

> Because the one-drop rule operated as an unquestioned assumption held by researchers, racial identity was not understood as a negotiable reality, nor was it an area where individuals had options. Because anyone with black ancestry was assumed to be black, black identity models were used to assess the racial identity development of mixed-race people. In this context, mixed-race people who resisted categorization as exclusively black were often seen as 'confused' and were pathologized by researchers. (Rockquemore and Laszloffy, 2005: 2)

They put forward a model that reflects the attempts to struggle against the dichotomies of ascriptive identities – either black or white – by stressing the diversity of self-identifications they encountered in the five years of research carried out since the late 1990s. Their model is called Continuum of Biracial

Identifications (COBI) (Rockquemore and Laszloffy, 2005: 5) and is basically a line running from black to white. People position themselves at any point along the line, they argue, but the majority are somewhere in the middle. The position might alter at different times in the respondents' lives. The model also reflects the interaction between social responses to the individual's appearance and the self-image that person has. Rejection and validation play a part in how individuals then see themselves.

The authors use the case study of the light-skinned bi-racial woman 'Kathy' (Rockquemore and Laszloffy, 2005: 11–13), who began by identifying as bi-racial, but leaning toward the white end of the scale, and ended up bi-racial leaning toward the black end. Her acceptance and rejection among the students at the three education institutions as a teenager and young adult had been quite different. The experiences began at a public school (50 per cent black, 50 per cent white), in which she had identified as bi-racial but was not accepted by the black students. In her next school, a private Catholic one, there were a small number of black and bi-racial students with whom she bonded. They validated her identification as bi-racial rather than black or white. Prior to her attending college, she went to a black students' induction course and made friends with a number of her future black and bi-racial peers. She was encouraged by this experience to explore her black side more and ended up identifying more with that element of her heritage. The acceptance of her choice as bi-racial had differed – from its interpretation as being hostile to black people (in her first school), to a normal one (Catholic school), and finally to one in which her blackness could be further explored. The COBI model enables a resistance to be developed against the dichotomy of black vs white, not through rejection of these two identities per se, but through the negotiation of the spaces in between as spaces in their own right, not just a gap between the only two options.

Moreover, based on her field interviewing, Rockquemore (2002) notes the gendered way in which bi-raciality is experienced. The appearance of women seems to be focused on more acutely than that of men, particularly hair, skin, eyes and mouth (the racial giveaways, if you like). The visual compartmentalisation processes of which these women are often subject have effects on their view of themselves and their relationship to blackness and whiteness:

> In experiencing the gendered nature of racial identity development, female respondents reported feeling the awkwardness of not being accepted by Black women yet being routinely categorized as Black by whites in their daily environment. This explains why some biracial men and women develop a Black identity, and yet that process is more fraught with psychological distress for women who feel less group acceptance. (Rockquemore, 2002: 495)

Either/Or, or Both/And?

All of this fieldwork raises questions about binary oppositions in the way identity is usually understood, and which are confounded by the stories people tell about their own lives, and the analysis made of these stories by researchers. There are two interrelated binaries that dominate discussions of 'race', and which are challenged by the array of empirical work already accomplished. The first binary is that between bodies and cultures. A strong theme in this book is of the ideological work accomplished in racism aimed at linking physical appearance to a static and predetermined culture; at dissolving the social into the natural. In this way, a person's cultural scope can be read off the body. This is what we do when we look at someone and think, there goes a 'white', 'Latino/a', 'black' person, etc. The visual supply of racialised conclusions structures the way we categorise. The second set of binaries is between different racialised bodies. Each racialised group has a line drawn around it, inside which are its physical, cultural and social characteristics. There may be some overlap culturally, but in this model there is always a distinct set of characteristics. This way of imagining 'race' is endorsed and bolstered by the rule of hypodescent. However, the research around 'mixedness' explodes those simplistic associations and dichotomies.

Changing Backgrounds, Changing Identities

First, let's look at some observations on 'race' and culture. Winddance Twine's 'brown-skinned white girls' (1996) live in principally white suburban American space and have absorbed class privilege. Their brown skin is due to their mixed parentage (in each case, one of their parents is African American), yet their socialisation has been very similar to that of their white schoolmates and friends because of social class and geographical location. When they move to a different type of urban space and embark on lives as students in a multiethnic context, they reconstruct their identities to reflect their bi-raciality or blackness depending on the individual case. Parents are aware of the possibility of their African American children not being black 'enough'. In theory, culture can remove a black person from blackness or restore them to it. Dalmage's (2000) white parents who live in suburbia take measures to racialise their bi-racial or adopted African American children by taking them to black churches, play groups and other cultural settings in order for them to normalise blackness. Some of the black middle-class parents interviewed by Karyn Lacy (2007) also deploy similar strategies, going out of their way to socialise in neighbourhoods where they no longer live, but where friends and family do, so they do not become too distant from their cultural blackness. So this is not only an issue for parents of bi-racial children, but for those of black children in socio-geographic positions that are overwhelmingly white and middle-class.

Whiteness as a set of norms and values is not only available to people of European ancestry. Bodies that are racialised can be socialised into any culture. If this is true, then, how can assumptions be made about people with parents from different racialised groups? What would be their *natural* culture? Some of that experience of identification is picked up in fieldwork and it constitutes a negotiation between: the image such individuals have of themselves; the image other social actors have of them; and the prevailing ways of making social sense of racialised identities in the places where, and at the times when, that person lives/works/is educated, etc. These identities are contingent and not set in stone. Even when they begin in one place, they can sometimes be read-justed in the light of experiences, knowledge, etc. – this is something which emerges clearly from the stories told to researchers (like those of the 'brown-skinned white girls' and 'Kathy' above).

Before we move on to the next section, it should be noted that there is a very uneven coverage given to the various combinations of ancestry in the existing work on 'mixed race'. The main thrust so far has been the experiences of people with one black and one white parent. This combination of heritages is the most frequent one in the UK, and one of the rarest in the USA. In the latter, it is made more interesting by the position of blackness being so looked down upon in comparison to other identities. There is much less work done with Asian-White and Asian-Black people, although there is some more of this now being published, especially in the USA (Root, 1996; Mahtani, 2002a, 2002b). In the UK Census 'Mixed' section, there is no specific named box to tick if one of your parents is not black or from the Indian subcontinent ('Asian' in British terms). You have to opt for 'Other Mixed'. Indeed, the least researched group consists of people with neither a black nor a white parent, which is a point made by Mahtani and Moreno (2001), but which has not yet been picked up on in any meaningful way by researchers.

Demographics and Political Investment in Racial Identification

The Census is not a neutral instrument reflecting social facts, but an indicator of what are considered as political problems to be quantified and made the subject of a discourse. The categorisation of populations into ethnic and racial groups using the Census is particularly fraught with problems over who decides what the categories are, and who decides who is placed in which cat-egory. As 'race' is a social not a biological fact, there is no consensus or scientific basis for these categories, which means they are open to change. Indeed, the Census categories have evolved considerably in North America and the UK over the years. In the former, as of the 2000 Census there have been over 100 ways to identify oneself racially and ethnically, as respondents are allowed to fill in more than one box (Box 8.2). The starting point of this logic is that 'races' are real entities to which people can choose to belong.

Box 8.2   Racial Categories in the US Census 2010[4]

This Census showed the population of the USA to be 308.7 million, with 299.7 million identifying themselves as belonging to one race, and 9.1 million as belonging to more than one race. This latter figure is up slightly on the 2000 figure. Definitions of these categories can be found in Appendix 2, and more information and links to original documentation at Appendix 3.

WHITE: 231 m (223.5 m white only, + 7.4 m ticked 'white' plus another 'race') = 74.8 per cent of the US population (down 2.3 per cent since 2000).

BLACK/AFRICAN AMERICAN: 42 m (13.6 per cent) (38.9 m + 3 m Black and another 'race'). 'People who reported their race as both black and white more than doubled from about 785,000 in 2000 to 1.8 million in 2010'.

HISPANIC OR LATINO: 50.4 million (16.3 per cent) of the US population. 'Hispanic' or 'Latino' must be offered as options (and), not alternatives (or). They are *ethnicities*, in the terms of the Census. Therefore, people ticking the box 'Hispanic' or 'Latino' are required also to choose a 'race' from the list provided.

ASIAN: 17.3 m (5.6 per cent) (14.7 m Asian only + 2.6 m more than one race)

AMERICAN INDIAN/ALASKAN: 4.1 m identified as American Indian/Alaskan (of whom 1.6 m chose more than one race) and **0.87 m** chose the 'Other Pacific Islander' category.

TWO OR MORE RACES: just over 9 m people (2.9 per cent) identified themselves as 'bi-racial' or 'multiracial' at the 2010 Census. People who reported both White and Black numbered 1.8 m; White and Some Other Race, 1.7 m; White and Asian, 1.6 m; White and American Indian and Alaska Native, 1.4 m. The next largest group was 'Black and Some Other Race', which had 315,000 people in it.

The inclusion of a category for 'bi-racial' or 'multiracial' people first appeared on the 2000 Census, as the result of lobbying by groups such as the Association of Multiethnic Americans (AMEA) and Project RACE (Reclassify All Children Equally).[5] We will look at the arguments for and against such a category below.

In the UK, the options have also grown since the first question on ethnic group was introduced in 1981. Ostensibly, the purpose of the British Census categories is to provide information for planning purposes and to enable the equal opportunity legislation to have a baseline against which to assess the recruitment, promotion, etc. of minorities. Lobbying has also procured representation for various groups, such as the Irish (O'Keeffe, 2007) and Mixed/Dual heritage people whose backing for separate categories came from the (now defunct) Commission for Racial Equality (CRE) and the support organisation People in Harmony (PiH). The approach adopted here is a separate category rather than the tolerance of ticking more than one box (which is the American solution).

Table 8.1   Percentages of each 'racial' group in the US Census 2000 and 2010

Race	Percentage, 2000	Percentage, 2010
White only	75.1	72.4
Black only	12.3	12.6
Asian only	3.6	4.8
American Indian/Alaskan	1.5	0.9
Pacific Islander	0.1	0.2
'Some Other Race'	5.5	6.2
More than one	2.4	2.9
Total	100	100

Source: Census Bureau (2000, 2010).

Box 8.3   Ethnic Categories in the England and Wales 2011 Census

The first thing to note is that the constituent parts of the UK do not have identical category lists to choose from. Here I am looking only at England and Wales, which are grouped together (Table 8.2). The second point is that 'race' is not used in the Census, in favour of 'ethnicity'.

Note the expansion of categories from the UK Census 1991, 2001 to 2011 (Tables 8.3, 8.4 and 8.5). The sub-categories in particular show the acknowledgement of 'Mixed' as an identity, from not on the radar (1991), to a limited coverage of strands within the 'Mixed' umbrella term. Moreover, the measurement of this Mixed group shows its expansion as a proportion of the population from 1.3 per cent (2001) to 2.0 per cent (2011) (Appendix 4).

Table 8.2   UK population by ethnicity, 2011

Ethnicity	Percentage
White	87.1
Gypsy-Traveller	0.1
Asian or Asian British: Total	6.9
Black or Black British: Total	3.0
Mixed or Multiple: Total	2.0
Other Ethnic Group: Total	0.9
Total	100

Table 8.3   Full ethnic categories in England and Wales 2011 Census

---

White

1. English/Welsh/Scottish/Northern Irish/British
2. Irish
3. Gypsy or Irish Traveller
4. Any other White background, please describe

Mixed/Multiple ethnic groups

5. White and Black Caribbean
6. White and Black African
7. White and Asian
8. Any other Mixed/Multiple ethnic background, please describe

Asian/Asian British

9. Indian
10. Pakistani
11. Bangladeshi
12. Chinese
13. Any other Asian background, please describe

Black/African/Caribbean/Black British

14. African
15. Caribbean
16. Any other Black/African/Caribbean background, please describe
17. Arab
18. Any other ethnic group, please describe
19. Other ethnic group

Table 8.4   Ethnic categories in UK 2001 Census

A White
British Irish
Any other White background, please write in

B Mixed
White and Black Caribbean
White and Black African
White and Asian
Any other Mixed background please write in

C Asian or Asian British
Indian
Pakistani
Bangladeshi
Any other Asian background please write in

D Black or Black British
Caribbean African
Any other Black background please write in

E Chinese or other ethnic group
Chinese
Any other, please write in

Table 8.5   Ethnic categories in UK 1991 Census

White
Black-Caribbean
Black-African
Black-Other please describe
Indian
Pakistani
Bangladeshi
Chinese
Any other ethnic group. Please describe

The arguments put forward by the advocates of a separate category for the Multiracial Movement in America and the CRE/PiH in the UK are similar. First, the person can identify according to their personal choice, rather than be obliged to tick a box that does not correspond to a set of experiences that differs from one of the 'un-mixed' categories. It is argued that the binary construction of 'race' in America – the rule of hypodescent – solidifies all the stock racial group boundaries. Self-identification with a range of appropriate labels is conceptualised by the Multiracial Movement as a right being withheld from all who might fall into that category:

> Opting for a 'check one or more' race format over the traditional single-race, 'check one only' box format on the Race and Ethnic Question, represents a long overdue victory for those who have stood for, lobbied, or otherwise endorsed the acknowledgement, celebration and respect for human diversity. What has been dismantled by this shift in public policy is the mythical notion that race is fixed rather than fluid, or that any governmental agency's perception of racial identity takes priority over an individual's right to self-identify. (Douglass, 2000)

Explicit multiraciality, it is maintained, challenges monolithic and dichotomous understandings of what 'race' is, and better reflects the fluidity of 'race' in twenty-first century America. There are also people who point to the increasing numbers of multiracial individuals and couples as evidence that America is 'postracial', a line of colour-blind argument (see Chapter 9) that became more strident over Obama's presidency (Gallagher, 2015).

The arguments against such a recategorisation are based on critiques of the political framework within which such claims are made, and disputes over what the objectives are. The American debate is particularly split, with the Multiracial Movement being accused of wanting to abandon African American political goals and get closer to whiteness, as the 'New Coloured People'

(Spencer, 2000) or the 'neo-mulattoes' (Horton, 2006). Gordon (1997: 67) critiques multiracials for not wanting to be black, which he argues is one of the two fundamental principles of racism (the other is 'wanting to be white', which he acknowledges does not have to be the case for multiracials). Moreover, Rainier Spencer (2006) points out that as such a high proportion of the African American population are 'mixed' in any case, what is the difference in racial logic, between bi-racials and 'mono-racials'? Concern is thus expressed about the consequent fragmentation of the African American population, which might impact upon the implementation of equality legislation and policies, by providing the political right with justifications for deprioritising them. Moreover, as the number of racial interest groups multiplies, yet the proportion of people claiming whiteness holds up, it becomes more difficult to mount coherent projects for racial equality. In summary, the Multiracial Movement is accused of sapping the demographic strength of black America, in a context where this merely means that the dominant position of whiteness goes unchallenged.

Is 'Multiracial' a Unitary Category?

According to the fieldwork, there are areas of similarity in the experiences of multiracial and 'mono-racial' minorities. These can be summarised as degrees of rejection by the major racialised groups, not only the dominant one, with the added weight of constituting a racialised minority. The striking thing about reading the accounts of identity among 'mixed race' people is the scope for altering the cultural orientation that is not available to people who are not mixed (although even in describing this I cannot shake off the terms and ideas that make these experiences intelligible).

'The common characteristic that multiracial people share is that they have had to learn to thrive in a society that does not acknowledge their multiple heritages or acknowledge that they are an emerging community', argues AMEA President Leonora Gaddy (AMEA, 2001). Yet in the same article, another AMEA activist, Matt Kelley, is quoted as saying that multiracials are 'people of color', and warning the other racial communities to 'Stop pushing us out. Widen your definition of your community to include us.' Kelley's comment is more revealing of the ambiguity of 'mixed race' as a community which appears simultaneously to be part of other communities, and comes together around a political objective. This seems to be a 'status group' in the Weberian sense, which in its campaigning for Census recognition, becomes a 'party' (Weber, 1946).

The complexities of the US situation are evident from the many contributions to the growing literature (Zack, 1993; Root, 1996; Ifekwunigwe, 2004; Davis, 2006). Yet there is a concentration on black–white bi-raciality that does not correspond to its numerical frequency vis-à-vis other combinations, and the lack of international perspectives. The black–white dynamic is more fraught with power discrepancies, the legacies of slavery and 'masculine insemination' than the other possibilities. There is a lack of attention to mixtures that have *no* white component. This in itself indicates that the racialised line that is most absorbing for researchers and activists appears to be the one dividing whiteness from its Others. Is this a way to accord more salience to the phenotypical element of 'race', and therefore create a paradox? By saying 'mixed race' is challenging the idea of 'race', do we not call into play the very thing that is supposed to be effaced: the relevance of the natural world (which presents bodies in particular ways), and again subject these bodies to the same visual regime of racialisation? Might this actually bolster the hierarchies integral to racism rather than stripping it of its power to wound?

Historian George Sanchez concludes that mixing alone does not threaten power: 'Racial mixing has never in itself destroyed racial privilege, as the places of Africans and natives throughout nearly all Latin American countries has proved' (Sanchez, 2004: 278).

Box 8.4   Lou Jing, Oriental Angel

The question of whether 'mixed race'/bi-racial people challenge the idea of 'race' itself is sometimes an abstract one, often a concrete one. What are you? Who are your parents? Where are your people from? are questions that seek categorical fixity in a space of fluidity. Occasionally a 'mixed race' person can challenge the idea of the nation, as was the case of Lou Jing, a contestant in a music talent contest (Go on, Oriental Angel!) in Shanghai, China in 2009. Wing-Fai Leung's analysis (2015) of the discourse surrounding Lou Jing's brief exposure to the Chinese and Chinese diasporic public raises a number of interesting issues. Lou Jing's father is African American, and he left before she was born, so she was raised by her Chinese mother in Shanghai. Lou speaks Mandarin and Shanghai dialect and has gone on record saying she is Chinese and Shanghainese.

However, online commentators came to other conclusions. Her mother, Sun Min, was criticised for shamelessness and dishonouring the nation by having a child with a black man, while Lou Jing was identified as neither Chinese nor Han (the dominant ethnic group) despite her cultural indistinguishability from her peers. Bloodlines matter to many of the interlocutors: her blackness cannot be surmounted by her Chinese culture. A range of comments saw Africans as inferior to Chinese and Europeans, and as potential threats to Chinese life. As one social media correspondent writes: 'One can either be an Oriental or have Black skin. Those are not compatible attributes' (2015: 297). Indeed, Leung underscores the much more positive reception that Eurasians receive in the media and Chinese culture more generally, emphasising that it is not the idea of 'mixedness' that troubles some Chinese, as the 'type' of mix.

Others bemoaned the comments and ideas they saw as racist, and suggested Lou Jing represented a modern China that is open and mixes with other parts of the world. The two logics sit side by side: on the one hand, bloodlines trump integration; and on the other, integration trumps bloodlines.

New Nations, New People? Challenges to Theories of Nation and Racial Identity in Brazil

Do 'mixed race' people represent the post-racial future: the end of 'race' as a salient social division? If one argument is that 'mixedness' per se challenges the social viability of 'race', then increasing numbers of 'mixed race' people logically must constitute a more potent threat to existing racial divisions.

In the experience of societies in which mixing has been ongoing for centuries, such as some of those in Latin America, a complicated set of patterns has emerged. Brazil is the example usually cited. However, if 'mixedness' is a majority experience, it does not seem to have altered the overarching social hierarchy: whiteness equals power and blackness does not (Miller, 2004). There is a very large range of terms for identifying one's 'race' in Brazil, and on further inspection, they turn out to be a long list of ways to say that one is not white (Bailey et al., 2013; Telles and Paschel, 2014).

As in many other Latin American republics, the official ideology is one of embracing *mestizaje* (Spanish) or *mestiçagem* (Portuguese) (mixedness), but the reality as translated into policies and actions is about constructing a nation around European norms, both ideological and physical. This has included encouraging European immigration in the nineteenth century (Garner, 2007a), implementing eugenics policies (Stepan, 1991; Dávila, 2003), and the development of cultural norms that favour European culture, especially the features of its beauty contestants (Edmonds, 2007).

In the nation-building story, blackness and whiteness mark degrees of modernity. For example, Weinstein (2003) argues that the state of Sao Paolo illuminates the process of making claims about which discourses are modern (free trade, democracy) and which are to do with tradition (slave populations, degeneracy). Claims were usually made by Sao Paolo elites by using models of development in which Sao Paolo is put forward as the only modern area of Brazil, particularly in relation to the backward, mainly black Bahia province to its north-east (2003: 249).

The short experiment of the *Estado novo* ('New State', 1937–45) which emphasised 'mixedness' of course did so at the expense of black organisation, and focused away from divisions of 'race' and class. This made the space for political blackness relatively limited (Hanchard, 1998, 1999). Black cultural and political movements are quite a recent phenomenon. Yet, since 2005–6, some states in Brazil have celebrated a 'Mixed Race Day' holiday (*Dia do Mestiço*)[6] after lobbying by the *Movimento Pardo-Mestiço Brasileiro* (Brazilian

Brown–Mixed Race Movement), which is campaigning for separate representation to black Brazilians (against the government's practice of counting them
as black, even when they have no black ancestry). It is easy to see why black
Brazilian political organisations might feel threatened by this, having worked
long and hard to create a non-white space for countering white European
dominance. They might see this as similar to the *Estado novo*'s project of not
seeing the outcomes of racial discrimination. Indeed, if 'mixedness' is virtually
the norm, is it so challenging to the racialised status quo?

We have to refocus on the different levels of discourse and experience
that this kind of question evokes. Individual people, as we have seen, do not
have predetermined trajectories in which their racialised identity remains
stable. It is contextual and developmental, based as much on ascription as
self-construction. So, if people identify as mixed, *pardo*, *mestizo*, etc. in their
nation states, in order to have their experience validated, this is one level of
discourse. Some of those people may, depending on the context in which
their status is worked out (see Box 8.1), also be absorbed into a white
dominant majority or elite.

Indeed, this is one strand of Eduardo Bonilla-Silva's predictions for the
future of the USA, his 'Latin-americanization' of 'race' (2002). In this structure,
a continuum of racialised positions is complicated by increased mixing and
variable identification by Hispanics and Asians. However, at the bottom,
socio-economically, remain those with darker skin. The middle of the spectrum
is thus extended but the principal lines remain intact. Some lighter-skinned
people may become 'honorary whites', but changing where the boundaries are
established does not mean that the boundaries disappear. Racism reworks
itself to structure relations in different periods.

Indeed, we may already have passed the point at which 'mixedness' stops
being a threat to the racial order, given the ideological work that such bodies
perform in advertising. Danzy Senna's acid remark (2004: 207): 'If you spot a
Cablinasian,[7] please contact the Benetton Promotions Bureau', neatly encapsulates the commodification of 'beautiful' mixed people who are the future of
the country (Ropp, 2004: 266), and who come to stand as visual metaphors
for globalisation (Sanchez, 2004). Indeed, Sanchez goes on to state that not
only will it still be dark-skinned and indigenous peoples who are at the bottom
of the pile in terms of access to power and other resources (near the poorer
whites, mixed and others), but there is also a question of timing (2004: 279).
Is 'mixed race' in the US linked to America's imperialism, as a result of the
military occupation of the Philippines, Vietnam, Japan, Korea, etc., just as the
'territorial and sexual' conquest of Mexico and of Native Americans led to
absorption within a white-dominated United States (see Chapter 4)?

Conclusions

- 'Mixedness' per se really challenges only the existing sets of categories, not
  the category of 'race' itself. It is clearly open to regressive as well as politically

progressive 'racial projects'. In the Latin-americanisation thesis that seems to be shared in different ways by critics of the Multiracial Movement, you still have whites at the top and blacks at the bottom. The guys in the middle might be playing musical chairs, but it is not in any substantial way that the category 'white' seems to be diminishing through the mixed category, and what Christian (2004) foregrounds as 'white supremacy' is still the crucial framing element.

- Indeed, paying attention to 'mixed race' is a fine line to walk without actually reinscribing 'race', rather than deconstructing it: 'Indeed for racial boundary crossing to matter at all, difference has to be constantly maintained so that the act of crossing bears significance to the society' (Sanchez, 2004: 279–80).

- However, there are personal and political collective identifications involved in this puzzle. People identifying as bi-racial on a personal level and acknowledging their mixed family may also identify with one or other of their parents' groups, depending on the context, as does President Obama. Often their personal experiences include being questioned and/or rejected by both of their parents' communities. The two options need not be in tension but are often spoken about as if they are.

- Once more, in the discourse about 'mixedness', other key dimensions of identity such as class and gender seem to have become submerged as we are drawn into 'race' talk. It may seem an odd thing for a scholar of racism to be criticising an over-emphasis on racialisation, but in the logic of my argument, made throughout this book, I think it reads predictably. Racism intersects with gendered and classed oppression, and losing sight of the intersections of those forms of discrimination leads us away from the concrete experiences of the people we study as sociologists. Rockquemore and Laszloffy (2005), Small (2001), Tizard and Phoenix (2002) and Ali (2003), for example, all argue that gender and class, respectively, also structure the lifeworlds of 'mixed race' people.

Points for Reflection

In what ways does 'mixedness' support or undermine the existing racialised hierarchy?

Does 'mixed race' mean the same thing in different places and at different times? What evidence do you have to support your answer?

What seem to be the important factors determining 'mixed race' people's identifications with one or the other parent's racialised identity?

Further Reading

King-O'Riain, R.C., Small, S., Mahtani, M., Song, M. and Spickard, P. (eds) (2014) *Global Mixed Race*. New York: NYU Press.

Based around observing the changes that increased mobility of people, ideas and goods has brought to notions of social difference, this international comparative text examines 'mixed race' experiences in a variety of national contexts.

Ifekwunigwe, J. (ed.) (2015) *Mixed Race Studies: A Reader*, 2nd edition. London: Routledge.

The first comprehensive collection of writings on 'mixed race' drawn from international sources and framed with the editor's contributions on the genealogy of this field of study.

Twine, F.W. (2011) *The White Side of Black Britain*. Durham, NC: Duke University Press.

An intimate visual ethnography of the lives of white mothers of 'mixed race' children in Leicester (UK), and their reflections on identity and community.

Notes

1. http://criticalmixedracestudies.org/wordpress/.

2. This is the frequent refrain of Helen Lovejoy, wife of Reverend Lovejoy in *The Simpsons*, one of my children's favourite television shows.

3. This is something akin to the storyline of James Weldon Johnson's novel, *Autobiography of an Ex-Colored Man* (1990 [1917]).

4. Breakdowns of various categories can be accessed through the Census Bureau website at: www.census.gov/prod/www/decennial.html.

5. See Project RACE: www.projectrace.com/. The AMEA's website is now being replaced. An archive can be found at: https://web.archive.org/web/20060813110446/http://www.ameasite.org/.

6. See www.nacaomestica.org/mixed_race_day.htm.

7. 'Cablinasian' is the racial identification that champion golfer 'Tiger' Woods attributes to himself. It covers Caucasian-Black-Native American-Indian-Asian.

9

New Racisms?

In this chapter we will

- Identify how 'new racisms' have been theorised
- Critique the idea of 'new' and 'old' forms of racism
- Examine some cultural aspects of racist ideas and practices

Norms and values change from one period to the next in different social contexts. The ways in which 'race' is articulated through the ideological dimension of racism is also transformed over time. As we will see, there is no consensus about the precise changes, or how they are to be interpreted. However, there is a consensus that there is something distinctive about the late twentieth and early twenty-first century compared to the rest of the twentieth century. In this chapter, we shall look at some of the suggestions advanced about what these changes are, and how to understand them, both in Europe and the USA.

We shall begin by looking at three European contributions to the theorisation of racism that have specifically identified elements that are 'new' in the period since the 1974 oil crisis: those of Martin Barker (1981), Etienne Balibar (Balibar and Wallerstein, 1991) and Pierre-André Taguieff (2001). After this, we will identify how elements of what they describe can be used in political discourse, first by representatives of the nationalist far right, and then by other actors, before going on to see how changes in formulating 'race' have taken place in the USA in the post-civil rights era.

European 'New' and 'Neo-Racism'

Martin Barker (1981, 1990) coined the term 'new racism' to describe the configuration of ideological forces dominant at the beginning of the neoliberal Conservative administrations that remain in power until 1997. He links the discourse of socio-biology to the realm of politics. Socio-biology is a set of scientific approaches to human behaviour that emphasises genetics and group behaviours observable in both animal and human worlds, a kind of updated

Social Darwinism shorn of its explicitly racialised element (Morris, 1968; Dawkins, 1976; Wilson, 1976). There is a narrative about natural, primal drives to stay with one's own kind and defend the 'us' from the 'them'. The following quote from the work of Richard Ardrey encapsulates the socio-biological account of group dynamics:

> The biological nation ... is a social group containing at least two mature males, which holds as an exclusive possession a continuous area of space, which isolates itself from others of its kind through outward antagonism, and which through its defence of its social territory, achieves leadership, cooperation and a capacity for concerted action. (Ardrey, 1967: 191)

Barker's interest in socio-biological accounts of inter-group conflict lies in the idea that such conflicts are genetically programmed into us. Racism and nationalism are thus naturalised, that is, described as primal feelings that cannot be changed by social action. Worse still, from the social scientist's perspective, the act of aggression that locates danger in the outgroup is actually explained as an act of 'kin altruism'. Racism is thus transformed from a form of hatred into merely a form of love for one's own people: a refrain used by far-right politicians since the 1980s. Les Back (2002) talks of this in his study of far-right internet dating sites, where he states that 'hate speaks the language of love' (see Box 9.1). Moreover, the socio-biologist angle is still put forward, in Charles Murray's review of Nicholas Wade's *A Troublesome Inheritance* (Murray, 2014) for example.

French political scientist Pierre-André Taguieff first located the development of two parallel forms of racism in the 1980s (1990, 2001). He began talking about what he termed 'differentialist racism', which can be distinguished from 'discriminatory racism'. The latter is framed within an imperial/colonial relationship that understands human diversity as being explicitly on a scale running from civilised to barbarous, and is as much about biology as culture. Indeed, Taguieff stresses the overlap and flow between the two spheres. 'Racism', he argues, 'does not just biologize the cultural, it acculturates the biological' (1990: 117).

'Differentialist racism' then is what he observed in the French and wider European context from the 1980s onwards, that is, a political instrumentalisation of the key terms of the previously anti-racist language of respect for difference and cultural diversity. In the French republican context, talking explicitly about 'race' in the political discourse is not acceptable. The far-right *Front national* (FN) (among others) developed a form of argument around difference ('le droit à la différence') in a cultural setting that implicitly places Christian, Catholic, white Europe on one side and everything else, especially Islam, on the other. This line of reasoning is linked by Taguieff with the far right's other areas of interest, such as anti-statism and nationalism.

So from being the clarion call of left progressive forces, the 'right to be different' became a slogan that encapsulates the nostalgic and reactionary imagining of communities as pure and monolithic blocs that should not be spoiled by mixing. Cultures are understood to be exclusive and static groups of people, unchanging across time and place, so that then FN leader, Jean-Marie Le Pen, can state that 'I love Maghrebins [people of North African, usually Muslim origin], but their place is in the Maghreb' (Taguieff, 1990: 116).

From this perspective, the characteristics and specific location of each culture is fixed. The movement of peoples entailed in the post-Second World War migratory landscape can only disrupt this fixity.

Differentialist racism is not ostensibly about biological 'race' at all, but about defending the right to have a distinct culture (and a space to have it in, see Box 9.1). This rights-based argument is the dimension of the ideas that political groups want to project (Williams and Law, 2012). However, argues Taguieff, this right to be different is really about the obsession of differentialist racism with mixing: cultures cannot mix without damage being done. At the root of the defence of culture is a vision in which the proximity of cultures alone necessarily leads to conflict, and this conflict is accelerated by mixing between people. This process of *métissage* is anathema to the differentialist racist point of view because it destroys the supposed purity of the original culture and leads to its degradation. Taguieff's argument neatly underlines the new and not so new elements of the 'new racism'. While the appropriation of the anti-racist left's vocabulary and its reorganisation into a white nationalist ideology is specific to the period, the theme of civilisations failing due to mixing and losing their purity can be traced back at least as far as de Gobineau's work in the 1850s.

We shall now turn to another French thinker, whose work focuses on political theory at a further level of abstraction. Etienne Balibar's broad argument is that like class and nationalism, racism is on one level 'functional' to capitalism: the salience and content of the ideologies change as the forms of capitalism alter (Balibar and Wallerstein, 1991). In the late 1980s, what he calls 'crisis' racism (1991: 219) deflects anxieties about the decline of the economy and life chances onto migrant groups, so that they are blamed for bringing disorder and economic problems and lowering the West's cultural level. In his discussion of new forms of racism, Balibar begins by locating the phenomenon historically:

> This new racism is a racism of the era of 'decolonization', of the reversal of population movements between the old colonies and the old metropolises, and the division of humanity within a single political space. (1991: 21)

The main argument of the new racism is 'differentialist' (see above), that is, that cultural difference in the world's populations is not only evident, but desirable and necessary. When the distance between the geographical spaces in which the world's cultures are lived out shrinks, then it is a natural step for this to lead to conflict between cultures defending themselves. In this logic, those who advocate the bringing together of cultures and indeed their mixing (the anti-racists) are actually generating racism. The perspective that seeks to keep cultures separate is thus the true anti-racism.

The dominance of the cultural element of racist ideas (at the expense of the pseudo-biological element that had been the focus of discourses of 'race' until the Second World War) is not new per se. As Balibar notes, European anti-Semitism is essentially cultural in character and goes back to medieval times (Chapter 3). The obsession with the cultural field means that the idea of 'racism without races' (1991: 21) derives from this longstanding stream of racism. However, for Balibar, what distinguishes the twentieth-century forms of 'new racism' is the naturalisation of conflict around cultures, alongside the implicit, rather than explicit, hierarchisation of cultures. All forms of racism include the idea that the world's cultures are hierarchically related, in other words, there are some superior ones and some inferior. Although the new racism proclaims itself egalitarian but separatist, Balibar notes that the idea of superiority pervades it, emerging 'in the very type of criteria applied in thinking the difference between cultures' (1991: 24). All integration or assimilation of people whose origins lie outside Europe is seen as progress for the latter.

The legacy of the 'new racism' is that the cultural frame still dominates the language and politics of the mainstream and far right in Europe. Political parties such as the Italian *Lega Nord* (LN), the *Alleanza nazionale* (AN) and the *Movimento Sociale Italiano* (MSI) with its links to Mussolini's Fascist Party, have shaped the country's debates on immigration and national identity. Since the 1990s, civilised Italy (the North) is put forward as having to defend its cultural integrity against both the backward cultures of the South (especially for the LN/AN) and foreign ones brought in by people from outside the EU, or *extracommunitari*. This discourse is particularly focused on African and Eastern European immigrants, sparking frequent discussions of citizenship, immigration legislation and initiatives for integrating immigrants. The 'honest national' discourse, however, can readily link space to 'culture' (a surrogate for 'race'). Sometimes there is a Freudian slip, as Umberto Bossi, Secretary General of the Italian *Lega Nord*, demonstrates in an interview with *Epoca* magazine (20 May 1990):

> The cultural differences are too much. The difference in skin colour is detrimental to social peace. Imagine if your street, your public square, was inhabited by people different from you: you would not feel part of your own world.

This is a statement formulated as a reasonable argument, and one hears echoes of this in fieldwork with white Europeans since the Second World War. The key lies in the term 'different'. Some differences are ignored and others are seen as unbridgeable, and the link between space, 'race' and culture seems very clear. Indeed, a case could be made that this basic equation of difference with detriment, and its threat to territory underpins the newer generation of right-wing nationalist/Islamophobic movements in Europe such as UKIP, *Pegida*, English Defence League, *Alternative für Deutschland*, True Finns, Sweden Democrats, Britain First, etc.

Box 9.1   Not Hate But Love: The British Far Right

As noted above, the charge of racism is frequently parried by far-right nationalist groups with the claim that they do not hate, but act out of love. Britain First's website (2016) states, in the menu labelled 'Racism', that:

> The only people we 'hate' are the *white* left-wing politicians and journalists who are wrecking our beautiful country.

> Our opposition to immigration is based on space, *not* race.

> Britain First is opposed to *all* mass immigration, regardless of where it comes from – the colour of your skin doesn't come into it – Britain is full up.

> Britain is heavily overcrowded – we cannot take in any more immigrants, especially when we have so many unemployed in our own country.

> Britain First is not 'racist' in any way and we do not hate any other ethnic groups.

> All we ask is that if people come to this country they abide by the law and respect our heritage and way of life.

> Just because we *love* our own nationhood, traditions and culture, doesn't mean we 'hate' anyone else.

Love not hate is a tradition on the right. The British National Party (BNP), at one time (1999–2010) the most well-organised and popular far-right party in the UK, expressed a similar party line after its leadership was assumed by Nick Griffin, who brought the presentation of the party toward the mainstream in order to compete more effectively for votes. The BNP's motivation, it was argued, is not hatred, nor is it racism, but love for one's own country and one's own people. Their website FAQs section included the following question and answer:

Q: 'The politicians and the media call the BNP "racist"? Is this true?'

A: 'No. "Racism" is when you "hate" another ethnic group. We don't "hate" black people, we don't "hate" Asians, we don't oppose any ethnic group for what God made them, they have a right to their own identity as much as we do, all we want to do is to preserve the ethnic and cultural identity of the British people.' (BNP website, in Atton, 2006: 577)

(Continued)

Like the French *Front National* in Taguieff's work, the BNP appropriated the left's 1960s language. It uses 'equality', 'community', 'identity' and 'rights' to establish the departure point of claims that white British people are the collective victims of racism and oppression in 'their own' country. Britain First is careful to suggest that it is a multiracial organisation, while the English Defence League (EDL) maintains that is only against the Islamification of the UK.

The BNP's site constructed white identity as repressed, under threat from minorities, and in need of defence. Indeed, 'racism', argues Chris Atton, 'is presented as a reasonable reaction to the imputed racism of the Other' (2006: 580). Minorities come out of this argument as not suffering from racism at all, but in fact being those who exert it against the indigenous population, with the assistance of politically correct authorities and other institutions. Thus, the adoption of previous left-wing and progressive concepts has enabled the far right to recast its potential voters as the abandoned, oppressed majority. This is an image that a considerable number of people seem to recognise, emerging strongly in qualitative interviewing of white UK people (Garner, 2015), and partly explaining the success of the Leave campaign in the 2016 EU Referendum.

Culture, Blood and Non-Belonging

The establishment of an imagined natural bond exclusively tying a people to a place, and defining the bloodline of the people within the framework of the nation state is the legacy of the eighteenth century (see Chapter 5), building on the ideological work done by the French and American revolutionaries. Remember how Herder's natural set of analogies renders this perfectly:

> The most natural state ... is one nation, with one national character ... a nation is as much a natural plant as a family. Only with more branches. Nothing therefore appears so directly opposite to the end of government as the unnatural enlargement of states. The wild mixture of races and nations under one sceptre. (Herder, 1784–91: 249–50)

In contemporary Europe, this bond justifies 'defensive' strategies of securing territory against the encroachment of those perceived as non-members of the nation. By its act of opening the possibility of dialogue (or miscegenation), the transgression of members of the *ethnos* (those outside the democratic, rights-exercising community) into the *demos* (the democratic, rights-exercising community) legitimises verbal and physical violence as a response. The neatest summary of the relationship of 'race' and culture as tools of domination in Western thought is provided by Robert Young (1995: 54) in this thought-provoking account of the genesis of culture in colonialism:

Culture has always marked difference by producing the other; it has always been comparative, and racism has always been an integral part of it: the two are inextricably clustered together, feeding off and generating each other. Race has always been culturally constructed. Culture has always been racially constructed.

What is important for us to grasp is the way that the discourse of 'new racism' wields the power to enact constrained and sublimated violence: a discourse that hinges on an assumed membership of a culture among its audience, the perception that this culture is threatened, and upon a broad belief that 'white' European/North American Christian culture is superior – although people may deny thinking that one 'race' is superior, as political leaders making the transition into respectable politics may stress. They are not inferior or superior, just 'different'. And it is the quality of this difference, its absolute 'unbridgeableness', and its bearers' incapacity to transcend it, that makes the deployment of cultural difference as an organising principle so treacherous.

The vagueness and popular understandings of culture as static enable them to be easily accessed by people seeking to demarcate themselves from their Others. The now defunct US National Socialist website dedicated to Ireland (www.nsrus.com), whose banner heading was 'No to a Black Ireland', contained a forum ('Concerned Citizens') on which the following was posted on 1 March 2002:

> Now the Government is spending millions on anti-racism. How in the world can you lump totally backward cultures and modern cultures in together and expect them all to get along. That's impossible. It would take generations and by then you would not have a white society and you would not have an Irish culture.

The discourse here evinces the usual anxieties over mixture and disappearance of cultural specificity that can be found, respectively, in writings going back to the nineteenth century and anti-immigration discourse since the 1950s in Europe. Moreover, the putative pathological incapacity for intra-cultural dialogue and the chasm separating cultures (developed vs undeveloped) are a synonym of 'race'. Take out the term 'culture' here, and replace it with 'race', and the message remains unaltered.

Indeed, the unvoiced supposition in the cultural struggle is that difference overrides similarity. While it is relatively easy to pinpoint the reliance of far-right political parties in Europe on new racism, it is also instructive to look at some of the ideas that form the basis of the way people discuss immigration in the mainstream political arena and the challenges this presents for society. One such example is David Goodhart's well-known provocative article in the political journal *Prospect* (2004: 30–7), which questions the capacity of Britain to sustain its welfare state in the face of increasing ethnic diversity (Box 9.2).

Box 9.2   Excessive Diversity and Dangerous Immigration

David Goodhart is a British journalist who was editor of political magazine *Prospect* (1995–2010) and director of the Demos think tank (since 2011). He has written a set of texts challenging what he refers to as 'left-wing myths' about British multiculturalism (Goodhart, 2004, 2013). The underlying argument is that first, people only trust others like them so the welfare state cannot function in a multicultural society. In *The British Dream* (2013), he argues that immigration (both highly skilled and low skilled) is deleterious to white UK people's economic progress. As Portes (2013: 7) notes, the (un-evidenced) causal link between immigration and poor economic outcomes for white UK people is now a mainstream assumption in British politics, and some of the support for the Leave campaign in the 2016 Referendum is attributable to it. His work is therefore seminal for understanding contemporary British racist thought:

> The diversity, individualism and mobility that characterise developed economies – especially in the era of globalisation – mean that more of our lives is spent among strangers. Ever since the invention of agriculture 10,000 years ago, humans have been used to dealing with people from beyond their own extended kin groups. The difference now in a developed country like Britain is that we not only live among stranger citizens but we must *share* with them. We share public services and parts of our income in the welfare state, we share public spaces in towns and cities where we are squashed together on buses, trains and tubes, and we share in a democratic conversation – filtered by the media – about the collective choices we wish to make. All such acts of sharing are more smoothly and generously negotiated if we can take for granted a limited set of common values and assumptions. But as Britain becomes more diverse, that common culture is being eroded. (Goodhart, 2004)

The key assumption here is that an ethnic/cultural form of diversity above all others is inimical to social solidarity. In support of his main thesis (diversity diminishes solidarity), Goodhart cites increasingly hostile opinions toward immigration, and toward perceived free-riding in general, as ways in which British taxpayers are losing sympathy with the national trend toward diversity of values. However, the empirical basis for suggesting that people's values differ very much – *by ethnicity alone* – is scant. In the fullest comparative exploration of ethnic minorities' values (Modood et al., 1997), it is clear that there is a spectrum of cultural overlap with mainstream British values as well as distinct areas of difference. Yet the former is much larger than the latter. This is not to suggest that, hypothetically, what culturally separates a British Muslim from a

British Sikh, and both from a secular white Briton, for example, is not important to each of them, but that the assertion that there is so little in common as to raise problems about social solidarity cannot so lightly be assumed. What, for example, if these three were all men, or all women, all from the same town, all sat next to each other in a school classroom? Moreover, Modood's argument (2004) that Muslim solidarity might be increasing as a function of post-2001 attacks and suspicion, and that segregation in the northern English towns that witnessed rioting is a result of poverty and white flight rather than a case of Muslims simply 'choosing' to live separate lives, is borne out by the fieldwork carried out by Phillips (2006) and Hussain and Bagguley (2005) respectively.

Typically, Goodhart refers to Robert Putnam's (2000) highly influential work as an example of diversity reducing solidarity. However, even Putnam now argues that while diversity leads to social isolation and lower levels of trust, both between and within ethnic groups, and he makes two important qualifications (Putnam, 2007). The first is that this phenomenon is only a short-term one. Over generations that situation dissipates. Second, there are institutional success stories that show that such attitudes can be overcome by contact on an equal footing, like the US armed forces. Goodhart's assertion that 'most of us prefer our own kind' (2004: 31), in an article devoted to the salience of ethnic difference in public policy, seems to signify that it encapsulates a special kind of difference that is more problematic than class, age, gender or religion, for example. He then makes a jump to advocating the exploration of a two-tier system of welfare in which migrants access a lower level of resources (which is already the case). For the first part of the article, we have been reading 'ethnicity' as a code for 'race', yet here it equates with migrant status (labour migrant or asylum-seeker). However, the proportion of Black, Asian and Minority Ethnic (BAME) people in Britain lies at around 13 per cent (2011 Census). What place, therefore, do those who are British but 'ethnic' in these terms occupy in the progressive dilemma that Goodhart illustrates? What is assumed about their values being different? Different from whose? Are class values so close in a nation experiencing a reversal in the direction of social equality in terms of wealth and income, that we can assume that the white populations are homogeneous, and necessarily different in important ways from those of BAME British of the equivalent social class? The object of this commentary is to highlight the lack of evidence to back up a serious assertion that both has, and has nothing to do with 'race'. Goodhart's piece demonstrates elements of the new racism: culture is the great divide; the lines between the domains of the physical (colour) and the psychological (humans are prone inevitably to ingroup and outgroup divisions and social action [Goodhart, 2004: 31]) are blurred. This is refracted through entirely mainstream and acceptable political discourse. Indeed, in recent fieldwork with white UK people (Garner, 2015), the cultural heritage of Britain is very clearly seen as a resource to be defended against encroachment – particularly from Muslims, but in general from 'immigrants'.

We shall now turn to the forms of racial discourse observed in the USA as being constitutive of a new formulation. There are similarities to the European forms, but also some clear differences.

The New Racisms in the USA: Colour-Blindness, Apathy and 'Whiteness as a Burden'

A number of American scholars have identified a pattern of indifference, ignorance and disengagement with racial topics on the part of white people since the 1990s (Bobo et al., 1997; Carr, 1997; Crenshaw, 1997; Kenny, 2000; Gallagher, 2003), but here we will look at three illustrative pieces of work, each illuminating one strand of the central problematic: colour-blind racism. These are Eduardo Bonilla-Silva's *Racism Without Racists* (2013); Tyrone Forman and Amanda Lewis's article on 'racial apathy' (2006); and Karyn McKinney's ethnography of white undergraduates' responses to a course on 'race' (2004).

What exactly is 'colour-blind racism'? Isn't colour-blindness something positive to be aimed for? Not in the terms of the scholars who use the concept, as the emphasis is placed more on the blindness side of the equation. Forman and Lewis summarise colour-blind racism's central beliefs as the following:

> (1) most people do not even notice race any more; (2) racial parity has for the most part been achieved; (3) any persistent patterns of racial inequality are the result of individual and/or group-level shortcomings rather than structural ones; (4) most people do not care about racial differences; and (5) therefore, there is no need for institutional remedies (such as affirmative action) to redress persistent racialized outcomes. (Forman and Lewis, 2006: 177–8)

The most in-depth and provocative exploration of colour-blind racism (henceforth CBR) is Eduardo Bonilla-Silva's *Racism Without Racists* (2013). The original was published in 2003, and the third edition is the one I am using here. Like Joe Feagin (2006: 126–8), he argues that there are dominant frames (or pathways for creating meaning available to people), and in relation to CBR, there are four central ones: abstract liberalism, naturalisation, cultural racism and minimisation of racism.

Box 9.3 'Racism without Racists'

Bonilla-Silva's now classic survey of American discourse on 'race', *Racism Without Racists* (2013), is a reference point for work investigating contemporary racialised discourse. Bonilla-Silva has captured the anatomy of American race talk, establishing a set of frames through which people talk about 'race' in a format characterised as 'colorblind racism' (Carr, 1997). Colour-blindness is a discourse that claims not to see colour, only people. Indeed, in this view of the social world, racism is created only by people evoking it. It relegates 'race' and racism to the past and is grounded in the assumption that the Civil Rights Act of 1965 definitively abolished inequalities, so that everyone since then has been operating on a level playing field. Bonilla-Silva uses a basis of more than 1,000 respondents (in two separate surveys), followed up with over 120 interviews. He analyses the recurrent narratives that emerge from this fieldwork, and concludes that discursively, racism is flourishing, but it is constituted through ways of talking about the social world that deliberately and painstakingly avoid directly addressing 'race'. The colour-blind frames Bonilla-Silva identifies are presented in Table 9.1.

Table 9.1 Bonilla-Silva's four frames of colour-blind racism (2013: 74)

Frame	Explanation
Abstract liberalism	Equal opportunities exist, and the US gives everyone a fair chance: ahistorical.
Naturalisation	People stick with their own (self-segregation). That's just how it is.
Cultural racism	Cultural failings, not biology, explain both poor and successful outcomes of various minorities. Why can't blacks and Latinos be more like Asians?
Minimisation	Playing down claims of racism, accusing people of 'playing the race card'. People who bring up 'race' cause racism.

I think we could find similar narrative patterns in the UK – indeed, I compare this work explicitly to mine (Garner, 2015) on England. Conceiving of racism as a historical force with little impact on the present; feeling under threat from 'alien cultures' that are understood as backward; and the idea that people stick together in ghettos are frequent themes in our interviews. This is to note that configurations of how racism functions on the level of a discourse are similar in both the USA and England. However, there are of course many issues specific to these two geographical spaces: a retreat from Britishness to Englishness in England, and a focus on affirmative action in the USA, for example. However, we might think of these four frames as overlapping and mutually nourishing elements of a bigger set of patterns.

Simply put, in an era when it has become taboo to speak directly about 'race' and attribute differential achievements to it, the discourse around 'race' has shifted to one in which it is constantly alluded to: and this can also be the case for black and Latino respondents in Bonilla-Silva's sample, who share the dominant way of thinking for which this discourse is a vehicle.

In 'abstract liberalism', ideas associated with liberalism such as individual rights and freedoms and the free market are used to argue against policy remedies for collective inequalities. Affirmative action, for example, is seen as an infringement of the rights of individuals and the scapegoating of people in the present for past actions (Harris, 1993). This view of competing individuals ignores or neglects the structural aspects of racism that were identified in Chapter 6. 'Naturalisation' is the argument that residential and other forms of segregation are explained by people's 'natural' drive to live with their own kind. This transforms the white suburb and the minority inner-city 'ghetto' into identical products of choice. Cultural racism is the attribution of cultural deviance and backwardness to minorities, which explains patterns of social exclusion that have outlived the civil rights era. Examples of this can be seen in Lewis's (2003) study of Californian primary schools looked at in Chapter 11. Finally, the 'minimalisation' frame diminishes the significance of racism and racist acts. This can be done by narrowing the definition of racism to include only explicitly racist acts, by arguing that this is all in the past, suggesting that only a few aberrant individuals are now actually racist, or, lastly, blaming minorities for being over-sensitive and seeing racism where it does not exist.

In his qualitative interviews, four principal storylines emerge. Bonilla-Silva maintains that the stories people tell about 'race' are the 'emotional glue' (2013: 119) that binds their claims about what that means in their lives. The stories are both a means to demonstrate to the interviewer that the speaker is not racist, and to show how the speaker is positioned vis-à-vis the contemporary question of racial inequality. The three-part structure of the mechanism is first to confess that a friend or relative holds or held racist views. Then an example is given of these views or actions, and finally the speakers distance themselves from this view. The substantive content of the four principal storylines that surround this 'trinity' structure are reducible to the following. The first is 'the past is the past', whereby the speaker supposes an absolute rupture between the past and the present, in which racism ceases in 1964. An overlap with this is the next storyline: 'I did not own slaves'. As the past is the past, the speakers distinguish themselves from any responsibility for past discrimination (even genealogically), and thus inoculate themselves against further claims for compensation or personal responsibility.

The third line is comparative: 'if other ethnics made it why not Blacks?' Here the parallel drawn is between Irish, Italian, Jewish and other white ethnic groups in American history and their successful rise through society after an initial phase of poverty and discrimination. This supposes that the obstacles in front of all groups are the same, which, like the first two, ignores the structural element of racism that was identified in Chapter 6.

The final line, which we shall see in more depth in the work of McKinney (below), is 'My job/promotion went to a Black man'. Here, the sense of entitlement of white interviewees is revealed through their assertion that either their job or promotion was unfairly given to an unqualified minority. In these stories, notes Bonilla-Silva, the minority is always assumed to be less qualified than the speaker. So these recurring lines shape the mainstream white response to discrimination in the post-civil rights era. And that response says that 'race' no longer matters, but the authorities and minorities with a chip on their shoulder make it matter, in ways that are perceived to be disadvantageous to white people in general.

Box 9.4 'Reverse Racism'

The concept of 'reverse racism' is only possible to imagine from within the 'culture of racial equivalence' analysed by Miri Song (2014) (see Box 9.5). Given the definitions of racism we examined in Chapter 1, and the examples we have drawn on throughout the book, it must be clear that racism is a power relationship with a specific history. It is a social relationship not an individual one, and produces a pattern of empirically observable disadvantages among the groups that are on the receiving end of this relationship. From a sociological perspective, reverse racism or 'anti-white racism' is difficult to imagine on a politically meaningful scale. It might be possible in some specific local contexts (access to jobs, violence aimed exclusively at white people for example), but there is no evidence that it is a social fact, or that a pattern of disadvantageous outcomes for white people qua white people exists. However, just because it has no basis in scholarly research does not prevent it being a political concept that has traction, or that could mobilise people. Indeed, I think the '(transatlantic) conceptualisation of putative reverse racism is thus a constitutive part of racism in its colour-blind form' (Garner, 2015: 147). In the USA, reverse racism is a driver for conservative social movements like the Tea Party, and has played a significant role in the rising popularity of Donald Trump. Norton and Sommers (2011: 215) found that in a survey of whites and blacks' views on racial prejudice since the 1950s, the conclusion among white respondents from the 1990s onwards, was that:

> Whites have replaced Blacks as the primary victims of discrimination. This emerging perspective is particularly notable because by nearly any metric – from employment to police treatment, loan rates to education – statistics continue to indicate drastically poorer outcomes for Black than White Americans.

Moreover, the French magazine *Valeurs Actuelles* published a poll in December 2013, stating that 47 per cent of those surveyed agreed that reverse racism was 'quite a widespread phenomenon in France'. This statement was supported by 83 per cent of *Front national* supporters, 58 per cent of Union for a Popular Movement (UMP; centre-right) supporters and 28 per cent of left-wing voters. This is a considerable finding, and should alert us to the pertinence of *the idea of* 'reverse racism', which I would qualify as a mobilising fantasy of contemporary political discourse. Scholars should reflect on the objectives of using such a concept as a political strategy, but should not discount it from analysis just because it is not borne out as an empirical phenomenon.

The question of how living in segregated ghettos affects black and Latino people's outlook on 'race' is frequently posed in America, and assumptions are made about its role in cultures of poverty and dependency. Yet, what happens to white people's racial solidarity, asks Bonilla-Silva, when they live in segregated white areas? The most obvious thing is that they think that segregation is perfectly normal and not to do with racism. The residential segregation is mirrored in the workplace, friendship and leisure activities, and this too is seen as unproblematic. Instead, the cultural generalisations: 'they are lazy', 'they are not like us', 'we are nice people' take the place of interactions and feed what Bonilla-Silva refers to as the 'white habitus': the norms and values of white segregated living. Indeed, the answers to the question on intermarriage in the survey reveal this absence of interaction. 'People cannot like or love people they don't see or interact with', he concludes (2013: 172).

Yet there is also a stream of white people in the survey who question the existing status quo, who see structural discrimination as a reality, and understand that they have a role in challenging it (see also Clarke and Garner, 2009). Contrary to the received wisdom that suggests that more educated middle-class people are more tolerant and liberal, he finds that working-class women are more likely to show empathy and understand discrimination. This he attributes to their increased interaction (as equals) with minority women, especially in the workplace. Bonilla-Silva's other possibly surprising finding is that minorities themselves are invested, albeit to a lesser degree, in the four pillars of CBR. While it is clear that they see racism as pervasive and structural, which is not the case for most white respondents, the 'cultural racism' and 'naturalisation frames' emerge as directly influencing minorities. Abstract liberalism also influences them indirectly. Given this proof of the penetration of CBR, Bonilla-Silva concludes: 'I regard the ideology of color-blindness as the current dominant racial ideology, because it binds whites together and blurs, shapes and provides many of the terms of debate for blacks' (2013: 219). A dominant ideology, he reminds us, 'is effective not by establishing ideological uniformity, but by providing the frames to organize difference' (2013: 219). Why is this important? Because having shifted from the paradigm in which whites were argued to be superior and others inferior, the new form of racism (as ideology) is equally unconducive to solving racial inequality because it allows people to live out their lives as if it had already been eliminated, and thus lets it continue by not supporting attempts to introduce reform. Bonilla-Silva sums this up:

> By regarding race-related matters as non-racial, 'natural', or rooted in 'people's choices', whites deem almost all proposals to remedy racial inequality necessarily as illogical, undemocratic, and racist 'in reverse'. (2013: 303)

Tyrone Forman coins the term 'racial apathy' (2004) to cover what he understands as a new form of racial prejudice in the USA: one that is growing and has negative consequences for equality. He followed this up with an article co-written with Amanda Lewis (2006), whose work on Californian schools is highlighted in Chapter 11. The bare bones of the argument are the following. In the post-civil rights era, the form of racial attitude identified in surveys has been less to do with maintaining actively antipathetic attitudes toward minorities, but more with indifference. First, the increasing proportion of non-committal answers to survey questions seems to hide more negative than positive attitudes, while second, the level of apathy about racialised inequalities outstrips that expressed in relation to other forms of inequality (Forman and Lewis, 2006: 179). There is a correlation between apathetic/indifferent answers on the question of discrimination against racialised minorities and hostility toward public policy measures aimed at reducing it. Therefore, this indifference is not neutral, but culminates in hiding negative feelings about helping to reduce inequalities. This structured and very selective apathy condones the racial status quo and acts against remedial policy. This can be linked to work on prejudice suggesting that the distancing between dominant and minority people takes the form of placing the latter in a position where they are understood as so different from the former that no empathy can be achieved. Second, it depends on 'strategic evasion' of the realities of social inequality (Bobo, 2004).

However, this is all derived solely from large-scale survey data ('Monitoring the Future', an annual survey of high-school seniors, whose sample was around 2,500, and the 2005 Chicago Area Survey, whose sample was 279 adults aged 21 and over). Forman and Lewis go a step further and interview white people in a Mid-Western town who used to go to a high school that was racially mixed prior to desegregation in the 1950s, and who graduated in 1968. This choice was made in order to understand how a group that can be expected to have more positive and engaged association with minorities think about 'race relations' in the twenty-first century. While a few interviewees still maintain connections and interactions with minorities, and are interested in overcoming inequalities, most are now suburban-based and racially apathetic.

The general pattern is one of withdrawal into 'a culture of avoidance' (Forman and Lewis, 2006: 188), that is avoidance of contact with non-whites, a lifestyle of 'not seeing', 'not knowing' and 'not caring', which, the authors claim, is not arbitrary, but chosen and cultivated through choices of residential settlement and school attendance. One interviewee goes as far as to say, of his interest in events: 'If it doesn't happen on my driveway I'm not interested' (Forman and Lewis, 2006: 189). In the interviewees' social understandings, the long period of racial discrimination in American history has ceased, and its relevance has been erased. History starts after civil rights (the mid-1960s), which means that all that happened before is discounted in explanations of contemporary poverty. In this way, the reasoning is that individuals have the choice to engage at school, to get qualifications and to work hard for a living. Not all those who refuse to take these choices (as the argument runs) are African Americans or Latinos, but the latter are more likely to because of cultural deficiencies.

We noted in Chapter 6 that there are historical reasons why residential segregation is so high in American urban spaces. To recap, the white suburban space in which they live has been created by generations of state intervention (through the Federal Housing Association, by lenders' racialised policies on mortgage lending, both described by Lipsitz [1998]), and white middle-class adults' choices of living there. This makes it not only more difficult for minority families to access the funds (as their household wealth is on average sixteen times less than white families [Sullivan et al., 2015]), but also creates a space which is perceived as monolithically white and unwelcoming. One of Forman and Lewis's interviewees expresses shock that an African American work colleague refuses to drive out to her house. The suburbanites then justify this segregated pattern of residence as arising from blacks' unwillingness to live with them, which is again disproved in Massey and Denton's data (1994).

Forman and Lewis conclude that 'racial apathy' is not merely an absence of information, but a cultivated resource of whiteness. It is enabled by a package of socially produced ignorance or 'mis-cognition' that allows people to claim they are nice and have good values, while actively disengaging or de-racing their lives to make their physical and mental surroundings into white places that at best maintain the status quo of racial inequality, and at worst exacerbate it.

Karyn McKinney's (2004) work on teaching white undergraduates provides further evidence of the way that the meanings of 'race' have been profoundly altered in the post-civil rights era. She bases the book on the journals that her students wrote on their reactions to her teaching, and their reflections on their racialisation as white. In one chapter, McKinney demonstrates the recurrent theme of whiteness as an economic liability in the contemporary social world. The feelings of whiteness 'under siege' coalesce around the topic of affirmative action. Students express anxieties about losing out to people of colour in university entrance, scholarships and employment. They perceive that the balance has shifted from a time when there was discrimination against minorities (only in the past), to the present, when the odds are stacked against them on the basis of their whiteness. One student, Jerry, even says that for the first time, he wishes he was black:

> Had I been black I would be a National Merit Scholar and had I been black I would not be taking a small loan to be here … I am sure that when I do graduate college and attempt to trade bonds, on Wall Street, I will probably, for the second time wish I was black. (2004: 163)

The context, as Jerry notes, is of perceived competition: with two strands. The first is that the principal competitors are African Americans, and second is the baseless assumption that affirmative action always constitutes quotas and rigid targeting practices (Dhami et al., 2006). This generates a script that the speaker or a friend or family member lost out to an unqualified black applicant. Indeed, such is the frequency of this script (also noted by Bonilla-Silva) that 'unqualified' becomes almost redundant. The scenario is always one in which the qualified white male is sacrificed to the quota-related success of the perennially unqualified Other.

This sense of entitlement, in which the competition is always given unfair advantage, can only be understood as a result of the failure of the white students to grasp the reality of discrimination at a national level. They see affirmative action as 'quotas', and imagine that there is a level playing field that no longer requires compensatory action, despite the consistent patterns of racialised inequality identified in surveys on employment, income, wealth, access to loans, etc. However, McKinney's students are very poorly informed about the topic that inspires such distress and resentment in them. The knowledge that the students do not have might significantly alter the frame they use to think about competition (although see Box 2.4 for a counter-argument). There are substantial amounts of legacy quotas (for children of alumni); gender-based advantages; and a relatively tiny proportion of minority-only scholarships (4 per cent of all scholarships in higher education). Moreover, the points systems for assessing students' applications are based neither solely on grade point average of standard assessment tests, nor on ethnicity.

The students' conviction that there is no longer discrimination against minorities requiring remedial action makes them conclude that existing practices comprise 'reverse discrimination'. This is not only labelled unfair, but immoral, and seen as running counter to the American ethic of hard work and responsibility. Indeed, for these young people the contemporary period is characterised by meritocracy: open, free education, and the opportunity to achieve regardless of origins. The colour-blind norm, then, banishes 'race' from the public domain. Those that refer to it in order to further themselves are 'hypocrites' or the real racists, because 'what racism is now' (McKinney, 2004: 162–3) is discrimination against white males.

The racialised frame is now one in which white racial superiority is ostensibly denied, and instead, judgements are made on the basis of a bogus collective appeal by minorities for the redress of grievances that are no longer pertinent. McKinney writes:

> The argument is not necessarily that people of color are 'lazy', or 'unmotivated', or whatever other traditional stereotypes are employed, but that *if they are not*, why do they, in today's meritocratic society, request or need 'extra help' in the form of affirmative action, 'quotas' or scholarships ... This linguistic maneuver is characteristic of the new discourse of whiteness. It affords these white respondents and others in their generation a supposed neutral stance in the problem of race: they are the defenders of people of color against claims of innate inferiority, but are also, in effect, judge and jury of the legitimacy of their stories, able to silence or at least discount parts of them that violate today's racial discursive etiquette. (2004: 181)

That etiquette is the colour-blind one that best represents American values. Indeed, on the basis of McKinney's work, colour-blindness seems to have assumed a significance far outweighing actual discrimination: 'for many white people, it is not continuing inequality in current race relations, but the inappropriate invocation of race that threatens American democratic values' (2004: 181).

These three pieces of research using different methods – quantitative survey data, qualitative interviews and learning journals/ethnography – have provided us with different perspectives on how 'race' is experienced and understood by white Americans in the early twenty-first century. The argument is put forward that 'colour-blind racism' is a new departure specific to the post-civil rights era. It depends on a refusal to acknowledge the continuing significance of racism in distributing differentiated life chances, and stems in part from the very segregated lives that most white Americans live. Most live in areas where minorities account for fewer than 1 per cent of their local neighbours, and go to schools where an average of 80 per cent of their peers are also white (cf. the experiences of African Americans, of whom between 16 and 25 per cent attend schools that are virtually 100 per cent minority).

The dominant discourse of colour-blindness also treats 'race' per se as a taboo topic, so that talking about the existing inequalities is constructed both as exaggeration and the unjustified deployment of 'race' to further the agendas of people who are not prepared to work hard for their goals. Instead, 'race' is addressed indirectly, through talk of 'bad schools', 'certain people', 'crime', etc. The aspiration toward colour-blindness, where people are always, to quote Martin Luther King, judged by the 'content of their character', has been ideologically conflated with slow and uneven actual movement in that direction. Ultimately, this mechanism works counter-productively: the idea that a level playing field already exists seriously hampers discussion of what it would take to practically reach that situation, a conclusion encapsulated in Charles Gallagher's concept of 'colorblind egalitarianism' (2015).

Box 9.5   A Culture of 'Racial Equivalence'

A key element of contemporary public discourse about racism is the emphasis on the idea that it is no longer an issue, and when it is, this is due solely to individuals rather than being a property of social relationships. Consequently, in the logic of post-racial racism, everyone is on a level playing field and anyone can be racist about anyone else. Miri Song (2014) analyses this logic, through public utterances on social media in the UK, and calls it 'racial equivalence'. This form of racialised discourse is distinguished by its reliance on the idea that all references to 'race' are racist per se, and that everyone is equally vulnerable to racism.

Song argues that the term 'racism' has lost most of its analytical power in public discourse. It has become conflated with the evocation of the idea of 'race' per se, rather than used to describe a system producing discriminatory outcomes sustained in everyday actions that can only be understood in a context of unequal power relations. On the contrary, claims that incidents and comments are 'racist' are proliferating and actually cloud an understanding of its severity and capacity to harm. 'These frequent and commonplace assertions of racism in the public sphere', she argues (2014: 125), 'paradoxically end up trivializing and homogenizing quite different forms of racialized interactions.'

With no clear public understanding that racism is a social (not personal) force, as a power relationship with a history, it is reduced in the culture of racial equivalence to personal interrelations. Making claims underpinned by membership of a racialised minority group is today understood as politically illegitimate. In this way the culture of equivalence compresses a large spectrum of ideas and practices into one that is undifferentiated by context, history or relative power. What black people say to each other thus ends up on the same level as oppressive practices drawn directly from colonial history. The outcome of this is that we focus not on what impact the comment or act has, and what ideological work it does, but instead on the idea that 'race' has been made visible in the first place: in the culture of racial equivalence that is the racist act per se.

What can the 'culture of racial equivalence' tell us about the status of racism in contemporary life? First, it points to a public confusion and awkwardness generated by wanting to ignore it because it's finished, but having to keep addressing it because it won't go away. However, without an explanatory framework that enables racism to be understood as a complex system, we are left dealing with a stream of single fragments; never a pattern that would enable us to see the bigger picture (Garner, 2015).

Conclusions

So is there anything 'new' about 'new racism'?

- It is clear that there is an emphasis being placed on the role of culture in defining difference, as opposed to phenotypical difference, in the late twentieth/early twenty-first centuries. However, with regard to the historical record, I would argue that the period when bodies were so important to racial ideologies at the expense of culture might well be the 'blip', while the reliance on culture comprises the continuity. The period prior to the eighteenth century witnessed both the development of anti-Semitism and the British colonisation of Ireland, for example. Both these seem to me to be performing the same discursive and material functions as racism from the late eighteenth century. Using the term 'new racism' can best be seen not as ushering in a completely new way of talking about 'race', but as recognising a new historical configuration.

- We have also witnessed half a century of post-colonial developing-world immigration into Europe; the decline of the welfare states; and the economic restructuring that followed the 1970s oil crisis, with European and North American economies moving painfully away from manufacturing toward the service sector. The 'new racism' describes how longstanding currents of ideas and practices have been reformulated to be effective in a different age, with cultural difference as its core concept.

- However, while the theoretical work on cultural forms of racism is covered here, some other elements have been added because of their value in defining the post-racial period: the 'culture of racial equivalence'; reverse racism and whiteness-as-a-burden (but not in the imperial sense). In Chapter 10, the focus will be on a site from which these three elements draw considerable potency in the twenty-first century: immigration.

Points for Reflection

Is there something different about public expressions of racism in the twenty-first century so that it can no longer be described in the same way as before?

In the hyper-mobile twenty-first century, why do you think mainstream attitudes toward Gypsy-Travellers are still so negative?

'Racism is racism regardless of creed or colour'. This is a tweet I received. How would you respond?

Further Reading

Bonilla-Silva, E. (2013) *Racism Without Racists: Color-Blind Racism and the Persistence of Racial Inequality in America,* 4th edition. Lanham, MD: Rowman and Littlefield.

Classic survey and interpretation of US attitudes to 'race', developed into a four-part categorisation of the components of colour-blind racism.

Gallagher, C. (2015) 'Colorblind Egalitarianism as the New Racial Norm', in K. Murji and J. Solomos (eds) *Theories of Race and Ethnicity,* pp. 40–56. London: Routledge.

Article demonstrating how colour-blind racism in its 2015 format draws heavily on the narrative that suggests that racial equality has been achieved in the US in the post-civil rights period. According to this narrative there are no further obstacles to social advancement except culture and individual ambition.

Song, M. (2014) 'Challenging a Culture of Racial Equivalence', *British Journal of Sociology* 65(1): 107–29.

Identifies and establishes an essential strand of colour-blind racism in popular culture that makes power relations invisible.

10

Immigration

In this chapter we will

- Explain how immigration and racism have historically been connected through ideas of the nation
- Look at case studies of immigration policies and their impacts
- Provide some theoretical tools to help understand the immigration–racism relationship
- Suggest how immigration and racism are linked in the twenty-first century

Why is there a chapter on immigration in a book on racism? This type of link is exactly what contemporary public discourse in the West identifies as problematic. For many, framing discussions of immigration in proximity to the concept of racism is an example of political correctness, whereas being concerned about the consequences of immigration is not a reflection of racism. For others, the two are inextricably bound: you cannot discuss immigration in the abstract. It is always about particular people in particular places at particular times, and the regulations governing movement deal differently with different groups of people. But is this dealing differently with different people enough to make it of interest to scholars of racism, and isn't the subject immigration policy rather than immigration per se? The vast academic literature on migration has not always been very clearly connected to race (Romero, 2008; Treitler, 2015). Indeed, while most of that body of work uses other paradigms and either glosses over or ignores the sociology of 'race' and ethnicity, few are as spiky toward it as Adrian Favell, who in relation to migration *within the EU*, comments that:

> Postcolonial theories of race, ethnicity and multiculturalism that clutter the shelves of bookstores and the pages of syllabi in the Anglo-American-dominated field of 'ethnic and racial studies' are also ineffective and largely irrelevant. (Favell, 2008: 706)

In earlier chapters I have set out arguments about racism that identify a basis that is as much cultural as physical, and have covered nationalist movements and whiteness, both of which will be drawn on in this chapter. I clearly do not share Favell's conclusion, and hope to convince you that racialisation is an effective and relevant prism for understanding contemporary immigration, even that of white Europeans within Europe. Even if Muslims are the prime targets in the sights of *Pegida*, *Alternative für Deutschland*, the EDL and the family of right-nationalist parties currently active, Eastern and Central European migrants also figure on the agenda.[1]

What I aim to do in this chapter is present a reading of immigration policies to establish that 'race' is a relevant variable and that racialised ideas of nation are, and have always been important to such policies. I argue that there are 'structures' of immigration (patterns of policy rationales), and 'structures' of anti-immigration discourse. This idea of basic and recurring patterns enables us to understand the trajectories of the policies. Next I will provide some case studies enabling the issues to be studied in finer grain. The final part of the chapter will look at the idea of 'borders' (between nations; people within a nation) being located in different places for different groups of people, and how the knock-on effects of public conversations about immigration also impact on people who are not immigrants.

Who is an Immigrant?

An immigrant is someone who travels to another nation for more than a holiday in order to study, work and/or reside. The International Labour Organisation estimates that as of 2016, there are 244 million migrants, 150 million of whom are workers.[2] While we could argue about how long and whether someone on a working holiday is a migrant (I would argue that this is to do with visas), the key point is that migrants are defined in national law as foreign nationals having to either obtain a visa in order to cross a border under a particular set of conditions, or they are explicitly exempt from such a necessity. The other point to note is that immigration status is not inherited: children and grandchildren of migrants are not immigrants, even though equivalents of terms such as 'second-generation', 'of immigrant origin', or 'non-indigenous' are frequently deployed to denote lineage.

As movement from East Africa into other parts of the world has been the longue-durée narrative of humanity, it could be argued that nothing is more mundane or intrinsic to the human condition than migration. However, contemporary discussions about migration have little time for historical comparisons, focusing instead on pressing matters of national identity, the economy and scarce resources. Counter to this, I insist that the relationship between immigration and racism cannot possibly be understood without a historical overview, however brief, to identify the *structures* of immigration policy (Table 10.1) and of discourse on immigration (Table 10.2).

My argument is not that everything to do with immigration policy and everything that people who have immigrant status experience is racialised, but that all of it unfolds within a structure that is racialised. Thus an approach of focusing only on some of the elements that are not *explicitly* racialised (4 and 5, and possibly 6 in Table 10.1) in relation to immigration policies produces a perspective that abstracts the policy from the lived experiences and socio-cultural contexts in which people actually cross borders and build lives under immigrant status. I would encourage scholars of racism to adopt a critical stance vis-à-vis such literature.

Table 10.1 Structures of immigration policy

First order structures

1 To encourage and include particular groups of migrants
2 To discourage and exclude particular groups of migrants

Second order structures

3 To strategically expand the population
4 To develop the economy
5 To fill labour market gaps
6 To demonstrate that the State is in control of national borders ('symbolic politics' [Cornelius, 2004: 304])

Immigration policy has always been tightly tied to ideas about who belongs to the nation, and why, in terms of building new nations or keeping the putative cultural balance of older ones. Its functions have always been to simultaneously include and in doing so exclude, particular populations. It is not until the second half of the nineteenth century that what we now recognise as immigration policy emerges; with the anti-Chinese and Japanese migration laws in the USA and Canada in the 1880s; White Australia in 1901 and the UK Aliens Act of 1905 (Box 10.1).

This time frame is particularly important. The last quarter of the nineteenth century witnessed the USA overtaking the UK as the world's most powerful economy, and the beginning of its rivalry with Japan. Lake and Reynolds (2008) demonstrate that the Anglophone world leaders and their advisors were part of international circuits discussing the world of global politics from a racialised perspective: Anglo-Saxon nations were viewed as natural leaders and drivers of civilisation, so the entry of Japan into the arena caused anxiety. For the UK, whose main source of immigration was Ireland, and still holding a sizeable overseas empire, the question was a different one: it did not see itself as building a nation or in competition with Pacific states, but as a natural ally of the USA and the Dominions. The Commonwealth of Australia, on the other hand, viewed itself as an outpost of Anglo-Saxon civilisation assailed by Asian Others. Its immigration policy was designed to protect the nation-building project from infiltration: protecting jobs and the nation against cultural and moral threats undermining united working men's associations and the government.

Box 10.1   Anti-Immigration Laws in the Anglophone World, 1880–1907

Some laws specific to Chinese and Japanese immigration were passed in late nineteenth-century North America:

The 1882 Chinese Exclusion Act (USA); the 1885 Chinese Immigration Act (Canada); and the 1907 'Gentlemen's Agreement' (USA)

Asian immigrants (especially Chinese) who had originally come to work in railway construction and mining, and others who had then moved on to large urban areas on the Pacific coast, had been blamed for stealing employment from their North American hosts, and corrupting their morals. Unions as well as political elites had campaigned to prevent further immigration, and various measures ranging from an outright ban on Chinese migrants, through to allowing only businessmen and spouses of existing migrants to remain (e.g. the Gentlemen's Agreement between the US and Japanese governments), via placing a special 'head tax' on immigrants, were instigated. It was the 1960s before immigration from China and Japan resumed.

The first important piece of legislation passed by the Commonwealth of Australia after Federation in 1900 was the 1901 Immigration Restriction Act. Again targeting primarily Chinese immigrants, alongside Pacific Islanders, this Act was to defend the employment market from cheaper Asian labour. The other objective was to shut off immigration except from Northern and Western Europe, seen as the source of the most civilised and advanced people, who were allegedly the ideal population to populate Australia's vast territories. The policy was known informally as 'White Australia' and stayed in place until the 1960s.

The first immigration law in UK history was the 1905 Aliens Act. A response to campaigns by unions and elites, the Act targeted the flow of poor Eastern European Jews fleeing the pogroms of the 1880–1900 period. Some of them settled in the East End of London, Manchester and other towns. Opposition to their settlement focused on working practices (working on Sunday); overcrowding; the threat to British culture; and undermining the labour market. However, Britain had a longstanding and successful Jewish population prior to the 1880s, and the resulting legislation was a compromise, identifying the poorest Jewish travellers (in 'steerage' class), for scrutiny by customs and immigration officials and excluding wealthier ones.

This clutch of immigration laws, passed in a 25-year period, demonstrated some common elements: a racialised filtering of people identified as threatening to the labour market and national culture; and an unusual alliance between elites and the organised working class around a project based on the idea of national purity. It demonstrates the basis of immigration policies, which were unashamedly racialised at this point in history.

The first explicit immigration control policies were constructed with clear objectives: to close down labour market entry to specific racialised groups; to enable State management of public anxiety; to develop a new nation; or defend an established one from external threat. Such threats had been identified in the bodies and cultures of Asian and Jewish migrants to nations that had an understanding of themselves as racialised Anglo-Saxon countries. The term 'race' is not used in any of these policies but they do not make sense without the concept. Foreigners are assumed to be intrinsically different from nationals, but some are more problematically different than others. Also a potential tension appears in the State's need to placate public opinion, while at the same time recognising the economic utility of immigration. The policies were developed as populist responses involving the organised working class as well as conservative politicians. We will now look briefly at how this tension can be expressed in a case study of the USA and Mexican immigration.

Case Study: The USA's Mexican Immigration Policy

Since the war between the USA and Mexico ended in 1848, and the subsequent annexation of large areas of California, Nevada, Arizona and Utah by the former, the regulations surrounding the rights of Mexican nationals to live and work in the USA have changed a number of times. A few examples drawn from Douglas Massey's (2009) study of immigration policy will demonstrate the sometimes contradictory rationales involved in immigration policy in the twentieth century.

We saw above that the USA sought to close down entry to Chinese and Japanese nationals at the end of the nineteenth century. This decision, culminating in the 1907 'Gentleman's Agreement' between the USA and Japan to eliminate Japanese immigration so that it would not need to be banned (therefore avoiding humiliation for Japan), actually created workforce shortages in railway construction, mining, farming and later, in factories. This was filled by bringing migrant workers from Mexico under a government recruitment programme – 16,000 had arrived by 1909.

Between the two World Wars, the USA vacillated between encouraging and discouraging migration from Mexico. Conscription created labour shortages filled by more migrants, but then quota laws were introduced to control the movement of revolutionary political ideas in the 1920s. The economic boom saw numbers of migrants rise again, but the establishment of the US Border Patrol in 1924 reduced the flow of undocumented workers, called 'illegals', from this point on. By 1930, the US Census had a separate category for 'Mexicans', who are listed as a 'race'.

When the USA entered the Second World War, conscription again drew white American workers out of the workforce. This time the government set up the 'Bracero' programme: an indentured labour scheme (workers fulfil

(Continued)

(Continued)

a contract and are rewarded at the end of it). The numbers were capped, and illegal immigration enforced by Border Patrol, but employers were short of workers and hired many more people than was legally stipulated. More than 400,000 *braceros* were brought into the USA annually between 1955 and 1959. The number of 'illegals' falls correspondingly, as documentation becomes easier to acquire. The Bracero programme was abolished in 1965, after civil rights campaigners led a successful campaign against it. They argued it was discriminatory, exploitative and humiliating.

The US adopted a new Immigration Act in 1964, which instigate a new visa system capping Western Hemisphere countries (including Mexico) at 20,000 per year. This produced a spike in undocumented immigration.

Massey argues that the during the Reagan administrations (1980–8) the discourse on immigration shifted from the health of the economy to the defence of the nation, and security. The movement of people was discussed in more hostile and warlike terms, and public opinion began to shift. Longstanding stereotypes of Mexicans as 'venal' and 'lazy' were embellished to posit them as also 'dirty', 'dangerous to America' and 'absorbing taxpayers' money'.

After 1985, the rules changed drastically: the Border Patrol saw a large increase in its budget. Its increased activity meant that the circular, seasonal migration pattern of previous decades was now interrupted. The odds against crossing undetected rose, as did the odds against anyone returning once they had successfully crossed. The stakes of getting into the USA were therefore higher after 1985, and so increasing numbers of people tried their luck each year.

The changes to immigration policy in the century covered by this very brief outline shows that the state of the economy, the regulations imposed and external factors all combine to frame immigration policy at different moments. The argument is never that 'race' is the only variable in immigration policy, but that immigrants are assumed (a priori) and constructed as being intrinsically different from the receiving nationals: indeed Mexicans officially become a 'race' for the 1930–40 period. They can therefore be dealt with under a different set tried rules from other groups.

In terms of the Mexican migrants involved in this long story we can note two important elements: first, the Bracero system emerged from and unfolded in a racialised organisation of society. The labour shortage was to fill the gap left by white agricultural workers; the Mexicans were often discriminated against (especially in Texas), and were segregated in ways similar to those experienced by African Americans. Moreover, the conditions under which *braceros* actually worked were often worse than those stipulated in their contracts, in terms of payment, food and the health risks attached to the work and living conditions. Thus different standards were applied to them than were applied to white American workers in the equivalent roles.

Second, in contemporary public discourse about Mexicans from the 1980s onwards, the important technical distinction between non-national immigrant and citizen is collapsed, accompanying the expansion of the category 'Latino'. All Mexicans, and all are constructed as either illegals (accepting worse pay than Americans and thus reducing the scope for employment), or benefit frauds. On the back of a set of racialising practices that depict 'Latino men as criminal and Latina women as breeders' (Golash-Boza, 2016: 137) the Federal government passed immigration reform Acts that led to 5 million people being deported (Golash-Boza, 2015). Moreover, in Celia Lacayo's study of white Californians' attitudes (2017) to Mexicans/Latinos, the latter are also viewed as a homogeneous criminal, dirty and threatening group, culturally incapable of advancement.

The practice of simultaneously attributing permanent outsider status to citizens due to their perceived links with immigration, and also negative characteristics to them *as a group* is a significant part of the relationship between immigration and racism. It is neglected by studies that focus exclusively on people with immigrant status, and we shall return to this in the section on 'Multiple Borders' below. Before looking at the second case study, of the European Union, we need to understand the playing field that immigrants work within: the parameters on movement afforded by passports.

Passport Power

Indeed, passports are not all equivalent in terms of the access they afford their bearers. The passports of the most economically and militarily powerful nations allow their holders to cross more borders without extra visa applications than the weaker ones. The website 'Passport Index' constructs a passport league table every year, demonstrating exactly how many countries each national passport gives its holders visa-free access to. The top and bottom passports/countries in 2016 are shown in Table 10.2.

Apart from the clear relationship between economic power (as a bloc or as an individual country), political stability and freedom of movement, this hierarchy generates, reflects and sustains the EU visa allocation system identified by Bigo and Guild (2005), where applicants from particular countries (near the bottom of the table) are evaluated according to the risks attached to the country as a whole, rather than their individual application. To better understand the relevance of the passport 'league table', we now need to examine the EU's immigration policies.

Table 10.2   Ranking of passports by visa-free access granted, 2016

Rank	Nation	Countries passport-holders can access without visas
1	Germany; Sweden	157
2	Finland; Italy; Switzerland; France; Spain; UK	156
3	Denmark; Netherlands; Belgium; South Korea; Norway	155
4	Singapore; Luxembourg; Austria; Portugal; USA	154
5	Greece; Ireland; Japan	153
6	Canada; New Zealand	152
Bottom places		
88	Bangladesh; Iran; South Sudan; Ethiopia	36
89	Syria	34
90	Somalia	32
91	Iraq	30
92	Pakistan	27
93	Afghanistan	24

Source: Passport Index: www.passportindex.org/byRank.php (accessed 30 June 2016).

The European Union and the Racialisation of Immigration

Immigration policies are implemented using classificatory regimes that distinguish between nationals and foreigners, and then between different categories of foreigners. Each category is allocated a set of criteria for entrance and conditions regulating their activities once within the national territory. These criteria are not based on 'race' in any obvious way, but by nationality. In the early twenty-first century, for the developed economies, the more stringent conditions are, as a general rule, placed on nationals of developing countries.

In terms of the structures presented in Table 10.1 (above), filling labour shortages and exercising symbolic powers seem the most relevant second order structures to this phase of immigration policy.

So when applied to contemporary immigration policies, what can racialisation mean? First, the official framing of discourse on immigration alters dramatically over time. We noted above that the first immigration laws (in Canada and the USA) in the 1880s were clearly racist, explicitly either banning or taxing only Chinese migrants.

However, in Europe, more than a century later, there are no outright bans on nationals of any country immigrating, nor are there exclusions of people by racial group per se. Indeed, all the EU nations must have equality legislation outlawing racial discrimination and providing redress to its victims. Moreover, particular visa schemes target workers from outside the EU; for seasonal work-ers, at one end, up to professionals in specific areas of employment – such as medicine, computing and civil engineering – at the other end of the spectrum (Box 10.2). Added to this, with the accession of the new Central and Eastern European countries to the EU in 2004, there are hundreds of thousands more white migrant workers in the West. However, we should remember that racial-isation does not depend on zero sum logic. Policies now do not either exclude people completely or not exclude them at all. Instead, they favour some catego-ries of people over others, which means two things. First the obstacles to surmount are not the same for all nationalities (see 'Passport Power' section above); and second, differential levels of resources and rights are allocated to different categories of immigrant once they are on national territory.

It should also be noted that public policy and attitudinal responses to phenomena are neither always 'national' nor always rational. In other words, they do not develop purely due to internal factors, because debates on immi-gration are affected by external events, e.g. the collapse of the Berlin Wall in 1989, the ramifications of the 9/11 attacks outside the USA, the 7/7 bombings in Britain, wars that generate large flows of asylum-seekers, etc. They are not purely rational because different kinds of migrants get lumped together in popular and political debates, so that people end up not knowing the differ-ences between asylum-seekers, people with refugee status and labour migrants. Public expectations of immigration policy are therefore confused. Other UK research shows that for many people, belonging to a nation corresponds pri-marily with skin colour, and anyone who is not white might at certain times be assumed to be a foreigner (Lewis, 2005; Garner et al., 2009).

From this starting point, I would argue that the immigration policies of EU member states have been racialised over the last few decades. The changes brought about under the Schengen Agreement on the freedom of movement of workers, and the subsequent harmonisation of EU nations' immigration policies, have produced a two-tier regime (Garner, 2007b) of EU and non-EU nationals. We could then think of this as having given rise to a three-part division: unproblematic European migration; problematic European migration; problematic non-European migration.

Schengen and 'Unproblematic' European immigration

The Schengen Agreement now has the support of the majority of EU states and it means freedom of movement for EU nationals across the borders of the signatory countries. A non-EU national can obtain a Schengen visa allowing travel within all the Schengen states for a set period (usually three months for tourists). The second element of importance is the recognition by the Treaty of Maastricht (1992) of the reciprocal rights of EU nationals in each other's countries. The knock-on effects are that as internal borders become less impor-tant, the efforts exerted on strengthening external borders have increased.

The most relevant distinction in the twenty-first century EU immigration regime is not between Germans and Italians, or between Portuguese and Irish, but between EU nationals and non-EU nationals (or as they are called in EU jargon, 'Third Country Nationals', or TCNs).

Almost all of this intra-European migration is unproblematic, in that no visas are required, and no local resistance is encountered: British migration to France (Scott, 2006: Benson, 2011), Swedish migration to Spain, for example (Lundström, 2014). Moreover, some immigrants are viewed as honorary insiders rather than outsiders. Guðjónsdóttir and Loftsdóttir's (2016) study of Icelandic immigrants in Norway shows how they are understood not as immigrants at all but extended family, whereas the term 'immigrant' is reserved for non-white migrants.

Box 10.2   'Managed Migration' Schemes

As well as general visa schemes within immigration policy, there are streams focused specifically on attracting particular kinds of migrant: typically those with skills and those seeking education. These schemes sit alongside the more exclusionary elements of policy, and are aimed at complementing it but sometimes contradict it. A loose term for these types of scheme is 'managed migration'. Here, the State seeks to attract people by creating special visa schemes, or granting extra benefits to migrants with a particular profile, or developing a points-based system that favours migrants with particular skills. In terms of the labour market, it is highly skilled workers (typically those from the healthcare, IT and civil engineering sectors) who are usually the targets. In the EU, schemes such as the Highly Skilled Migrant Programme (UK and Netherlands), Highly Skilled Worker Residence Card (France), Red White Red Card (Austria), or the Blue Card scheme (Germany) enable non-EU nationals to enter and reside within the EU. The conditions attached to these visas are usually neither particularly liberal nor conducive to settlement and integration (being short-term and granting minimal benefits and family reunion rights). However the conditions are more advantageous than other visas. Obtaining them depends on high levels of education and therefore typically favours non-EU nationals with enough social and economic capital to have obtained university degrees.

In any case, this managed migration into EU countries focuses on a different level of the economy from the entry-level jobs that were available in the 1950s for example. What is the link with racialised mobility? Since the Schengen Area (and its UK/Ireland variation, the Common Travel Area) emerged as a functioning space in the 1980s, non-EU nationals can no longer come to the UK, find work and then change visas, as was previously the case. EU nationals can indeed reside, seek work and change jobs without visas. Highly skilled migration is now the only way that non-EU nationals can legally come to work full-time in the UK. So over the last three decades, the balance of opportunities has swung away from migrants drawn from former European colonies, and toward Europeans who have access to entry-level work as well as other levels. What will happen in this regard when the UK negotiates its exit from the EU remains to be seen.

At the same time, intergovernmental action has resulted in a two-tier immigration regime in which EU nationals have rights very close to those of citizens. Although this has developed over a 25-year period through a number of individual, connected routes, the overall effect has been the racialisation of the EU immigration regime. White European manual workers now have a vast advantage over non-white, non-European manual workers. Even if someone from the latter category somehow found a visa scheme that allowed him/her to work legally in an EU country, that person would need to live there continuously for a certain number of years (probably five to eight depending on the country), and qualify and wait for the naturalisation process to finish (which means years of paying taxes without having rights). Remember that living continuously in an EU country is hampered by the fact that visas are often quite short-term, maybe 12–24 months, and sometimes non-renewable. Therefore, nationality and employment status count much more than other criteria towards obtaining access to labour markets. The obstacles in front of non-EU workers are much stiffer than those facing their European counterparts.

'Problematic' White Migrants

However, as racialisation is always relational, for every group of extended family, there is a group of outsiders, and in the post-Berlin Wall version of Europe where Eastern and Central Europeans can access labour markets inaccessible until the early twenty-first century, they occupy that role. This structural position (foreign workers in low-paid work perceived as competition for local working-class people) is far from new. Noiriel (1988) points to the problems of integration experienced by Polish, Italian and Portuguese workers in nineteenth- and twentieth-century France, while Irish workers experienced similar issues. The groups in the French case were all Catholic, suggesting that such tensions are never monocausal. While Icelanders are greeted like cousins returning home in Norway, Van Riemsdijk (2013) finds that the professional experience of Polish migrant nurses there is more likely to be queried and looked down upon because of suspected backward civilisation and non-equivalent qualifications. Central and Eastern Europeans in the UK appear to be well aware that they are in a hierarchical position between white UK people, on the one hand, and non-white UK/immigrants of colour, on the other (Fox et al., 2015). Moreover, Poles in Britain have experienced a variety of discriminatory actions (verbal and physical abuse) as well as being categorised as simultaneously hard-working and reliable, but drunk and scrounging (Dawney, 2008; Lee-Treweek, 2010; Ryan, 2010; Moore, 2013). They were also targeted for abuse and violence in the immediate aftermath of the UK Brexit vote of June 2016.

The other group of problematic white migrants is Gypsy-Travellers (Solimene, 2011; Carrera et al., 2013). We noted the history of prosecution and persecution of Travelling people in Europe in Chapter 3. The histories within Eastern bloc regimes were quite varied but with definite hotspots such as Romania (Barany, 2002). Now, as people head West for better opportunities, the responses to them are just as varied. While Sweden, the UK and Ireland formally accepted all nationals of new accession countries (known as 'A8') in 2004 rather than imposing a temporary ban on residence as the other EU nations did, this does not mean that Travellers were welcomed. Indeed, media coverage has been particularly hostile, identifying them as scroungers, beggars and thieves who would invade and absorb resources (Fox et al., 2015), and threaten the European way of life (Loveland and Popescu, 2015). France deported hundreds of Roma in 2011 (Ram, 2014) despite them being EU nationals, while in Italy, vigilantes have attacked and destroyed Gypsy-Traveller camps (Woodcock, 2010). These Travellers are categorised as lawless and unproductive Others with even less entitlement to resources than the indigenous Travellers in each country.

Notwithstanding popular understandings of 'race' as rooted purely in physical appearance, and racism as therefore impossible between white Europeans, I argue elsewhere (Garner, 2007a) that there are 'contingent hierarchies' in which white Europeans position other ostensibly white Europeans in subaltern places according to culture, religion and/or nationality. Working-class Eastern and Central Europeans, and Gypsy-Travellers, particularly Roma, fill this slot in the second decade of the twenty-first century.

'Problematic' Non-EU Nationals

Apart from nationals of countries with powerful economies and passports (see Table 10.2) such as the USA, Canada, Japan, South Korea, New Zealand, etc., the vast majority of non-EU nationals find themselves greatly disadvantaged by the EU immigration regime purely on the basis of their nationality. It is now more difficult than it was prior to the 1990s to access European countries. They have to comply with the criteria for a Schengen visa (or a UK and Ireland one). One important criterion states that in order to change status (from a tourist to migrant worker or student, for example) the visa-holder must leave the Schengen Area and return to their country of normal residence, or failing that, the nearest with diplomatic representation.

Therefore, the old ties of former colonies and the metropolis that had enabled people to move relatively easily to Britain, France, the Netherlands, Belgium, Spain and Portugal for instance, under preferential conditions, have now been minimised relative to those countries' new responsibilities to each other's nationals.

Moreover, even to set foot in the EU is much harder for people from some countries than it is for others. Allied with the differential power of passports is the de facto categorisation of different populations as threats. Bigo and Guild (2005) clearly demonstrate the degree of difficulty that different nationals have in accessing a visa for the EU, depending on security threats and the perceived risk of people overstaying the visa. Effectively for many non-EU nationals, the border is the consulate of the receiving country when they make a visa application.

So to recap, the racialisation of the EU's immigration regime does not mean that *all* members of particular racialised groups have different rights than others. There are of course plenty of EU nationals and people on various work visas who are not racialised as white, and do get access. The key dividing line is EU national/non-EU national, which has come to underpin the EU immigration regime. In this binary schema, non-EU nationals are a priori suspect and need investigation, and must demonstrate proof of their intentions and economic solvency. They cannot compete for work on the same basis as EU nationals because of differential access to visas, and the control of the EU labour market imposed through minimum advertising times before jobs can be offered to non-EU nationals. Moreover, within the range of non-EU national status there is a hierarchy at whose head sit the wealthy developed-world countries, and at the foot are those with serious economic and/or political instabilities, and which are linked to terrorism.

Multiple Borders

I have already alluded to the idea in the preceding sections, by placing border in the plural, that to understand the racialisation of immigration we also need to take account of how borders are of differing types, and present themselves differently for different people. Even something as mundane as going through passport control at an airport demonstrates the filtering system. On arrival at an airport in the EU, passengers are filtered into two queues: 'EU nationals' and 'All other passports'. People in the latter queue are subject to different scrutiny than the EU nationals one, where often a very brief look at the passport suffices. Bigo and Guild (2005) suggest that the border for someone applying for a visa in many developing-world countries is the consulate where the application is made. For others with more powerful passports, the border is at immigration control at point of entry. Travellers on the train between the UK and France are checked while in between the two countries. However, not all borders are equally policed. The most militarised borders in the world must be North/South Korea and Mexico/USA for example, while some of the internal European borders within the Schengen Area are not controlled. However, it is also important to think of borders as being virtual, in that states can activate them both directly and indirectly, an important demonstration of 'symbolic power' (Cornelius et al., 2004).

In Box 10.3 one 'border-generating' response is described. Arizona State Law SB 1070 gave police the right to stop and require identity papers hundreds of miles north of the Mexican border, while other states adopting similar legislation do not even adjoin that border. A culture of checking identity documentation, which has developed rapidly in many countries (such as the USA, the UK and Australia), means that universities, schools and local police are now effectively back-up customs and immigration officials. In places where police can carry out random checks (instead of those linked to the committing of a crime), who is required to show paperwork is open to the officers' discretion. The identification of who is an immigrant and who is not cannot be done just by looking at someone, and this is where the question of the racialisation of immigration moves into a different space. A host of qualitative and quantitative studies demonstrate three key social phenomena:

1. Immigration is viewed by a substantial proportion of Europeans and North Americans as bringing serious threats to culture and the economy.

2. White people habitually overestimate the number/proportion of people of colour, and the number of immigrants and/or asylum-seekers in their country/city/region.

3. White people customarily group people with different immigration statuses and nationalities together and see them as problematic.

These trends in findings, taken together, indicate that the question of immigration is never limited to those who are technically immigrants: it always cascades into the social relationships between those who see themselves as belonging to the nation and those whose belonging they reject. In short, some groups of ethnic minorities have not yet been seen as full members of the nation. This might still be linguistically institutionalised in such phrases as 'second-generation', 'd'origine immigrée', 'allochtoon'/'autochtoon', etc., or by other means. However we might conceptualise this process of recognising and not recognising citizens and immigrants, racialised perceptions play a role in who people think belongs in either category, or why they think that.

Box 10.3   Arizona SB 1070

Arizona is a large US south-western border state with a 30 per cent Latino population (at the 2010 Census). Introduced into the Arizona Senate as Senate Bill (SB) 1070, the 'Support Our Law Enforcement and Safe Neighborhoods Act' (2010), gave powers to police to stop people to check their immigration status; and made illegal immigration (and sheltering, transporting or hiring) illegal immigrants a misdemeanour. This Bill caused a local and national controversy, raising issues about what rights citizens and non-citizens should have, the actual economic impacts of immigration, and above all, racial profiling. The Bill's advocates argued that these powers made it easier to control illegal immigration, and that those with the right papers had nothing to fear. For its opponents, the Bill gave carte blanche to police to enforce immigration checks in a racist pattern, by making anyone looking 'Latino' fair game. Indeed, work on the impact that raids on Latino districts, workplaces and schools (Romero, 2011) actually had indicated that these raids were a source of insecurity, fear and resentment. Indeed, national public opinion according to opinion polls stood at 60:40 in favour of the Bill.

The Bill was challenged by the Department of Justice later in 2010, and in the Supreme Court decision, *Arizona* v. *USA* (2012), some elements of SB 1070 were struck down. However, the capacity to investigate immigration status for those detained if there is 'probable cause', remains. Moreover, other states later introduced versions of SB 1070. Most of these Bills were defeated at state level, but some remain on the books, including the even stricter Alabama Law HB 56 (2011). The Alabama state line is more than 800 miles from the Mexican border.

Making Immigrants into Objects of Fear

The story of Mexicans in the US is illustrative of the changes that immigration policy produces: sometimes increasing mobility, sometimes reducing it, always creating categories of people and placing those categories under different kinds of regulations. However, as part of this categorisation process, ideas of immigrants as fundamentally different from 'us' in the receiving nation, and of immigrants as undesirable bodies encroaching on 'our' space are standard features of discourses on immigration. Indeed we can see that the first rule of the structures of anti-immigration discourse (Table 10.3) is that immigrants are utterly different from 'us', whoever the 'us' may be. These structures of anti-immigration, reproduced with minor variations in different geographical, political and historical contexts, are profoundly racialising or lend themselves to that process. They can be summarised as a set of claims, as shown in Table 10.3.

Table 10.3   Discursive anti-immigration structures

Claim
Immigrants take jobs from nationals
Immigrants absorb welfare that should be given to nationals
Immigrants cause increased pressure on public resources
Immigrants have more children than nationals
Immigrants bring crime (especially violence, prostitution, child abuse)
Immigrants' (less-developed) cultures threaten the existing national one
Immigrants bring disease

We will look at two examples of discourse surrounding immigrants: Resident Koreans in Japan and asylum-seekers in provincial England. Such discourses are of course prevalent not only in the West. It is important to understand that these discourses are not just words, but that they are part of practices in which material resources are also denied, and the subordinated group's relationships to power are more tenuous than that of the group making the claims. In other words, they are grounded in unequal power relations.

Japan: *Zaitokukai* vs *Zainichi*

In 2009, the Japanese anti-immigration campaigning group *Zaitokukai* made headlines by demonstrating on a park outside a Korean school. Speakers using megaphones addressed the school staff and children in insulting terms and linked them to foreign policy tensions between North Korea and Japan, as well as 'reclaiming' the park that had been used as playing fields by the school pupils, for Japanese territory (Itagaki, 2015). This was part of a series of demonstrations in various Japanese cities, against 'Resident Koreans' (*zainichi*) whose status is that of permanent residents but not citizens (denizens). A social movement of opposition began to develop (Tsutsui and Shin, 2008). Five elements of this situation are instructive for us: Japan's relationship to the idea of 'race'; Japan's colonial past; Resident Koreans' status in Japanese society; the Resident Koreans' actual position; and some overlaps with contemporary tensions elsewhere (North America and Europe).

Japan's Relationship to the Idea of 'Race'

As noted in Box 5.4, Japan had a twentieth-century empire including all of Korea (1910–45), parts of China (Manchuria, 1931, Inner Mongolia, 1936, Nanjing and other areas 1937–47) plus territory occupied in South East Asia in the Second World War. The Japanese ruling classes were feudal and the Emperor was viewed as a godlike person (much as European monarchs prior to the French Revolution). In this context, ideas of noble breeding were widespread, and the idea of Japanese exceptionalism and the purity of the race flourished (Armstrong, 1989). Although the colonies were understood as being part of the Japanese family, this family was an extended one, with the Koreans and Chinese seen as of inferior stock and civilisation, and thus distinct from the Japanese. The Japanese saw themselves as both more cultured and better bred than their imperial peoples; again, much as those at the heart of other empires. It is important to keep this in mind when looking at the *Zaitokukai* response to *zainichi*.

During the colonial period, 2 million Koreans came to work in Japan. Although most returned after the Second World War, around 600,000 stayed on (Itagaki, 2015). These *zainichi* ended up typically in the lowest-paid work and the worst quality housing (Tsutsui and Shin, 2008). Self-help organisations for North and South Koreans evolved, and they campaigned together on issues such as citizenship and pensions. However, these two communities differed in their take-up of Japanese education. South Koreans integrated into the Japanese system, campaigning to have Korean taught as a language in the curriculum, while North Koreans preferred to run their own schools, using Korean as one of the languages of teaching, as well as studying Korean culture (Tsutsui and Shin, 2008).

Resident Koreans occupied an intermediate status between Japanese citizens and immigrant workers (mainly from other Asian states and African countries, referred to as *sangokujin* [developing-world nationals]) (Eisenberg, 2009). It is interesting that at the moment when the *Zaitokukai* begins to raise its profile and engage in more focused activities, enabled by internet technology, the Resident Koreans' actual position is of increasing integration into Japanese society since the 1990s (e.g. upward mobility and higher rates of intermarriage). The school and its surrounding territory form the focus of that escapade, according to Itagaki (2015), because of the revival of Japanese nationalism in the twenty-first century. Japanese nationalists have revised history to show Japan in a more favourable light. The Chinese are claimed to have exaggerated or even invented the Japanese army's excesses in Nanjing, and the Koreans similarly exaggerate the question of the 'comfort girls' (women forced into prostitution for the use of the Japanese armed forces). Moreover, North Korea's abduction of Japanese citizens fuels the *Zaitokukai* onslaught on Korean schools. So in this view, Japan is actually the victim, and the nationalists are defending its honour (Itagaki, 2015).

We might draw some parallels between the Japanese and contemporary European and North American cases, although the mainstream conceptions of 'race' differ. The Japanese one is explicitly to do with bloodlines and culture: a pure nation striving to maintain its level of civilisation and culture against relatively backward migrant cultures dragging it down. However, the battle of cultures and civilisations is a familiar element of anti-immigrant and anti-multiculturalism discourses (Lentin and Titley, 2011) engaged in by a variety of actors from fringe right-wing nationalist groups through to senior politicians and US presidential candidates.

However, although they are structurally at a disadvantage (as non-citizens), even the Resident Koreans have more rights than the asylum-seekers in provincial England to whom we will turn next.

Box 10.4   Asylum and Detention

Asylum has always been a distinct stream within immigration: its driver is political instability, and its regulations are international rather than national. The United Nations High Commission for Refugees (UNHCR) is responsible for keeping figures. The way it divides up the population 'of concern' to the UNHCR includes refugees, and asylum-seekers as well as internally displaced and stateless persons (see Appendix 5 for UNHCR definitions). The population of concern numbered over 65 million as of 30 June 2016, with 21 million refugees.

Despite discourses in various Western countries that lament the rising numbers of asylum-seekers, the majority of them reach only as far as a neighbouring developing-world country. Only 6 per cent of the 65 million displaced persons are hosted in Europe and 12 per cent in the Americas. Effectively the map of asylum source and host countries and other conflicts is virtually a map of political instability, wars and other conflicts. In 2016, the largest source countries were Syria, Afghanistan and Somalia (each sending more than 1 million people), while the biggest refugee-housing countries are Turkey, Pakistan, Lebanon (all hosting more than 1 million), Iran, Ethiopia and Jordan.

The number of asylum-seekers reaching Europe or Australia then is actually a very small fraction of the total. However, increasingly harsh asylum regimes in the West have been constructed since the 1990s, as numbers grew due to the collapse of the Iron Curtain, civil wars, the War on Terror, and various associated regime changes. Asylum-seekers are now seen in Europe and Australia, at least, as problematic and to be dealt with through a different stream of policy that is aimed at deterring others.

Detention is now an established part of this policy in the UK, the US and Australia (Aas and Bosworth, 2013), and deportation is increasingly linked to minor infractions in the USA (Golash-Boza, 2015). Asylum-seekers have not committed or been charged with committing a crime, yet many are held in detention at any given moment. This can be in purpose-built centres, old hotels and motels, private rented accommodation, or in camps. Camps on islands are a particular feature of the global response to asylum, which Alison Mountz (2011) calls the 'enforcement archipelago'. Asylum-seekers are effectively subject to a parallel legal, welfare and penal system. They are overwhelmingly from developing-world countries and are racialised as part of the process of becoming a 'refugee' (as can be seen in the English example below). Different types of detention (offshore, onshore, centre) and the regime that controls the holding space impact differently on different categories of person in terms of security, vulnerability to attack, and mental health issues. There is an overlap between the growing detention population (some of them literally held in prisons), the Prison Industrial Complex (Box 6.4), the privatisation of detention and incarceration, and the European 'migration crisis' (Box 10.5).

Racialising Asylum-Seekers

Asylum-seekers themselves are relatively powerless, being dealt with under different regulations from citizens, and indeed, often subject to more draconian measures than other categories of migrant. In some countries, asylum-seekers are held in detention centres or camps, with very ill-defined timelines for having applications processed. Those in the case we are going to examine are not. They are housed in different places around the city of Bristol in South-West England. Although the example is from 2003–4, it still demonstrates link between attitudes and power.

The UK government began its policy of 'dispersal' in 2000. The objective was to alleviate the concentration of asylum-seekers being held or housed in the areas immediately surrounding the ports and airports of South-East England. As part of the plan for dispersal, the purpose of some government buildings was changed to turn them into asylum holding centres. In the town of Portishead, near Bristol, in 2004, an office space on a small industrial estate was taken over by the Ministry of Defence for use as an asylum processing centre; in other words, a place where asylum-seekers were to go and obtain ID, have interviews about their cases, etc. Because the building's use had changed purpose, the local authority had to open a public consultation, during which around 200 communications were submitted by the public. More than 90 per cent were against the asylum-seekers coming to Portishead. My article on this process (Garner, 2013) goes into detail (for a summary see Table 10.4), but here we can identify three illustrative elements:

1. Asylum-seekers are characterised as one homogeneous mass (despite the diversity of the people from Asia, Africa, South America, the Middle East and Europe). It should be noted that no asylum-seekers had come to the centre at the time these protests were registered.

2. The racialisation of the asylum-seekers (an a priori very diverse group) is relational. In other words in the discourse of the protest letters, 'they' are constructed unlike 'us'.

3. The focus of the protestors' engagement with the proposed office is based around two elements. The first are sets of arguments saying that there is insufficient infrastructure to deal with the people coming to a semi-rural location; and second, a depiction of asylum-seekers in which they are culturally deficient in a number of ways that will bring negative experiences to the locals. People say explicitly that asylum-seekers do not belong in the quiet, family-oriented semi-rural space and should remain in cities. The racialisation process is thus indirect, using proxies, as in Eduardo Bonilla-Silva's (2013) famous formulation of 'racism without racists'.

Table 10.4 Summary of binary relational discourse about asylum-seekers in Portishead, UK (drawn from Garner, 2013)

Portishead residents	Asylum-seekers
'us'	'them'
quiet	noisy
safe	dangerous
wealthy	poor
hardworking	lazy
taxpayers	scroungers
law-abiding	criminal
ethical	unethical

Indeed, although the Portishead citizens claim that they are the victims of government policy and their rights are not being respected, even this exercise of citizens' rights is also a demonstration of the protestors' power to judge the asylum-seekers, and to define them in a number of negative ways. The asylum-seekers have no voice in this process: they are merely dispersed and will have to travel to the office in order to progress their cases.

Finally, a more generalisable point about the way people make the identities of less powerful people is that like the Japanese protestors discussed above, the people in Portishead – and other places in England (Modell, 2004; Hubbard, 2005) – have come to occupy a victim position even though ostensibly they have more resources (power, rights, security and options) than those against whom they are protesting. Indeed, immigrants of all kinds trigger powerful emotional responses about threats, risk and security among those who have much more security than the groups against which they protest.

Box 10.5 European 'Migration Crisis'

Before 2014, people had literally been dying to get into Europe for decades (just as they had been dying to get into the USA from the South). NGOs collecting figures suggested around two to three deaths per day as an average for the period between 1990 and 2010. However in the post-2014 period, this figure has risen to more than 10 per day according to the International Organization for Migration (Brian and Laczko, 2014).

The 'migration crisis' began in 2014, when the number of asylum applications more than doubled compared to the previous few years, and almost returned to its peak level of 1992 (more than 600,000), which doubled again in 2015. The crisis is fuelled by instability, as can be seen in the top three nationalities represented in the asylum-seeking population in Europe: Syrian, Iraqi and Afghan. All these are war zones, and the latter two are experiencing wars initiated by Western powers this century. Moreover, the development of IS, and the collapse of Syrian and Libyan civil society have accelerated movement out of the Middle East: there have simultaneously been fewer barriers to movement, and more reason to move.

The response from EU nations has been to work clearly within the 'us'/'them' binary, identifying migrants as security threats, and aiming to process them on the external borders of Europe in the Balkans, Hungary, the Greek islands and Turkey. This experience is cast in public discourse in terms of a 'migrant crisis' because the mobile people fleeing disorder are racialised as a mass of undeserving, dangerous, potential criminals, just like the asylum-seekers in provincial England (Garner, 2013). It should be underlined that the fact that these asylum-seekers do not belong to one racialised group in no way discounts the response from being racist. The diverse group is understood as a homogeneous mass with specific characteristics. This message is illustrated in then UKIP leader Nigel Farage's 'Leave' poster during the EU Referendum of June 2016, in which a long line of refugees is depicted, with the words 'Breaking Point' superimposed on it.

Moreover, after Italy's abandonment of Operation Mare Nostrum (a navy exercise aimed at preventing drownings and turning back boats) in 2014, the EU's underfunded and piecemeal replacement has allowed thousands of potentially preventable deaths in the Mediterranean Sea. This lukewarm response to serious safety issues suggests that the lives of such migrants hold less value for EU nations than those of their own citizens, a phenomenon of anti-empathy that, in relation to the construction of stereotypes about African American women absorbing welfare (Hancock, 2004) and the killing of young African American men in the USA (Hancock, 2012), Ange-Marie Hancock calls 'the politics of disgust'.

While the political discourse on the 'migrant crisis' is studded with references to the resources required to deal with the large numbers of people, the discursive structures within which this discussion takes place are the classic ones we have already noted in Table 10.1. The structures engaged with by European governments (although the picture in European civil society seems much more fluid) lie firmly in the exclusionary category, aimed at filtering less desirable bodies out of national space. Moreover, these bodies are first made less desirable through racialisation. When they are framed repeatedly as dangerous, disease-ridden, lazy and needy, it is not surprising that an 'affective economy' (Ahmed, 2004) develops in which these migrants become the source of a crisis rather than a symptom of one.

Conclusion: Immigration Structures, Borders and Belonging

- We began by arguing that immigration regimes are racialised and intensely political, in that they are founded in and help reproduce global and national social hierarchies. Although they reflect and bear the precise social and historical baggage of the nation that makes them, they all fit within the structures set out in Table 10.1. Their rationale and objectives are to produce certain outcomes in the receiving society's demography and/or economy.

- The ways in which these structures work is through the production and reproduction of different kinds of borders: physical and geographical ones; regulatory ones; and discursive ones.

- It seems an obvious point, but immigration regimes are influenced by physical and geographical borders. Some borders are militarised, while others are not. Some borders are more police-able than others, typically sea borders are harder to control than land ones, but even there geographical features such as mountains, rivers and deserts have an impact on how thoroughly a border can be controlled. Decisions about policing borders are political ones in that government and cross-government agencies are funded by taxation.

- Many Europeans and North Americans are used to crossing borders on land, at ports or at airport customs and immigration checks. However for people whose passports are less powerful, it is rare to reach that physical border without having passed through some other process, such as applying for a visa at a consulate. Regulatory borders (where identity checks of various kinds are carried out) can also be devised so that they occur at different points of interaction with agencies and institutions, like a health service or a university, and these apply to students, workers, patients. As we saw in the Arizona SB 1070 example, such regulatory borders are highly political and have significant impact as they usually fall disproportionately on some groups of people (which is of course the point of them).

- Discursive borders are less controllable than the first two, as the State may initiate or respond to the borders people make when they talk about who belongs and who does not belong to the nation, in different ways. In the scholarly work on racism, there is an important section of literature on the way people racialise themselves and other groups by talking about them as having particular types of characteristics which do/do not fit into the nation's putative range of characteristics. Many references to this work have been made throughout this book. In terms of immigration the key point to retain is that when people refer to immigrants/immigration, we do not know exactly what they are talking about (Ford et al., 2012); and second, they often include people who are not immigrants in discussions about belonging. In this case, the non-immigrants – who are discursively tagged with such phrases as 'of immigrant origin', 'ethnic minorities', 'second-generation migrants', or some equivalent in each language – are actively racialised in this dis-cursive act. As I argue elsewhere (Garner, 2015), racial identity becomes, in Sara Ahmed's (2004) terms, 'stuck to' the topic of immigration through the repetition of ideas.

- Thinking about these three types of borders in relation to each other could point us toward a better understanding of the racialised stakes of immi-gration. In the second decade of the twenty-first century, the crisis of the nation state can be summarised by sovereignty over borders; and control of population. Popular perceptions that the State has either lost control or is no longer working in the interests of the group that sees itself as indigenous have led to political actions spanning mainstream and far-right movements and parties. The response called for is greater controls over some bodies, and is accompanied by the psychologically violent use of discourse aimed at drawing borders using values, criminality, etc., that reject some bodies' claims to belong to the nation. Indeed, in relation to access to resources, and loyalties to the State, the values and authenticity of particular groups of people are called into question in a way that people whose ancestors are not immigrants (or who are white immigrants from a few generations ago) are not. In this configuration of immigration, the receiving nation is assailed by criminal, violent, backward and rapacious Others. Victimhood is embraced in this discourse and racism simultaneously avowed as self-defence, or disa-vowed as love for one's own group, or nothing to do with 'race'. In this view-point, 'multiculturalism is genocide', and the need to preserve 'our' culture is held up as an equivalent of 'their' demands to preserve theirs. Indeed culture is a battlefield, and as we note in Chapter 12, Muslims are constructed not as a 'race' but as the bearers of a threatening culture.

- As noted in the first chapter, 'race' here is clearly not a pre-existing prop-erty of human groups, but a social product of these patterned processes of words and actions. In other words, immigration is one of the mechanisms that make 'race'.

Points for Reflection

Think about discussions of immigration in your country: in what ways does immigration appear as a threat?

What are the 'structures' of your government's current immigration policy, in terms of defining who is welcome and who is unwelcome?

What has 'race' got to do with immigration?

Further Reading

Hainmueller, J. and Hopkins, D. (2014) 'Public Attitudes Toward Immigration', *Annual Review of Political Science* 17: 225–49.

Comparative international quantitative analysis of public opinion about immigration in the twenty-first century. Shows emerging patterns of negative opinion based on cultural more than economic issues.

Romero, M. (2008) 'Crossing the Immigration and Race Border: A Critical Race Theory Approach to Immigration Studies', *Contemporary Justice Review* 11(1): 23–37.

Concise and focused critique of existing paradigms in US migration studies, combined with advocacy of critical race theory as a means of approaching the topic.

Erel, U. (2011) 'Complex Belongings: Racialization and Migration in a Small English City', *Ethnic and Racial Studies* 34(12): 2048–68.

Interviews in an English town show different levels of categorisation of migrants and ethnic minorities, who are racialised around issues of 'neighbourliness'. The consensus of white residents, the more neighbourly you are, the closer you are to 'belonging'.

Notes

1. Indeed, from the perspective of a scholar writing in Britain in 2016, with a referendum on the nation's membership of the European Union having been fought partly around immigration from Europe, it is important to understand.

2. The ILO's homepage is: www.ilo.org/global/topics/labour-migration/lang—en/index.htm.

11

Whiteness

In this chapter we will

- Examine the history of theorising the racialisation of white identities
- Provide a working definition of whiteness
- Summarise and synthesise research carried out on whiteness
- Establish how the concept of whiteness impacts on our understanding of racisms

Social scientists began interrogating what white racialised identities meant at the end of the nineteenth century. The first to do so were African Americans: W.E.B. Du Bois (1998 [1935]) and Ida Wells (1893) are the pioneers of the corpus. It could be argued that many critical studies that fall into the category of 'race' and ethnic studies between the early 1900s and the 1990s are about white identities. However, the renewed and explicit academic interest in 'whiteness' dates back to the work of American labour historian David Roediger, whose study of the white American working class, *The Wages of Whiteness* (1991), opened the door to a multidisciplinary migration toward the issues he raised. Acknowledging that whiteness had previously been invisible in framing questions about the labour movement, and more broadly, identifying pieces of history that reflected poorly on even the more radical white Americans, were important steps in shifting the analysis toward how the dominant groups in US society developed identities in relation to minorities.

This shift takes the focus away from minorities as somehow problematic per se, and pays closer attention to the ways that white people are racialised actors rather than neutral observers, and the complexities of the positions they hold. However, there have also been criticisms. Most important is the accusation that studies focusing on the way white people are divided by class and gender so that they do not all benefit equally from whiteness lead us to lose sight of the bigger picture: racisms work in the West by valuing whiteness over other forms of identity, and by generating a series of benefits and dis-benefits

(Mills, 2004). However, the discourse that questions whether racism is still relevant in the contemporary USA is very widespread, and indeed, this 'colour-blind racism' constituted the backdrop to Chapter 9. Moreover, there are other criticisms, namely that the whole problematic is tied closely to the USA and does not have much to say to activists and scholars in other places.

Additionally, there are serious political implications to stressing that 'white' might be a real identity. Groups from the anti-racist left to the white nationalist right often share the starting point that 'race' is a real thing, and that they are white (Hughey, 2012). Their ideas of what to do about that might be very different, but the idea of white as an unchallengeable identity (reflecting blackness, Asian-ness or Latino-ness, for example) might well be endorsed by studies of white identities unless they are very carefully qualified. So, as in the cases of all the topics looked at in this book, there are political stakes in studying, reflecting upon and being active around questions of racism beyond (as well as inside) the confines of the classroom.

In this chapter, some key elements of the US literature will be identified and summarised, before we look at the way in which whiteness can be used critically as an approach for examining contemporary Europe. This necessarily overlaps with what has been labelled the 'new racism' since the early 1980s (Chapter 9). Here, whiteness can be used, with clear caveats, to help understand current discourses about nation, 'race' and belonging.

American Work on Whiteness

There are a number of principal themes from the American literature on whiteness,[1] which I will explain here. In answer to the question 'what is whiteness?', I would argue that it is a number of things at once, and the most important of these are: a power relationship; a frame for understanding social relationships; and a making explicit of how white identities are racialised. There is no one all-encompassing definition because the dynamics of power are very local and tied into the historical circumstances of a particular place.

Terror

The starting point for understanding whiteness in the American context is that of terror. For centuries, the use of violence against the population of Native Americans and enslaved Africans, then freed slaves, generated understandings of interaction with white Americans among those communities based on fear and resentment. The narratives of the slavery period are full of this arbitrary use of different forms of violence: removal from land, psychological violence, rape, lynching. The systematic use of violence to keep order and control of the non-European population of the American colonies and then the nascent USA is reflected in a vein of literature including essays, novels, poetry, theatre, political campaigning and social science going back more than a century. Writers such as

James Baldwin, bell hooks and Toni Morrison have engaged directly with white-ness as it looms over the African American experience.[2] Baldwin, for example, identifying the psychological violence of racism, refers to the cumulative effect of 'the millions of details twenty-four hours of every day which spell out to you that you are a worthless human being' (1985: 404). Given this type of presence in the imaginary of people of colour, it may seem odd that the idea of invisibility has been used to characterise whiteness, but this is the next theme to emerge.

Invisibility/Visibility

There are three ways in which invisibility crops up in terms of white identities. The first is the context of whiteness as the norm, and the second is to do with the power of whiteness to make itself the norm. The third is the power to make individuals who are not white invisible *in a collective*. These are connected.

First, in a number of studies, white people say they do not think of them-selves as being 'white', that is, as not having a racial identity, or that 'race' didn't matter where they grew up because there were no minorities there. This supposes that 'race' is only for people who are not white, so that a 'normal' identity is white. It therefore does not have to be addressed in racial terms. Many of Ruth Frankenberg's (1994) Californian women speak about feeling white only when they arrived in larger multiracial towns where they were exposed to a greater variety of people. This experience is repeated many times in stories that white British people from provincial towns tell about when they visit urban areas with more obvious demographic diversity (Tyler, 2003; Byrne, 2006; Clarke and Garner, 2009). Ann Phoenix (1996, 2005) and Steven Farough (2004) find, respectively, that young people and white males con-struct their identities as being individual vis-à-vis those of minorities as being collective and informed by 'race' in a way theirs is not. This becomes a differ-ent point when we talk about how norms are invisible. The dominant groups in society, whether by class, 'race' or gender, generate and sustain ideas that justify their dominance and make it natural and normal. Only people whose identities fall outside the dominant group's therefore need to be defined differ-ently. Richard Dyer's central point in his study of whiteness in film and photography (1997) is that white is the framing position: a dominant and normative space against which difference is measured. In other words, white is the point from which judgements are made, about normality and abnormal-ity, beauty and ugliness, civilisation and barbarity. Simply put, whiteness is the default setting for 'human': everything else is deviant and requires explanation. Whiteness goes without saying.

However, one task of critical scholars is to articulate what 'goes without saying', and therefore unpick what it means. Toni Morrison's essay on race in the history of American literature (1993) identifies African Americans as the invisible segment of the population. As we have noted from the work that links whiteness to terror, whiteness is usually far from invisible to people who are not racialised as white. The question of invisibility depends on who you are and what you are looking at. It also applies to the effects that whiteness can have on others. In Morrison's terms, it renders black people invisible.

The third function of whiteness is to make individual black people invisible vis-à-vis an idea of blackness, as in Ralph Ellison's *Invisible Man* (1952). This occurs in D. Marvin Jones's (1997) interpretation of the 1989 Charles Stuart case in Boston. Jones argues that 'race' as a social practice evacuates individuality from those objectified and reduces them to a list of imputed bio-cultural characteristics. Stuart and his brother murdered his pregnant wife, then wounded Stuart in order to trick the police. They then blamed the murder on a black man in jogging pants with a raspy voice. This led to a highly intensive police operation in the area where the killing had taken place, in which many black men were questioned. Stuart's brother later confessed that the scheme was a scam to claim life insurance. The surrounding media and political discourse had included calls for the restoration of the death penalty in the state. Stuart's story had been readily believed, despite a lack of evidence. He eventually committed suicide and Boston's black community reacted angrily to the scrutiny to which it had been unfairly subject. Jones asserts that assumptions of black criminality thus form the basis of white responses to black subjects at particular moments, when 'race' constitutes a line dividing innocence from guilt. White Americans are willing to accept the story because this is how they expect black men to act. The police and media response was founded on the idea that any black man could have killed the woman because it is in the nature of black men to do things like this. However, when discussing crimes perpetrated by white criminals, a different logic applies: it is not *in the nature* of white people to do these things, although some may do. This is a significant distinction as it recognises whites as individuals and free agents, but blacks as a collective bound by nature.

Box 11.1 (Adverse) White Possession in Australia

Adverse possession is a legal term in Common Law that means a person can obtain deeds to land which does not originally belong to them by proving occupation of that land for a given period of time. It is implied that the prior owner has de facto given up claim.

Australian scholar Aileen Moreton-Robinson (2004, 2005) argues that the most important fact about Australia is that it is built on possession of native land. Yet this is barely engaged with in discussions about national identity. All the cultural discourses are about the relationship with Britain's culture. Ultimately, Moreton-Robinson sees the elision of ethnic difference between Irish, English, Scots and Welsh, and, after the 1901 Immigration Restriction Act, the merging of those identities into whiteness – into which other European settlers are then admitted:

While blackness was congruent with Indigenous subjugation and sub-ordination, whiteness was perceived as synonymous with freedom and citizenship. (2005: 27)

Indeed, in Australian culture the importance of the landscape becomes key: the Australian cultural 'founding ancestors' were all 'struggling against the landscape', she writes: 'It is the landscape that must be conquered, claimed and named, not Indigenous people, who, at the level of the subconscious, are perceived to be part of the landscape and not human' (2005: 26).

So if Australian values are intrinsically bound up in overcoming hardship and conquering the landscape (and not conquering people), then the myth of peaceful possession can continue. Violent possession cannot be acknowl-edged because that would challenge the underpinning Australian values of tolerance and 'fair play'.

When indigenous Australians challenge possession they are usually unsuccessful. The Mabo ruling in 1993 is a rare case where native title to land was recognised. However, subsequent Australian High Court rulings have prioritised Common Law over tradition (that is, occupancy and use of land are privileged over original ownership). The case of the Yorta Yorta peo-ple's claim (1995–2002) demonstrates the functioning of white logic over indigenous logic, in what Moreton-Robinson calls 'the possessive logic of patriarchal white sovereignty' (2004).

The ruling hinged on whether the Yorta Yorta could demonstrate continu-ous occupation of the land in question. They had amassed a substantial amount of physical evidence, yet this was not deemed sufficient. The Yorta Yorta occupation and use of the land was ruled to have been interrupted when the Europeans came, and new property laws came into being (Common Law). Common Law allows for 'adverse possession', so the Crown's claim to the land could be proven by occupation, de facto showing the court that the indigenous people could not evidence continuous use of the land through tradition. In contrast, the Mabo ruling had recognised that indigenous own-ership had been reduced over a period of time rather than lost completely at a stroke. The Court stated that the Yorta Yorta's petition for the return of the land demonstrated that they no longer had possession of it. Moreton-Robinson points out that if something is stolen it does not become the property of the thief, and asking for it to be returned does not signal that the original owner has lost legal right to it. The Court's logic of property ownership thus functions very differently from that of the indigenous people. In their terms, they belong physically and spiritually to the land. No other indigenous people would ever claim that land, which is synonymous with the Yorta Yorta people themselves. So the logic of possession based on land being a commodity that can be bought, sold and occupied by anyone trumps the indigenous logic of stewardship and intimate identification with the land.

Possession thus emerges as a white colonial way of knowing and under-standing social facts (an epistemology). However the key point is that this logic is not acknowledged as being partial and the product of one type of civilisation, but is assumed to be universal and superior.

Cultural Capital

'Cultural capital' is one of the terms developed by Pierre Bourdieu (1986) to describe non-economic forms of 'wealth' distributed unevenly throughout society. It grants advantage that provides unequal access to employment, education, etc. Simply put, cultural capital can be thought of as consisting of ways to behave, think and express oneself that are valued, as well as the holding of types of knowledge that are valued hierarchically, especially that pertaining to high culture (Bourdieu, 1977). While the concept was first developed to enable an exploration of class distinctions and reproduction, it can also be used in relation to whiteness.

Du Bois first focuses on the non-economic advantages in being white in America, in his history of the Reconstruction (1998 [1935]: 707), when he discusses what he terms the 'public and psychological wage' of whiteness. He was searching for reasons as to why the white poor in the Southern states supported their elites against the newly freed slave population rather than allying with them to press for better living and working conditions. His conclusion was that whiteness insulated them from the idea of ever being slaves, the lowest possible status in American society. The distance between them and the former slaves was more important to them than that between poor and wealthy white southerners.

This 'public and psychological wage' has been looked at in a number of ways, and can be seen clearly in two pieces of work. One is the essay by Peggy McIntosh (1988), in which the author conceptualises privilege as a 'knapsack' full of things that give her advantages over people of colour. The list of 46 items includes things she does not have to do (act as a representative of her 'race'; take notice of minority groups' agendas or minority people with impunity); things she can take for granted (move into an area that she can afford to live in); being treated at least neutrally by her neighbours; curricula which reflect the contribution of people her colour; cosmetics and prosthetics which match her skin tone; and things she can do without worrying (move around different public spaces without being the focus of attention). McIntosh's list is a starting point for thinking about what she calls 'unearned advantage'. Frequently, models of racism we are presented with suggest that there are clear ways in which some groups are discriminated against, but do not make explicit how the dominant groups (usually white, but not always in every place) gain advantage from it. Reflection on this point brings us to a position where we can distinguish the intentions and ideas that individual people hold, from the systemic disadvantages and advantages that we are provided with. Charles Mills' neat summary of this, in his *Racial Contract* (1997: 11), is that the tacit contract to maintain a racially hierarchical society can be the object of criticism without it ceasing either to function, or to advantage white people as a group: 'All whites are beneficiaries of the Contract, though some whites are not signatories to it.' This does not mean that everyone in that category benefits equally, but that there is a benefit vis-à-vis groups racialised as not being white.

Amanda Lewis's study of three California primary schools (2003), for example, shows how teachers' expectations of behaviour, language use, achievement and family support follow a racialised pattern. The white pupils are not subject to the same kind of attention as their black and Latino classmates and this lack of scrutiny works to their advantage.

While the message emerging from work on schooling in both the USA and Britain (Johnson and Shapiro, 2003; Byrne, 2006) is that as a general rule, white parents seek schools with minimal proportions of minorities, there is also another side to cultural capital. Bourdieu (1984) uses it to talk only about the advantageous aspects enabling the middle classes to reproduce their patterns of education and thus employment. There is another scenario: the desirability of 'multicultural' capital. Diane Reay and her team's (2007) study of middle-class parents in England showed that there is a segment of that population who send their children to particular types of state secondary school, with a mixed class and ethnic composition. This strategy is aimed at extending the amount of cultural capital their children develop in terms of having experience of different types of people from themselves. This, it is argued, will be an asset to them in terms of employment and social networking in multicultural Britain. In the other form of cultural capital, there is a benefit to be accrued from non-elite culture. In their study of young people in a small provincial English town, Watt and Stenson (1998) show that the capital gained through having attended the town's multiethnic secondary schools enables the former students to negotiate urban spaces with more confidence than their middle-class suburban peers. The latter, due to the restricted social circles in their schools, have less knowledge of the town centre, of the different districts and of the people who live in them, making them wary of much of the town.

Contingent Hierarchies[3]

In addition to a set of borders between people categorised as 'white' and 'non-white', there is another set of internal borders produced by racialisation. In other words, there are socially observable degrees of whiteness between the groups that seem to be unproblematically white. Examples here include Southern, Central and Eastern European immigrant groups in Western Europe and North America, Jews, Gypsy-Travellers/Roma, as well as the numerous and important divisions based on class, gender, sexuality, region, etc. identified in the literature on both America and Britain (Daniels, 1997; Nayak, 2003; Hartigan, 2005).

In European and North American societies, there is a history of imputing defective natural and cultural characteristics to members of the lower classes that goes back to feudal times in Europe. The thread of this is that there is a hierarchical socio-economic order in society, an order that reflects the natural traits of those groups. The hierarchy is thus because the dominant group deserve to be dominant, and the subordinate deserve to be subordinate.

The social world is therefore explained by the natural world, and culture is an expression of these distinctive 'natures'. The social mobility opened up by the end of feudalism and the beginning of the industrial world ended the notion that the feudal orders were completely distinct from each other. Instead, the new urban and to a lesser extent rural working classes were conceptualised by the dominant groups as both biologically and culturally inferior.

By the mid-nineteenth century, when ideas about class, 'race' and gender as social hierarchies were fully developed and linked to science (see Chapter 7), bodies of work dealing with the flaws inherent in working-class lives and culture were being published. Reports of the 'dangerous classes' linked their difficult economic positions and involvement in crime as deriving from genetic and cultural shortcomings not shared by the upper orders of society. Such flaws could be transmitted environmentally or through the bloodline, and some of the writing around the topic of racial purity in the late nineteenth and early twentieth century, the period of Social Darwinism and eugenics, focused on this reproductive mechanism. Eugenics-influenced discourse (see Chapter 7) emphasised the perils of mixing good with bad genes. It was argued that antisocial behaviour derived from poor family etiquette and practices. In the scenarios popularised in the press, the idea of 'racial poisons' became significant, all the more so as 'weaker' blood was believed to multiply faster than the 'stronger'. Gertrude Davenport, the wife of America's leading eugenicist Charles Davenport, stated in a popular magazine in April 1914 that 'the greatest menace of imbecility is not that the imbecile may break into our house and steal our silver, or that he might set fire to our barn, but that he may be born of our flesh' (Hartigan, 2005: 95).

Similarly, in the Freudian fight for civilisation taking place within the Self, race theorist Winthrop Stoddard asserts that class status coincides with racial value:

> Let us understand once and for all [he warns] that we have among us a rebel army – the vast host of the unadaptable, the incapable, the envious, the discontented, filled with instinctive hatred of civilization and progress, and ready on the instant to rise in revolt. Here are foes that need watching. Let us watch them. (Stoddard, 1922: 87)

Of course, if the argument could be used to note a distinction between classes, then it could equally apply to different ethnic groups, even the nominally white ethnic groups. By the late nineteenth century, not only was there a notion of the racial superiority of whites over everyone else, but putative league tables of superiority within each of these broad 'races' had been put forward (see Chapter 7). The Anglo-Saxon was claimed to be at the summit of the white 'race', above the Celts, Latins, Persians and Jews (who sometimes appeared as a separate 'race' in the many attempts to classify human diversity that emerged from this period). In both Britain and North America, the racial status of ostensibly white groups such as the Catholic Irish, Eastern European Jews and Gypsy-Travellers has been the subject of discussion, social comment, social action and State policy. Indeed, Britain's first piece of immigration legislation, the 1905 Aliens Act (see Chapter 10), was formulated as a result of campaigning against the arrival of Jews fleeing persecution in Eastern Europe. In the contemporary UK, there has been a recent presence of Central and Eastern European migrants, often in areas where there had been little previous history of migration, such as the more rural east, and parts of the north-west. Many of the statements of hostility made about them resemble the accusations of dirtiness, undercutting labour markets and lawlessness made about waves of immigrants going back to the Irish in the early nineteenth century.

This point leads us back to where we came in, with American labour historians' excavation of the relations between different immigrant groups and the host populations in American urban space (Roediger, 1991). The principal finding of Barrett and Roediger (1997) is that the cultural line separating white from black in the USA was not as clear as had been supposed. New European migrants who were neither protestant nor Northern European were not constructed as fully white (that is, fitting in with the dominant culture and capable of democracy). They often worked in jobs that free Black Americans had done, lived in or near places that they had lived, and in the case of the Catholic Irish, were compared unflatteringly with Black Americans (Garner, 2004). Indeed, so dangerous were Southern and Eastern European Catholics and Jews in the eugenicists' view, that the harshest quotas in the 1924 Immigration Act were applied to countries such as Italy, Poland and Russia.

The theoretical engagement with whiteness in the USA has produced a large number of books and articles that discuss and refine ideas (Nayak, 2007). However, for the purposes of this introduction, we are going to concentrate on some empirical fieldwork to get a feel for what can be analysed on the ground.

Box 11.2 'White Protectionism' and Penal Spectatorship

In their interesting and speculative study, Dirks et al. (2015) set out to look for patterns in the online responses to mugshots of people arrested for non-violent offences in the USA. These mugshots are posted on websites and the public is invited to comment. Their hypothesis was that white commentators would neutralise the offences of, and defend the more conventionally attractive-looking white women.

The theoretical hook they used is 'white protectionism' (Wray, 2006), which is discursive work white people do to protect other whites who commit racist acts and make racist statements. Dirks wondered whether this protectionism would extend to defending criminals as individuals. The focus on women must be understood in the context of the traditional framing of women who commit crimes as aberrant, either 'bad' or 'mad', and more

(Continued)

(Continued)

frequently victims rather than perpetrators of crimes. Moreover, black women offenders are not discursively treated in the same way: they have been stereotyped for centuries as more aggressive, more masculine and less morally correct than white women, so crime is not the aberration that it is considered for white women. This is the discursive background against which Dirks' team studied online responses to the mugshots, which 'serve to stigmatize, dehumanize, criminalize, and to entertain' (2015: 171). The main findings are:

- The majority of comments are made by men (62.3%), and most by whites (83.0%) (p. 165).

- '59.3% of comments ... mentioned the woman's body or her physical appearance, 38.9% focused on the details of her crime, and 12.4% discussed her punishment' (p. 166).

- 'Men of color are far more likely to post body comments (78.0%), followed by white men (57.1%), women of color (56.5%), and white women (53.6%)' (p. 167).

- 'Men of color and white women (14.6%) are more likely to discuss punishment than white men (10.6%) and women of color (0%) ... Furthermore, white female commenters are more likely to suggest help for the arrestee, as opposed to punitive comments made by men of color and white men' (p. 168).

- There was initial support for the hypothesis on white protectionism: most positive comments are made by: white men (67%); white women (64.9%); women of colour (60.0%); men of colour (59.0%).

- 'We find significant race and intersectional differences with regard to protectionism with white women being the most likely to neutralize with their comments (39.8%), followed by white men (32.2%), women of color (26.1%), and far fewer men of color (17.1%)' (p. 170).

These findings demonstrate a degree of 'white protectionism', and tell us that engagement with this criminal justice/entertainment space is gendered and racialised. A study of comments made about mugshots of people of colour on the same website would complement this piece of research. However, the commentators have no input into the judgement of these offenders. When we consider the findings of the Vilanova study (Viglione et al., 2011), a leaning toward downplaying the crimes of lighter-skinned women begins to appear more serious. The Vilanova study looked at the sentencing of 12,000 black women in North Carolina between 1995 and 2009. It found that lighter-skinned women were sentenced more leniently than darker-skinned women for similar crimes, and served on average smaller proportions of their sentences. This pattern is also indicated by some social psychology research on black men's sentencing in the USA.

Themes from Fieldwork on Whiteness

There are a number of overlaps in the findings of the fieldwork carried out in the USA and Britain (Garner, 2009a). The theme of invisibility/visibility; the roles of cultural capital and shared values in making 'white' meaningful vis-à-vis others; the contingent class and ethnic hierarchies within the white group – all these appear with their distinctive local accents. One clear shared finding is that white is frequently now proposed as a disadvantaged identity in the face of government and cultural schemas that favour minorities (Garner, 2015). In the USA, this claim coalesces around affirmative action (or at least what people imagine affirmative action to consist of – for clarity, see McKinney, 2004; Dhami et al., 2006), while in the UK it does so around so-called 'political correctness'. Underlying this victimhood is a profound sense of not having benefited from social change, and loss of ground. However, the precise history of the USA and the experiences of colonial violence there have made terror and systemic psychological and physical violence more immediately relevant to accounts of whiteness as power. This is not to say that there are none of these things in Europe. Indeed, the more striking element of the European experience is of whiteness mediated through a colonial history into a post-colonial present. The following fieldwork will demonstrate some of these overlaps and distinctions.

Case Study: Hartigan's 'Racial Situations'

John Hartigan's ethnography of inner-city Detroit (1997, 1999) is focused largely on a district called Briggs, which is home to low-income white and black families. While there are other sections dealing with gentrification of a nearby inner-city area, and a struggle over schooling in a mainly white suburb, Hartigan develops his analysis primarily from his observations of life in Briggs. He finds that the way people there make sense of whiteness and blackness is a very complicated mixture of codes. Incidents can end up racialised, but do not necessarily begin that way. On the other hand, the cordial relations between black and white in the area are explained, he believes, by the long period of common socialisation: many of the inhabitants were at school with each other and have remained in the area. The personal knowledge they have of each other's family histories appears to keep people focused on individuals rather than on the collective narratives of black and white. In the earlier piece, Hartigan had reported that when he told some interviewees that he was studying 'race relations', they suggested he should go to a housing project across the highway, indicating that it was a zone too dangerous for whites (1997: 191):

(Continued)

(Continued)

> In this [their own] neighborhood, they were one family among many, white and black, who held elaborate and lengthy knowledge of each other reaching back over the tumultuous past three decades. But across the intersection [that is, in that particular project] they were simply 'whites', partly for their skin color and partly in terms of location and being out of place.

The invisibility feared by Hartigan's white respondents thus thematically mirrors that of the black people who Jones (1997) maintains are objectified by whiteness.

In the codes of discourse and action that Hartigan identifies, the role of 'race' differs widely. It is sometimes irrelevant, sometimes part of the mix and sometimes the basis of action. There are different registers of language and behaviour that are acceptable in some contexts and not in others. Additionally, 'race' is frequently understood through the frames of class. An example of this is a multiracial baseball game played by the family of Hartigan's main white informant, Jessie (1999: 140–4). They arrange to play a serious game against a team of local black people whom they had met the week before. One of Jessie's brothers, David, refuses to play because he doesn't want to play against blacks. His decision is viewed by the Briggs-based family as more evidence of David's weirdness and efforts to distance himself socially from them: David already lives elsewhere in a wealthier neighbourhood. More people join the game as the afternoon goes on, and by the end, the two teams are racially mixed. David's girlfriend, Becky, from a white suburb of Detroit, expresses her discomfort about the proximity of black people. This manifests itself in her leaving early and not wanting to lend her glove to black players, which is what she tells Jessie. The resulting family feud is interpreted through the lens of class. Jessie's Briggs-based family see Becky as a spoilt middle-class girl who is out to 'spoil' David too. Her inability to function in a racially mixed setting is seen by the family as proof of her snobbery (not her racism, which is not explicitly referred to as such). For Becky and David, argues Hartigan, their 'striving for social mobility and higher class standing was articulated through an assertion of the need for careful racial boundary maintenance by avoiding interracial situations' (1999: 142).

Case Study: Lewis's 'Racialised School Situations'

Amanda Lewis (2003) argues that the school is not a racially neutral haven of equality but a site in which children learn about 'race', and the adults they encounter impose understandings of 'race' upon them and each other. Her study is of three primary schools in California: a mixed inner-city one, a mainly white suburban one and a special bilingual (Spanish–English) suburban one.

All the schools address the issue of 'race' differently, from denial that it is an issue at all through to explicitly placing racism on the agenda to be addressed. However, Lewis finds that despite the different starting points, there are common areas.

At the mainly white 'Foresthills' school, the consensus is that 'race' is not an issue because of the demographic composition of the school. Staff and parents are adamant that 'race' plays no part in their lives, and the school's engagement with multiculturalism and inequalities is rudimentary. However, Lewis asserts that this school encapsulates the dominant way of thinking about 'race' in America: colour-blind racism (see Chapter 9). The process of racialisation, and the discriminatory effects of housing policy over the past century, for example, have created white suburbs like Foresthills that provide the intake of this school. Moreover, this residential segregation is bolstered by social and workplace segregation, which means that the school's student body lives in virtual isolation from non-white people. The understandings of discrimination are that it is mainly just the response of minorities with a chip on their shoulder, and that in fact there are cultural deficiencies that give rise to the problems of poverty and segregation.

At 'West City', a school in a mainly white neighbourhood into which Latino and African American kids are bussed daily, 'race' is not denied as such, but given a cultural spin. Lewis finds that teaching staff have racialised expectations and understandings of the pupils' lives. Problems in school among African American children are understood by the mainly white staff as stemming from the dysfunctional families of the latter, and the lower value attached to education. The few minority staff in the school feel the pressure of having to be the ones who explicitly raise the issue of racism and racist assumptions, and the minority children generally do worse academically than the white ones. Lewis asserts that the combination of expectations, different assumptions and engagement of staff with the different types of pupil contributes to unequal outcomes. It is easier to attribute this to the children's culture than accept that there is something in their own practices and assumptions that needs remedying.

'Metro2' is a special bilingual school sought after by white middle-class parents, and which contains a large proportion of Latino students. Although it serves a mixture of socio-economic groups, the white pupils are generally from the better-off end of the spectrum and their parents dominate the school's agenda. It is in part a study of how cultural capital functions in a school, even from the point of applying for a place, which requires handling a number of forms (Ball, 1993). Although the school is bilingual, Spanish is the official language and there is no English as a Second Language teaching available. English is the first language in only two classrooms. This means that the learners of Spanish get a better educational deal than the learners of English, who provide models to the other students but do not get the same service in return. Despite a lot more attention being paid to minority identities and the issue of social equality, the outcomes still tended

(Continued)

(Continued)

toward those of 'West City'. 'The white children in this school', writes Lewis, 'were the only white children I interviewed who were aware of and able to talk about racism and discrimination as factors in mobility and opportunity' (2003: 108). However, the social segregation she witnesses, outside of formal lessons, takes place in the schoolyard, and outside the walls of the school. Even in the school itself, the racial lines are sometimes clear: the three spelling groups follow racial lines. Most of the top group are white, most of the few African Americans are in the bottom group and most of the Latinos are in the two bottom groups (2003: 115).

The interpretations of difference held by the white staff and parents of these three schools are based firmly in ideas about culture and responsibility. The concept of structural discrimination is acknowledged most often at Metro2, but this does not eliminate the cultural approach. This goes hand-in-hand with the colour-blind ideology, which asserts that it is solely people's merit that counts. Rather than being an aspiration, this is understood as a fact, and therefore collective failure is interpreted as the failure of individuals within the group. However, the phenotypical dimension of 'race' is still present. In the case of bi-racial children at Metro2, for example, this comes to the fore in a series of misrecognitions, when the culture and appearance of children do not tally with preconceptions (2003: 115). Hector is a light-skinned Hispanophone Latino who is consistently seen as a white Anglophone, and not given credit for his English-language skills. Enrique's parentage is black Mexican, and he is proud of his Chicano culture, however he is seen as African American and not acknowledged as a Latino. Finally, brown-skinned Omar, whose parentage is German American and Bolivian, is questioned when he claims European heritage.

Box 11.3   Blackface

On Saturday evenings until I was a teenager, the BBC used to broadcast the *Black and White Minstrel Show* featuring a troop of white music and dance performers, blacked up. The show was at one time extremely popular, with audiences of over 20 million in the 1960s. By 1978 it had been cancelled, but the theatre version of the show continued in one form or another until the early 1990s.

US historian Eric Lott (2013) argues that minstrelsy in America (from the 1830s) was to do with the ambivalence of white vis-à-vis black masculinities. Inhabiting black masculinity in this way enabled a sanctioned transgression into an envied space, at the same time as raucous and bawdy working-class performances that hinted at empathy. The tradition also saw cross-dressing, as men played black women as well in aggressive and masculine ways.

Lott points to themes of emasculation and violence done to the black body that he interprets as expressions of controlling black masculinities and sexuality. David Roediger (1991) suggests that blackface is the ultimate performance of whiteness: a method by which new European immigrants learned whiteness by caricaturing blackness. The stereotypes of African Americans as idle, sensual and sexual were the characteristics to which white immigrants were encouraged to be opposite. Thus, blacking up enabled them to both ridicule blacks and enjoy representational power over them.

Black performers also performed in blackface in nineteenth-century America: but black and white audiences read their work differently, which leads us to the question of what contemporary blackface (and indeed 'yellowface') is about, and who gets to say what it's about. For a long time, Hollywood has been casting white actors in the roles of black and Asian characters, just as has happened in theatre for centuries.[4] Asian American actor Michelle Villemaire has recently spoofed Hollywood's yellowface tradition by posing in character in photographs alongside the 'yellowed' cast member on her website, 'Homemade Mimi' (Yahoo News, 2016). However, the question of interpreting black/yellowface recurs in global settings: American students blacking up for their 'Compton Cookout' in 2010 to mock 'Black History Week', and similar examples, especially Halloween costumes; the Dutch 'Zwarte Piet' Christmas tradition that is coming under increasingly acute scrutiny because of the protests by black Dutch people; and Swedish art and politics (Hübinette and Räterlinck, 2014).

The global entertainment industry contains plenty of examples: fashion shoots of Claudia Schiffer, Kate Moss and Ondria Hardin to name a few; some Asian popular entertainment and advertising, and US and British television comedy have all had examples of these practices, from *How I Met Your Mother* to *Little Britain* and *Come Fly With Me*. The Hollywood film *White Chicks* (2004) is often cited as a comparable example. The argument runs, if whiteface is ok, why is blackface wrong? We need to be aware of the history of the practice and the potential punishments. Blackface – a practice that began while slavery was still flourishing – is essentially about caricaturing and dehumanising black people. Similar arguments apply to the appropriation of Native American imagery, for example. Whiteface cannot dehumanise a group of people in a structurally weak position. Although many white people are indeed in structurally economically weak positions, there are also many who are in much more powerful positions, and the primary reason explaining the weak social locations is not 'race'.

Is this practice relentlessly racist, or can subverting its messages ever change its structural position? Under what conditions can or could blackface subvert racism?

Byrne's Mothers Looking for the 'Right Mix'

Bridget Byrne (2006) studies white mothers choosing primary schools for their children in South London. She explains that she is seeking to counteract: 'the assumption … that we (everyday white people in Britain who are not particularly racist) cannot be interesting as "race" has nothing to do with us' (Byrne, 2006: 1). The analysis of how the 'we' she refers to is constructed is a project requiring her to hear and see 'race' in 'contexts where it is not explicitly felt as present' (2006: 2). Byrne argues that 'race' needs to be understood as performative, and 'more specifically as a product of perceptual practices' (2006: 74). She observes that questions about 'race' in her interviews were frequently met with a lowering of the speaker's voice. There were evasions (talking about other identities when asked directly about 'race'), and silences: talking about 'race' is awkward. Indeed, a common strategy deployed was not to see difference, that is, to talk as if whiteness is not a social location.

Yet, in not seeing their whiteness, the women definitely see blackness. Black men, for example, emerge as simultaneously threatening and desirable. In narrating themselves, Byrne's white women subjects often evoke whiteness as an absence of 'race' during provincial, often rural, childhoods, followed by an awareness-raising confrontation in the cosmopolitan metropolis. For them, as for Ruth Frankenberg's interviewees (1994), 'race' is something seen and done only when face-to-face with the 'Other'.

At the 'core of motherhood', writes Byrne, 'lie the intersections of race, class and gender' (2006: 106). She proceeds to demonstrate this in her examination of the ways in which the social networks of both mothers and children, and the choice of schools, are highly classed and raced acts. While there are obvious cultural and material conflicts over resources, what is fascinating is the view of multiculturalism as a form of cultural capital. Many of the mothers are pro-multicultural: exposure to difference is deemed good for the children. Yet there is what former French president François Mitterrand once termed a 'threshold of tolerance'. For these mothers, there has to be the 'right mix', which involves just enough minority (and/or working class) children to make it interesting, but not so many as to make them think that the school's standards will be brought down (even this is not true). Byrne's conclusion is that in the eyes of their mothers, children must learn to be white and middle class *in the right way*. Her emphasis on performativity leads her to state that: 'the security and stability of the white middle-class norm requires constant repetition and recitation in order for it to be ensured for their children' (2006: 137). The mothers thus nurture their children's whiteness by careful management of the contexts in which they learn about difference.

Box 11.4   Complaining about Racism at School

Amira is the mother of Jonathan, a primary schoolboy in Myers and Bhopal's (2015) fieldwork on racism in rural English schools. The black family had moved to a rural location and Amira's son experienced bullying. This necessitated repeat meetings with the headteacher. At the original meeting:

> The head teacher didn't know what to say, it was like she was in denial and couldn't believe that boy had called Jonathan these names.

> I think she thought we were lying. Or that Jonathan was lying. And she said to us, 'we don't have racism or bullying in our school, and if the children do say those things, it's not racist, it's like saying you have ginger hair'. (2015: 8)

The school did not effectively deal with the issue, Jonathan was physically hurt, and in the end he was moved to another school, which affected his confidence. Amira and her husband made an official complaint. Instead of dealing with the issues raised in it, the school's and then the County Council's responses were to blame the family.

> ... the evidence they accumulated to demonstrate their son was being racially bullied were seen as exaggerations by the Head. More troublingly the weight of evidence they accumulated was used by the local education authority's solicitor as evidence of such exaggeration. Amira received a letter from the County's Chief solicitor suggesting their continued pursuit and documentation of their concerns constituted bullying by the family of the school. Furthermore they could be barred from school premises and communicating directly with the school, (it was suggested that all future communications with the school would need to go through the County's solicitor). (2015: 14)

The headteacher and the school's position demonstrates a 'white frame' (Feagin, 2006) and 'epistemological ignorance' (Mills, 1997). Although obligated to adhere to particular anti-discriminatory policies by the 2000 Race Relations (Amendment) Act, the decision-makers at the school clearly decided to discount the evidence because they did not think that it fitted with the school's view of itself and its OFSTED rating. In the school's ethos, kids are all the same; teasing about ginger hair is an equivalent of racism; 'race' is not a justifiable basis for claiming victimhood; and the school community is incapable of enacting racism. The normal functioning of the school is ordered (for the headteacher and its white pupils), but disordered and unsafe for this black child. So great is the cognitive dissonance that the mother's insistence that the school fulfil its obligation to make it safe for her child is constructed as aggressive and unreasonable. The 'public and psychological wage' of whiteness is expressed here in the power to present the black child's experience as fictitious and exaggerated.

Tyler's Semi-Rural English Middle Classes

Katharine Tyler's ethnographies of the English village of Greenville in Leicestershire (2003, 2006) show that semi-rural space is defended using the development of middle-class values of belonging through adherence to ways of being and behaving. Tyler finds clear class distinctions within the village between the white inhabitants, but her fieldwork focuses on the ways in which racism is articulated there. There are a small number of wealthy South Asian families in Greenville, and these are seen as 'abnormal' because they do not fit notions of respectability and normality. In other words, they do not engage in the usual activities there such as charity work (women) and going to the pub (men) (2003: 394). Particular episodes illustrate the way 'race' emerges in people's understandings of the Asians. One family extended its house against local opposition generated by anxieties of the villagers about what the space would be used for. The white villagers predicted that the house would be used as a combined residence, business premises and temple. One villager states that: 'They are very nice people but eyebrows are raised when the hordes of friends and relatives come from Leicester. It isn't done in Greenville' (2003: 405). Tyler concludes that 'wealthy Asians are thought to live in extended families, are perceived to be excessively wealthy, extravagantly religious, run disruptive businesses from their homes and cook smelly foods' (2003: 409).

For the middle classes in semi-rural Leicester (a medium-sized city in the East Midlands with a relatively large South Asian descended population), tranquillity is a prized value. While solidarity (for the poor elsewhere) is demonstrated through the routines of charity work, the real test of belonging in Greenville is to attain invisibility. Talking of one particular Asian family in the village, one resident tells Tyler (2003: 400) 'They are as good as gold ... we never see them.' Hiding oneself and keeping the noise down are viewed as the correct way to behave, a value that contradicts the justification given for not forging more intimate relations, which is that 'Asians don't mix'.

There are binding themes in all the snippets of fieldwork glimpsed here: the precarious invisibility and visibility of whiteness and the cultural capital this brings into play; the capacity of whiteness to link people across class and gender into positions of relative power in particular contexts; the pieces of history that whiteness enables white people to not have to take into account; and the diminution of overtly racialised language.

Box 11.5   Decolonising the University: #whyismycurriculumwhite and #rhodesmustfall

Student anti-racist activism in British universities has developed in recent years chiefly around some social media-based campaigns, the most high profile of which are #whyismycurriculumwhite and #rhodesmustfall. They focus on developing a critical evaluation of universities as 'white spaces', in other words where whiteness is a norm; the contributions and struggles of racialised minorities are not incorporated into the various canons or the built environment; and the institutions' historical connections to colonialism are celebrated, or at least not recognised as problematic. #whyismycurriculumwhite was taken up in a number of British universities from 2014, in the form of study groups and ongoing campaigning around representation and discrimination.[5] A typical retort to the criticism of canons as not reflecting diversity is that the work students study is the best of the best regardless of its producers' identities, and that arguing for more diversity is artificially lowering standards for political ends. This response could be understood as another version of the 'less qualified minority took my job/scholarship' riff, assuming as it does that white achievement is always on merit, and ignoring the patterns of structural discrimination that make access to academic knowledge production easier for the dominant groups (especially the white middle and upper classes, and especially men). As noted in Chapter 4, standpoint theory argues that perspectives are largely experiential, and white middle-class male is not a neutral position from which to produce knowledge but a privileged one.

The #rhodesmustfall campaign began at the University of Cape Town in 2015, and focused on demands to remove a statue of Cecil Rhodes as a symbolic representation of a wider move to 'decolonise' higher education in South Africa. After a series of protests, the university removed the statue in April 2015, but further campaigning around student accommodation and course content continued. The decolonising concept had caught on, both in other South African campuses, and in Oxford, where Oriel College has a statue of Rhodes. Students there demanded the statue's removal, recognition of Oriel's connections to colonialism and better representation of minority groups. Although the Students Union voted to remove the statue, any hope of achieving that goal was quashed in January 2016, when key Oriel benefactors threatened to withdraw funding if the statue were removed. The Oxford campaign drew criticism that the students were seeking to 'rewrite history'. Actually the campaign sought more, not less discussion of history, but rather from a much more critical, 'decolonising' position than the standard one, which views the British Empire as a 'benevolent NGO that went everywhere in the world', as one of the contributors to the *Why is my Curriculum White* film puts it. The legacies of the British Empire are alive and kicking in higher education.

Conclusions

- Whiteness is simultaneously a shorthand for a historical system of power (which Charles Mills calls 'white supremacy'); a multidisciplinary area of study; and a set of positionings and identifications with discourses into which people are socialised. It is also a recognition that in the ongoing fiction of 'race', white is also a category.

- There are clearly different levels of whiteness to understand. The example of colonial possession of native land, the school's response to a parent trying to protect her son from bullying, and patterns of comments online about offenders' mugshots all fall within our area of interest. Yet the colonial legacy has significant impacts of a different order, and can in a way be seen as influencing the school's response, and because American history is so tightly tied into the expansion of European colonies, it is also important to the mugshot example. While the micro-level examples identified in the fieldwork are studies of how whiteness works on an everyday basis, the macro-level material makes the micro-level material intelligible.

- Whiteness studies has now been under way in its new form, as a reflexive body of work per se for nearly two decades, and according to Gallagher and Twine (2007: 5) began its 'third wave' a decade ago.

- The corpus on whiteness as conceptualised and operationalised outside of the USA is growing, and the fieldwork reveals the complexities of local racial regimes and underscores the intersectional approach's claim (Chapter 4) that people live out intersections of identities. On some axes, they are dominated and on others, part of the dominant group.

- The ongoing power of whiteness, which is reflected in each of the chapters of this book, is not as invisible or as potent for all those racialised as 'white'. Indeed, in some cases it is more difficult to see how it benefits people on the lowest socio-economic rungs of the ladder. However, as has been argued since the beginning of social science's engagement with whiteness, its benefits are not confined to the economic sphere. Analyses that focus exclusively on that aspect will necessarily miss the point, which is that the ideological and social interpretations of white identities can (maybe provisionally) compensate for low status in the economic arena.

- In much of the fieldwork, the understandings of what constitutes racism and what the 'problem' actually consists of are increasingly individual rather than collective, and locate problems in the past rather than the present (Box 6.3). On the one hand, white people see themselves as individuals, yet minorities (unless they know them personally) are conceptualised as groups.

- On the other hand, discrimination is seen as a thing of the past, which is now minimal and used as an excuse by minority individuals for not achieving.

- There are pertinent critiques of the substance of whiteness studies. Two of the most glaring gaps in the work so far are the absence (with a few notable exceptions) of sustained studies of the intersection of gender and whiteness since the black feminist critique of the early 1980s, and the overriding concentration on working-class subjects as opposed to middle-class ones (again with a few exceptions). The broader criticism that whiteness as a paradigm puts white people back in the centre of the frame is a more nuanced one: 'whiteness' and 'white people' are not the same thing.

Points for Reflection

What is whiteness?

How can the concept of whiteness help us understand the dynamics of contemporary racisms?

Is the concept relational? In other words, does 'white' only have meaning when placed against 'black', 'Asian', etc., or does it mean something in and of itself?

Further Reading

Mills, C.W. (1997) *The Racial Contract*. Ithaca, NY: Cornell University Press.

Mills' text on history and politics locates 'race' at the heart of the Enlightenment project of democracy, he is at pains to stress the distinction between white and non-white understandings of political inequalities.

Harris, C. (1993) 'Whiteness as Property', *Harvard Law Review* 106(8): 1707–91.

Classic statement, using case studies critically interpreted, of how whiteness has been historically constructed by the US legal system as a form of capital equivalent to property.

Garner, S. (2007) *Whiteness: An Introduction*. London: Routledge.

Critical synthesis of social science work on defining and critiquing whiteness, with examples drawn from various historical, political and geographical contexts.

Notes

1. Interested readers can find a much more detailed investigation in Garner (2007a).

2. See Baldwin (1965, 1985), bell hooks (1992, 2000) and Toni Morrison (1993).

3. See also my amended chapter on 'Contingent Hierarchies' in Routledge's electronic resource: The Social Issues Collection: A Routledge/University Readers Custom Library for Teaching (www.socialissuescollection.com/).

4. As a modern counterpoint, the Royal Shakespeare Company's *Hamlet* production in 2016 was played by a primarily Black British cast, with three white actors.

5. A film, *Why is My Curriculum White*, is viewable at: www.youtube.com/watch?v=Dscx4h2l-Pk.

12

Islamophobia

In this chapter we will

- Examine definitions of Islamophobia

- Trace the contextual discussions about fundamentalism

- Provide an insight into how Islamophobia is currently theorised

- Look at some case studies in which the theories are embodied

The term 'Islamophobia' emerged relatively recently as a concept discussed in the social sciences.[1] However, it covers a phenomenon which is far from new: the process of homogenising Muslims and attributing negative, backward and exotic otherness to them as a group. We will critically present some definitions of Islamophobia and its establishment as a sociological phenomenon in the twenty-first century. Clearly, there is racism addressed toward Muslims, and has been for some time, so the question is, do we need this new term? If so, what does it describe? What does it do? Could its content be dealt with under 'racism'?

In this chapter, we are going to first provide some context for the production of ideas about Islam, shorthanded as the relationship between the 'West' and the 'East'. This involves engaging with work by Said and Huntington. These bring out different aspects of the overarching relations at play in the construction of Islam. The second section tries to begin the work of separating the idea of 'fundamentalism' from Islam. The third looks more closely at definitions of Islamophobia, particularly in terms of what is at stake in understanding it as a form of racism rather than religious prejudice. We then discuss two arenas that might shed light on some of the cultural tensions: dress codes and socio-economic indicators. Finally, I offer some ways to think critically about Islamophobia as a set of ideas.

It has already been established in previous chapters that the distinction between phenotype and culture as the basis of discriminatory discourses and practices is actually a false dichotomy. In reality, they are two faces of the same phenomenon that have become increasingly entangled in the forms of 'new racism' emerging in the West over the last three decades (Chapter 9). There is even a case to say that culture preceded physical difference as the basis of discrimination: Balibar (Balibar and Wallerstein, 1991) suggests that anti-Semitism is paradigmatic of this, while Garner (2004, 2009b) points to the colonisation of Ireland and the racialisation of the Irish in the USA and Britain as later versions. Moreover, following on from the discussion in Chapter 10, in which a highly diverse group of people are clustered together under a temporary administrative status (asylum-seeker), this chapter provides another case study of Othering: the construction of Islam, a diverse set of practices with different sects or streams, crossing all the world's continents and involving people from all of what were labelled in the nineteenth century, the 'races' of the world.

Big Theories: 'Orientalism' and Clashes Between Civilisations

Said: The Idea of 'Orientalism'

Edward Said (1979) argues that over a period going back to the late eighteenth century, expert knowledge, developed in the academies of the West, created an exotic object: the 'Orient'. This space was completely different from the West: backward rather than modern and full of people ('Orientals') who are congenitally corrupt rather than honest; indolent rather than industrious; fanatical rather than objective; and selfishly dangerous rather than altruistically interested in the truth. I have used pairs of adjectives deliberately. Said's contention is that Western scholars have created the imaginary place, 'the Orient' and the people who populate it, 'Orientals', as opposites of the cherished image they have of themselves as Westerners. This process and set of practices is what he terms 'Orientalism'.[2] Indeed, the question of power to create representations lies at the heart of Said's thesis:

> ... the phenomenon of Orientalism as I study it here deals principally, not with a correspondence between Orientalism and Orient, but with the internal consistency of Orientalism and its ideas about the Orient ... despite or beyond any correspondence, or lack thereof, with a 'real' Orientalism. (Said, 1979: 5)

The representation is highly sexualised, as demonstrated in the paintings to which Said refers[3] and the 'anthropological' travel writings generated by scholars' engagement with the Middle East. Oriental men are conceptualised as weak and effeminate, yet a danger to white women, whom they covet. Oriental women, on the other hand, are mysterious, submissive and exotic. He finally contends that the policy-making circles of Western powers have understood the East in this Orientalist fashion because of the provision of this kind of information from experts. As Grosfoguel and Mielants (2006) argue, knowledge produced in the Western academy becomes the dominant norm, regardless of its accuracy, and it sets frames that construct Islam and Muslims in a specific way, as backward, aggressive and misogynistic. All discussions then take place within this framework. Grosfoguel and Mielants label this 'epistemic racism'.

Said's work has become a cornerstone of post-colonial studies, attracting a plethora of critical writings. Overall, there are some obvious gaps in the work, such as his overriding focus on the Middle East at the expense of other parts of Asia and North Africa (indeed omitting a large part of the Muslim world), the lack of follow-up to the gendered understandings he identifies in the writings of European and American scholars, and the implicit claim that everyone from the West who studies Eastern cultures is an Orientalist. Elsewhere, he is at pains to critique essentialist understandings of culture and people. Scholars who argue that the 'Orient' has a similarly reductive and politicised understanding of the 'Occident', that can be referred to as 'Occidentalism' (Carrier, 1992; Buruma and Margalit, 2004), may well have a point. Said's work is also open to the critique that the 'West' is as much of a misrepresentation as the 'East'. However, it is not clear that the power relations are the same: the Muslim world's relative economic and political weakness (with the exception of the oil-rich Gulf States) vis-à-vis the imperial and neo-colonial West means that, as Werbner (2005) points out, the anti-Americanism of Muslims can serve as a protest against geopolitical domination rather than the response of equals.

However, what remains is a thought-provoking argument that threads power relations to images circulating freely in Western culture, and which lie at the root of prejudice against Islam and Muslims.

Huntington: The 'Clash of Civilisations' Thesis

Political scientist Samuel Huntington published an article in the journal *Foreign Affairs* (1993) using a phrase drawn from a paper by 'Orientalist' scholar Bernard Lewis (1990) a few years previously. It was in part a response to historian Francis Fukuyama's thesis of 'the end of history' (1992), which claimed that liberal capitalism had defeated communism and that global *ideological* conflict was now to all extents and purposes over. The journal article received so much acclaim that Huntington worked the paper up into a full-length monograph (1996). His argument is straightforward. After the Cold War and the fall of the Berlin Wall, the world will realign along cultural (or civilisational lines):[4]

> It is my hypothesis that the fundamental source of conflict in this new
> world will not be primarily ideological or primarily economic. The great

divisions among humankind and the dominating source of conflict will be cultural. Nation states will remain the most powerful actors in world affairs, but the principal conflicts of global politics will occur between nations and groups of different civilizations. The clash of civilizations will dominate global politics. The fault lines between civilizations will be the battle lines of the future. (1993: 22)

The blocs Huntington labels 'civilisations' are 'the highest cultural groupings and the broadest level of identity short of that which distinguishes humans from other species' (1993: 24). 'Fault line conflicts' occur between neighbouring countries belonging to different civilisations (e.g. India and Pakistan) or within states that are home to populations from different civilisations (e.g. the former Yugoslavia). 'Core state conflicts' are on a global level between the major states of different civilisations (e.g. the Iraq war). Yet, the principal confrontation, he maintains, will be between the Judeo-Christian West and Islam (1993: 31–9). The conflicts between Islamic and other civilisations are particularly intense and violent. 'Islam', he asserts, 'has bloody borders' (1993: 35).

While Huntington found favour within neo-conservative policy circles especially, his thesis has been roundly criticised over two main areas. First, his conceptualisation of civilisations assumes homogeneity and ignores internal divisions. These blocs appear vast, discrete and culturally static. There are two forms of conflict arising: the divisions within the region of the world he terms 'Islam' can be ethnic as well as religious. It is questionable to imagine that a swathe of the world running from Northern through Eastern Africa to the Middle East, the Indian subcontinent and Indonesia has no significant internal divisions. The references he uses are drawn entirely from elites and from overviews of conflicts. Indeed, there is no empirical basis put forward for stating that this is in fact the primary way in which billions of people identify themselves. Secondly, the attribution of all conflict to exclusively cultural differences ignores any political, ideological or even economic basis for differences that might arise. In Huntington's perspective, everything is pursuant to clearly defined cultural boundaries. The idea that countries can contain people from different cultures without conflict, or that political ideas can be implemented at different times in different places, is absent. Indeed, Huntington's broad thesis actually chimes with that of the Islamist organisations deploying political violence (that is, groups that claim Islam as their source, but whose objectives are wholly political), a point made by Said (2001) in his review of Huntington's book.

So the two groups that have the greatest investment in the 'clash of civilisations' thesis are the two groups most capable of fuelling such a clash: strategic policy-makers in the West, and Islamic groups that use political violence. This brings us neatly to the question of 'fundamentalism'.

Box 12.1   Un-American Muslims

Saher Selod's (2015) middle-class professional Muslim interviewees in the USA had mostly grown up and/or been educated and worked in the USA for years, and were feeling comfortably part of the nation until the 9/11 attacks. However, their post-9/11 experiences have reconfigured them as intrinsically un-American. Indeed, many have changed their behaviour (by hiding or downplaying their affiliation to Islam as a way of managing their public and working lives) because their American co-workers link them dis-cursively to terrorism, backward civilisations and the oppression of women. This oppression is read through wearing the headscarf, and is much harder to avoid (like men who shave off their beard) if you are a woman who wants to wear the headscarf. Most importantly, Selod argues that the recurring comments linking Muslims to terrorism, to un-American activities and to cultural practices that lie outside the mainstream, serves to de-Americanise them. The ordinariness and professional status of these Muslim Americans does not inoculate them against racialisation. The power available to those who de-Americanise is clear from these stories.

The potent combination of physical and cultural elements that non-Muslims deploy to identify and 'Other' Selod's respondents demonstrates that Islamophobia is a form of racism rather than of religious prejudice (Garner and Selod, 2015). This process generates narratives about Muslim-ness that people are slotted into on the basis of physical, reli-gious, cultural and national genealogies rather than the values and behav-iours of the people themselves. This reduction of complexity and diversity to a narrow range of putative characteristics is of course constitutive of racist discourses, and here, of Islamophobia.

'Fundamentalism'

One of the ideological outcomes of the latest phase of political conflict between Islamist groups and nation states both in the Islamic world and the West, is the collocation 'Islamic fundamentalism'. Yet the term 'fundamental-ism' was coined in relation to Protestant churches in the USA in the 1920s as a mark of differentiation from what were seen as liberal and deviant churches. In Steve Bruce's (2000) work, like that of Karen Armstrong (2002), examples of fundamentalism are drawn from the major world religions. Bruce concludes that fundamentalism is 'a rational response of traditionally religious peoples to social, political and economic changes that downgrade the role of religion in public life' (Bruce, 2000: 116). Indeed, he points out that seen from the viewpoint of the 'fundamentalist', it is the people who do not observe the scriptures that are deviant. The norm of detaching oneself selectively from such texts is relatively recent in the Judeo-Christian world: the nineteenth century is the secularising century. However, he does argue that monotheistic religions (Christianity, Judaism and Islam) can give rise to more intense and dogmatic forms of fundamentalism. Eisenstadt (1995) uses the term 'fundamentalism' to refer to the attitude of religious groups that reject complex traditions, including scholarly and juridical interpretive ones, in favour of a 'return' to an idealised era or scriptures, often, he adds, with the added agenda of imposing their vision through political or violent means. In relation to contemporary acts of political violence committed by individuals or groups that see themselves fighting back for Islam against the West, Eisenstadt's definition at least captures the political dimension, whereas Bruce's fundamentalism is exclusively religious. In Bruce's terms, an Islamic fundamentalist could well have an interpretation of the Qu'ran that leads him or her to despise aspects of Western civilisation, but they would not act on this in the kinds of ways that others deploy political violence.

Parekh's early exploration of the subject (1991) tends toward Eisenstadt's. In fact, he argues that far from being traditionalist and conservative, fundamentalism is an attempt to engage with modernity: it provides a reading of scripture designed to be the basis of political activism engaging with the secular world, rather than humble contemplation. He makes a very useful distinction between 'ultra-orthodoxy' and fundamentalist understandings of the scripture, and forward-looking 'politico-religious projects' (Parekh, 1991: 41) based on a narrow and selective reading of scripture. Indeed, Parekh asserts that only religions 'of the book' (Islam, Christianity and Judaism) can experience 'fundamentalism' in the terms he sets out, because they are based around the direct inspiration of one set of writings that is understood as the word of God revealed. Other religions can have political movements based on writings, but not with a relationship established between scripture (as the word of God) and political action. The degree to which the various groups within the Islamic faith either do or do not reflect the 'true' messages of the Qu'ran, or what that means, lies well beyond the scope of this book. There are obviously a number of different paths within Islam – Sunni, Shi'ite, Sufi, Wahhabi, etc. – that have different emphases, traditions and understandings about what exactly constitutes ethical behaviour. If you add to this that the religion includes white Europeans and North Americans as well as Black Africans and African-descended people, people of Middle Eastern, North African and Indian subcontinental origin as well as Indonesians, this world faith starts to become less easy to visualise as a monolithic bloc, and that is even before we start to think about linguistic, regional, class and gender distinctions in the way Islam is experienced.

In a way, the *homogeneous* global community of all Muslims is, like Marx's international proletariat, a virtual reality, an aspiration of activists. What I am seeking to do here is suggest an accurate understanding of what the term 'Islamic fundamentalism' might actually mean: groups of people who see their position as at the vanguard of this *ummah*, taking the battle to the West and to those seen as its acolytes, with a long-term objective of overthrowing non-Islamic states and replacing them with states run according to what they think is a specific interpretation of the Qu'ran. It is to be noted that in this definition the political project dimension (as in Parekh [1991] and Eisenstadt [1995]) is the most significant. Indeed, the groups and individuals actually signified by the term 'Islamic fundamentalist' in this sense are those who actively support or condone political violence used not just against Westerners, but against other Muslims who are deemed not Muslim enough. The development of the Wahhabi jihadist 'IS'[5] since 1999 encapsulates the particular – and limited – appeal of this form of political action, attracting fighters from other countries to its jihadist project of establishing a caliphate in Iraqi/Syrian territory.

However, the most salient point about current discourse on Islam is that no definition of fundamentalism is offered. The vaguer the term remains, the easier it is to stretch it to fit anyone, including the overwhelming majority of Muslims: people who have no interest whatsoever in the political project of overthrowing states and replacing them. This space is exploited by anti-Islamic groups across the world: from Pamela Geller's American Freedom Defense Initiative to Geert Wilders in the Dutch parliament, and the cyberworld of discussions of the 'true nature' of Islam, the conclusion is that there is no such thing as a 'moderate Muslim' (Box 12.3). Yet Quraishi's (2005) British study, for example, suggests that Muslims feel their religious identity is 'soiled' as a result of depictions of adherents to Islam being considered fanatics, terrorists or fundamentalists. What the linking of the terms 'Islamic' and 'fundamentalist' actually accomplishes in contemporary discourse is to fuse in the minds of the Western public two different communities. On the one hand, we have Muslims in general (in all places at all times), some of whom might well have a developed critique of some Western practices and values derived from their reading of Islam (as do many Christians, Jews and secular people). On the other, there are the small number of people committed to a politics of violence and the establishment of an Islamic state to replace both existing states in Islamic countries, and Western states.

This focus is not meant to turn the gaze away from the political violence enacted by nation states, either against their own citizens or those of other countries. The 'war on terror' has involved a variety of state terrorist practices: the bombing of civilian populations; the suspension of the rule of law; imprisonment outside international law; shoot-to-kill policies; racial profiling. Indeed, the relationship of state and non-state forms of violence to one another needs to be thought of as more intimately linked. Al-Qaeda did not materialise out of nothing; it has a lineage going back to the Muslim Brotherhood in Egypt and the attempts to eradicate it by the Egyptian state. There are also links between superpowers' incursions into Muslim countries and the sponsorship of and recruitment to organisations wedded to political violence (Hiro, 2002).

We have noted Said's (2001) claim that both Islamophobes and Islamists believe the world is neatly split into two main civilisational blocs in confrontation. There is a kind of symmetry of understandings here. For the latter, the

West indiscriminately oppresses Islamic people, both in the West and in the Islamic world, thereby creating the *ummah* of oppression and resistance. Those who justify attacking people and objects within Muslim states in retaliation for bombings aimed at Westerners are also buying into this idea that *all* Muslims everywhere are fair game because they are somehow the cause of the actions of tiny numbers of people. In Adams and Burke's research on post-9/11 attitudes in England (2006: 992), 'Andrea' expresses exactly this sentiment:

PB: How do you feel about the media coverage?

Andrea: They was showing [Muslim people] being quite scared to go down the street, because they were getting attacked, Muslims over here, and spat at. I must admit, if I was walking down the street and I would see one of these, you know those dresses that they wear from head to toe, and I'd get angry cause I'd think, you know, 'your bloody beliefs, and all the rest of it, that did all that'. Even though I'd know they weren't personally to blame I'd still feel 'if it weren't for you bloody people'.

PB: You felt an anger towards ...?

Andrea: But it is a contradiction because I did, yeah, but at the same time I do know there are normal nice people that don't agree with it as well.

The readiness with which one can switch between these discourses is a clue to the normative racialisation of Muslims. As with asylum-seekers, a diverse group of ethnically distinct people can be categorised as innately dangerous. The cartoons of the Prophet Mohammed in the Danish newspaper in 2005 work on the same principle. The Prophet in that case represents all Muslims. He is carrying bombs to signify that in this world view, all Muslims are potential terrorists. The discursive process of making the terms 'Muslim', 'fundamentalism' and 'terrorist' adhere to one another is engaged in by the media and the State in its formulation of security policy that profiles all Muslims as potential terrorists, and it becomes the norm: to the point where it is accepted policy to make (male) bodies racialised as Islamic into a priori objects for punishment and suspicion (Bhattacharyya, 2008).

The outcome is to reduce the complexity of Islam to a one-dimensional figure that signifies terror. This is not to deny that some Muslims have used political violence to intimidate and kill opponents, just as have people from other religions and secular groups. The point is that the process of linking the three terms, 'Muslim', 'fundamentalist', 'terrorist', turns all Muslims everywhere into potential terrorists, or 'suspect communities' (Hillyard, 1993) regardless of their personal convictions, or at the very least into accomplices who should publicly denounce links even if there are none. Moreover, each time there is a terrorist attack, the link between the terms is underscored.

Definitions of Islamophobia

In 1996, the Runnymede Trust established the Commission on British Muslims and Islamophobia and published its report, *Islamophobia: A Challenge for Us All*, a year later (Commission on British Muslims and Islamophobia, 1997). The report set out eight distinctive features of Islamophobia. Each of these features contained 'closed' and 'open' views toward Islam (see Appendix 6). The common reading was that the closed views should be interpreted as prejudiced, whereas the open views should not. However, if these are the only options, this presents a problem. Where can opinions between these two end points on a continuum be classified? Few binary systems represent all the shades of the social world.

Islamophobia or Muslimphobia?

There is much debate over what racist dispositions Islamophobia constitutes. Millward (2008) suggests that 'narrow' and 'broad' positions can be adopted. Fred Halliday (1999) exemplifies Millward's 'narrow' position. He contends that Islamophobia denotes a fear of the religion of Islam (ideas and practices) rather than fear of Muslims per se, which should be labelled 'anti-Muslimism' (Halliday, 1999: 898). This is also the stance of Miles and Brown (2003), for example. Their question is, should Islamophobia be included under the term 'racism' because it is about a religion rather than a 'race'? Earlier writing had put forward the idea that it could not be considered racism because of the cultural, rather than racial, target. Muslims as a group are multiracial, therefore, the logic ran, Islamophobia could not be about 'race' (if 'race' is understood only as phenotype and not to do with culture).

Taking on a 'broad' position, Modood (1997: 4) argues that it is about both religion and 'race'. Islamophobia, he asserts, is more a form of 'cultural' racism than a religious intolerance. He, like Barker and Balibar in their different ways (Chapter 9), argues that cultural racism is a form of 'new' exclusion which is as pernicious as 'traditional' forms that focused on the body (Modood, 1992, 2007). We have seen that in the 'new racisms', the ideological centre has shifted so that 'race' seems now to be as much about insurmountable cultural differences as biological difference. These unbridgeable differences are often expressed around membership of national communities, so that the excluded group have some flaw(s) that mark them as undeserving of membership, such as African Americans in the literature on 'colour-blind racism', and European Muslims in the 'new racism'.

The issue of what exactly Islamophobia does is addressed directly by social anthropologist Pnina Werbner (2005: 5–6). She suggests that there are two broad conceptualisations of racism. One states that there are a variety of unique forms of racism, each specific to a group of targets and the historical context in which it arises (this is exactly the line I pursue in this book).

The other tends to see these specifics as simple layers of artifice cloaking the basic function of racism: to subjugate and/or destroy the Other. If the latter idea is correct, what is the point of using Islamophobia as a way to understand discourse and social action? To answer this, Werbner proposes a way to see what is specific about Islamophobia to the contemporary period. Her rationale involves using three 'logics' of racism (2005: 7) drawn from the work of Wieviorka (1995) and Bauman (1993). These are:

- self-purification = physical expulsion/elimination

- subordination = physical exploitation of labour

- assimilation = cultural destruction.

Corresponding to each of these logics, she designs a fantasised figure represent-ing the type of person to which this logic is principally addressed: the 'slave', the 'witch' and the 'Grand Inquisitor'. However, these, she adds, are not merely fantasies but real fears displaced onto real people, and 'what these people come to represent symbolically' (Werbner, 2005: 7). The symbolic threats are described in language drawn from psychoanalytic accounts of racism.

In the case of the subordination logic, the figure is the slave: out-of-control, order-threatening and perpetrating revenge through violence, theft and sexual aggression. Corresponding to the logic of assimilation is the witch, who:

> ... crystallizes fears of the hidden, disguised, malevolent stranger, of a general breakdown of trust, of a nation divided against itself. Your neighbour may be a witch who wants to destroy you. He or she is culturally indistinguishable in almost every respect because the witch masquerades as a non-alien. (Werbner, 2005: 7)

Here one thinks of Jews in Europe and various trading 'middleman minorities' (Bonacich, 1975), such as the Chinese in Malaysia and the Caribbean, Asians in the USA, Indians in East and Southern Africa, etc.

The logic most pertinent to Islamophobia, argues Werbner, is reliant on changes in the dominant ethos and values of Western society. Sexual threat and libido in the permissive West are now less threatening, while a society based on individual capital accumulation and consumption as an aspiration and measure of social worth renders the 'greedy' middleman minorities somewhat less terrifying than a century ago. So the figure that must be expelled in the act of self-purification is the 'Grand Inquisitor'.

This figure is chosen because Europe's intellectual history since the Middle Ages has been aimed at escaping the Inquisition, that essentialising, rights-denying, difference-swallowing space of punitive clerical control. 'What is scary about Islam', she contends, 'is the way it evokes the spectre of puritanical Christianity, a moral crusade, European sectarian wars, the Crusaders, the

Inquisition, the attack on the permissive society' (Werbner, 2005: 8). The function that such a figure performs is to create a bloc out of groups that are usually in tension with each other: the political far right, middle-class elites and the unsatisfied working classes:[6]

> The Islamic Grand Inquisitor is not a disguised and assimilated threat as the Jew was; 'he' is not subservient and bestial like the black slave. He is upfront, morally superior, openly aggressive, denying the validity of other cultures – in short, a different kind of folk devil altogether. (2005: 8)

This thought-provoking train of ideas indicates that there is a purpose to the term 'Islamophobia', in that it suggests something specific to the historical moment. Yet, despite the sophistication of this model, the class and gender aspects of the puzzle are not developed. We shall return to that later.

However, while there is some technical dispute over whether Islamophobia is a form of, rather than a separate concept from, racism, there is something of a consensus that the 2001 attacks in the USA marked a point that has seen a change in the way Muslims are perceived in the West. While Meer (2006) and Modood (2005) both claim that there have been positive changes, with more exposure of a variety of Muslims in the public domain meaning that it becomes more difficult to collapse them all into the category 'fundamentalist', more scholars see 2001 solely as the starting point of a worsening of the hostility shown toward Muslims. A rise in the number of attacks on Muslims across the West was observed in the immediate period after the September 2001 attacks (Allen and Nielsen, 2002). The media and the far right are identified as playing an active role in the development of anti-Islamic opinions (McDonald, 2002; Richardson, 2004; Larsson, 2005; Sheridan, 2006). The effects of this are clear in fieldwork done with white UK respondents in contemporary Britain, where Muslims have assumed the position of most threatening Other (Clarke and Garner, 2009). Abbas (2007) is therefore summarising other scholars' thoughts when he contends that both the volume and level of anti-Islamic sentiment in Western societies have intensified.

However, while there might be consensus that there is more hostility toward Muslims than before, and that this is linked to various responses to the attacks on Western targets since 2001, there is also a line of critique that suggests there are limits to the utility of Islamophobia. Is it a form of racism, a form of religious prejudice, or even secular critique? Can the term also be used, for example, as a way to silence criticism of practices that some consider unacceptable, or as a useful 'straw man' on which to blame everything negative in Muslims' lives? In other words, does every criticism or negative action toward Muslims or Islam constitute Islamophobia? Are Muslim women campaigning to be able to worship in mosques they are excluded from using Islamophobic arguments? Are Muslims who target other Muslims in wars and with political violence Islamophobic? There are voices that make qualified claims of this kind, such as Malik (2005), and others who point to the potential dangers of it (Richardson, 2004).

Religious authority of any kind comes into its most serious tension with secular society over how a body of ideas can be criticised when there seem to be opposite ways of understanding social relations: over the separation of the public and private spheres, over the role of women, over the way the leading figure in a given religion can be spoken of or represented. As students of the sociology of racism, we ought to exercise caution here, because the problem is that in the actual discourses that occur, arguments move very quickly from the specific to the general. In other words, attention has to be paid to not generalising a specific practice to all Muslims (or Jews, or Christians, or Sikhs, or Hindus and so on) everywhere, at all times, as we will see below in Delphy's (2006) engagement with the French law of 2004 against wearing headscarves to school. This is especially true when the same practices are also engaged in by people who are not part of the faith group under scrutiny.

Islamophobia: Racism, Religious Prejudice, Political Correctness?

In the first two chapters of the book I set out some basics of understanding racisms. There are three elements: power relationship, ideas and practices. Moreover, 'race' is never a given starting point, but is always the outcome of social relationships (racialisation). Although as Nasar Meer (2013: 386) points out,

> With some important exceptions, it is striking to observe the virtual absence of an established literature on race and racism in the discussion of Islamophobia; something that is only marginally more present in the discussion of antisemitism.

The departure point for the corpus from which 'race' is absent is that 'race' is not a property of the group identified but of the social relationships that engage the more and less powerful social groups. The main argument against Islamophobia being considered a form of racism is that Muslims do not constitute 'a race', therefore critiquing them cannot be racism. The counter-argument presented in this book is that it does not matter if Muslims are a priori a 'race', only that the ideas and practices of non-Muslims generate patterns of behaviour and outcomes that group people under the heading 'Muslim', then deal with them as if they share particular characteristics (beyond the religious affiliation to a global and non-unified religion). Here 'race' is, as Tyrer points out, 'a MacGuffin' (a red herring) (2013: 23). The empirical work carried out across the world demonstrates that Muslims' experiences follow patterns of being identified for differential treatment, particularly if they are women who wear headscarves or veils. However, it would still be true to say that the status of Islamophobia as a form of racism is highly contested. In a post-racial era it is still not strategically useful to groups opposed to Islam, or any other target, to be linked publicly and explicitly with the idea of racism. Indeed, beyond the academy there are important stakes attached to not acknowledging that Islamophobia is racism. Sayyid (2011: 2) sets these stakes out clearly:

> Because Muslims are not a race, any and all forms of discrimination and violence disproportionately directed at them is thinkable and doable. Because Muslims are not a race the systemic violations directed against them cannot be racially motivated. Because Muslims are not a race their subjugation is not racism. Thus most themes associated with previous expressions of racism can be (and increasingly are) brought back into style. Muslim extremists can join the black mugger, the Gypsy thief, the Jewish anarchist as the stars of racism's narratives.

Part of the epistemological battle (around what ideas mean, and what counts as knowledge) is the status of criticism in civil society. It is justifiable in liberal democracies to criticise religious ideas and practices, but not the racialised identity of those who profess them. The refusal to acknowledge Islamophobia as racist is therefore important for people engaged in the political struggles around Islam to be able to legitimately criticise Muslims – and this qualification should be clear – not just the wholly critiquable individuals who commit acts of murder, rape, political violence of all kinds, but to make critiques of Muslims apply always to them *as a group*: in other words to constantly have up their sleeve the argument that although a few Muslims may have done x, y or z, they could all potentially do them because they are all like that.

Indeed, as theoretical scholarship on Islamophobia develops, its systemic and complex functioning is being advanced theoretically. Abdellali Hajjat and Marwan Mohammed argue that Islamophobia is a 'total social fact' (2013: 18), in other words:

> … a social phenomenon that involves 'the whole of society and its institutions': political, administrative, legal, economic, media and intellectual. Islamophobia 'viscerally' engages individuals and social groups consciously and unconsciously, which mostly explains the 'hysterical' and 'emotive' elements of the controversies surrounding the Muslim question.

Within this social phenomenon, they carefully distinguish ideas, prejudices and practices, with the hypothesis that 'Islamophobia is the consequence of the construction of a "Muslim problem" whose "solution" lies in disciplining bodies and minds that are presumed to be Muslim' (2013: 20). Constructing the 'Muslim problem' is therefore understood as a project of State and institutions, aimed at collapsing Muslims who engage in political violence with all the rest, from a departure point which sees them as permanently unable to be part of Western civilisation, within a framework alluded to by Said (1979), Sayyid (2011) and Grosfoguel and Mielants (2006).

We shall now look at two areas that should help us establish some contours of the discourse on Muslims that are useful to any discussion of Islamophobia. The first is an exploration of the issues around one of the most contentious interfaces between Muslim and secular societies in recent years: dress codes. The second is a brief socio-economic outline of Muslims in the UK, which presents a dimension that is usually left out of the culturally focused discourse of difference that constitutes the basis for Islamophobia.

Islamic Women's Dress

Women wearing traditional Muslim dress (including anything from a head-scarf – the famous *foulard* in French – through to the *jilbab* to the full dress, *niqab* and *burqa*) raise questions about what types of difference are permitted and not permitted, about public and private space, and about gender relations. Westerners generally read such codes as over-dressing and narrowly as signs of oppression and excessive religiosity in secular settings. Here, we return to Said's observations about the West's power to construct Islam. The West's construction of the Orient is gendered as well as racialised: the univocal interpretation of Muslim women as submissive and oppressed is expressed in terms of clothing, interpreted as the outward manifestation of their oppression by Muslim men. This is not to say that women have not been the subject of violence perpetrated by men as 'punishment' for not dressing in the way they are expected to by some men with a particular understanding of the Qu'ran's injunction to dress modestly. The point is that the most oppressive behaviour becomes generalised in the discourse as the most frequent, as the norm. The second element of this process is that women who claim they choose to dress with headscarves, *jilbabs*, etc. to demonstrate their piety, are dismissed as being submissive and backward, or as just doing it to please Muslim men. In fact, empirical research, where Muslim women actually talk about their dress codes, reveals a highly complex set of factors. The wearing of particular clothing at particular times can be about the choice of which self to present at a given moment and why. Individuals do not all dress the same way all the time (Dwyer, 1999; Zempi, 2016). In terms of clothing, public space seems demarcated much more strongly from the private space than is the norm in secular understanding, and political choices sometimes overlap with religious ones, as Rinaldo (2007) concludes in her study of women in Indonesia:

> Among women's groups in Indonesia, the veil serves both to inculcate piety *and* to express identity, both intentionally and unintentionally. If we were to study these women only in terms of identity politics, we would certainly overlook their religious devotion and their efforts to produce themselves as pious subjects. But to examine them only in terms of their religious piety would be to neglect crucial elements of their political commitments ... Perhaps because of this complicated function and this very public role, clothing is an important part of how subjectivity is produced and reproduced. (2007: 18)

Clare Dwyer's (1999) interviews with young Muslim women in Britain reveal a continuum of practices that revolve around dressing to fit different contexts (school, leisure outside family, leisure with family, private space). The choices are sometimes to do with resistance, and sometimes bowing to expectations, but they are made within the context of a consensus that there is an obligation to wear at least a headscarf in certain contexts in order to retain the identity of a Muslim woman. This consensus is clearly not shared by every Muslim. As seen in the case of France and the 2004 law, there is a variety of interpretations among leading Muslim scholars. The idea of referring to empirical studies of Muslim women is not to be proscriptive, and suggest all Muslim women should wear headscarves, but merely to reflect the fact that many Muslim women wear headscarves and other articles of clothing *out of choice*. The headscarf is a symbolic border: verbal and physical attacks on Muslim women sometimes involve pulling off their veils, a symbolic act of humiliation, explored by Allen (2014) in terms of the impacts on women's lives.

Box 12.2   Do Muslim Women Need Saving?

Muslim women, as Said notes, have been objectified by the Western gaze as submissive, exotic and oppressed by backward men for centuries. The contemporary Islamophobic moment has heightened the intensity of this gaze. Muslim women (collapsed into one all-encompassing category denying any forms of agency) are helpless victims to be fought for; criticised for covering and actively uncovered in acts of individual and State violence; and when hailed as political actors, expected to limit themselves to engagements with the relationship between them and Muslim men.

When First Lady Laura Bush addressed the USA in November 2001, her agenda was to establish that the US armed forces about to invade Afghanistan were fighting to secure freedom from oppression for Muslim women oppressed by Taliban and Al-Qaeda terrorists. This type of mission statement is far from new, but it was a high-profile rendering of the helpless-Muslim-woman theme that has animated media, NGO and government interventions for decades. Lila Abu-Lughod's analyses of this theme (2002, 2013) provide plenty to reflect upon.

Pointing out that reducing Muslim women to symbols of helplessness reinforces Western feelings of superiority and obscures complex situations, she states: 'we need to be suspicious when neat cultural icons [the Muslim woman] are plastered over messier historical and political narratives, so we need to be wary when Lord Cromer in British-ruled Egypt, French ladies in Algeria, and Laura Bush, all with military troops behind them, claim to be saving or liberating Muslim women' (Abu-Lughod, 2002: 785).

Abu-Lughod finds herself writing a counter-cultural account against the dominant frames, and has to stress that she is not glossing over the actual discriminatory practices that impact upon Muslim women in Muslim countries, but challenging this depiction of such a diverse group in so many contexts as a simplistic, reductive 'figure': the Muslim woman. The process by which such figures are arrived at, she argues, ignores the contexts of war and poverty that frame their lives to a greater extent than just the local cultural variations.

As Christine Delphy points out below, Western feminists also use this narrative of saving as their departure point. There are multiple interpretations of the headscarf, veil and *burqa* by the women that wear them (Zempi, 2016), but the dominant Western reading is that they all signify oppression and policing of individualism by men. Indeed, the paradox of the theme that Muslim women are to be saved is that they frequently bear the brunt of the post-9/11 and 7/7 hostility, and an emerging form of specific attack (presumably recast as liberation) involves uncovering their heads, a physical manifestation of the ideas encapsulated in discourses on women's dress (Straw, 2006) and legislation like the French *burqa* ban of 2010. Those ideas have been drawn upon to posit Muslim women as the ultimate symbol of otherness, with *burqa* and/or veil-clad women appearing on political materials produced by right-wing nationalist parties across Europe throughout the current century.

Moreover, the perceived need to protect Muslim women extends to school-age girls, as Mirza (2015) notes in her study of English secondary schools. She finds that schools engage differently with Muslim girls and white non-Muslim girls, in that issues are attributed to culture in relation to the first group and class in relation to the latter (2015: 40–1). In the context of three Muslim school pupils fleeing the country to join ISIL in 2015, there is a very narrow focus on protecting Muslim women from their own cultures. 'Muslim young women are produced as abject, voiceless victims of their cultures and thus open to state surveillance in terms of cultural practice, but yet absent from the mainstream policy discourse which should protect them as equal citizens' (2015: 41). Yet even when they are invited to be central actors in policy, as in the PREVENT scheme analysed by Naaz Rashid (2014), this comes with conditions: they are expected to engage exclusively with the same paradigm of breaking free of patriarchal control. When they seek to broaden the agenda to include the economy and foreign policy, the reception by the State interlocutors is not positive.

Muslim women engage in a variety of feminist organisations working at different levels, and come with a range of political vantage points (Ali, 2012) that articulate with more general anti-globalisation and anti-racist movements. However, the characterisation of them as in need of saving is an enduring colonial and Islamophobic framing. We could fruitfully reflect on the discourses on radicalisation, the vulnerability of Muslim women, and what clothing means in a moment of backlash against multiculturalism (Lentin and Titley, 2011).

In France, the issue of dress codes has been taken a step further and a law in 2004 enshrined the principle that ostentatious religious symbols could not be worn in public (that is, state) schools. By 2010, there was a law against wearing a veil or *burqa* in public. It should be made clear that the republicans in

France fought for centuries to have the Church formally separated from the State, and the principle of secular public institutions (*la laïcité*) is one of the founding values of the French republic, dating back to the law of 1905. The 2004 legislation came after repeated *affaires du foulard* (Headscarf Affairs), the first of which was in 1989, where stand-offs had taken place between pupils wearing Islamic headscarves and schools that prevented them from entering, on the grounds that the school was a secular space. Over the period 1994–2003, around 100 pupils were thus banned from returning to school if they continued to wear headscarves. The government had occasionally been forced to intervene, and as the courts overturned around half of these expulsions, it became clear that the existing laws and regulations were open to too broad an interpretation (so that not every case ended up with the same outcome). After the Stasi Commission (Commission de Réflexion sur l'Application du Principe de Laïcité, 2003) had taken evidence, the government acted on its report and introduced the law that was passed in March 2004. We are going to look at the response of one high-profile French feminist scholar, Christine Delphy,[7] to the feminist discourse around the law, in order to draw some key points out, relating to the way the problem was constructed.

Delphy (2006) concentrates only on the feminist discourse about wearing the veil and/or headscarf in France (1999–2004). She does so to tease out the issues of anti-sexism and anti-racism, which were presented implicitly as the two options (anti-sexism for those in favour of the law, and anti-racism for those opposed). Delphy's arguments are reminiscent of the criticisms made by black and minority women about Western feminism (see Chapter 4): minority women's voices were ignored or downplayed; practices engaged in by all men were projected uniquely onto Muslims; French women assumed that they and their society was less sexist than that of Muslim women.

Firstly, the headscarf itself, she argues, became the subject of a hyperbolic attack in which power was attributed to it that it does not possess. It is described in turns as 'diabolical', a very important form of oppression of women, and as a sign enabling other women to be identified for rape. Secondly, in a binary opposition, French society became an opposite of Muslim society, in that patriarchal relations and male violence toward women evaporated from it, so that all the negative things that happened to women in France were linked with Muslims. It should also be borne in mind that the places where violence toward women and their oppression take place, according to the discourse, is very heavily loaded with class interpretations. The *banlieues* (suburbs of major cities in which large-scale public housing is concentrated) represent a space of working-class, and underclass, crime, immorality and violence in the French collective imagination. Young people – substantial proportions of whom are descended from immigrants – from such places occasionally engage in political shows of strength (from the early 1990s to the riots of November 2005). We should note that by saying *banlieue* the focus is surreptitiously seeping onto non-Muslim, non-immigrant working-class French people as well. During the period leading up to the passage of the law, the Commission heard evidence from very few Muslim women, and discussions in feminist circles included only those who were in favour of the law.

What happened in this process of distancing, argues Delphy, is that French feminists ended up reproducing the same set of relations as their opponents had in the past. First, the debates split women into two discrete groups: Muslims and non-Muslims. Then they read into this division a discrepancy of civilisation – modern (secular) vs backward (Muslim) – in which women are only victims. So, instead of looking at the intersection of 'race' and gender to see the specific position into which Muslim women are placed (simultaneously victims of racism and of sexism, but also agents), they placed them in a position where they were seen exclusively as victims of sexism, whose source was solely racialised men. Somehow, in this process, non-Muslim French society and its men had disappeared from the power equation. Indeed, some of the most vehement advocates of sexual equality in the public discourse underlying this law were French men who had made no contribution to gender equality discourse prior to this. The background to this story, argues Delphy, was the cumulative power of a number of campaigns for solidarity with Muslim women in various parts of the world, alongside the post-2001 'war on terror', which had made Muslim women into objects to be saved by French feminists. Indeed, the space in which to be French, Muslim and a woman (all at the same time) is virtually untenable given the parameters of the discussion Delphy describes. However, as Muslim responses show, this is exactly the identity prized by many people in contemporary France.

Delphy's contribution to interrogating assumptions in public discourse on Islam in the West is rich and provocative, touching as it does on class, gender, 'race' and sexuality. However, one of the major aspects of the position of Muslims in the West is very often overlooked in the academic attention paid to the issue: socio-economic inequalities. The next section will look at this in relation to the UK.

Box 12.3   Online Islamophobia

One notable feature of Islamophobia is its internet base. A set of prominent websites such as Bare Naked Islam, JihadWatch, Gates of Vienna and Stop Islamicisation of America, inter alia, maintain a stream of articles, news excerpts and links to similar sites and publications arguing that Islam is taking over the West (Islamification) with the help of liberal elites, and that multicultural societies are its vehicle. Images of veiled women, news of Muslims committing crimes (especially violent and/or sexual ones) and of violent acts carried out by terrorists are the usual fare of such sites, whose aim is to hammer home a message that Islam is a violent, misogynist and

(Continued)

(Continued)

hate-filled religion, and that there is no such thing as a 'moderate Muslim'. This powerful arsenal of well-funded sites is complemented by the various far-right nationalist parties across the world whose websites argue in a similar vein, although with a more local focus.

Online Islamophobia has numerous elements (web presence and social media being the most important) and different modes of engagement such as hashtagging. Awan (2016), for example, identifies spikes in Islamophobic social media activity in response to atrocities carried out, citing the #KillAllMuslims hashtag following the Paris attacks of November 2015; and #FuckMuslims on September 11. These collective acts, with people posting aggressive messages under hashtags, go hand-in-hand with trolling and threats on Muslim internet users that Awan identifies as traumatic, confidence-sapping experiences, particularly as mechanisms to stop it recurring are so ineffective, and the political will to do so seems lacking.

As stated above, a key part of the message conveyed is that all Muslims are equally dangerous. When US television company TLC broadcast *All American Muslim* in 2013–14, a controversy erupted (Chao, 2015) about its depictions of middle-class American(ised) Muslims: boycotts were threatened, and sponsors pulled out of the show, criticised by some as propaganda attempting to portray an acceptable and normal face of Muslims. This normality was interpreted by the Islamophobic actors engaged in the debate as deliberately trying to present a false picture of the generally zealous and aggressive religion that is the message disseminated elsewhere on the net.

Socio-Economic Indicators: Muslims in the UK

One of the mechanisms through which racialisation functions is by suppressing difference *among* the majority and minority groups, and to express it all as the difference *between* majority and minority. Looking at some of the statistical indicators allows us to identify some patterns.

In terms of geographical distribution, 4.28 per cent of the UK population were Muslims at the 2011 Census, and 47 per cent were born in the UK. British Muslims make up 12.8 per cent of London's population (37.8 per cent of British Muslims), and 39 per cent live in the North-West, the West Midlands and Yorkshire. There are concentrations of the Muslim population in Birmingham, Manchester, Leeds/Bradford and Lancashire towns such as Bolton, Preston and Oldham. Muslims from different national origins are differentially spatially distributed: Middle Eastern in North London, Indian in West London and Bangladeshis in East and North London, while Pakistanis are split across the East and West of the city (Mayor of London, 2006: 18–33). Two-thirds of Muslims are Asian and one-third non-Asian (including 8 per cent white). The labour force participation rate of Muslims is 19.8 per cent (vs 34.9 per cent for the nation), and the unemployment rate is 7.2 percent (vs 4.0 per cent nationally).

Forty-six per cent of Muslims now live in the poorest 10 per cent of local authority districts (compared to 32 per cent in 2001). Overall, Muslims have an 18 per cent higher risk of poverty than other groups (either religious or secular). This has a number of knock-on effects. One is poor health outcomes. While the proportion of Muslims declaring that their health was 'bad' is over-all similar to the national level of 5.1 per cent, for those in the over 50 category, it is double the national average. Housing status also compares unfavourably to the national levels: 43.1 per cent of Muslim households own their own home (or with a mortgage) vs 63.3 per cent nationally; while 27 per cent are in social housing (17.6 per cent nationally). However, these figures hide internal differences. Pakistani Muslims have higher rates of home-ownership and lower rates of social housing than the national average, while Bangladeshis have lower and higher respectively[8].

So on a number of indicators, Muslims in the UK are worse off than the average. Within those parameters, there are discrepancies between different groups, with Bangladeshis particularly over-represented near the bottom of the table. Moreover, there are positive changes in terms of levels of education (from 39 to 26 per cent 'no educational qualifications' between 2001 and 2011), and in younger women's education levels in particular. The proportion of Muslims in the 'Higher professional occupation' category is 5.5 per cent (vs 7.6 per cent overall). There is greater comparability in the 'Small employers and own account workers' category, where both the national and Muslim figures are over 9.0 per cent.

What might all this tell us about Muslim experience in the UK? While there is a growing middle class, the majority experience is framed by the working-class positions that most migrants have come to in Britain. Moreover, that experience is virtually always of an urban context, where the risk of poverty is growing and unemployment is higher than the national average.

While achievement is relatively low but growing in some areas, experiences of racism and a feeling of exclusion are unfortunately typical. This provides a position of marginality that frames questions expressed exclusively in religious terms, as if 'Muslim' was one's sole identity, unaffected by gender, 'race', class, age, etc. For example, there are implications of having a principally urban-based and relatively young population, as is the case of British Muslims. Their 14.4 per cent incarceration rate (Shaw, 2015)[9] is partly due to the youthful demographic, which puts a higher proportion of Muslims into the peak age cohort for offending, as well as the fact they are more likely to reside in urban areas which are subject to over-policing (Quraishi, 2005). Moreover, the over 50s group experiences health outcomes that are twice as poor as those of the national average, while the under 50s are indistinguishable from the national average. It is commonplace to focus on cultural distinctions between Muslim and non-Muslim populations, but this neglects a number of other relevant issues, notable socio-economic ones.

Conclusions

We have examined some of the background, theoretical interventions on Islamophobia and empirical material on Muslims' experiences. I am ever more convinced not only that 'Islamophobia' denotes a separate form of racism targeted at Muslims, just as 'anti-Semitism' demotes a precise pathology of racism directed against Jews, but that it is also a paradigmatic form of racism for our era: a blend of bodies and culture placed under state discipline, and with its clearly visible gendered and classed elements. These are particular racisms having much in common with other strands but also their own historical and geopolitical pathologies. Islamophobia's 'closed' and 'open' definitions are a starting point for discussion, but no more than that. However, very few people may find themselves completely in either of its columns. People's opinions can be contradictory and irrational as well as logical and rational.

- Islamophobia illustrates the intertwined nature of the physical and the cultural in recurring formations of 'race' and racism. As has been argued throughout this book, racism utilises ideas drawn from both the biological and the cultural domains. However, some extremely important structural and cultural issues are missed out by focusing on Islamophobia *solely* as a set of ideas about culture, even some as fascinating as the question of gendered dress, for example. Prejudice and the monopoly of the cultural realm distract our attention from systemic processes that are revealed in patterns of employment, education and segregation. The obstacles to integration in various Western regimes, and cultural flashpoints around them, are not derived solely from ideas about religion.

- Whatever definition of Islamophobia we end up with, it cannot prevent a progressive critique of social practices rationalised through specific *interpretations* of Islam which are clearly not the object of consensus among Muslims. These include, for example, political violence against civilians (this is obviously not only applicable to Islamists), anti-democratic government, and gendered punishments meted out for dress violations, adultery or other breaches of ethical codes. Opposition to these should figure on a progressive agenda in any case, whether or not they are being carried out by people who are Muslims.

- Islam is engaged in an ongoing dialogue within itself as well as with other world faiths. The cry of 'Islamophobia' ought not be allowed to silence calls for social justice. However, as a point of principle, the essential starting point is not to see any of these things as *intrinsic* to Islam, and thus not prevalent in other religions or secular practices. The fight for democracy is not confined to the Islamic world, and it is only in relatively recent times that European nations that see themselves as the vanguard of rights gave the entitlement to vote to adult women, for example. There are still gendered discrepancies in the life chances, employment patterns, wages and pensions of men and women in the West, and levels of violence committed by men against women, as Delphy points out (2005, 2006), are still very high.

- The way in which Islamophobia functions is precisely by collapsing a complex set of positions into one – a negative one, which is projected onto Muslims, and then evacuating the non-Muslim communities of any similar practices or norms. It operates, like all racisms, on binary principles (civilisation vs barbarity), where culture is one mediation of such difference, but the actors are in more complex positions than merely those defined by culture: they are also socially located by gender, class and education.

Points for Reflection

Could you set out the key points of the argument that Islamophobia is a useful concept?

Is Islamophobia about 'race', religion, both, neither?

Can you explain the gendered aspects of Islamophobia?

Further Reading

Vakil, A. (2010) 'Who's Afraid of Islamophobia?', in S. Sayyid and A.K Vakil (eds) *Thinking Through Islamophobia: Global Perspectives*, pp. 272-9. London: C. Hurst.

Final summarising chapter of collection that provides a synthesis and starting point for thinking about Islamophobia, and the social and political conditions that generate the contestation of this concept.

Abu-Lughod, L. (2013) *Do Muslim Women Need Saving?* Cambridge, MA: Harvard University Press.

This book confronts the idea that Muslim women are mainly victims of culture for the West to save, and instead demonstrates the diversity and complexity under the category 'Muslim women'.

Selod, S. (2015) 'Citizenship Denied: The Racialization of Muslim American Men and Women post-9/11', *Critical Sociology* 41(1): 77-95.

Interviews with American Muslims show how they are discursively stripped of their American-ness, racialised and thus turned into threats to US culture and values.

Overall Reflections on the Material Covered by this Book

One of the points for reflection in Chapter 1 was 'Can you think of any ways in which "race" and racism have impacted on your life?' Do you still have the same answer as you did then?

What are the core features of racism and what are the aspects that we can identify as being open to variation?

If you were given the task of setting topics for further study in this field (not covered by this book), what would they be and why?

Notes

1.   Rana (2007) argues that it dates back to the 1970s.

2.   Said can be seen talking about Orientalism on YouTube: uk.youtube.com/watch? v=_njKVdFL6Kw.

3.   One such key image is the Snake Charmer by Jean-Léon Gérôme, 1870, which adorns the cover of *Orientalism*. The painting can be seen at: www.jeanleongerome.org/Snake- Charmer.html.

4.   These civilisations are 'Western, Confucian, Japanese, Islamic, Hindu, Slavic-Orthodox, Latin American and possibly African' (Huntington, 1993: 25).

5.   The name of this organisation is 'Islamic State'; Daesh; ISIL (Islamic State of Iraq and the Levant'; ISIS (Islamic State of Iraq and Syria). News corporations in the West refer to it as so-called Islamic State.

6.   Werbner may well have captured here the alliance that won the UK's EU Referendum for the 'Leave' campaign in June 2016.

7.   Delphy was one of the founder members of the women's liberation movement in France in 1968, and published a very influential collection of essays on feminist organisation and theory, *L'ennemi principal* (1970). She went on to found the journal *Nouvelles Questions Féministes*, and is one of the leading figures in the French national research body, the CNRS.

8.   The Muslim Council of Britain (2015) produced a useful report synthesising the Census figures.

9.   Less than 1 per cent of this figure is accounted for by prisoners held on convictions for terrorist offences.

Appendices

Appendix 1: Racial Disparities in Wealth, USA, 2000

Even for middle-class subjects, the racial wealth and income disparities exist between white, black and Latino households. Although the 2000 *income* discrepancy tapers to its lowest point – 0.76 (that is, where African Americans on average earn 76 per cent of what their white counterparts do) – the other measurements of wealth used by the authors tell a different story. Net financial assets (NFA) (including property in the form of land, housing, stocks and shares, savings, etc.) and net worth are far lower for African Americans than whites. Also, because of borrowing for house purchases, 63 per cent of black households own zero or negative NFA, while only 28 per cent of white ones fall into that category. More black households therefore require two people to be working, so if income were cut off, far fewer could remain solvent – either at current level or poverty level – than white households. The *closest* point between black and white middle-class couples in terms of wealth is in the group earning over $50,000, where the wealth ratio is 0.52. Further down the socio-economic scale, the discrepancies are larger than this, with white wealth averaging at eight times that of African American wealth.

Source: Oliver, M. and Shapiro, T. (2006) *Black Wealth/White Wealth: A New Perspective on Racial Inequality*, 2nd edn. New York: Routledge.

Appendix 2: Racial Definitions from the US Census, 2010

'White' refers to a person having origins in any of the original peoples of Europe, the Middle East, or North Africa. It includes people who indicated their race(s) as 'White' or reported entries such as Irish, German, Italian, Lebanese, Arab, Moroccan, or Caucasian.

'Black or African American' refers to a person having origins in any of the Black racial groups of Africa. It includes people who indicated their race(s) as 'Black, African Am., or Negro' or reported entries such as African American, Kenyan, Nigerian, or Haitian.

'American Indian or Alaska Native' refers to a person having origins in any of the original peoples of North and South America (including Central America) and who maintains tribal affiliation or community attachment. This category includes people who indicated their race(s) as 'American Indian or Alaska Native' or reported their enrolled or principal tribe, such as Navajo, Blackfeet, Inupiat, Yup'ik, or Central American Indian groups or South American Indian groups.

'Asian' refers to a person having origins in any of the original peoples of the Far East, Southeast Asia, or the Indian subcontinent, including, for example, Cambodia, China, India, Japan, Korea, Malaysia, Pakistan, the Philippine Islands, Thailand and Vietnam. It includes people who indicated their race(s) as 'Asian' or reported entries such as 'Asian Indian', 'Chinese', 'Filipino', 'Korean', 'Japanese', 'Vietnamese' and 'Other Asian' or provided other detailed Asian responses.

'Native Hawaiian or Other Pacific Islander' refers to a person having origins in any of the original peoples of Hawaii, Guam, Samoa, or other Pacific Islands. It includes people who indicated their race(s) as 'Pacific Islander' or reported entries such as 'Native Hawaiian', 'Guamanian or Chamorro', 'Samoan' and 'Other Pacific Islander' or provided other detailed Pacific Islander responses.

'Some Other Race' includes all other responses not included in the White, Black or African American, American Indian or Alaska Native, Asian, and Native Hawaiian or Other Pacific Islander race categories described above. Respondents reporting entries such as multiracial, mixed, interracial, or a Hispanic or Latino group (for example, Mexican, Puerto Rican, Cuban, or Spanish) in response to the race question are included in this category.

Appendix 3: US Census Briefs

WHITE – Census Bureau, The White Population: 2010, p. 1, www.census.gov/prod/cen2010/briefs/c2010br-05.pdf

BLACK – Census Bureau, The Black Population: 2010, p. 1, www.census.gov/prod/cen2010/briefs/c2010br-06.pdf

HISPANIC/LATINO – www.census.gov/prod/cen2010/briefs/c2010br-04.pdf

ASIAN – www.census.gov/prod/cen2010/briefs/c2010br-11.pdf

TWO OR MORE RACES – www.census.gov/prod/cen2010/briefs/c2010br-13.pdf

Appendix 4: Proportions of White/Non-White Groups in UK Census (2001 and 2011)

Ethnic group	Percentage of total 2001	Percentage of minority population	Percentage of total 2011	Percentage of minority population
White	92.0	n/a	87.0	n/a
Mixed	1.2	15.0	2.0	14.7
Asian	4.0	50.0	6.3	45.0
Black	2.0	25.0	3.0	22.0
Chinese	0.4	5.0	0.7	4.7
Other	0.4	5.0	1.0	6.7
Non-white minorities	8.0	100	100	100

Appendix 5: United Nations High Commission on Refugees Definitions

The UNHCR works for the global 'population of concern'. That population (www.unhcr.org/uk/who-we-help.html) is broken down in the UN statistics into the following groups:

Asylum-seeker

An asylum-seeker is someone whose request for sanctuary has yet to be processed. Every year, around 1 million people seek asylum.

National asylum systems are in place to determine who qualifies for international protection. However, during mass movements of refugees, usually as a result of conflict or violence, it is not always possible or necessary to conduct individual interviews with every asylum-seeker who crosses a border. These groups are often called 'prima facie' refugees (www.unhcr.org/uk/asylum-seekers.html).

Refugee

Refugees are people fleeing conflict or persecution. They are defined and protected in international law (the 1951 Geneva Convention, and the 1967 New York Protocol) (see: www.unhcr.org/uk/1951-refugee-convention.html), and must not be expelled or returned to situations where their life and freedom are at risk.

Internally Displaced Person (IDP)

Internally displaced people (IDPs) have not crossed a border to find safety. Unlike refugees, they are on the run at home.

While they may have fled for similar reasons, IDPs stay within their own country and remain under the protection of its government, even if that government is the reason for their displacement. As a result, these people are among the most vulnerable in the world (www.unhcr.org/uk/internally-displaced-people.html).

Stateless People

Today, at least 10 million people around the world are denied a nationality. As a result, they often aren't allowed to go to school, see a doctor, get a job, open a bank account, buy a house or even get married.

Stateless people may have difficulty accessing basic rights such as education, healthcare, employment and freedom of movement. Without these things, they can face a lifetime of obstacles and disappointment (www.unhcr.org/uk/stateless-people.html).

Appendix 6: 'Closed' and 'Open' Views of Islam

Distinctions	Closed views of Islam	Open views of Islam
1. Monolithic/ diverse	Islam seen as a single monolithic bloc, static and unresponsive to new realities.	Islam seen as diverse and progressive, with internal differences, debates and development.
2. Separate/ interacting	Islam seen as separate and other – (a) not having any aims or values in common with other cultures; (b) not affected by them; and (c) not influencing them.	Islam seen as interdependent with other faiths and cultures – (a) having certain shared values and aims; (b) affected by them; and (c) enriching them.
3. Inferior/ different	Islam seen as inferior to the West – barbaric, irrational, primitive, sexist.	Islam seen as distinctively different, but not deficient, and as equally worthy of respect.
4. Enemy/ partner	Islam seen as violent, aggressive, threatening, supportive of terrorism, engaged in 'a clash of civilisations'.	Islam seen as an actual or potential partner in joint cooperative enterprises and in the solution of shared problems.
5. Manipulative/ sincere	Islam seen as a political ideology, used for political or military advantage.	Islam seen as a genuine religious faith, practised sincerely by its adherents.
6. Criticism of West rejected/ considered	Criticisms made by Islam of 'the West' rejected out of hand.	Criticisms of 'the West' and other cultures are considered and debated.
7. Discrimination defended/ criticised	Hostility toward Islam used to justify discriminatory practices toward Muslims and exclusion of Muslims from mainstream society.	Debates and disagreements with Islam do not diminish efforts to combat discrimination and exclusion.
8. Islamophobia seen as natural/ problematic	Anti-Muslim hostility accepted as natural and 'normal'.	Critical views of Islam are themselves subjected to critique, lest they be inaccurate and unfair.

Source: Commission on British Muslims and Islamophobia (1997) *Islamophobia: A Challenge for Us All*. London: Runnymede Trust. Reprinted with permission.

References

Aas, K. and Bosworth, M. (eds) (2013) *Migration and Punishment: Citizenship, Crime Control, and Social Exclusion*. Oxford: Oxford University Press.

Abbas, T. (2007) 'British Muslim Minorities Today: Challenges and Opportunities to Europeanism, Multiculturalism and Islamism', *Sociology Compass* 1(2): 720–36.

Abu-Lughod, L. (2002) 'Do Muslim Women Really Need Saving? Anthropological Reflections on Cultural Relativism and its Others', *American Anthropologist* 104(3): 783–90.

Abu-Lughod, L. (2013) *Do Muslim Women Need Saving?* Cambridge, MA: Harvard University Press.

Adams, M. (2006) 'A New Definition of Racism', Townhall blogs. Available at: http://town-hall.com/columnists/MikeSAdams/2006/04/10/a_new_definition_of_racism.

Adams, M. and Burke, P.J. (2006) 'Recollections of September 11 in Three English Villages: Identifications and Self-Narrations', *Journal of Ethnic and Migration Studies* 32(6): 983–1003.

Adamson, W. (1986) 'Interview with Gayatri Spivak', *Thesis Eleven* 15: 91–7.

Adorno, T., Frenkel-Brunswik, E., Levinson, D.J. and Sanford, R.N. (1950) *The Authoritarian Personality*. New York: Harper.

Ahmed, S. (2001) 'The Organisation of Hate', *Law and Critique* 12(3): 345–65.

Ahmed, S. (2004) 'Affective Economies', *Social Text* 79 22(2): 117–39.

Ali, S. (2003) *Mixed-Race, Post-Race: Gender, New Ethnicities and Cultural Practice*. Oxford: Berg.

Ali, Z. (2012) *Féminismes islamiques*. Paris: La Fabrique.

Allen, C. (2014) 'Exploring the Impact of Islamophobia on Visible Muslim Women Victims: A British Case Study', *Journal of Muslims in Europe* 3(2): 137–59.

Allen, C. and Nielsen, J. (2002) *Summary Report on Islamophobia in the EU after 11 September 2001*. Vienna: European Union Monitoring Centre on Xenophobia and Racism.

Allport, G. (1954) *The Nature of Prejudice*. Reading, MA: Addison-Wesley.

AMEA (Association of Multiethnic Americans) (2001) 'AMEA Responds to Multiracial Census Data'. Available at: http://multiracial.com/index.php/2001/03/12/amea-responds-to-multiracial-census-data/.

American Society for Aesthetic Plastic Surgery (1999) *ASAPS 1999 Statistics on Cosmetic Surgery*. Available at: www.surgery.org/sites/default/files/ASAPS1999 Stats.pdf.

American Society for Aesthetic Plastic Surgery (2003) *2003 ASAPS Statistics –
8.3 Million Cosmetic Procedures: American Society for Aesthetic Plastic
Surgery Reports 20 Percent Increase.* Available at: www.surgery.org/sites/
default/files/2003%20ASAPS%20Statistics-%208.3%20Million%20
Cosmetic%20Procedures.pdf.

American Society of Plastic Surgeons (2009) *2008 Cosmetic Demographics.*
Available at: https://d2wirczt3b6wjm.cloudfront.net/News/Statistics/2009/
cosmetic-procedures-ethnicity-2009.pdf.

American Society of Plastic Surgeons (2015) 2014 *Plastic Surgery Statistics
Report.* Available at: https://d2wirczt3b6wjm.cloudfront.net/News/Statistics/
2015/plastic-surgery-statistics-full-report-2015.pdf.

Amos, V. and Parmar, P. (1984) 'Challenging Imperial Feminism', *Feminist
Review* 17(1): 3–19.

Anderson, B. (1983) *Imagined Communities: Reflections on the Origin and
Spread of Nationalism.* London: Verso.

Anderson, W. (2006) *The Cultivation of Whiteness: Science, Health and Racial
Destiny in Australia.* Durham, NC: Duke University Press.

Andreassen, R. (2014) 'The Search for the White Nordic: Analysis of the
Contemporary New Nordic Kitchen and Former Race Science', *Social
Identities* 20(6): 438–51.

Anthias, F. (1990) 'Race and Class Revisited – Conceptualising Race and
Racisms', *Sociological Review* 38(1): 19–43.

Anthias, F. (1999) 'Institutional Racism, Power and Accountability', *Sociological
Research Online* 4(1). Available at: www.socresonline.org.uk/4/lawrence/
anthias.html.

Anthias, F. and Yuval-Davis, N. (1993) *Racialized Boundaries: Race, Nation,
Gender, Colour and Class and the Anti-racist Struggle.* London: Routledge.

Appelbaum, N., MacPherson, A. and Rosemblatt, K. (2003) *Race and Nation in
Modern Latin America.* Chapel Hill, NC: University of North Carolina Press.

Appiah, A. (1990) 'Racisms', in D. Goldberg (ed.) *Anatomy of Racism,*
pp. 3–17. Minneapolis: Minnesota University Press.

Aptheker, H. (1946) *The Negro People in America: A Critique of Gunnar
Myrdal's 'An American Dilemma'.* New York: International Publishers.

Ardrey, R. (1967) *The Territorial Imperative.* London: Collins.

Armstrong, B. (1989) 'Racialization and Nationalist Ideology: The Japanese
Case', *International Sociology* 4(3): 329–43.

Armstrong, K. (2002) *The Battle for God: Fundamentalism in Judaism,
Christianity and Islam.* New York: Alfred Knopf.

Aspinall, P. and Song, M. (2013) *Mixed Race Identities.* New York: Springer.

Atton, C. (2006) 'Far-Right Media on the Internet: Culture, Discourse and
Power', *New Media and Society* 8(4): 573–87.

Australian Human Rights Commission (1997) *Bring them Home: Report of
the National Inquiry into the Separation of Aboriginal and Torres Strait
Islander Children from Their Families.* Sydney: AHRC. Available at: www.
hreoc.gov.au/social_justice/bth_report/index.html.

Awan, I. (ed.) (2016) *Islamophobia in Cyberspace: Hate Crimes go Viral.*
Aldershot: Ashgate.

Back, L. (2002) 'Aryans Reading Adorno: Cyber-Culture and Twenty-First Century Racism', *Ethnic and Racial Studies* 25(4): 628–51.

Bailey, S.R., Loveman, M. and Muniz, J.O. (2013) 'Measures of "Race" and the Analysis of Racial Inequality in Brazil', *Social Science Research* 42(1): 106–19.

Baldwin, J. (1965) *Going to See the Man*. New York: Dial Press.

Baldwin, J. (1985) *The Price of the Ticket: Collected Non-Fiction 1948–1985*. New York: St. Martin's Press.

Balibar, E. and Wallerstein, I. (1991) *Race, Class, Nation: Ambiguous Identities*. New York: Verso.

Ball, S. (1993) 'Education, Markets, Choice and Social Class: The Markets as a Class Strategy in the UK and the USA', *British Journal of the Sociology of Education* 14(1): 3–19.

Banton, M. (1977) *The Idea of Race*. London: Tavistock Press.

Banton, M. (1996) 'Racism', in E. Cashmore (ed.) *Dictionary of Race and Ethnic Relations*, 4th edn. London: Routledge.

Banton, M. (1997) *Ethnic and Racial Consciousness*. Harlow: Addison Wesley Longman.

Barany, Z. (2002) *The East European Gypsies: Regime Change, Marginality, and Ethnopolitics*. Cambridge: Cambridge University Press.

Barker, M. (1981) *The New Racism: Conservatives and the Ideology of the Tribe*. London: Junction Books.

Barker, M. (1990) 'Biology and the New Racism', in D. Goldberg (ed.) *Anatomy of Racism*, pp. 18–37. Minneapolis: University of Minnesota Press.

Barnes, N. (1994) 'Face of the Nation: Race, Nationalisms and Identities in Jamaican Beauty Pageants', *The Massachusetts Review*, 35(3/4): 471–92.

Barot, R. and Bird, J. (2001) 'Racialization: The Genealogy and Critique of a Concept', *Ethnic and Racial Studies* 24(4): 601–18.

Barrett, J. and Roediger, D. (1997) 'Inbetween Peoples: Race, Nationality and the "New Immigrant" Working Class', *Journal of American Ethnic History* Spring: 3–44.

Barth, F. (1969) *Ethnic Groups and Boundaries: The Social Organization of Culture Difference*. Boston: Little Brown.

Bauman, Z. (1989) *Modernity and the Holocaust*. Cambridge: Cambridge University Press.

Bauman, Z. (1993) *Life in Fragments*. Oxford: Blackwell.

BBC News (2013) 'Mystery Girl Maria's Parents Found in Bulgaria by DNA', 25 October. Available at: www.bbc.co.uk/news/world-europe-24673804.

Beck, U. (1992) *Risk Society: Toward a New Modernity*. London: Sage.

Beck, U. (2000) 'Living Your Own Life in a Runaway World: Individualisation, Globalisation and Politics', in W. Hutton and A. Giddens (eds) *On the Edge: Living with Global Capital*, pp. 164–74. New York: The New Press.

Beeman, A., Glasberg, D.S. and Casey, C. (2011) 'Whiteness as Property: Predatory Lending and the Reproduction of Racialized Inequality', *Critical Sociology* 37(1): 27–45.

Benson, M. (2011) *The British in Rural France: Lifestyle Migration and the Ongoing Quest for a Better Way of Life*. Oxford: Oxford University Press.

Bhattacharyya, G. (2008) *Dangerous Brown Men: Exploiting Sex, Violence and Feminism in the War on Terror*. London: Zed Books.

Bigo, D. and Guild, E. (eds) (2005) *Controlling Frontiers: Free Movement into and within Europe*. Aldershot: Ashgate.

Billig, M. (1995) *Banal Nationalism*. London: Sage.

Bishop, R. and Robinson, L. (1998) *Night Market: Sexual Cultures and the Thai Economic Miracle*. New York: Routledge.

Blackmon, D. (2008) *Slavery by Another Name: The Re-Enslavement of Black People in America from the Civil to World War II*. New York: Doubleday.

Bliss, C. (2012) *Race Decoded: The Genomic Fight for Social Justice*. Stanford, CA: Stanford University Press.

Bobo, L. (2004) 'Inequalities that Endure? Racial Ideology, American Politics and the Peculiar Role of the Social Sciences', in M. Krysan and A. Lewis (eds) *The Changing Terrain of Race and Ethnicity*, pp. 13–42. New York: Russell Sage Foundation.

Bobo, L., Kluegel, J. and Smith, R. (1997) 'Laissez-Faire Racism: The Crystallization of a Kinder, Gentler, Anti-Black Ideology', in S. Tuch and J. Martin (eds) *Racial Attitudes in the 1990s: Continuity and Change*, pp. 15–44. Westport, CT: Praeger.

Bonacich, E. (1975) 'A Theory of Middleman Minorities', *American Sociological Review* 38: 583–94.

Bonilla-Silva, E. (1997) 'Rethinking Racism: Toward a Structural Interpretation', *American Sociological Review* 62(3): 465–80.

Bonilla-Silva, E. (2002) 'We are All Americans!: The Latin Americanization of Racial Stratification in the USA', *Race and Society* 5(1): 3–16.

Bonilla-Silva, E. (2013) *Racism Without Racists: Color-Blind Racism and the Persistence of Racial Inequality in America*, 4th edn. Lanham, MD: Rowman and Littlefield.

Bourdieu, P. (1977) *Outline of a Theory of Practice*. Cambridge: Cambridge University Press.

Bourdieu, P. (1984) *Distinction: A Social Critique of the Judgement of Taste*. London: Routledge.

Bourdieu, P. (1986) 'The Forms of Capital', in J.G. Richardson (ed.) *The Handbook of Theory: Research for the Sociology of Education*, pp. 241–58. New York: Greenwood Press.

Bouteldja, H. (2015) 'State Racism(s) and Philosemitism or How to Politicize the Issue of Antiracism in France?', Speech at House of Literature, Oslo, 3 March: Available at: http://indigenes-republique.fr/state-racisms-and-philosemitism-or-how-to-politicize-the-issue-of-antiracism-in-france/.

Bracey, G. (2015) 'Toward a Critical Race Theory of State', *Critical Sociology* 41(3): 553–72.

Brah, A. (1996) *Cartographies of Diaspora: Contesting Identities*. London: Routledge.

Brian, T. and Laczko, F. (eds) (2014) *Fatal Journeys: Tracking Lives Lost During Migration*. Geneva: International Organisation for Migration. Available at: https://publications.iom.int/system/files/pdf/fataljourneys_countingtheuncounted.pdf.

Broberg, G. and Roll-Hansen, N. (2005) *Eugenics and the Welfare State: Sterilization Policy in Norway, Sweden, Denmark, and Finland*. East Lansing: Michigan State University Press.

Brown, M. (2002) 'Crime, Governance and the Company Raj: The Discovery of Thuggee', *British Journal of Criminology* 42(1): 77–95.

Bruce, S. (2000) *Fundamentalism*. Cambridge: Polity Press.

Brunsma, D. (ed.) (2006) *Mixed Messages: Multiracial Identities in the 'Color-Blind' Era*. Boulder, CO: Lynne Rienner.

Burleigh, M. (2001) *A New History of the Third Reich*. London: Pan.

Buruma, I. and Margalit, A. (2004) *Occidentalism: The West in the Eyes of its Enemies*. New York: Penguin.

Byrne, B. (2006) *White Lives: The Interplay of 'Race', Class and Gender in Everyday Life*. London: Routledge.

Calhoun, C. (1997) *Nationalism*. Milton Keynes: Open University Press.

Camiscioli, E. (2001) 'Producing Citizens, Reproducing the "French Race": Immigration, Demography and Pronatalism in Early Twentieth-Century France', *Gender and History* 13(3): 593–621.

Carbado, D., Crenshaw, K., Mays, V. and Tomlinson, B. (2013) 'Intersectionality: Mapping the Movements of a Theory', *Du Bois Review* 10(2): 303–12.

Carby, H. (1982) 'White Woman Listen! Black Feminism and the Boundaries of Sisterhood', in *The Empire Strikes Back*, pp. 212–31. Centre for Contemporary Cultural Studies. London: Hutchinson.

Carmichael, S. and Hamilton, C. (1967) *Black Power: The Politics of Liberation*. New York: Random House.

Carr, L. (1997) *Color-Blind Racism*. Thousand Oaks, CA: Sage.

Carrera, S., Bigo, D. and Guild, E. (eds) (2013) *Foreigners, Refugees or Minorities? Rethinking People in the Context of Border Controls and Visas*. Aldershot: Ashgate.

Carrier, J. (1992) 'Occidentalism: The World Turned Upside-Down', *American Ethnologist* 19(2): 195–212.

Cartwright, S. (1860) 'Slavery in the Light of Ethnology', in E. Elliott (ed.) *Cotton is King and Pro-Slavery Arguments*. Augusta, GA: Pritchard, Abbott and Loomis.

Cavallaro, J. and Manuel, A. (1997) *Police Brutality in Urban Brazil*. New York: Human Rights Watch/Americas.

Chakraborti, N. (2010) 'Beyond "Passive Apartheid"? Developing Policy and Research Agendas on Rural Racism in Britain', *Journal of Ethnic and Migration Studies* 36(3): 501–17.

Chamberlain, H. (1911 [1899]) *The Foundations of the Nineteenth Century* (trans. John Lees). London and New York: John Lane.

Channel 4 (2013) 'Second Roma Child Taken by Irish Police for DNA test', 23 October. Available at: www.channel4.com/news/ireland-roma-child-blonde-maria-found-police-dna-test.

Chao, E.C. (2015) 'The-Truth-About-Islam. Com: Ordinary Theories of Racism and Cyber Islamophobia', *Critical Sociology* 41(1): 57–75.

Childs, E. (2005) *Navigating Interracial Borders: Black–White Couples and Their Social Worlds*. New Brunswick, NJ: Rutgers University Press.

Christian, M. (2004) 'Assessing Multiracial Identity', in J. Ifekwunigwe (ed.) *Mixed Race Studies: A Reader*, pp. 303–12. London: Routledge.

Chua, A. (2011) *Battle Hymn of the Tiger Mother.* London: Bloomsbury Publishing.

Clarke, S. and Garner, S. (2009) *White Identities.* London: Pluto.

Collomb, G. (1999) 'Entre ethnicité et national: A propos de la Guyane', *Socio-anthropologie* 6. Available at: http://socio-anthropologie.revues.org/113.

Combahee River Collective (1982 [1977]) 'A Black Feminist Statement', in G. Hull, P. Scott and B. Smith (eds) *All the Women Are White, All the Blacks Are Men, But Some of Us Are Brave: Black Women Studies*, pp. 13–22. Old Westbury, NY: The Feminist Press.

Commission de Réflexion sur l'Application du Principe de Laïcité dans la République (2003) *Rapport au Président de la République.* Paris: La Documentation Française. Available at: www.ladocumentationfrancaise. fr/var/storage/rapports-publics/034000725.pdf.

Commission on British Muslims and Islamophobia (1997) *Islamophobia: A Challenge for Us All.* London: Runnymede Trust.

Cornelius, W., Tsuda, T., Martin, P. and Hollifield, T. (eds) (2004) *Controlling Immigration: A Global Perspective.* Stanford, CA: Stanford University Press.

Cornelius, W., Martin, P. and Hollifield, T. (1996) *Controlling Immigration: A Global Perspective.* Stanford, CA: Stanford University Press.

Cox, O.C. (1948) *Caste, Class and Race.* New York: Doubleday.

Crenshaw, K. (1989) 'Demarginalising the Intersection of Race and Sex: A Black Feminist Critique of Anti-Discrimination Doctrine, Feminist Theory and Anti-Racist Politics', *University of Chicago Legal Forum* 139: 383–94. Available at: http://chicagounbound.uchicago.edu/cgi/viewcontent.cgi? article=1052&context=uclf.

Crenshaw, K. (1991) 'Mapping the Margins: Intersectionality, Identity Politics, and Violence against Women of Color', *Stanford Law Review* 43(6): 1241–99.

Crenshaw, K. (1997) 'Color-Blind Dreams and Racial Nightmares: Reconfiguring Racism in the Post-Civil Rights Era', in T. Morrison and C. Lacour (eds) *Birth of a Nation'hood*, pp. 97–168. New York: Pantheon Books.

Cutler, D., Glaeser, E. and Vigdor, J. (1999) 'The Rise and Decline of the American Ghetto', *Journal of Political Economy* 107(3): 455–506.

Dalmage, H. (2000) *Tripping on the Color Line: Black–White Multiracial Families in a Racially Divided World.* New Brunswick, NJ: Rutgers University Press.

Daniel, G.R., Kina, L., Dariotis, W.M. and Fojas, C. (2014) 'Emerging Paradigms in Critical Mixed Race Studies', *Journal of Critical Mixed Race Studies*, 1(1): 6–65.

Daniels, J. (1997) *White Lies: Race, Class, Gender, and Sexuality in White Supremacist Discourse.* New York: Routledge.

Davenport, C. (1911) *Heredity in Relation to Eugenics.* New York: Henry Holt & Co.

Dávila, J. (2003) *Diploma of Whiteness: Race and Social Policy in Brazil, 1917–1945.* Durham, NC: Duke University Press.

Davis, A.Y. (1998) 'Racialized Punishment and Prison Abolition', in T. Lott and J. Pittman (eds) *Blackwell Companion to African-American Philosophy*, pp. 360–9. London: Basil Blackwell.

Davis, A.Y. (2001a) 'Race, Gender, and Prison History: From the Convict Lease System to the Supermax Prison', in D.F. Sabo, T.A. Kupers and W. James (eds) *Prison Masculinities*, pp. 35–45. Philadelphia: Temple University Press.

Davis, A.Y. (2001b) *Women, Race and Class*. London: Virago.

Davis, F.J. (1991) *Who is Black? One Nation's Definition*. University Park, PA: Pennsylvania State University Press.

Davis, F.J. (2006) 'Defining Race: Comparative Perspectives', in D. Brunsma (ed.) *Mixed Messages*, pp. 15–32. Boulder, CO: Lynne Rienner.

Davis, M. (1992) *City of Quartz: Excavating the Future in Los Angeles*. New York: Vintage.

Davis, M. (2001) *Late Victorian Holocausts: El Niño Famines and the Making of the Third World*. New York: Verso.

Dawkins, R. (1976) *The Selfish Gene*. Oxford: Oxford University Press.

Dawney, L. (2008) 'Racialization of Central and East European Migrants in Herefordshire', Working Paper 53, University of Sussex: Sussex Centre for Migration Research.

Delgado, R. and Stefancic, J. (1995) *Critical Race Theory: The Cutting Edge*. Philadelphia, PA: Temple University Press.

Delgado, R. and Stefancic, J. (1997) *Critical White Studies: Looking Behind the Mirror*. Philadelphia, PA: Temple University Press.

Delphy, C. (1970) 'L'ennemi principal', *Partisan*, 54–5.

Delphy, C. (2005) 'Gender, Rage and Racism: The Ban of the Islamic Headscarf in France', in M. Thapan (ed.) *Transnational Migration and the Politics of Identity*, pp. 228–51. London: Sage.

Delphy, C. (2006) 'Antisexisme or anti-racisme? Un faux dilemme', *Nouvelles Questions Féministes* 25(1): 59–83.

Denis, A. (2008) 'Review Essay: Intersectional Analysis', *International Sociology* 23(5): 677–94.

DeSalle, R. and Tattersall, I. (2014) 'Mr. Murray, You Lose the Bet', *Genewatch* 27(2). Available at: www.councilforresponsiblegenetics.org/genewatch/GeneWatchPage.aspx?pageId=532.

Despres, L. (ed.) (1975) *Ethnicity and Resource Competition in Plural Societies*. Berlin: Walter de Gruyter.

Dhami, R., Squires, J. and Modood, T. (2006) *Developing Positive Action Policies: Learning from the Experiences of Europe and North America*. Department of Work and Pensions Research Report No. 406. Leeds: Department of Work and Pensions. Available at: www.tariqmodood.com/uploads/1/2/3/9/12392325/developing_positive_action_policies.pdf.

Dirks, D., Heldman, C. and Zack, E. (2015) '"She's White and She's Hot, So She Can't Be Guilty": Female Criminality, Penal Spectatorship, and White Protectionism', *Contemporary Justice Review* 18(2): 160–77.

Doane, A. (2006) 'What is Racism? Racial Discourse and Racial Politics', *Critical Sociology* 32(2–3): 255–74.

Douglass, R. (2000) 'Upgrading America's Conversations on Race: The Multi-Race Option for Census 2000', Association of Multi Ethnic Americans, June 2000. Available at: http://amea.site/census/upgrade2k.asp.

Du Bois, W.E.B. (1998 [1935]) *Black Reconstruction in the United States, 1860–1880.* New York: Free Press.

Du Bois, W.E.B. (2003 [1920]) *Darkwater: Voices From Within the Veil.* Amherst, NY: Humanity Books.

Duster, T. (2003) *Backdoor to Eugenics*, 2nd edn. New York: Routledge.

Duster, T. (2006) 'Lessons from History: Why Race and Ethnicity Have Played a Major Role in Biomedical Research', *Journal of Law, Medicine and Ethics* 34(3): 487–96.

Dwyer, C. (1999) 'Veiled Meanings: Young British Muslim Women and the Negotiation of Differences', *Gender, Place and Culture* 6(1): 5–26.

Dyer, R. (1997) *White.* London: Routledge.

Eccleston, B. (2016) 'Travellers Group Says Councils Should Provide Permanent Sites Rather than Spend £20m a Year on Evictions', *Coventry Evening Telegraph*, 8 January. Available at: www.coventrytelegraph.net/news/coventry-news/travellers-group-says-councils-should-10704031.

Edmonds, A. (2007) 'Triumphant Miscegenation: Reflections on Beauty and Race in Brazil', *Journal of Intercultural Studies* 28(1): 83–97.

Ehrenreich, B. and Hochschild, A. (eds) (2003) *Global Woman: Nannies, Maids, and Sex Workers in the New Economy.* New York: Metropolitan Books.

Eisenberg, J. (2009) 'From Neo-Enlightenment to Nihonjinron: The Politics of Anti-Multiculturalism in Japan and the Netherlands', *Macalester International* 22(1): 76–107.

Eisenstadt, S. (1995) 'Fundamentalism, Phenomenology, and Comparative Dimensions', in M.E. Marty and R.S. Appleby (eds) *Fundamentalisms Comprehended*, pp. 259–76. Chicago: University of Chicago Press.

Elliott, A. (2008) *Making the Cut: How Cosmetic Surgery is Transforming Our Lives.* London: Reaktion Books.

Ellison, R. (1952) *Invisible Man.* New York: Random House.

Equality Authority (2006) *Annual Report 2006.* Dublin: Equality Authority.

Erel, U. (2011) 'Complex Belongings: Racialization and Migration in a Small English City', *Ethnic and Racial Studies* 34(12): 2048–68.

Essed, P. (1991) *Understanding Everyday Racism: An Interdisciplinary Theory.* London: Sage.

European Union (2000) 'Council Directive 2000/78/EC of 27 November 2000: Establishing a General Framework for Equal Treatment in Employment and Occupation'. Available at: http://eur-lex.europa.eu/LexUriServ/LexUriServ.do?uri=CELEX:32000L0078:en:HTML.

Evans, S. (2014) 'Victims of a Craze for Cosmetic Surgery', *BBC News Online*, 15 December. Available at: www.bbc.co.uk/news/magazine-30295758.

Eze, E. (1997) *Race and the Enlightenment: A Reader.* Boston: Blackwell.

Fanning, B. (2002) *Racism and Social Change in the Republic of Ireland.* Manchester: Manchester University Press.

Fanon, F. (1967a) *Black Skin, White Masks*. New York: Grove Press.

Fanon, F. (1967b) *The Wretched of the Earth*. New York: Grove Press.

Farough, S. (2004) 'The Social Geographies of White Masculinities', *Critical Sociology* 30(2): 241–64.

Favell, A. (2008) 'The New Face of East–West Migration in Europe', *Journal of Ethnic and Migration Studies* 34(5): 701–16.

Feagin, J. (2006) *Systemic Racism: A Theory of Oppression*. New York: Routledge.

Fenton, S. (2007) *Ethnicity*, 2nd edn. Cambridge: Polity Press.

Flannery, E. (2004 [1985]) *The Anguish of the Jews: Twenty-Three Centuries of Antisemitism*, 2nd edn. Mahwah, NJ: Paulist Press.

Ford, R., Morrell, G. and Heath, A. (2012) '"Fewer but Better"? Public Views about Immigration', in A. Park, E. Clery, J. Curtice, M. Phillips and D. Utting (eds) *British Social Attitudes: The 29th Report*, pp. 26–44. London: NatCen Social Research. Available at: www.bsa.natcen.ac.uk/media/38852/bsa29_full_report.pdf.

Forman, T. (2004) 'Color-Blind Racism and Racial Indifference: The Role of Racial Apathy in Facilitating Enduring Inequalities', in M. Krysan and A. Lewis (eds) *The Changing Terrain of Race and Ethnicity*, pp. 43–66. New York: Russell Sage Foundation.

Forman, T. and Lewis, A. (2006) 'Racial Apathy and Hurricane Katrina: The Social Anatomy of Prejudice in the Post-Civil Rights Era', *Du Bois Review* 3(1): 175–202.

Foucault, M. (1977) *Discipline and Punish: The Birth of the Prison* (trans. Alan Sheridan). New York: Vintage.

Foucault, M. (2003) *Society Must Be Defended: Lectures at the Collège De France, 1975–76*. London: Allen Lane.

Fox, J., Moroşanu, L. and Szilassy, E. (2015) 'Denying Discrimination: Status, "Race", and the Whitening of Britain's New Europeans', *Journal of Ethnic and Migration Studies* 41(5): 729–48.

Frankenberg, R. (1994) *White Women, Race Matters*. Madison: University of Wisconsin Press.

Fraser, S. (ed.) (1995) *The Bell Curve Wars: Race, Intelligence, and the Future of America*. New York: Basic Books.

Frederickson, G. (1988) *The Arrogance of Race*. Hanover, NH: Wesleyan University Press.

Freedman, M. (1960) 'The Growth of a Plural Society in Malaya', *Pacific Affairs* 33(2): 158–68.

Freimuth, V., Crouse Quinn, S., Thomas, S., Colea, G., Zook, E. and Duncan, T. (2001) 'African Americans' Views on Research and the Tuskegee Syphilis Study', *Social Science and Medicine* 52(5): 797–808.

Fukuyama, F. (1992) *The End of History and the Last Man*. New York: Free Press.

Fuller, T. (2006) 'A Vision of Pale Beauty Carries Risks for Asia's Women', *New York Times*, 14 May. Available at: www.nytimes.com/2006/05/14/world/asia/14thailand.html?pagewanted=2&_r=2&sq=skin%20whitening&st=nyt&scp=7.

Furnivall, J.S. (1939) *Netherlands India: A Study of Plural Economy.* Cambridge: Cambridge University Press.

Gallagher, C. (2003) 'Color-Blind Privilege: The Social and Political Functions of Erasing the Color Line in Post-Race America', *Race, Gender and Class* 10(4): 1–17.

Gallagher, C. (2015) 'Colorblind Egalitarianism as the New Racial Norm', in K.Murji and J. Solomos (eds) *Theories of Race and Racism*, pp. 40–56. London: Routledge.

Gallagher, C. and Twine, F.W. (2007) 'The Future of Whiteness: A Map of the "Third Wave"', *Ethnic and Racial Studies* 31(1): 4–24.

Galton, F. (1905) 'Eugenics: Its Definition, Scope and Aims', *Sociological Papers* 1: 45–51.

Gans, H. (1979) 'Symbolic Ethnicity: The Future of Ethnic Groups and Cultures in America', *Ethnic and Racial Studies* 2(1): 1–20.

Garner, S. (2004) *Racism in the Irish Experience.* London: Pluto.

Garner, S. (2007a) *Whiteness: An Introduction.* London: Routledge.

Garner, S. (2007b) 'The European Union and the Racialization of Immigration, 1986–2006', *Race/Ethnicity: Multidisciplinary Global Contexts* 1(1): 61–87.

Garner, S. (2007c) 'Babies, Blood and Entitlement: Gendered Citizenship and Asylum in the Republic of Ireland', *Parliamentary Affairs* 60(4): 137–51.

Garner, S. (2009a) 'Empirical Research into White Racialized Identities in Britain', *Sociology Compass* 2(6): 1–14.

Garner, S. (2009b) 'Ireland: From Racism without "Race", to "Racism without Racists"', *Radical History Review* 104: 41–56.

Garner, S. (2013) 'The Racialisation of Asylum in Provincial England: Class, Place and Whiteness', *Identities*, 20(5): 503–21.

Garner, S. (2015) *A Moral Economy of Whiteness.* London: Routledge.

Garner, S. and Selod, S. (2015) 'The Racialization of Muslims: Islamophobia and Empirical Studies', *Critical Sociology* 41(1): 9–19.

Garner. S., Cowles, J., Lung, B. and Stott, M. (2009) 'Sources of Resentment, and Perceptions of Ethnic Minorities among Poor White People in England', National Community Forum/Department for Communities and Local Government. Available at: http://webarchive.nationalarchives.gov.uk/2012 0919132719/http://www.communities.gov.uk/documents/communities/pdf/1113921.pdf.

Giddens, A. (1984) *The Constitution of Society: Outline of a Theory of Structuration.* Cambridge: Polity Press.

Giddings, P. (1984) *When and Where I Enter: The Impact of Black Women on Race and Sex in America.* New York: William Morrow.

Gilens, M. (1999) *Why Americans Hate Welfare: Race, Media and the Politics of Antipoverty Policy.* Chicago: University of Chicago Press.

Gillborn, D. (2005) 'Education Policy as an Act of White Supremacy: Whiteness, Critical Race Theory and Education Reform', *Journal of Education Policy* 20(4): 485–505.

Gilman, S. (1991) *The Jew's Body.* New York: Routledge.

Gilroy, P. (1987) *Ain't No Black in the Union Jack.* London: Hutchinson.

Gilroy, P. (2000) *Against Race: Imagining Political Culture Beyond the Color Line.* Cambridge, MA: The Belknap Press of Harvard University Press.

Glenn, E. (2008) 'Yearning for Lightness: Transnational Circuits in the Marketing and Consumption of Skin Lighteners', *Gender and Society* 22(3): 281–302.

Gobineau, A. de (1853–55) *Essai sur l'inégalité des races humaines*. Paris: Firmin Didot.

Goffman, E. (1963) *Stigma: Notes on the Management of Spoiled Identity*. Englewood Cliffs, NJ: Prentice-Hall.

Golash-Boza, T. (2015) *Deported: Immigrant Policing, Disposable Labor and Global Capitalism*. New York: New York University Press.

Golash-Boza, T. (2016) 'A Critical and Comprehensive Theory of Race and Racism', *Sociology of Race and Ethnicity* 2(2): 129–41.

Goldberg, D. (2000) *The Racial State*. Boston: Blackwell.

Goldberg, D. (2005) 'On Racial Americanization', in K. Murji and J. Solomos (eds) *Racialization: Studies in Theory and Practice*, pp. 87–102. Oxford: Oxford University Press.

Goldberg, D. (2009) *The Threat of Race: Reflections on Racial Neoliberalism*. Hoboken, NJ: Wiley.

Goodhart, D. (2004) 'Too Diverse', *Prospect*, 20 February.

Goodhart, D. (2013) *The British Dream: Successes and Failures of Post-War Immigration*. London: Atlantic Books.

Gordon, A. (1999) 'Globalism and the Prison Industrial Complex: An Interview with Angela Davis', *Race and Class* 40(2–3): 145–57.

Gordon, L. (1997) *Her Majesty's Other Children*. Lanham, MD: Rowman and Littlefield.

Gotham, K. (2000) 'Urban Space, Restrictive Covenants and the Origins of Racial Residential Segregation in a US City, 1900–50', *International Journal of Urban and Regional Research* 24(3): 616–33.

Graham, K. (2016) 'The British School-to-Prison Pipeline', in K. Andrews and L. Palmer (eds) *Blackness in Britain*, pp. 130–42. London: Routledge.

Gramsci, A. (1971) *Selections from the Prison Notebooks of Antonio Gramsci* (ed./trans. Q. Hoare and G. Nowell-Smith). New York: International Books.

Grant, M. (1915) *The Passing of the Great Race*. New York: Charles Scribner's Sons.

Green, D. (ed.) (2000) *Institutional Racism in the Police Force: Fact or Fiction*. London: Civitas. Available at: www.civitas.org.uk/pdf/cs06.pdf.

Greenslade, R. (2005) *Seeking Scapegoats: The Coverage of Asylum in the UK Press*. London: Institute for Public Policy Research.

Grosfoguel, R. and Mielants, E. (2006) 'The Long-Durée Entanglement between Islamophobia and Racism in the Modern/Colonial Capitalist/Patriarchal World-System: An Introduction', *Human Architecture* 5(1): 1–12.

Guðjónsdóttira, G. and Loftsdóttir, K. (2016) 'Being a Desirable Migrant: Perception and Racialization of Icelandic Migrants in Norway', *Journal of Ethnic and Migration Studies*. Available at: http://dx.doi.org/10.1080/1369 183X.2016.1199268.

Hainmueller, J. and Hopkins, D. (2014) 'Public Attitudes Toward Immigration', *Annual Review of Political Science* 17: 225–49.

Hajjat, A. and Mohammed, M. (2013) *Islamophobie: Comment les élites françaises fabriquent le 'problème musulman'*. Paris: La Découverte.

Halkias, A. (2003) 'Money, God and Race: The Politics of Reproduction and the Nation in Modern Greece', *European Journal of Women's Studies* 10(2): 211–32.

Hall, S. (1980) 'Race, Articulation and Societies Structured in Dominance', *In UNESCO, Sociological Theories: Race and Colonialism*. París: UNESCO.

Hall, S. (1988) 'New Ethnicities', in K. Mercer (ed.) *Black Film Black Cinema*, pp. 27–31. London: Institute of Contemporary Arts.

Hall, S., Critcher, C., Jefferson, T., Clarke, J. and Roberts, B. (1978) *Policing the Crisis: Mugging, the State and Law and Order*. London: Macmillan.

Halliday, F. (1999) 'Islamophobia Reconsidered', *Ethnic and Racial Studies* 22(5): 892–902.

Hanchard, M. (1998) *Orpheus and Power: The Movimento Negro of Rio de Janeiro and Sao Paulo, Brazil, 1945–1988*. Princeton, NJ: Princeton University Press.

Hanchard, M. (ed.) (1999) *Racial Politics in Contemporary Brazil*. Durham, NC: Duke University Press.

Hancock, A.-M. (2004) *The Politics of Disgust: The Public Identity of the Welfare Queen*. New York: NYU Press.

Hancock, A. (2011) *Solidarity Politics for Millennials: A Guide to Ending the Oppression Olympics*. New York: Springer.

Hancock, A.-M. (2012) 'Trayvon Martin, Intersectionality, and the Politics of Disgust', *Theory and Event* 15(3). Available at: http://muse.jhu.edu/article/484428.

Hancock, A.M. (2013) 'Empirical Intersectionality: A Tale of Two Approaches'. *UC Irvine Law Review* 3(2): 259–96.

Harap, L. (1987) *Creative Awakening: The Jewish Presence in Twentieth-Century American Literature, 1900–1940s*. Santa Barbara, CA: Greenwood Publishing.

Haraway, D. (1988) 'Situated Knowledges: The Science Question in Feminism and the Privilege of Partial Perspective', *Feminist Studies* 14(3): 575–99.

Harding, S. (1991) *Whose Science? Whose Knowledge? Thinking from Women's Lives*. Ithaca, NY: Cornell University Press.

Harell, A., Soroka, S. and Ladner, K. (2014) 'Public Opinion, Prejudice and the Racialization of Welfare in Canada', *Ethnic and Racial Studies* 37(14): 2580–97.

Harris, C. (1993) 'Whiteness as Property', *Harvard Law Review* 106(8): 1707–91.

Hartigan, J. (1997) 'Locating White Detroit', in R. Frankenberg (ed.) *Displacing Whiteness*, pp. 180–213. Durham, NC: Duke University Press.

Hartigan, J. (1999) *Racial Situations: Class Predicaments of Whiteness in Detroit*. Princeton, NJ: Princeton University Press.

Hartigan, J. (2005) *Odd Tribes: Toward a Cultural Analysis of White People*. Durham, NC: Duke University Press.

Haywood, K. and Yar, M. (2006) 'The "Chav" Phenomenon: Consumption, Media and the Construction of a New Underclass', *Crime, Media, Culture* 2(1): 9–28.

Herder, J.G. (1784–91) *Ideas for a Philosophy of a History of Humanity*, cited in E. Eze (1997) *Race and Enlightenment: A Reader*. Boston: Blackwell.

Herrnstein, R. and Murray, C. (1994) *The Bell Curve: Intelligence and Class Structure in American Life*. New York: Free Press.

Hill-Collins, P. (1990) *Black Feminist Thought*. New York: Routledge.

Hillyard, P. (1993) *Suspect Community*. London: Pluto.

Hiro, D. (2002) *War Without End: The Rise of Islamist Terrorism and the Global Response*. London: Routledge.

Hobsbawm, E. and Ranger, T. (1983) *The Invention of Tradition*. Cambridge: Cambridge University Press.

Holloway, S. (2003) 'Outsiders in Rural Society? Constructions of Rurality And Nature – Society Relations in the Racialisation of English Gypsy-Travellers, 1869–1934', *Environment and Planning D: Space and Society* 21: 695–715.

Holloway, S. (2005) 'Articulating Otherness? White Rural Residents Talk About Gypsy-Travellers', *Transactions* 30: 351–67.

Holmes, O. (2016) 'Thai Ad with "White Makes You Win" Message Lambasted for Racism', The *Guardian*, 8 January. Available at: www.theguardian.com/world/2016/jan/08/thai-advert-white-makes-you-win-skin-whitening-lambasted-for-racism.

hooks, b. (1982) *Ain't I a Woman? Black Women and Feminism*. Boston: South End Press.

hooks, b. (1992) *Black Looks: Race and Representation*. Boston: South End Press.

hooks, b. (2000) *Where We Stand: Class Matters*. New York: Routledge.

Horsman, R. (1981) *Race and Manifest Destiny: The Origins of American Anglo-Saxonism*. Cambridge: Cambridge University Press.

Horton, H.D. (2006) 'Racism, Whitespace and the Rise of the Neo-Mulattos', in D. Brunsma (ed.) *Mixed Messages: Multiracial Identities in the 'Color-Blind' Era*, pp. 117–21. Boulder, CO: Lynne Rienner.

Hubbard, P. (2005) ' "Inappropriate and Incongruous": Opposition to Asylum Centres in the English Countryside', *Journal of Rural Studies* 21(1): 3–17.

Hübinette, T. and Räterlinck, L. (2014) 'Race Performativity and Melancholic Whiteness in Contemporary Sweden', *Social Identities*, 20(6): 501–14.

Hughey, M. (2012) *White Bound: Nationalists, Antiracists, and the Shared Meanings of Race*. Stanford: Stanford University Press.

Hunter, M. (2007) 'The Persistent Problem of Colorism: Skin Tone, Status, and Inequality', *Sociology Compass* 1(1): 237–54.

Huntington, S. (1993) 'The Clash of Civilizations and the Remaking of World Order', *Foreign Affairs* 72(3): 22–49.

Huntington, S. (1996) *The Clash of Civilizations and the Remaking of World Order*. New York: Simon & Schuster.

Husbands, C. (1987) 'British Racisms: The Construction of Racial Ideologies', in C. Husbands (ed.) *'Race' in Britain*. London: Hutchinson.

Hussain, Y. and Bagguley, P. (2005) 'Citizenship, Ethnicity and Identity: British Pakistanis after the 2001 "Riots"', *Sociology* 39(3): 407–25.

Hylton, K. (2005) '"Race", Sport and Leisure: Lessons From Critical Race Theory', *Leisure Studies* 24(1): 81–98.

Ifekwunigwe, J. (1999) *Scattered Belongings: Cultural Paradoxes of 'Race', Nation and Gender*. London: Routledge.

Ifekwunigwe, J. (2001) 'Re-Membering "Race": On Gender, Mixed Race and Family in the African Diaspora', in D. Parker and M. Song (eds) *Rethinking 'Mixed Race'*, pp. 42–64. London: Pluto.

Ifekwunigwe, J. (2004) *Mixed Race Studies: A Reader*. London: Routledge.

Ignatieff, M. (2000) 'Less Race, Please', in D. Green (ed.) *Institutional Racism and the Police: Fact or Fiction?*, pp. 21–4. London: Institute for the Study of Civil Society.

International Council on Human Rights Protection (2000) 'The Persistence and Mutation of Racism'. Available at: www.ichrp.org/files/reports/26/112_report_en.pdf.

Ioanide, P. (2015) *The Emotional Politics of Racism: How Feelings Trump Facts in an Era of Colorblindness*. Stanford, CA: Stanford University Press.

Irish Traveller Movement (2013) 'ITM Statement in Response to Roma Children Taken into Care', 23 October. Available at: http://enarireland.org/statement-in-response-to-roma-children-taken-into-care/.

IRP (Institute on Race and Poverty) (2002) 'Long Island Fair Housing: A State of Inequity'. Available at: www.eraseracismny.org/storage/documents/housing/Long_Island_Fair_Housing_A_State_of_Inequity.pdf.

Itagaki, R. (2015) 'The Anatomy of Korea-Phobia in Japan', *Japanese Studies* 35(1): 49–66.

Jacobson, M. (1998) *Whiteness of a Different Colour: European Immigrants and the Alchemy of Race*. Cambridge, MA: Harvard University Press.

James, C.L.R. (1963) *Beyond a Boundary*. London: Hutchinson.

Jasper, J. (2006) 'Emotions and the Microfoundations of Politics: Rethinking Ends and Means', in S. Clarke, P. Hoggett and S. Thompson (eds) *Emotions, Politics and Society*, pp. 14–30. Basingstoke: Palgrave.

Jessop, B. (1990) *State Theory: Putting the Capitalist State in its Place*. Cambridge: Polity Press.

Johnson, H. and Shapiro, T. (2003) 'Good Neighborhoods, Good Schools: Race and the "Good Choices" of White Families', in A. Doane and E. Bonilla-Silva (eds) *White Out: The Continuing Significance of Racism*, pp. 173–88. New York: Routledge.

Johnson, J.W. (1990 [1917]) *Autobiography of an Ex-Colored Man*. New York: Penguin.

Jones, D.M. (1997) 'Darkness Made Visible: Law, Metaphor and the Racial Self', in R. Delgado and J. Stefancic (eds) *Critical White Studies: Looking Behind the Mirror*, pp. 66–78. Philadelphia: Temple University Press.

Jones, J. (1993) *Bad Blood: The Tuskegee Syphilis Experiment*. New York: Free Press.

Jones, S. (1994) *The Language of the Genes: Biology, History and the Evolutionary Future*. London: Flamingo.

Joseph, P. (ed.) (2006) *The Black Power Movement: Rethinking the Civil Rights–Black Power Era*. New York: Routledge.

Kahn, J. (2006) 'Race, Pharmacogenomics, and Marketing: Putting BiDil in Context', *The American Journal of Bioethics* 6(5): W1–W5.

Kahn, J. (2007a) 'Race-ing Patents/Patenting Race: An Emerging Political Geography of Intellectual Property in Biotechnology', *Iowa Law Review* 92(2): 354–416.

Kahn, J. (2007b) 'Race in a Bottle', *Scientific American*, July. Available at: www.sciam.com/article.cfm?id=race-in-a-bottle.

Kandeh, J. (1992) 'The Politicization of Ethnic Identity in Sierra Leone', *African Studies Review* 35(1): 81–99.

Kenny, L. (2000) *The Daughters of Suburbia: Growing up White, Middle Class and Female*. New Brunswick, NJ: Rutgers University Press.

Kent, M. and Wade, P. (2015) 'Genetics against Race: Science, Politics and Affirmative Action in Brazil', *Social Studies of Science* 45(6): 816–38.

Keskinen, S. (2016) 'From Welfare Nationalism to Welfare Chauvinism: Economic Rhetoric, the Welfare State and Changing Asylum Policies in Finland', *Critical Social Policy*, 36(3): 352–70.

King-O'Riain, R. (2006) *Pure Beauty: Judging Race in Japanese American Beauty Pageants*. Minneapolis: University of Minnesota Press.

King-O'Riain, R.C., Small, S., Mahtani, M., Song, M. and Spickard, P. (eds) (2014) *Global Mixed Race*. New York: NYU Press.

Klug, B. (2004) 'The Myth of the New Anti-Semitism' *The Nation*, February 2. Available at: www.thenation.com/article/myth-new-anti-semitism/.

Knox, R. (1850) *The Races of Men: A Philosophical Inquiry into the Influence of Race over the Destinies of Nations*. London: Henry Renshaw.

Kuper, L. and Smith, M.G. (eds) (1969) *Pluralism in Africa*. Berkeley: University of California Press.

Kushner, T. (2005) 'Racialization and "White European" Immigration to Britain', in K. Murji and J. Solomos (eds) *Racialization: Studies in Theory and Practice*, pp. 207–26. Oxford: Oxford University Press.

Lacayo, C. (2017) 'Perpetual Inferiority: Whites' Racial Ideology Toward Latinos', *Sociology of Race and Ethnicity*, forthcoming.

Lacy, K. (2007) *Blue-Chip Black: Race, Class, and Status in the New Black Middle Class*. Berkeley: University of California Press.

Ladson-Billings, G. and Tate, W. (1995) 'Toward a Critical Race Theory of Education', *Teacher's College Record* 97(1): 47–68.

Lake, M. and Reynolds, H. (2008) *Drawing the Global Colour Line: White Men's Countries and the Question of Racial Equality*. Cambridge: Cambridge University Press.

Lamont, M. (2000) *The Dignity of Working Men*. Cambridge, MA: Harvard University Press.

Larsson, G. (2005) 'The Impact of Global Conflicts on Local Contexts: Muslims in Sweden after 9/11 – the Rise of Islamophobia, or New Possibilities?', *Islam and Christian–Muslim Relations* 16(1): 29–42.

Lawler, S. (2005) 'Disgusted Subjects: The Making of Middle-Class Identities', *Sociological Review* 53(3): 429–46.

Lawler, S. (2012) 'White Like Them: Whiteness and Anachronistic Space in Representations of the English White Working Class', *Ethnicities* 12(4): 409–26.

Leclerc, G.-L. (1748–1804) *A Natural History, General and Particular*, cited in E. Eze (1997) *Race and Enlightenment: A Reader*. Boston: Blackwell.

Lee, J. and Zhou, M. (2015) *The Asian American Achievement Paradox*. New York: Russell Sage Foundation.

Lee-Treweek, G. (2010) '"Be Tough, Never Let Them See What it Does to You": Towards an Understanding of the Emotional Lives of Economic

Migrants', *International Journal of Work Organisation and Emotion* 3(3): 206–26.

Lentin, R. (2004) 'From Racial State to Racist State: Ireland on the Eve of the Citizenship Referendum', *Variant* 20. Available at: www.variant.org.uk/20texts/raciststate.html.

Lentin, A. and Lentin, R. (eds) (2006) *Race and State*. Newcastle: Cambridge Scholars Press.

Lentin, A. and Titley, G. (2011) *The Crises of Multiculturalism: Racism in a Neoliberal Age*. London: Zed Books.

Lentin, R. and McVeigh, R. (2006) *After Optimism: Ireland, Racism and Globalisation*. Dublin: Metro Eireann.

Lewis, A. (2003) *Race in the Schoolyard: Negotiating the Color Line in Classrooms and Communities*. New Brunswick, NJ: Rutgers University Press.

Lewis, B. (1990) 'The Roots of Muslim Rage: Why so Many Muslims Deeply Resent the West, and Why Their Bitterness Will not Easily be Mollified', *Atlantic Online*, September. Available at: http://tonyinosaka.googlepages.com/muslimrage-atlantic.pdf.

Lewis, M. (2005) *Asylum: Understanding Public Attitudes*. London: Institute for Public Policy Research.

Lijphart, A. (1969) 'Consociational Democracy', *World Politics* 21(2): 207–25.

Lijphart, A. (1977) *Democracy in Plural Societies: A Comparative Exploration*. New Haven, CT: Yale University Press.

Linnaeus, C. (1735) *The System of Nature*, cited in E. Eze (1997) *Race and Enlightenment: A Reader*. Boston: Blackwell.

Lipsitz, G. (1995) 'The Possessive Investment in Whiteness: Racialized Social Democracy and the "White" Problem in American Studies', *American Quarterly* 47(3): 369–87.

Lipsitz, G. (1998) *The Possessive Investment in Whiteness: How White People Profit from Identity Politics*. Philadelphia: Temple University Press.

Lipsitz, G. (2011) *How Racism Takes Place*. Philadelphia: Temple University Press.

Lipstadt, D. (1993) *Denying the Holocaust: The Growing Assault on Truth and Memory*. London: Penguin.

Lombroso, C. (1876) *L'Uomo Delinquente*. Milan: Hoepli.

Lott, E. (2013) *Love and Theft: Blackface Minstrelsy and the American Working Class*. New York: Oxford University Press.

Loveland, M.T. and Popescu, D. (2015) 'The Gypsy Threat Narrative Explaining Anti-Roma Attitudes in the European Union', *Humanity and Society* 40(3): 329–52.

Luibhéid, E. (2004) 'Childbearing Against the State? Asylum Seeker Women in the Irish Republic', *Women's Studies International Forum* 27: 335–49.

Lukács, G. (1971) *History and Class Consciousness*. Boston: MIT Press.

Lundström, C. (2014) *White Migrations: Gender, Whiteness and Privilege in Transnational Migration*. Basingstoke: Palgrave.

Mac an Gháill, M. (1999) *Contemporary Racisms and Ethnicities: Social and Cultural Transformations*. Buckingham: Open University Press.

Macdonald, M. and Twine, F.W. (2013) 'Residential Mobility and the Market' in F.W. Twine and B. Gardener (eds) *Geographies of Privilege*. New York: Routledge, pp. 205–30.

MacPherson, W. (1999) *The Stephen Lawrence Inquiry: Report of an Inquiry by Sir William MacPhersan of Cluny* (CM 4262-I). HMSO. Available at: www.gov.uk/government/uploads/system/uploads/attachment_data/file/277111/4262.pdf.

Mahtani, M. (2002a) 'What's in a Name? Exploring the Employment of "Mixed Race" as an Identification', *Ethnicities* 2(4): 469–90.

Mahtani, M. (2002b) 'Interrogating the Hyphen-Nation: Canadian Multicultural Policy and "Mixed Race" Identities', *Social Identities* 8(1): 67–90.

Mahtani, M. and Moreno, A. (2001) 'Same Difference', in D. Parker and M. Song (eds) *Rethinking 'Mixed Race'*, pp. 65–75. London: Pluto.

Malik, K. (2005) 'The Islamophobia Myth'. Available at: www.kenanmalik.com/essays/prospect_islamophobia.html.

Mallett, C. (2016) *The School-to-Prison Pipeline: A Comprehensive Assessment.* New York: Springer.

Malthus, T. (1798) *Essay on the Principle of Population.* London: J. Johnson.

Massey, D. (2009) 'Racial Formation in Theory and Practice: The Case of Mexicans in the United States', *Race and Social Problems* 1(1): 12–26.

Massey, D. and Denton, N. (1994) *American Apartheid: Segregation and the Making of the Underclass.* Cambridge, MA: Harvard University Press.

Mayor of London (2006) *Muslims in London.* London: Greater London Authority.

McCall, L. (2001) 'Sources of Racial Wage Inequality in Metropolitan Labor Markets: Racial, Ethnic, and Gender Differences', *American Sociological Review* 66(4): 520–41.

McCall, L. (2005) 'The complexity of intersectionality', *Signs*, 30(3): 1771–1800.

McDonald, H. (2013) 'Irish Police Return Blonde Girl to Roma Family', The *Guardian*, 24 October. Available at: www.theguardian.com/world/2013/oct/24/blonde-girl-roma-parents-returned-dna.

McDonald, K. (2002) 'From s11 to September 11 – Implications for Sociology', *Journal of Sociology* 38(3): 229–36.

McIntosh, P. (1988) 'White Privilege and Male Privilege: A Personal Account of Coming to See Correspondences through Work in Women's Studies', Working Paper 189, Wellesley College.

McKinney, K. (2004) *Being White: Stories of Race and Racism.* New York: Routledge.

McVeigh, R. (2009) '"The People Do What the Political Class Isn't Able to Do": Antigypsyism, Ethnicity Denial and the Politics of Racism without Racism', in G.S. Bhattacharyya (ed.) *Ethnicities and Values in a Changing World.* London: Routledge.

Meer, N. (2006) '"Get Off Your Knees": Print Media Public Intellectuals and Muslims in Britain', *Journalism Studies* 7(1): 35–59.

Meer, N. (2013) 'Racialization and Religion: Race, Culture and Difference in the Study of Antisemitism and Islamophobia', *Ethnic and Racial Studies* 36(3): 385–98.

Melwani, L. (2008) 'The White Complex', *Little India*, 18 August. Available at: www.littleindia.com/nri/1828-the-white-complex.html.

Mengel, L. (2001) 'Triples – the Social Evolution of an Asian Pan-Ethnicity', in D. Parker and M. Song (eds) *Rethinking 'Mixed Race'*, pp. 99–116. London: Pluto.

Miles, R. (1982) *Racism and Migrant Labour*. London: Routledge.

Miles, R. (1987) *Racism*. London: Routledge.

Miles, R. and Brown, M. (2003) *Racism*, 2nd edn. London: Routledge.

Miller, M. (2004) *Rise and Fall of the Cosmic Race: The Cult of Mestizaje in Latin America*. Austin: University of Texas Press.

Mills, C.W. (1997) *The Racial Contract*. Ithaca, NY: Cornell University Press.

Mills, C.W. (2003) *From Class to Race: Essays in White Marxism and Black Radicalism*. Oxford: Rowman and Littlefield.

Mills, C.W. (2004) 'Racial Exploitation and the Wages of Whiteness', in G. Yancy (ed.) *What White Looks Like: African-American Philosophers on the Whiteness Question*, pp. 25–54. New York: Routledge.

Mills, C.W. and Pateman, C. (2007) *Contract and Domination*. Cambridge: Polity Press.

Millward, P. (2008) 'Rivalries and Racisms: "Closed" and "Open" Islamophobic Dispositions Amongst Football Supporters', *Sociological Research Online* 13(6). Available at: www.socresonline.org.uk/13/6/5.html.

Milne, R.S. (1981) *Politics in Ethnically Bipolar States: Guyana Malaysia, Fiji*. Vancouver: University of British Columbia Press.

Mire, A. (2005) 'Pigmentation and Empire: The Emerging Skin-Whitening Industry', *Counterpunch*, 28 July. Available at: www.counterpunch.org/2005/07/28/the-emerging-skin-whitening-industry/.

Mirza, H.S. (2015) 'Dangerous' Muslim Girls? Race, Gender and Islamophobia in British Schools' in C. Alexander, D. Weekes-Bernard and J. Arday (eds) *The Runnymede School Report Race, Education and Inequality in Contemporary Britain*, pp. 40–43. London: Runnymede Trust. Available at: www.runnymedetrust.org/uploads/The%20School%20Report.pdf.

Modell, D. (dir.) (2004) *Keep Them Out*, Channel 4, 6 May.

Modood, T. (1992) *Not Easy Being British: Colour, Culture and Citizenship*. Stoke: Runnymede Trust and Trentham Books.

Modood, T. (1997) 'Introduction: The Politics of Multiculturalism in the New Europe', in T. Modood and P. Werbner (eds) *The Politics of Multiculturalism in the New Europe: Racism, Identity and Community*. London: Zed Books.

Modood, T. (2004) 'Muslims and the Politics of Difference', *The Political Quarterly* 74(1): 100–15.

Modood, T. (2005) *Multicultural Politics: Racism, Ethnicity and Muslims in Britain*. Edinburgh: Edinburgh University Press.

Modood, T., Berthoud, R., Lakey, J., Nazroo, J., Smith, P., Virdee, S. and Beishon, S. (1997) *Ethnic Minorities in Britain: Diversity and Disadvantage – Fourth National Survey of Ethnic Minorities*. London: Policy Studies Institute.

Mohanty, C. (1988) 'Under Western Eyes: Feminist Scholarship and Colonial Discourses', *Feminist Review* 30: 61–88.

Moon, K. (1997) *Sex Among Allies: Military Prostitution in US–Korea Relations*. New York: Columbia University Press.

Moore, H. (2013) 'Shades of Whiteness? English Villagers, Eastern European Migrants and the Intersection of Race and Class in Rural England', *Critical*

Race and Whiteness Studies 9(1). Available at: www.acrawsa.org.au/files/ejournalfiles/191Moore20131.pdf.

Moreton-Robinson, A. (2004) 'The Possessive Logic of Patriarchal White Sovereignty: The High Court and the Yorta Yorta Decision', *Borderlands e-Journal* 3(2). Available at: www.borderlands.net.au/vol3no2_2004/moreton_possessive.htm.

Moreton-Robinson, A. (2005) 'The House that Jack Built: Britishness and White Possession', *Australian Critical Race and Whiteness Studies Association Journal* 1(2): 21–9.

Morris, D. (1968) *The Naked Ape*. London: Corgi.

Morrison, T. (1970) *The Bluest Eye*. New York: Holt, Rinehart and Wilson.

Morrison, T. (1993) *Playing in the Dark: Whiteness and the Literary Imagination*. New York: Vintage.

Morton, S. (1839) *Crania Americana: A Comparative View of the Skulls of Various Aboriginal Natives of North and South America, to which is Prefixed an Essay on the Variety of Human Species*. Philadelphia: J. Dobson.

Mountz, A. (2011) 'The Enforcement Archipelago: Detention, Haunting, and Asylum on Islands', *Political Geography* 30(3): 118–28.

Murji, K. and Solomos, J. (eds) (2005a) *Racialization: Studies in Theory and Practice*. Oxford: Oxford University Press.

Murji, K. and Solomos, J. (2005b) 'Introduction', in K. Murji and J. Solomos (eds) *Racialization: Studies in Theory and Practice*, pp. 1–28. Oxford: Oxford University Press.

Murray, C. (2014) 'A Scientific Revolution is Under Way – Upending One of Our Reigning Orthodoxies', *Wall Street Journal*, 2 May.

Muslim Council of Britain (2015) *British Muslims in Numbers: a Demographic, Socio-economic and Health profile of Muslims in Britain drawing on the 2011 Census*: Available at: www.mcb.org.uk/wp-content/uploads/2015/02/MCBCensusReport_2015.pdf.

Myers, M. and Bhopal, K. (2015) 'Racism and Bullying in Rural Primary Schools: Protecting White Identities Post Macpherson', *British Journal of Sociology of Education* 36(1): 1–19.

Nagel, J. (2003) *Race, Ethnicity and Sexuality: Intimate Intersections, Forbidden Frontiers*. New York: Oxford University Press.

Nahman, M. (2008) 'Nodes of Desire: Romanian Egg Sellers, "Dignity" and Feminist Alliances in Transnational Ova Exchanges', *European Journal of Women's Studies* 15(2): 65–82.

Nature Biotechnology (2005) 'Illuminating BiDil' 23(8): 903.

Nayak, A. (2003) 'Ivory Lives: Economic Restructuring and the Making of Whiteness in a Post-Industrial Youth Community', *European Journal of Cultural Studies* 6(3): 305–25.

Nayak, A. (2007) 'Critical Whiteness Studies', *Sociology Compass* 1(2): 737–55.

Nelson, A. (2016) *The Social Life of DNA: Race, Reparations, and Reconciliation After the Genome*. New York: Beacon Press.

Noiriel, G. (1988) *Le Creuset français. Histoire de l'immigration, XIXe–XXe siècles*. Paris: Éditions du Seuil.

Norton, M. and Sommers, S. (2011) 'Whites See Racism as a Zero-Sum Game That They Are Now Losing', *Perspectives on Psychological Science* 6: 215–18.

Nozick. R. (1974) *Anarchy, State and Utopia*. New York: Basic Books.

Nye, R. (1949) *Fettered Freedom: Civil Liberties and the Slavery Controversy, 1830–1860*. East Lansing: Michigan State College Press.

O'Keeffe, G. (2007) 'The Irish in Britain – Towards Greater Visibility?', in W. Huber, M. Böss, C. Malignant and H. Schwall (eds) *Irish Studies in Europe*, pp. 121–32. Leuven: The European Federation of Associations and Centres of Irish Studies (EFACIS).

Oakley, A. (1974) *The Sociology of Housework*. London: Martin Robertson.

ODPM (Office of the Deputy Prime Minister) (2004) *Gypsy and Traveller Sites, Vol. 1: Thirteenth Report of Session 2003–04*. London: HMSO.

Offe, C. and Ronge, V. (1982) 'Theses on the Theory of the State', in A. Giddens and D. Held (eds) *Classes, Power, and Conflict*, pp. 249–56. Berkeley: University of California Press.

Okely, J. (1983) *The Traveller-Gypsies*. Cambridge: Cambridge University Press.

Oliver, M. and Shapiro, T. (2006) *Black Wealth/White Wealth: A New Perspective on Racial Inequality*, 2nd edn. New York: Routledge.

Omi, M. (2001) 'The Changing Meaning of Race', in N. Smelser, W.J. Wilson and F. Mitchell (eds) *America Becoming: Racial Trends and Their Consequences, Volume 1*, pp. 243–63. Washington, DC: National Research Council.

Omi, M. and Winant, H. (1994 [1986]) *Racial Formation in the US: From the 1960s to the 1980s*. New York: Routledge.

Parekh, B. (1991) *The Concept of Fundamentalism* (Meghraj Lecture, 1991). Coventry/Leeds: University of Warwick/Peepal Tree Press.

Parker, D. and Song, M. (eds) (2001) *Rethinking 'Mixed Race'*. London: Pluto.

Parker, D. and Song, M. (2006) 'New Ethnicities Online: Reflexive Racialization and the Internet', *The Sociological Review* 54(3): 575–94.

Pateman, C. (1988) *The Sexual Contract*. Cambridge: Polity.

Pearson, K. (1930) *Life, Letters and Labours of Francis Galton, Volume Three A: Correlation, Personal Identification and Eugenics*. Cambridge: Cambridge University Press.

Peiss, K. (1999) *Hope in a Jar: The Making of America's Beauty Culture*. New York: Holt.

Phillips, C. (2011) 'Institutional Racism and Ethnic Inequalities: An Expanded Multilevel Framework', *Journal of Social Policy* 40(1): 173–92.

Phillips, D. (2006) 'Parallel Lives? Challenging Discourses of British Muslim Self-Segregation', *Environment and Planning D: Society and Space* 24(1): 25–40.

Phoenix, A. (1996) 'I'm White – So What? The Construction of Whiteness for Young Londoners', in M. Fine (ed.) *Off White*, pp. 187–97. New York: Routledge.

Phoenix, A. (2005) 'Remembered Racialization: Young People and Positioning in Different Understandings', in K. Murji and J. Solomos (eds) *Racialization: Studies in Theory and Practice*, pp. 103–22. Oxford: Oxford University Press.

Pickering, C. (1854) *The Races of Men and Their Geographical Distribution*. London: H.G. Bohn.

Poliakov, L. (2003a) *The History of Anti-Semitism, Volume 1: From the Time of Christ to the Court Jews*. University Park: University of Pennsylvania Press.

Poliakov, L. (2003b) *The History of Anti-Semitism, Volume 2: From Mohammad to the Marranos*. University Park: University of Pennsylvania Press.

Poliakov, L. (2003c) *The History of Anti-Semitism, Volume 3: From Voltaire to Wagner*. University Park: University of Pennsylvania Press.

Poliakov, L. (2003d) *The History of Anti-Semitism, Volume 4: Suicidal Europe 1870–1933*. University Park: University of Pennsylvania Press.

Portes, J. (2013) 'An Exercise in Scapegoating', *London Review of Books* 35(12): 7–9. Available at: http://www.lrb.co.uk/v35/n12/jonathan-portes/an-exercise-in-scapegoating.

Putnam, R. (2000) *Bowling Alone: The Collapse and Revival of the American Community*. New York: Simon & Schuster.

Putnam, R. (2007) 'E Pluribus Unum: Diversity and Community in the Twenty-First Century – The 2006 Johan Skytte Prize Lecture', *Journal of Scandinavian Political Studies* 30(2): 137–74.

Quinn, D.B (1966) *The Elizabethans and the Irish*. Ithaca, NY: Cornell University Press.

Quraishi, M. (2005) *Muslims and Crime: A Comparative Study*. Aldershot: Ashgate.

Ragbir, A. (2012) 'Fictions of the Past: Staging Indianness, Identity and Sexuality Among Young Women in Indo-Trinidadian Beauty Pageants', *Caribbean Review of Gender Studies*, 6: 1–21.

Rahier, J.M. (1998) 'Blackness, the Racial/Spatial Order, Migrations and Miss Ecuador 1995–96', *American Anthropologist* 100(2): 421–30.

Raimon, E.A. (2004) *The 'Tragic Mulatta' Revisited: Race and Nationalism in Nineteenth-Century Antislavery Fiction*. New Brunswick, NJ: Rutgers University Press.

Ram, M.H. (2014) 'European Integration, Migration and Representation: The Case of Roma in France', *Ethnopolitics* 13(3): 203–24.

Rana, J. (2007) 'The Story of Islamophobia', *Souls* 9(2): 148–61.

Randall, V. and Waylen, G. (eds) (1998) *Gender, Politics, and the State*. London: Routledge.

Rashid, N. (2014) 'Giving the Silent Majority a Stronger Voice? Initiatives to Empower Muslim Women as Part of the UK's "War on Terror"', *Ethnic and Racial Studies*, 37(4): 589–604.

Rattansi, A. (2005) 'The Uses of Racialization: The Time–Spaces and Subject–Objects of the Raced Body', in K. Murji and J. Solomos (eds) *Racialization: Studies in Theory and Practice*, pp. 271–302. Oxford: Oxford University Press.

Rawls, J. (1971) *A Theory of Justice*. Cambridge, MA: Belknapp.

Reay, D., Hollingworth, S., Williams, K., Jamieson, F., Crozier, G., James, D. and Beedell, P. (2007) '"A Darker Shade of Pale?" Whiteness, the Middle Classes and Multi-Ethnic Inner City Schooling', *Sociology* 41(6): 1041–60.

Reid, S. (2008) *Never To Return: The Harrowing True Story of a Stolen Childhood*. Edinburgh: Black and White Publishing.

Renan, E. (1992 [1882]) *Qu'est-qu'une nation?: Et autres essais politiques*. Paris: Agora.

Rex, J. (1970) *Race Relations in Sociological Theory*. London: Routledge.

Rich, P. (1990) *Race and Empire in British Politics*. Cambridge: Cambridge University Press.

Richardson, J. (2004) *(Mis)Representing Islam: The Racism and Rhetoric of British Broadsheet Newspapers*. Amsterdam: John Benjamins.

Richardson, J. and O'Neill, R. (2013) '"Stamp on the Camps": The Social Construction of Gypsies and Travellers in Media and Political Debate', in J. Richardson and A. Ryder (eds) *Gypsies and Travellers: Empowerment and Inclusion in British Society*, pp. 169–86. Bristol: Policy Press.

Rinaldo, R.A. (2007) 'High Heels and Headscarves: Women's Clothing and Islamic Piety in Indonesia', paper presented at the annual meeting of the American Sociological Association, New York, 11 August. Available at: http://citation.allacademic.com/meta/p_mla_apa_research_citation/1/8/2/5/8/p182584_index.html.

Rivers-Moore, M. (2013) 'Affective Sex: Beauty, Race and Nation in the Sex Industry', *Feminist Theory* 14(2): 153–69.

Roberts, D. (2011) *Fatal Invention: How Science, Politics and Big Business Re-Create Race in the Twenty-First Century*. New York: The New Press.

Robinson, C. (1983) *Black Marxism: The Making of the Black Radical Tradition*. London: Zed Books.

Rockquemore, K.A. (2002) 'Negotiating the Color Line: The Gendered Process of Racial Identity Construction among Black/White Biracial Women', *Gender and Society* 16(4): 485–503.

Rockquemore, K.A. and Arend, P. (2002) 'Opting for White: Choice, Fluidity and Racial Identity Construction in Post Civil-Rights America', *Race and Society* 5(1): 49–64.

Rockquemore, K.A. and Laszloffy, T. (2005) *Raising Biracial Children*. Lanham, MD: Altamira.

Roediger, D. (1991) *The Wages of Whiteness: Race and the Making of the American Working Class*. London: Verso.

Rojek, C. and Turner, B. (2001) *Society and Culture*. London: Sage.

Romero, M. (2008) 'Crossing the Immigration and Race Border: A Critical Race Theory Approach to Immigration Studies', *Contemporary Justice Review* 11(1): 23–37.

Romero, M. (2011) 'Not a Citizen, Only a Suspect', in M. Kie-Jung, J. Costa Vargas and E. Bonilla-Silva (eds) *State of White Supremacy: Racism, Governance, and the United States*, pp. 189–210. Stanford, CA: Stanford University Press.

Roosevelt, T. (1906) *State of the Union*. Available at: www.let.rug.nl/usa/presidents/theodore-roosevelt/state-of-the-union-1906.php.

Rooster, G. (1930) 'A Review of Race Psychology', *Psychological Bulletin* 27(5): 329–56.

Root, M. (1996) 'The Multiracial Experience: Racial Borders as Significant Frontier in Race Relations', in M. Root (ed.) *The Multiracial Experience*. Thousand Oaks, CA: Sage.

Ropp, S. (2004) 'Do Multicultural Subjects Really Challenge Race? Mixed Race Asians in the United States and the Caribbean', in J. Ifekwunigwe (ed.) *Mixed Race Studies: A Reader*, pp. 263–70. London: Routledge.

Ryan, L. (2010) 'Becoming Polish in London: Negotiating Ethnicity Through Migration', *Social Identities* 16(3): 359–76.

Said, E. (1979) *Orientalism*. New York: Vintage.

Said, E. (2001) 'Clash of Ignorance', *The Nation*. Available at: www.thenation.com/article/clash-ignorance/.

San Juan, E. (2001) 'Problems in the Marxist Project of Theorising Race', in E. Cashmore and R. Jennings (eds) *Racism: Essential Readings*, pp. 225–46. London: Sage.

Sanchez, G. (2004) 'Y Tù qué?: Latino History in the New Millennium', in J. Ifekwunigwe (ed.) *Mixed Race Studies: A Reader*, pp. 276–82. London: Routledge.

Satzewitch, V. (1987) 'Racisms: The Reactions to Chinese Migrants in Canada at the Turn of the Century', *International Sociology* 4(3): 311–27.

Sayyid, S. (2011) 'Racism and Islamophobia', International Centre for Muslim and Non-Muslim Understanding, *MnM Commentary* 4: 1–4.

Scarman, L. (1986) *Scarman Report: The Brixton Disorders, 10–12 April, 1981*. London: Pelican.

Schulte-Sasse, L. (1996) *Entertaining the Third Reich: Illusions of Wholeness in Nazi Cinema*. Durham, NC: Duke University Press.

Schwarz, H. (2010) *Constructing the Criminal Tribe in Colonial India: Acting Like a Thief*. Chichester: John Wiley.

Scott, S. (2006) 'The Social Morphology of Skilled Migration: The Case of the British Middle Class in Paris', *Journal of Ethnic and Migration Studies* 32(7): 1105–29.

Selod, S. (2015) 'Citizenship Denied: The Racialization of Muslim American Men and Women Post-9/11', *Critical Sociology* 41(1): 77–95.

Senna, D. (2004) 'The Mulatto Millennium', in J. Ifekwunigwe (ed.) *Mixed Race Studies: A Reader*, pp. 204–9. London: Routledge.

Shaw, D. (2015) 'Why the Surge in Muslim Prisoners?', *BBC News Online*, 11 March. Available at: www.bbc.co.uk/news/uk-31794599.

Sheridan, L.P. (2006) 'Islamophobia Pre- and Post-September 11th, 2001', *Journal of Interpersonal Violence* 21(3): 317–36.

Sibley, D. (1995) *Geographies of Exclusion: Society and Difference in the West*. London: Routledge.

Silverstein, P. (2005) 'Immigrant Racialization and the New Savage Slot: Race, Migration, and Immigration in the New Europe', *Annual Review of Anthropology* 34: 363–84.

Sims, J. (2007) *Mixed Heritage: Identity, Policy and Practice*. London: Runnymede Trust.

Sin, B. (2016) 'Why a Skin-Whitening Selfie Camera is a Hit in China', *Forbes*, 16 March. Available at: www.forbes.com/sites/bensin/2016/03/16/a-skin-whitening-selfie-camera-is-a-hit-in-china-because-asia-has-a-racist-perception-of-beauty/#1030c4f36d47.

Sivanandan, A. (1990) *Communities of Resistance*. London: Verso.

Skeggs, B. (1997) *Formations of Class and Gender: Becoming Respectable*. London: Sage.

Skeggs, B. (2005) *Class, Self and Culture*. London: Routledge.

Skeggs, B. and Wood, H. (2008) 'Spectacular Morality: Reality Television and the Re-Making of the Working Class', in D. Hesmondhalgh and J. Toynbee (eds) *Media and Social Theory*, pp. 177–94. London: Routledge.

Skinner, D. (2006) 'Racialized Futures: Biologism and the Changing Politics of Identity', *Social Studies of Science* 36(3): 459–88.

Small, S. (1994) *Racialized Barriers: The Black Experience in the United States and England in the 1980s*. London: Routledge.

Small, S. (2001) 'Colour, Culture and Class: Interrogating Interracial Marriage and People of Mixed Descent in the United States', in D. Parker and M. Song (eds) *Rethinking 'Mixed Race'*, pp. 117–33. London: Pluto.

Smith, A.D. (1981) *The Ethnic Revival in the Modem World*. Cambridge: Cambridge University Press.

Smith, L. (2015) 'Gypsies and Travellers: Planning Provisions', Briefing Paper Number 07005, 4 January 2016. Available at: http://researchbriefings.files.parliament.uk/documents/SN07005/SN07005.pdf.

Smith, L.T (1999) *Decolonizing Methodologies: Research and Indigenous Peoples*. London: Zed Books.

Solimene, M. (2011) '"These Romanians Have Ruined Italy": Xoraxané Romá, Romanian Roma and Rome', *Journal of Modern Italian Studies* 16(5): 637–51.

Song, M. (2014) 'Challenging a Culture of Racial Equivalence', *The British Journal of Sociology* 65(1): 107–29.

Sowell, T. (1990) *Preferential Policies*. New York: William Morrow.

Spencer, H. (1864) *Principles of Biology, Volume 1*. London: Williams and Norgate.

Spencer, J.M. (2000) *The New Colored People: The Mixed-Race Movement in America*. New York: New York University Press.

Spencer, R. (2006) 'New Racial Identities, Old Arguments: Continuing Biological Reification', in D. Brunsma (ed.) *Mixed Messages*, pp. 83–116. Boulder, CO: Lynne Rienner.

Spruill, J.C. (1938) *Women's Life and Work in the Southern Colonies*. New York and London: W.W. Norton & Company.

Stepan, N. (1991) *The Hour of Eugenics: Race, Gender, and Nation in Latin America*. Ithaca, NY: Cornell University Press.

Stoddard, W. (1922) *Revolt Against Civilization*. New York: Scribner.

Stonequist, E. (1937) *The Marginal Man: A Study in Personality and Culture Conflict*. New York: Charles Scribner's Sons.

Straw, J. (2006) 'I felt uneasy talking to someone I couldn't see', *Guardian*, 6 October. Available at: www.theguardian.com/commentisfree/2006/oct/06/politics.uk.

Streeter, C. (2012) *Tragic No More: Mixed-Race Women and the Nexus of Sex and Celebrity*. Amherst: University of Massachusetts Press.

Sullivan, L., Meschede, T., Dietrich, L. and Shapiro, T. (2015) *The Racial Wealth Gap*. Waltham, MA: Institute on Assets and Social Policy, Brandeis University. Available at: https://iasp.brandeis.edu/pdfs/2015/RWA.pdf.

Taguieff, P.A. (1990) 'The New Cultural Racism in France', *Telos* 83: 109–22.

Taguieff, P.A. (2001) *The Force of Prejudice: On Racism and its Doubles* (trans. H. Melehy). Minneapolis: University of Minnesota Press.

Telles, E. and Paschel, T. (2014) 'Who Is Black, White, or Mixed Race? How Skin Color, Status, and Nation Shape Racial Classification in Latin America', *American Journal of Sociology* 120(3): 864–907.

Tizard, B. and Phoenix, A. (2002) *Black, White or Mixed Race? Race and Racism in the Lives of Young People of Mixed Parentage*, 2nd edn. London: New York.

Torre, C.D.L. (1999) 'Everyday Forms of Racism in Contemporary Ecuador: The Experiences of Middle-Class Indians', *Ethnic and Racial Studies* 22(1): 92–112.

Traveller Movement (2015) 'Note on Planning Application Success Rates for Traveller Sites Compared to Residential Dwellings'. Available at: www.travellermovement.org.uk/wp-content/uploads/2015/09/Note-on-planning-application-success-rates-for-Traveller-sites.pdf.

Treitler, V.B. (2015) 'Social Agency and White Supremacy in Immigration Studies', *Sociology of Race and Ethnicity* 1(1): 153–65.

Tsutsui, K. and Shin, H.J. (2008) 'Global Norms, Local Activism, and Social Movement Outcomes: Global Human Rights and Resident Koreans in Japan', *Social Problems* 55(3): 391–418.

Twinam, A. (2006) 'Purchasing Whiteness: Conversations on the Essence of Pardo-ness and Mulatto-ness at the End of Empire', paper presented at Lockmiller seminar, Emory University, 29 March.

Twine, F.W. (1996) 'Brown-Skinned White Girls: Class, Culture and the Construction of White Identity in Suburban Communities', *Gender, Place and Culture* 3: 205–24.

Twine, F.W. (2011) *A White Side of Black Britain*. Durham, NC: Duke University Press.

Tyler, I. (2008) '"Chav Mum, Chav Scum": Class Disgust in Contemporary Britain', *Feminist Media Studies* 8(1): 17–34.

Tyler, K. (2003) 'The Racialized and Classed Constitution of Village Life', *Ethnos* 68(3): 391–412.

Tyler, K. (2006) 'Village People: Race, Class, Nation and the Community Spirit', in S. Neal and J. Agyeman (eds) *The New Countryside: Ethnicity, Nation and Exclusion in Contemporary Rural Britain*, pp. 129–48. Bristol: Policy Press.

Tyrer, D. (2013) *The Politics of Islamophobia: Race, Power and Fantasy*. London: Pluto.

UNESCO (1950) *UNESCO and its Programme III: The Race Question*. Paris: UNESCO.

United Nations (1965) *International Convention on the Elimination of All Forms of Racial Discrimination: adopted and opened for signature and ratification by General Assembly resolution 2106 (XX) of 21 December 1965*. Available at: www2.ohchr.org/english/law/pdf/cerd.pdf.

Valdez, Z. (2011) *The New Entrepreneurs: How Race, Class, and Gender Shape American Enterprise*. Stanford, CA: Stanford University Press.

Van Deburg, W. (1992) *New Day in Babylon: The Black Power Movement and American Culture, 1965–1975*. Chicago: University of Chicago Press.

Van Riemsdijk, M. (2013) 'Everyday Geopolitics, the Valuation of Labour and the Socio-Political Hierarchies of Skill: Polish Nurses in Norway', *Journal of Ethnic and Migration Studies* 39(3): 373–90.

Vargas, J.C. and Amparo Alves, J. (2010) 'Geographies of Death: An Intersectional Analysis of Police Lethality and the Racialized Regimes of Citizenship in São Paulo', *Ethnic and Racial Studies*, 33(4): 611–36.

Viglione, J., Hannon, L. and DeFina, R. (2011) 'The Impact of Light Skin on Prison Time for Black Female Offenders', *The Social Science Journal* 48: 250–8.

Voegelin, E. (1940) 'The Growth of the Race Idea', *The Review of Politics* July: 283–317.

Voegelin, E. (2000 [1933]) *Race and State* (trans. R. Heim). Baton Rouge and London: Louisiana State University Press.

Wade, N. (2014) *A Troublesome Inheritance: Genes, Race and Human History*. New York: Penguin.

Wade, P., Beltrán, C.L.L., Restrepo, E. and Santos, R.V. (eds) (2014) *Mestizo Genomics: Race Mixture, Nation, and Science in Latin America*. Durham, NC: Duke University Press.

Warner, W.L. and Srole, L. (1945) *The Social Systems of American Ethnic Groups*. New Haven, CT: Yale University Press.

Watanabe, K. (1995) 'Trafficking in Women's Bodies, Then and Now: The Issue of Military Comfort Women', *Peace and Change* 20: 501–14.

Watt, P. and Stenson, K. (1998) 'The Street: "It's a Bit Dodgy Around There": Safety, Danger, Ethnicity and Young People's Use of Public Space', in T. Skelton and G. Valentine (eds) *Cool Places: Geographies of Youth Cultures*, pp. 249–66. London: Routledge.

Weber, E. (1976) *Peasants into Frenchmen: The Modernization of Rural France, 1870–1914*. Stanford, CA: Stanford University Press

Weber, M. (1946) *Essays in Sociology* (ed./trans./intro. H.H. Gerth and C. Wright Mills). Oxford: Oxford University Press.

Weber, M. (1978 [1922]) *Economy and Society (Vol. I)* (ed./trans. G. Roth and C. Wittich). Berkeley: University of California Press.

Weinstein, B. (2003) 'Racialising Regional Difference: Sao Paulo versus Brazil, 1932', in N. Appelbaum, A. MacPherson and K. Rosemblatt (eds) *Race and Nation in Modern Latin America*, pp. 237–62. Chapel Hill: University of North Carolina Press.

Weis, L. (2006) 'Masculinity, Whiteness, and the New Economy: An Exploration of Privilege and Loss', *Men and Masculinities* 8(3): 262–72.

Wells, I. (1893) 'Lynch Law'. Excerpt available at: www.historyisaweapon.com/defcon1/wellslynchlaw.html.

Werbner, P. (2005) 'Islamophobia: Incitement to Religious Hatred – Legislating for a New Fear?', *Anthropology Today* 21(1): 5–9.

Wetherell, M (2012) *Affect and Emotion: A New Social Science Understanding*. London: Sage.

Wetherell, M. and Beer, D. (2014) 'The Future of Affect Theory: An Interview with Margaret Wetherell', *Theory, Culture and Society*, 15 October. Available at: www.theoryculturesociety.org/the-future-of-affect-theory-an-interview-with-margaret-wetherall/.

Wetherell, M. and Potter, J. (1992) *Mapping the Language of Racism: Discourse and the Legitimation of Exploitation*. New York: Columbia University Press.

Whyte, P. (2009) *No Easy Road*. Kailyard Publishing.

Wieviorka, M. (1995) *The Arena of Racism*. New York: Sage.

Williams, S. and Law, I. (2012) 'Legitimising Racism: An Exploration of the Challenges Posed by the Use of Indigeneity Discourses by the Far Right', *Sociological Research Online* 17(2). Available at: www.socresonline.org.uk/17/2/2.html.

Wilson, E. (1976) *Sociobiology – The New Synthesis*. Cambridge, MA: Harvard University Press.

Wing-Fai, L.(2015) 'Who Could be an Oriental Angel? Lou Jing, Mixed Heritage and the Discourses of Chinese Ethnicity', *Asian Ethnicity*, 16(3): 294–313.

Wittgenstein, L. (1953) *Philosophical Investigations*. Oxford: Basil Blackwell.

Wolfe, P. (2002) 'Race and Racialization: Some Thoughts', *Postcolonial Studies* 5(1): 51–62.

Woodcock, S. (2010) 'Gender as Catalyst for Violence Against Roma in Contemporary Italy', *Patterns of Prejudice* 44(5): 469–88.

Wray, M. (2006) *Not Quite White: White Trash and the Boundaries of Whiteness*. Durham, NC: Duke University Press.

Wyly, E., Moos, M. and Hammel, D. (2012) 'Race, Class, and Rent in America's Subprime Cities', in M. Aalbers (ed.) *Subprime Cities: The Political Economy of Mortgage Markets*, pp. 242–90. Hoboken, NJ: Wiley.

X, Malcolm and Haley, A. (1969) *The Autobiography of Malcolm X*. New York: Random House.

Yancy, G. (2001) 'A Foucauldian (Genealogical) Reading of Whiteness: The Production of the Black Body/Self and the Racial Deformation of Pecola Breedlove in Toni Morrison's *The Bluest Eye*', *Radical Philosophy Review* 4(1–2): 1–29.

Young, R. (1995) *Colonial Desire: Hybridity in Theory, Culture and Race*. London: Routledge.

Yuval-Davis, N. (1997) *Gender and Nation*. London: Routledge.

Yuval-Davis, N. (2011) *The Politics of Belonging: Intersectional Contestations*. London: Sage.

Zack, N. (1993) *Race and Mixed Race*. Philadelphia: Temple University Press.

Zakharov, N. (2015) *Race and Racism in Russia*. London: Palgrave.

Zappone, K. (2003) (ed.) *Re-Thinking Equality: The Challenge of Diversity*. Dublin: Equality Authority.

Zempi, I. (2016) '"It's a Part of Me, I Feel Naked Without it"': Choice, Agency and Identity for Muslim Women who Wear the Niqab', *Ethnic and Racial Studies* 39(10): 1738–54.

Index

Page numbers in **bold** denote specific dedication to the subject